Courage Under Siege

STUDIES IN JEWISH HISTORY JEHUDA REINHARZ, General Editor

OTHER VOLUMES ARE IN PREPARATION

Courage Under Siege

Starvation, Disease, and Death
in the Warsaw Ghetto

CHARLES G. ROLAND

New York   Oxford
OXFORD UNIVERSITY PRESS
1992

Oxford University Press

Oxford   New York   Toronto
Delhi   Bombay   Calcutta   Madras   Karachi
Kuala Lumpur   Singapore   Hong Kong   Tokyo
Nairobi   Dar es Salaam   Cape Town
Melbourne   Auckland

and associated companies in
Berlin   Ibadan

Published by Oxford University Press, Inc.,
200 Madison Avenue, New York, New York 10016

Oxford iis a registered trademark of Oxford University Press

Library of Congress Cataloging-in-Publication Data
Roland, Charles G.
Courage under siege : starvation, disease, and death
in the Warsaw ghetto / Charles G. Roland.
p.   cm.   Includes bibliographical references and index.
ISBN 0-19-506285-X
1. Jews—Poland—Warsaw—Persecutions.
2. Holocaust, Jewish (1939–1945)—Poland—Warsaw.
3. Holocaust, Jewish (1939–1945)—Health aspects—Poland—Warsaw.
4. Jews—Health and hygiene—Poland—Warsaw.
5. Warsaw (Poland)—Ethnic relations.
I. Title.   DS135.P62W3355   1992
940.53′18′094384—dc20 91-45644

1 3 5 7 9 8 6 4 2

Printed in the United States of America
on acid-free paper

DEDICATED TO

EMMANUEL RINGELBLUM (1900–1944),
historian of the ghetto
and creator of *Oneg Shabbat,*
the secret archive that collected and preserved
so much from that tragic time,
who would have done this history better

AND

to the survivors

Acknowledgments

My special debt to the survivors of the Warsaw ghetto, the underground medical school, and gentile Warsaw is profound. These interviewees include some who have requested anonymity, and who therefore are identified only by pseudonym: Dr. Marek Balin, Timberlake, Ohio; Prof. Irena Borman Bessette, Kingston, Ontario, Canada; "Halina Berg," Warsaw and California; Dr. "Bronislawa Wygodzka," Lodz; Dr. Bronislaw Wisniewski, Elmhurst, New York; Dr. Henry Fenigstein, Toronto; Mrs. Eugenia Pernal, Toronto; Mrs. Millie Eisen, Grayslake, Illinois; Dr. Tadeusz Stabholz, North Canton, Ohio; the late Dr. Karolina Borman Bein Placek, South Orange, New Jersey; Dr. Ludwig Stabholz, Tel Aviv, Israel; Dr. Karola Karlowicz, Warsaw; Prof. Kazimierz Zakreczewski, Warsaw; the late Dr. Janina Zaborowska, Oakville, Ontario; Dr. Jan Merkel, Warsaw; "Grace Dover," Port Dover, Ontario; and Dr. Egon Tramer, Winnipeg, Manitoba.

Several donors have generously supported various elements in the research: Mr. Henry Kalinowicz, Montreal; [others in Montreal]; the John P. McGovern Foundation, Houston, Texas; Dr. Danuta Podkomorska, Winnipeg, Manitoba; the late Harold N. Segall, M.D., Montreal; and Dr. Anna Szetle, Winnipeg, Manitoba.

And for assistance of kinds too numerous and too varied to be spelled out in detail, though deeply appreciated:

In Canada: Rabbi Bernard Baskin, Hamilton, Ontario, who introduced me to Dr. Henry Fenigstein, my first interviewee on this subject, and who, in turn, directly or indirectly, has led me to all the others; Mrs. Mali Fenigstein, Toronto; Cora Miszuk, Hamilton, Ontario; and Professor Pauline Mazumdar, University of Toronto. Much general encouragement has been offered by two colleagues, though neither they nor any of those others named here bear any responsibility for my errors, omissions, or nuances of interpretation. They are Prof. Michael Kater, York University, Toronto, and Dr. William Seidelman, McMaster University, Hamilton, Ontario.

In the United States: Dr. Wladaslaw Lewin, Janusz Korczak Medical Society, Kew Gardens, New York; the Archives staff at the YIVO Institute, New York City; the staff at the Fortunoff Video Archive of the Holocaust, Yale University, New Haven, Connecticut; Ms. Denise B. Gluck, Director of Archives, American Jewish Joint Distribution Committee, New York City; the late Mrs. Martha Osnos, New York City; May Hill Russell Library, Monroe County Library System, Key West, Florida; and Prof. Fred Kasten, Department of Anatomy, Tulane University, New Orleans, Louisiana.

In Israel: Prof. Josef Kermisz, Director, Hadassah Modlinger and Judith Kleiman, Archives, and Judith Levine, Photographic Archives, Yad Vashem, Jerusalem; and Eva Feldenkreis, Archivist, Beit Lohamei Hagetaot, Israel.

In Germany: David Marwell, Ph.D., Director, Berlin Document Center, Wasserkäfersteig No. 1, D1000 Berlin 37, Germany.

In Poland: Prof. Alfred Sicinski and Prof. Sicinska, Warsaw; Dr. Daniel Grinberg, Director, and Mr. Robert Lewandowski, Zydowski Instytut Historyczny, Tlomackie 3–5, Warsaw; Mr. Mieczyslaw Jedruszczak, Warsaw.

For translations: Dr. Krzysztof Cena (Polish): Ms. Ewa Boniecka, McMaster University (Polish); Dr. Marek Balin, Timberlake, Ohio (Polish); Mr. Heinz Deppe, Burlington, Ontario (German).

I wish further to recognize the able assistance of the highly professional staff at Oxford University Press (New York), most particularly my editor, Nancy Lane, and Stanley George, Helen Greenberg, and Edward Harcourt.

Finally, I acknowledge the warm and unwavering support of Connie Roland, who now knows a great deal about the Warsaw ghetto, and who suffered vicariously and sympathetically during the many gloomy days that punctuated my immersion in this sad theme over so many years. She has read this book—some portions many times—has assisted in the organization of the illustrations, and has been a patient buffer to the grim and almost unremittingly painful material from which this book has been constructed.

Burlington, Ontario   C.G.R.
June 1991

Contents

Courage Under Siege

Introduction

Henryk Fenigstein held his wife Ala close as they struggled to keep their footing. They were caught in a weeping, struggling, frightened mass of Jews driven with shouts and blows into a waiting cattle car. The car was jammed with young men and women—the children and the elderly had long since died or been taken to Treblinka or Auschwitz.

For a moment, before the sliding door slammed shut, Fenigstein looked out toward the Warsaw ghetto. The air was heavy with smoke, and ashes littered the ground everywhere. The *Umschlagplatz*—the loading place—was filled with torn fragments of clothing, bits of paper, broken glass, and abandoned belongings of all kinds. He could see nothing but the chaotic confusion of the *Umschlagplatz* and the surrounding buildings. He had worked as a pathologist in those buildings for 18 months. Briefly, it occurred to the young doctor that that day in May 1943 was not only likely to be the last of his life, but that it also signified the end of an era. When he and his few surviving medical colleagues were marched out of the burning ruins of the ghetto, Jewish medicine in Warsaw ceased to exist. A tradition that extended over centuries was extinguished.

That tradition had been strong and fruitful when the Nazis marched into Poland in September 1939. Now, less than four years later, destruction was total.

It is my chief purpose in this book to describe this tradition and its destruction, particularly the events of the 30 months from the creation of the Warsaw ghetto in November 1940 until the end of the ghetto and Warsaw Jewry in May 1943. The story is painful, often horrifying, and deeply depressing; yet from the labors of the nurses and doctors and public health workers rises an encouraging and even inspirational note that rings true through the miasma of the endless Nazi brutalities.

For Poland, the war began 1 September 1939 with the wail of sirens, the crash of shells and bombs, and the news of German advances. Warsaw was bombed heavily that day. For the Jews of Warsaw, the day and the war began with a particularly poignant tragedy, one that contained the seeds of the future had one been able to read the signs. The first Jewish victims were the children at the CENTOS[1] institution at Otwock, a suburb 15 miles to the southeast. German bombs destroyed the institution, killing or maiming dozens of the Jewish children living there.[2] This was not the Holocaust yet, but it may be seen as symbolic that Jewish children, the lifeblood of this vibrant element of Polish life, were among the first to be destroyed.

The Holocaust—the deliberate destruction of most of the Jews of Europe—along with the genocide of enormous numbers of Gypsies and other non-Jewish inhabitants of Eastern Europe—is arguably the least understandable event since the Creation. Reactions to the Holocaust by those who were enmeshed in it are, however, more comprehensible. A very few committed suicide.[3] Some became totally obsessed with self-preservation at all costs. Many tried to ignore the grim reality and avoided facing up to its implications. Most behaved decently and even nobly as the situation deteriorated into oblivion.

The generally accepted estimate is that approximately 6 million Jews were destroyed during the war as a consequence of the Holocaust, along with millions of others who died in concentration camps, in prisoner-of-war camps, and of starvation and disease in numberless locales throughout the world, as well as in battle. Of Warsaw's 400,000 Jews, a few thousand survived. Estimates vary from as few as 5,000 to as many as 20,000; the smaller estimate seems more likely. In this book I shall attempt to tell the story of the ghetto in Warsaw itself, not from the viewpoint of politics, as has been done ably by Yisrael Gutman[4] and others, but explicitly as medical history.

In a sense, that viewpoint is perhaps the most natural and appropriate that a historian might choose. Everything about life in the Jewish quarter of Warsaw and, later, its ghetto focused on getting enough food to prevent starvation, and therefore to avoid the debilitation that made one more susceptible to disease; and, of course, on trying to prevent various diseases.

The efforts of the Jewish council, the *Judenrat*, were directed substantially to reacting to these problems. Created by the Nazis as a sort of municipal council, given power only to a limited degree within the ghetto, with no opportunity to debate policy imposed by the Germans and with totally inadequate means, the *Judenrat* nevertheless did what it could to keep the community functioning. Both its credibility and its actions were further compromised by two weaknesses in the leadership ranks. First, many of the best-trained and most experienced people were lost to the *Judenrat,* either from having left the city early in the war or from being removed from office—often killed—by the Nazis.[5] Moreover, as Gutman points out about the Jewish leaders in Warsaw and, by extension, elsewhere in Poland, "Their consciousness, forged by a classic European education, dismissed out of hand the possibility of a calculated system to murder masses of innocent and helpless victims."[6] The Jews of Poland were by no means unique in their difficulty in comprehending the barbarity that soon was to engulf them. Opinions differ sharply on how well the members of the *Judenrat* accomplished their impossible tasks.[7] Corruption flourished, often encouraged and even made possible by the occupying power, but the intent in principle was fundamentally beneficent.

At the same time, Jewish organizations worked vigorously to provide social welfare to the burgeoning masses who needed it desperately. Most of the relief agencies had existed before the war, often based on political parties or occupational groups. But the chief task from the autumn of 1939 on was physical survival of hunger and disease. Political activities in the classic sense did continue, but the scope of possible action was slight and the need for welfare overwhelming. The majority of the ghetto's inhabitants, preoccupied as they were with the struggle against hunger, disease, and overcrowding, "were hardly sympathetic to those who were 'playing around' with outlawed politics."[8]

Thus the disaster in Warsaw (and many other communities in Poland) can be seen as predominantly medical. Yet the attention paid to the medical aspects by general historians has been slight, giving little recognition to the fundamental nature of the struggle. Gutman, for example, while mentioning often the existence of hunger and disease, concentrates on organizational and political history, presenting scant detail about exactly what the diseases were or how they influenced the struggle for existence of individuals and of the community itself. The index to his book, *The Jews of Warsaw, 1939–1943: Ghetto, Underground, Revolt*, is symptomatic. It lists nothing medical whatsoever except one citation of four page numbers under "epidemics"[9]; the words "starvation," "typhus," "tuberculosis," "hospital," "Czyste Hospital," "vaccine," "physicians," and "nurses" appear nowhere. The textual allusions are limited to passing comments on typhus and starvation. Gutman makes no attempt to assess the importance of these problems in terms of the allocation of ghetto supplies, the impact on the population censuses, the psychological devastation that descended on a population confined within such an unhealthy area, or any of the other imaginable consequences and problems.

In the Jewish quarter of Warsaw and, later, in the ghetto, the residents knew from the beginning that the struggle was for their lives, individually if not collectively. The threat of disease and hunger was palpable long before any ultimate Nazi design was discerned. The struggles of the Jewish leaders were basic: Maximize the supply of food; keep the hospitals functioning; teach public health fundamentals to the populace. But the Jews also found ways to rise above merely coping with basic health needs.

One inspirational reaction was the creation of a medical school within the Warsaw ghetto, as described in Chapter 10. Carried out against German edicts and incredible odds, the school was modeled on standard European curricular lines. Its intent was to educate Jewish youth in medicine and, if the situation permitted and the war lasted that long, to graduate physicians to fill the depleted ranks of the Jewish medical profession. With the conventional wisdom of hindsight we can perceive the impossibility of the task. Yet the medical school operated for 15 months, the greater part of two academic years. Only a few students survived the ghetto and, in a variety of ways, avoided liquidation at Treblinka or in the labor camps. Some of them became physicians. A very few are still practicing medicine half a century after the school vanished in the chaos attending the eradication of the ghetto and its inhabitants.

Similarly, the research into hunger disease outlined in Chapter 5 was another instance of Jewish determination not to be limited to the mere fundamentals of survival. Given the vast numbers of starving men, women, and children in the ghetto, physicians undertook scientific studies of starvation. They had no illusions that the research would help them or their patients to survive. Rather, it was research of the purest kind, intended to advance human knowledge. And it did.

This book is an effort to tell the story of the unceasing pressure on the inhabitants of the Warsaw ghetto that resulted from constant hunger and the threat or the reality of catastrophic disease. I shall use, wherever possible, eyewitness testimony generously provided by a small group of survivors, most of them doctors, nurses, or medical students in the ghetto. Thus the book contains two interwoven stories. One is a general account of the demoralizing final years in the lives of half a million Jews within the Warsaw ghetto; the second is the particular experiences of a handful of men and women who were active in some medical capacity during the war and who survived this catastrophic era.

No discussion of the ghetto can succeed unless it gives some recognition to the scope of life there. Within Warsaw the ghetto was a living entity, a city within a city, until ultimately destroyed in April and May 1943. Its borders changed, its population swelled and shrank in conformance to Nazi regulations and actions. But it was truly a city, containing half a million souls, with all of the complexity that one expects from any grouping of this many human beings. Within the original Jewish population of Warsaw in the summer of 1939, there were some rich, many poor, and a multitude between these extremes. Most were fundamentally honest and decent, but a few were neither; crime existed in Jewish society as in all others, with the notable qualification that murder and rape were almost unknown. Moreover, there was a strong, deep-rooted tradition of mutual help among the Jews of Eastern Europe. Without this tradition, the ghetto might have disintegrated by itself, given the appalling conditions forced upon the Jews. Instead, its active destruction was begun by the Nazis in July 1942.

The Jews of Warsaw were not a unitary entity. No less than any other racial, religious, or ethnic group comprising hundreds of thousands of persons, Warsaw's Jews fit within a wide spectrum of types. At one extreme were the former Jews, or baptized Jews, or Christianized Jews. Thousands of Jews—or their parents or grandparents—had left Judaism and formally accepted another religious designation. In Poland, this usually meant baptism and entry into Catholicism. This process had been going on for centuries but had accelerated in the first few decades of the twentieth century.

At the other end of the spectrum were the Hasidim and other Orthodox Jews; these were the Jews most quickly identifiable as being Jewish, the men wearing the long beards, curled side locks of hair, and characteristic attire. For these, religious ceremony, dietary laws, and a rich panoply of daily observance based on holy writings were fundamental aspects of life.

And between the Orthodox and the converted there were numerous, often indefinable groupings representing various religious sects within Jewry, as well as a large group whose observance of religious customs was either nominal or nonexistent. A significant group were the so-called assimilationists, who were Jews, some observant and some not. But they tried to be good Poles as well, learning Polish and sending their children to Polish schools.[10]

Nor were the variations limited to religious practice. Within Warsaw and within Poland, there were well-educated Jews and illiterate, ignorant Jews; Jews who spoke Polish and French and knew neither Hebrew nor Yiddish, and Jews who spoke only Yiddish; sybaritic Jews and ascetic Jews; Jews who considered themselves Polish patriots and Jews who worked toward a Palestinian homeland; communist Jews and ultra-right Jews; honest Jews and thieves; fat Jews and thin. To best see this panoply, one should, perhaps, read some of the Warsaw novels of Isaac Bashevis Singer, who had lived in Warsaw before World War II—books such as *Shosha* and *The Family Moskat*, for example.[11]

One spectrum that will be encountered repeatedly has to do with money, with "financial means." As in all societies there was a spread here, too. Stefan Ernest has described this spectrum of wealth and its effects:

> Perhaps twenty, perhaps thirty thousand properly nourished people, members of the "social elite." In contrast are the masses of a quarter of a million beggars and totally destitute, who struggle just to postpone the hour of death from starvation ... and in the middle, between these two ends of the spectrum, a mass of about 200,000 "average people" who make do, more or less, and are still considered "personalities," still surviving, decently dressed, their bodies not swollen by hunger.[12]

Throughout this book I shall refer to Jews usually without making, again, these qualifications. But I ask the reader to remember the disparate, polyglot, varied reality behind this shorthand word. It was only the Nazis, with ruthless if idiosyncratic logic, who created unity from this diversity. They proclaimed that all of the various Jews just described would experience identical fates: first ghettoization, later extermination.

A NOTE ON WORDS

In writing about World War II in Europe, one encounters a phenomenon of language that requires some attention. The Nazis, masters of propaganda and misrepresentation—other words for lies—employed a number of words in ways other than those generally recognized, whether in German, Polish, Yiddish, Hebrew, French, English, or any other language.

The most common of these words were "Aryan," "relocation," "*Aktion*," "deportation," and "selection." I intend to suggest here how the Nazis used these words, and then shall not usually single them out further, leaving them to appear wherever appropriate in the following pages without the distinction of quotation marks. I hope the reader will understand, when reading these words, that they are used in the Nazi sense in effect between the early 1930s and 1945.

Aryan: In the narrowest sense, this word was used by the Nazis to designate the tall, blond, Nordic individuals who were the prototypes of Hitler's vision of the German "master race." But the word came to be used much more broadly as a shorthand term for non-Jewish. Thus writings about wartime in Warsaw frequently refer to "Aryan Warsaw," meaning that part of the city exclusive of the ghetto, and to "Aryan Poles" to indicate non-Jewish Poles. The word will be used in that wider sense in this book.

Relocation, *Umsiedlung*: This was the euphemism for extermination. Being "relocated to the east" meant being sent to a camp such as Treblinka or Sobibor and death.

Aktion: This was a raid, a rounding up of Jews (or Belgians or Czechs), usually for deportation or relocation. The *Aktion* might consist of apprehending whatever Jews happened to be in the street, or might involve clearing buildings or even blocks. Because the English equivalent, "action," is such a common and banal word, the original German will usually be used.

Deportation: Deportation was not as necessarily absolute as relocation. If one were deported to an extermination camp, one died. But deportation might be to a camp such as Auschwitz, where there was at least some slight chance of survival, as several interviewees for this book can testify. The same was true of Buchenwald, Dachau, and other similar labor camps.

Selection: this was not an innocent word; when "selected" by the Nazis, the usual end result was death. In a concentration camp, the inhabitants of a barracks might be surveyed and certain members selected because of illness. These men and women might be sent to the hospital, a seemingly innocuous and even desirable result. But all inmates knew that the so-called hospital tended to be a doorway to the gas chambers and the crematoria. In the Warsaw ghetto, selections from the workers in a ghetto industry or from an apartment building usually ended with the selectees being marched to the *Umschlagplatz* and transported to Treblinka.

In addition, I must comment on the word "antisemitism." The spelling of "antisemitism" is a source of some debate. Often a hyphen is used. Shmuel Almog points out that using the hyphen gives inappropriate dignity to the word "Semite," in this context not equated with historical Semitic peoples in the Near East but rather used as a synonym for "Jew." In this book the word is used without a hyphen.[13]

1

Medical Conditions and the Jewish Medical Profession in Poland Before World War II

Poland was a difficult place for Jews to live in the 1930s, though undoubtedly less so for a professional person than for a laborer. But antisemitism, while not universal, was reaching new heights of virulence, and every aspect of life was affected. No Jews were permitted to be professional officers in the Polish army, though exceptions were made occasionally, especially in the case of medical officers.[1] No Jews were in the police.

Obtaining a good education was complicated and difficult. In the preuniversity phases, if one's family had money, then ways of avoiding antisemitism existed; for example, there were excellent, but expensive, all-Jewish schools available for girls in Warsaw[2] and for boys.

A Jew's experience of antisemitism covered a wide range, dependent on many factors, particularly appearance and family wealth. Looking obviously Jewish was a guarantee of unpleasantness, at least. But having a "good" face, one without identifiably "Jewish" characteristics, could mean a relatively incident-free existence.[3]

In the universities, a *numerus clausus* was invoked: in medicine and in dentistry, no more than 10 percent of students could be Jewish.[4] The result was falling enrollment by Jews in Polish universities. In the 1928–29 academic year, 17.9 percent of medical students were Jewish; in 1937 that figure had declined to 10 percent.[5] Between these years, two political events fanned the flames of Polish antisemitism: Poland and Nazi Germany signed an agreement on political matters in 1933, and Marshal Jozef Pilsudski died in 1935.[6] Pilsudski had attempted to minimize antisemitism in Poland while he was premier.

Nor did admission of a Jewish student to the select 10 percent admitted to medical school end the acts of prejudice. These continued, not only unabated but often exaggerated by daily proximity to antisemitic fellow students and the indifference of most of the professors. Various humiliations were introduced by actively antisemitic professors and students. One was the "ghetto bench," an arrangement whereby Jews were allowed to sit only in a special area on the left side of the lecture hall. Another was the placing of yellow tags on those benches, bearing the resurrected medieval slogan, "Here sits a Jew."[7] A Catholic medical student remembers clearly the efforts of her nationalistic classmates to humiliate the Jews in the class in 1938. There was physical intimidation too, including the beating of Jews with rubber hoses in the dissecting room at Warsaw University.[8]

Although some university teachers refused to enforce a quota or the ghetto bench system, a large percentage did permit such practices. The number of Jews attending Polish universities declined rapidly. Even though "some Jewish students remained standing throughout their classes rather than sit on the ghetto benches, separate seating areas came to be common practice."[9] But some Jewish students were helped by their professors; Dr. Ludwig Stabholz received significant assistance from his otherwise notoriously antisemitic teacher, Prof. Edward Loth.[10] This happened both when he was a medical student and later, when he was teaching anatomy in the ghetto medical school.

Once admitted, the students followed a curriculum more or less typical of all European medical schools of the 1930s.[11] In 1938, 4074 students graduated in medicine in Poland, 24 percent of them women (1185 graduated in pharmacy, 52 percent women).[12] Presumably, about 400 of these (10 percent) were Jewish. Much worse was in store for Jewish university students, of course. Poles who had friends in Czechoslovakia would have learned what happened there when the Nazis arrived in 1938. All Jewish students were forced out of the universities, including medical students. Those who were in the final year were permitted to take their examinations, but only from a Jewish professor. Those in the earlier years were simply expelled.[13]

In general, Jews who planned or hoped to emigrate had difficulty getting their money out of Poland. One of the schemes used to get around this problem required the cooperation of medical (and other) students studying abroad, usually because of the *numerus clausus*. A Jew could send money out of the country if he were supporting a university student abroad. When Marek Balin was studying in Paris, family friends would send him money for "support," which he would deposit in their bank account, deducting 10 percent as his fee. This he used, along with his earnings as a waiter, to support himself in the university there.[14] So many Jewish students in Poland were poor that they sought aid from the American Joint Distribution Committee, which in 1938 provided 8170 zloty ($1600) to assist needy Warsaw students; of this amount, 667 zloty was assigned to the Association of Students of Medicine in Warsaw.[15]

Antisemitic attitudes permeated professional life after graduation. In 1937, the Association of Physicians of the Polish Republic, one of the leading medical organizations in the country, passed a by-law excluding Jews from membership. Not all members approved, and ultimately several chapters that refused to comply were disbanded.[16] Prof. Ludwig Hirszfeld, himself a baptized Jew, was a member of the Society of Preventive Medicine. This society had been created before the war by Dr. Zygmunt Srebrny and many others, Jews and gentiles. But "[i]t hurts me to remember that many physicians, even those of Jewish origin, did not want to speak in that society so that, God forbid, no one would suspect them of Semitophilism."[17]

So, medical students who were Jewish had a difficult time getting an education in Poland and practicing their profession afterward. What of their patients? The 1920s and 1930s were not easy years for the average Polish Jew. Poverty began, for many, with the destruction wrought by World War I; families were dislocated, orphans abounded, wages were low, and in the late 1930s in particular, antisemitism acquired new vigor and made the lives of the Jews even more difficult.

Out of the misery and suffering of the Jews of Europe during World War I arose an organization that played a decisive role in succoring them then and that continued its activities after the war. This group played an equally vital role in the ghetto of Warsaw, and throughout Poland, in the 1940s. The organization was the American Jewish Joint Distribution Committee, known variously as the American Joint Distribution Committee, the AJDC, the JDC, and perhaps most often simply as "Joint."

Joint was a wartime baby, whose grandfather was the American Jewish Committee (AJC), founded in 1906 with the aim of safeguarding the rights of Jews everywhere and of fighting discrimination. When World War I began, its impact on the Jews of Eastern Europe induced the AJC to set up the American Jewish Relief Committee (AJRC), which became the chief fund-raising agency for Jews in the United States and a parent of Joint. Ultimately, the AJRC joined forces with two other bodies with more or less parallel aims, the Central Relief Committee (CRC) and the People's Relief Committee (PRC), to give birth to the AJDC.[18] That joining together was memorialized in the word "Joint" in the name of the new committee.

After World War I, Joint continued trying to aid the Jews of Eastern Europe. In Poland it set up facilities to provide medical care, a desperate need inadequately met by the Polish government. Joint also addressed one of the most compelling problems of the time: providing care for hundreds of orphans, as well as children who had lost their parents in the confusion of wartime. By the early 1920s, Joint had begun to remove itself from direct involvement in the field, believing it more appropriate to have local initiative carry on. Thus it passed on its medical and preventive-medical activities to a new Polish-Jewish agency, *Towarzystwo Ochrony Zdrowia Ludności Żydowskiej*, or TOZ (Society to Protect the Health of the Jewish Population). TOZ was founded in 1922.[19] The work of Joint with orphans and needy children became the responsibility of *Centrala Opieki nad Sierotami*, or CENTOS (Organization for the Care of Orphans). CENTOS was a federation of Polish Jewish children's aid and orphan organizations created in 1924. By 1935 it included 90 percent of all Jewish child-aid institutions in Poland.[20]

The new organizations carried on the work previously done by Joint, with ongoing and substantial financial support from America. But to the highest degree possible, they were funded locally by fees and donations. Both TOZ and CENTOS, as will be discussed in the appropriate chapters, were crucial to supporting the inhabitants of the Warsaw ghetto. They finally disappeared as organizations when the Germans forced them to combine with and became divisions of *Żydowskie Towarzystwo Opieki Społecznej*, or ŻTOS (Jewish Welfare Association).

During the 1930s, many of Poland's Jews were in dire need of aid. In 1932, reports to Joint headquarters indicated that nearly 100,000 Jewish families—a total of over 400,000 persons—were on the verge of starvation.[21] This was almost one-third of all the Jews in Poland. Two years later, TOZ social workers surveyed the poorer parts of the Jewish district in Warsaw; their findings indicated the barely marginal existence of many Jews. Indeed, the observations provide a sort of *déjà vu* when one encounters the extremes of life in the ghetto seven and eight years later. Here is a single but typical example:

> *Mr. F-i (Stawki 22[22])* The family consists of 8 people: the parents, the grandmother and five children. All live in a kitchen which they rent from another family. The window faces a wall and the room is therefore dark all day. Two little children aged

10-11 look like children 6-7—pale, weak and sickly. The father had a stand with second-hand clothes which, due to his frequent illnesses, was sold at auction. At present, when he is well, he peddles in the street but that is very rare because he is sick in bed most of the time. His wife, a small wizened and shrunken woman, has learned to sew and is now a "seamstress"—she mends old underwear in a Warsaw market-place. However, her earnings are so small that they are not even sufficient for bread alone: she earns 25 groschen a day (five cents!).[23]

People in this situation had great difficulty obtaining adequate medical care. One consequence was that healers of many kinds flourished, offering cheap but often medically questionable aid. Janina David describes one individual of this type, a *feldscher* who called himself a "medical assistant" and who earned a living doing cupping, applying leeches, giving injections, and sometimes pulling teeth.[24] Something better was needed but frequently not available.

The expenditures of Joint were high during the 1930s, as the worldwide Depression had severe effects in Eastern Europe. In 1936, total expenditures in Poland amounted to $541,500, of which $47,400 (8.7 percent) was for medical work through TOZ and the direct support of hospitals and clinics; for the first nine months of 1937 the figures rose to $722,300 and $84,100 (10.8 percent), respectively.[25]

What did that expenditure provide? TOZ workers cited 14 activities for 1937, areas of support that emphasize their intention to stress preventive over curative medicine, though, of course, not to the exclusion of the latter. These activities were:

1. medical-advisory offices for mothers and nursing infants
2. medical advisory offices for general use and school children
3. "Dentistic-cabinets" (for examining teeth)
4. antituberculosis advisory offices
5. x-ray cabinets—healing of favus (a skin disorder)
6. cabinets for light treatment
7. hospitals
8. sanatoria
9. school hygiene offices
10. summer colonies
11. feeding of school children
12. propaganda about hygiene
13. lectures
14. rural physicians (76 physicians were assisted financially by TOZ in settling in provincial towns)[26]

As the war years came closer, the state of Poland's Jews continued to worsen. In 1937, TOZ fed 35,514 school children regularly, and CENTOS fed 20,590 plus all those boarded in CENTOS orphanages and homes.[27] One report emphasizes the problems in Wolhynia, a Polish province where pogroms were almost unknown but where the countrywide policy of boycotting Jewish enterprises cut especially deep. For example, in Ostrog, a town of 13,000, of whom half were Jews, the children were hungry. Fewer than half of the Jewish children attended school because there was no money for clothing, food, or tuition. Of 386 Jewish children surveyed by

CENTOS workers, only 67 were healthy; 29 were chronically ill, 31 were ill, 61 had scrofula, and 196 were labeled weak and anemic.[28] These are the kinds of persons who were forced into the Warsaw ghetto between 1940 and 1942. By 1938, Polish observers estimate that of 550,000 Jewish children of school age, more than half were suffering from malnutrition.[29]

Though only a minority of Polish Jews were in such a desperate condition as World War II approached, it was a large minority. Nothing that happened during the war improved their situation. Even more important than day-to-day hunger and absence of decent clothing were the long-term cumulative effects. When children or adults have been undernourished for months or years, they often exist on the brink of physical disaster. Unlike their better-fed compatriots, they succumbed with disastrous speed to further deprivation. And the future brought with it prompt and unremitting deprivation.

2

Nazi Rule Comes to Poland

> . . . there is no place for agitators, profiteers, or Jewish parasites in the area that has been placed under German sovereignty.
>
> Hans Frank, 26 October 1939[1]

THE BACKGROUND

During World War I, the composition that Poland was to have after the war was much discussed. Indeed, the subject was a major topic among the powers maneuvering to take fullest advantage of the Brest-Litovsk Treaty.[2] In 1916, the Germans announced their policy for a Kingdom of Poland, based on the premise that the Poles would show their gratitude by placing Polish battalions under German command. The Poles would not. Austria saw Poland united with Galicia, becoming part of the Habsburg monarchy. Hungary thought that Poland should become an Austrian province. The German High Command (as distinct from the government) envisaged a division of lands that would maximize their strategic advantages in the next war[3] by creating wide corridors in the Danzig-Thorn neck and in Upper Silesia to ensure limitless coal supplies. The Russians, not surprisingly, expected to have "Russian Poland" returned to them. The opinion of the Poles, though seldom sought or listened to, can be imagined.

Many forces shaped Poland between the wars and affected Polish attitudes toward Jews. The most important were nationalism, economic depression, and Nazism.

Pilsudski's defeat of the Soviet army on 16 August 1920[4] epitomized twentieth-century Polish pride in nationhood. But the defeat of the Russians was recognized by the Poles as a temporary respite. The essentially defenseless nature of Poland was unchanged. Poland is situated on a plain with few physical features that present serious problems for invading armies from either east or west. So nation building (or rebuilding) was carried out in an atmosphere of impending doom.

The worldwide economic depression affected Poland as seriously as most other nations. The struggle for jobs exacerbated the already strong Polish antisemitism. Economic boycott of Jewish businesses was a common and effective Polish response that helped the Poles and simultaneously dealt a serious blow to the Jews. Jews were not the only poor people in Europe in the 1930s, of course; many people hungered, many starved to death. Because of welfare agencies and philanthropy, poor Jews subsisted. But their poverty was real and essentially unchanged by these efforts to help.

The historian Lucy Dawidowicz spent a year in Poland between the summer of

1938 and the beginning of World War II. Her experiences were in Wilno, now Vilnius in Lithuania, but there is no reason to suppose that her introduction to true poverty would have been different had she been in Warsaw. She was shocked to find a Jewish babies' clinic filled with "ashen, skinny, withered, sad-eyed, cheerless, cranky, coughing, wailing, unbelievably filthy" children[5] and some areas of Wilno occupied by hordes of beggars "dressed in layers of tatters that had once been clothing. Some didn't have shoes, but had swaddled their feet in strips of rags."[6] To know precisely what these people looked like, one need only examine some of the extant photographs of Jews on the verge of death in the Warsaw ghetto. These unfortunates imported with them, into the ghetto, the certainty of their destruction.

Hitler made no secret of his insistence on land to provide for German *lebensraum*, or of his perception that it lay largely to the east of Germany. And immediately east of the Third Reich was Poland, as all Poles were nervously aware. Nevertheless, in 1934, Poland and Germany signed a 10-year nonaggression pact. This more or less friendly period was short-lived as 1939 came inexorably closer. But one characteristic of the mid-1930s was some agreement between Germany and Poland as to their mutual antisemitic feelings. Thus the *Volkischer Beobachter* published accounts in 1936 of the bombing of synagogues and Jewish shops in Poland and described for the German public the demands of Polish nationalist groups that Jewish emigration from that country be paid for by the international Jewish community.[7] In 1938 OZON, an official Polish political party, published a pamphlet that contained these words: "The first stage of this struggle is to lock the Jews in a ghetto, isolate them from their destructive work."[8]

By 1939, of course, the Nazis grouped Poles only slightly above the Jews and Gypsies, who were *untermenschen*, subhumans, to be treated as slave labor or worse. As late as 1943, Dr. Hans Frank, Governor-General of the *Generalgouvernement*, attempted to have the German propaganda ministry cease lumping the Poles together with the other two groups. He required labor from the Poles, who therefore needed to be treated with a modicum of good will.[9]

THE NAZI REGIME IN POLAND

Less than a month after their invasion, the armed forces of Nazi Germany compelled the capitulation of Poland. In Warsaw, hostilities ceased on 27 September 1939.[10] Repression of the entire population began immediately but was most severe in the case of the Jews.

Life changed rapidly for all Poles, Jews and Christians alike. By November 1939 the country had been divided into three parts. The Russians held the eastern segment. The remaining portion consisted of a large western and northern area annexed to Germany and made part of the Reich (Silesia, Warthegau, part of east Prussia) and central Poland, called the *Generalgouvernement,* with headquarters at Kraków under Hans Frank, whose threatening words began this chapter. The *Generalgouvernement* was divided into four districts, each with a governor: Kraków, Radom, Warsaw, and Lublin.[11] In October 1939 the *Generalgouvernement* contained 11,835,510 persons, of whom 1,457,376 were Jews.[12]

Throughout Poland, education ground to a halt under German rule.[13] The aim of German policy, for Christian Poles, was to permit only semiliteracy, sufficient for what was intended to be a population of manual laborers.[14] Heinrich Himmler, Reich Leader of the SS, is quoted as having said: "For the non-German population of the East there must be no schooling higher than the four-grade [sic] elementary school. The aim of such an elementary school must merely be this: Simple arithmetic up to no more than 500; writing one's own name; the lesson that it is a divine command to be obedient to the Germans, and to be honest, hard working, and good. I do not think that reading is required."[15]

The Jews were scheduled for relocation or, by 1941, for extinction, and thus their education required no planning on any long-term basis. In Warsaw, the last Jewish school officially closed its doors on 4 December 1939.[16]

The Nazis arrived in Poland with special plans for its Jews. As early as 21 September 1939, Reinhardt Heydrich, Chief of the Reich Security Head Office and Protector of Bohemia, issued orders to concentrate all Jews in cities as soon as possible, to begin to transfer all Jews in the Reich to Poland, to transfer the 30,000 Gypsies to Poland, and to carry out these transports using freight trains.[17]

Immediately after the war began, stories began to circulate about the actions of German personnel. Soon after the Nazis set up their government in the *General-gouvernement*, a man received a bill from the Germans for medical care of his son, a mental patient. On inquiring why the billing ceased on 19 October 1939, the father was informed that the Germans had shot his son on that date, along with the other mental patients in the institution.[18] That same autumn, a physician saw a German officer stop a Jewish woman in the street, take her fur coat from her, and give it to his female companion.[19] But this woman would have considered herself fortunate if she knew about the fate of some other Jewish women in Warsaw; suspected of concealing jewelry or gold, they were stripped, forced to stand on a table, undergo an amateur but presumably enthusiastic and forceful gynecological "exam," and then jump onto the floor, legs wide apart, so that the supposed hidden valuables would be dislodged from their vaginal canals.[20]

The attitude of the conquerors to the Jews is epitomized in a German officer who discovered a young gentile Polish boy observing an *Einsatzgruppe* at work, shooting Jews in a ditch they had just been forced to dig. Unaccountably, the officer neither shot the boy nor chased him away. At the sound of another volley of shots he looked at the boy, shrugged, and said contemptuously, "*Nur Juden.*" Only Jews.[21] Hans Frank made his feelings explicit, if anyone had doubted them, on 16 December 1941, when he said, "my outlook on the Jews is based on the hope that they will cease to exist."[22] By then, that outcome was about to be ensured.

At the beginning of the war the Jewish *Kehilla* had ceased to function, largely due to the flight of many of its prewar members. The *Kehilla* was a religious and social institution of the type that existed in every Jewish community. In its place, five members of the *Kehilla* remaining in Warsaw formed a "Buerger Committee" (Coordinating Committee). These men were Senator Mojzesz Koerner, Adam Czerniakow, Abraham Gepner, Maksymilian Apolinary Hartglas,[23] and Henryk Szoszkies. Their intention was to create a body with which the Polish authorities could discuss welfare and other problems and to which the Jewish population could appeal in case of need. Soon after the Germans occupied Warsaw on 28 September, they forcefully disbanded the Buerger Committee, and Czerniakow was ordered to establish an institution completely new to the Jews, a *Judenrat*.[24] All five of these men served on the *Judenrat* until sometime in the autumn, when Szoszkies escaped from Poland to the United States.

On 4 October, the Warsaw *Judenrat* was created by the Germans to replace both the *Kehilla* and the ad hoc Buerger Committee that had been formed by the Jews in September. Unlike the *Kehilla*, the *Judenrat* was a political and economic bureaucracy intended by the Germans to continue the activities of the *Kehilla* and, in addition, to be a means to force the Jewish community not only to carry out German orders but also to pay for their operation. The duties imposed on the *Judenrat* were those customarily associated with a municipality, including public health, police, distribution of supplies, postal services, and employment.[25] At the same time that they demanded that the *Judenrat* undertake these responsibilities, the Germans ensured the ultimate impossibility of the task by supplying, or permitting to be supplied, too little of everything except Jews.

On 4 November 1939, the victorious Germans first indicated their conviction that it would be necessary to create a ghetto. It is a revealing commentary on the lack of cohesion among the German conquerors that the order was issued by the SS in the name of the *Wehrmacht* military commander of the city. However, the latter knew nothing of the order, which was soon set aside.[26] But the basic idea was retained and planning proceeded.

On 23 November 1939, a decree ordered every Jew in Warsaw to wear a white armband bearing a blue Star of David on the right sleeve below the elbow.[27] Although many Jews tried to transform the armband into a symbol of pride, one of its immediate effects was to inflame further a violent antisemitic element of the Polish population by clearly identifying prospective subjects for humiliation, robbery, and injury. Identifying papers were marked prominently "Jude" (see Figure 2.1.)

Economic sanctions, forced labor, and indiscriminate confiscation of property, as well as beatings, rape,[28] and murder—carried out by Polish rowdies, by Germans themselves, and later by Ukrainian and other nationals in German service—became part of the routine of life for Warsaw's Jews from 1939 on. The routine hostility of a certain portion of the Polish people toward the Jews was significantly intensified during the war,[29] at least partly because this element felt themselves encouraged by the occupiers.

The social structure of the Jewish quarter, soon to become the ghetto, was distorted by various influxes of Jews from outside Warsaw, a process that began with the arrival of Polish Jews from destroyed villages after the German *blitzkrieg* of September 1939. Over the next three years the Nazis forced tens of thousands of refugees from Poland and Germany into the ghetto. A few of these, the German Jews, arrived relatively well off, with some personal belongings, money, and valuables, in more or less intact family units. The great bulk, however, had been forced to leave their homes with minutes' to hours' notice, taking with them no more than they could carry. By the time they arrived at Warsaw, they had often been robbed of these few possessions by their "guards," whether they were Germans, Poles,

Figure 2.1. *Ausweis,* or identity card, of Dr. Bernard Waksman (now Dr. Bronislaw Wisniewski) (reproduced courtesy of Dr. Wisniewski).

Ukrainians, or Latvians. They were humiliated, depressed, often unwell, and thoroughly cowed. Even the originally well-to-do among them usually had little left, and those whose lives had previously been lived on the margin were destitute, dependent on assistance from the Jewish community, which had little to give. It was especially among these last groups, the refugees, that the worst poverty was seen and that the twin foes of starvation and disease took the quickest and easiest toll.

The German governor of the Warsaw District, Dr. Ludwig Fischer, issued an order on 2 October 1940 establishing the boundaries of the ghetto and calling for its institution by 31 October.[30] The Jews were informed of this order on 12 October 1940, a date that presumably was not coincidental; it was Yom Kippur, the Day of Atonement.[31] This date was changed twice, but by 15 November 1940 the ghetto existed. At least 80,000 Christian Poles had been moved out of the area and around 140,000 Jews forced in.[32]

3

Life and Conditions in the Warsaw Ghetto

There is within us some hidden power, mysterious and secret, which keeps us going, keeps us alive, despite the natural law. If we cannot live on what is permitted, we live on what is forbidden.

Chaim Kaplan, 10 March 1940, Warsaw[1]

STAGES OF JEWISH EXISTENCE IN WARSAW DURING WORLD WAR II

The period from the beginning of World War II to the end of the war in Europe, September 1939 to May 1945, can be divided into seven stages with respect to the existence of the Jews in Warsaw.[2] Conditions differed from one phase to the next, sometimes profoundly. The stages, and the relevant German agencies in charge of the Jews, are as follows:

1. The War in Poland: September 1939; the *Wehrmacht* was in charge at this early stage.
2. The Takeover of the Jewish Community: early fall 1939; *Einsatzgruppe IV* took over briefly.
3. Impositions and Exactions: fall 1939 to the creation of the ghetto in November 1940; control effected by the German city administration, headed first by Helmuth Otto and later by Oskar Dengel and Ludwig Leist.
4. Ghetto Formation: November 1940 to early spring 1941; German district administration: Division *Umsiedlung* (Resettlement or Relocation), led by Waldemar Schön, in charge.
5. Ghetto Maintenance: spring 1941 to the first deportations to Treblinka, 22 July 1942; German district administration, the *Kommissar* for the ghetto being Heinz Auerswald.
6. The Deportations: from 22 July 1942 on; this deadly stage was managed by SS *Umsiedlung* staff headed by Hermann Höfle, from the staff of Odilo Globocnik, head of the SS for the Lublin district.
7. Furtive Survival until Germany Surrendered: May 1943 to May 1945.

This book describes and elucidates primarily stages 2 through 6, viewing them from the particular viewpoint of health and disease. Nevertheless, stage 1 cannot be omitted, since in it the physical and psychological conditions were established that would play so large a role in all the later stages.

19

THE WAR IN POLAND, SEPTEMBER 1939

In the period between 1 and 27 September, enormous damage was inflicted on Warsaw by Nazi bombs and artillery shells. In addition to regular ordnance, there was a rumor of bacterial warfare. After heavy bombing on 14 September, the following day German planes dropped propaganda leaflets. "These leaflets were not touched because the Radio had announced that they were soaked with bacilli."[3] There is no evidence that this was in fact the case; almost certainly the event is an illustration of the panic that occurs at such times.

According to one estimate, as many as 95 percent of all homes in the city were damaged to some degree, 10 to 25 percent of those being destroyed and perhaps 30 percent heavily damaged.[4] That part of Warsaw commonly referred to as the "Jewish quarter" (though many gentiles lived there as well) was especially heavily damaged. Isaiah Trunk cites a figure of 30 percent of Jewish homes, stores, factories, and workshops totally destroyed, including the two Jewish business centers located on or around Grzybow Square and Nalewki Street.[5] A contemporary report from Joint staff in Warsaw, however, states that as many as 40 percent of the houses in the Jewish district were destroyed.[6]

To understand the impact of this destruction on the Jews of Warsaw, and to see the ultimate reflection of such losses on matters involving survival within the ghetto, we must know something of Jewish living conditions in Warsaw before the war.

The districts of Muranów and Mirów, which contained the Jewish quarter, were full of shops and the homes of workers (mostly Jews), largely lower-middle-class and cottage workers. The latter operated their home industries especially in and around the following streets: Leszno, Karmelicka, Gliniana, Dzika, and Nalewki—names that will recur again and again in terms of life in the ghetto. The people there had modest homes, some very modest indeed. About 43 percent came from what was then called the lower middle class; 40 percent were working class.[7] Almost none of the homes in this area were single-dwelling houses, but rather apartment buildings, often very large, or two- or three-story buildings with shops on the street level and living quarters above.

A typical apartment contained one bedroom, a kitchen, and a living room, usually small. Sometimes there was a water faucet and sink in the kitchen and a stove. Toilets, dingy, dark, and smelly, were located in the courtyard or backyard, adjacent to a large receptacle for garbage. In general, the only baths were public establishments.[8] Some of the neighboring buildings had large textile or haberdashery shops in front, with "a bewildering variety of small shops in the yards and on the upper floors. Wholesale cosmetics, umbrellas, notions, various trade supplies, paper goods, bindery shops, religious articles, shoe stores, they were all there."[9] This description refers to Nalewki Street, in the heart of the Jewish quarter.

Irena Bakowska lived at Pawia 38, immediately across the street from Pawiak Prison, in one of the typical multistory buildings with inner courtyards that were so common in central Warsaw. Because both her parents were dentists, they had a large apartment in the five-story building, with windows looking out on the street and also into a courtyard. One wall of the hollow square of the building was the

Opus factory, where men's shirts were made. The other three walls contained apartments; thus residents could look into the factory from their dwellings.[10]

Because so much of this area was damaged and destroyed, there were many local "refugees," whose numbers were swollen when large numbers of refugees from surrounding towns and villages swarmed in, making the task of housing and feeding them all even more complicated. And because this severely damaged area was part of that small portion of Warsaw eventually set aside as the ghetto, it was much more difficult to provide housing than would otherwise have been the case.

A small proportion of Warsaw's Jews lived outside this area. Some of the most well-to-do lived in luxurious homes in the suburbs, particularly the formerly Jewish converts to Catholicism. These highly desirable residences could not be duplicated inside the ghetto. However, many of these people, when forced to move to the ghetto, were able to find housing on relatively fashionable streets such as Chłodna and Sienna.

The destruction wrought by the bombing and shelling of Warsaw in September 1939 created major physical problems, some of which were not completely corrected until after the war ended. Water and sewage systems were seriously damaged and electricity was available only irregularly, causing hardship for many Poles and Jews. The Jewish quarter, much of which became the ghetto, was harder hit than most areas of the city, and repairs simply were not made.

During the first winter of the war, a year before the ghetto was created, adequate heating was a problem for many Varsovians. In the home of Dr. David Wdowinski, the windows had been blown out during the September bombardment and could not be replaced. The family had to break up and burn their own furniture to keep from freezing.[11] That winter of 1939–40 was unusually cold, and Adam Czerniakow, chairman of the *Judenrat*, complained in February that even his office was almost never heated.[12] He would have noticed the cold more than usual at that time, since just three days before, he had been arrested and forced to await the pleasure of his Nazi superiors while standing in the snow at Krasinski Square. He discovered the literal meaning of "cooling his heels," since after four hours' wait one of his feet was frostbitten.[13] Ten days later, a Jew living at Franciszkańska 6 froze to death in his apartment.[14]

Not surprisingly, a sudden increase of frostbite was seen by the doctors in the bitter winter of 1939–40 and in the following two winters as well. Frostbite was not particularly common among the original residents of Warsaw; they often were cold but usually had enough garments to prevent actual freezing. With the refugees, it was different. They arrived destitute, often stripped of many of the clothes they had been wearing when they began their trek from the outlying villages and towns. Almost invariably their bundles, usually packed in haste in the face of orders to abandon their homes in 10 or 15 minutes, had been opened many times and anything valuable had been removed. This was done by the German guards and by Polish peasants. Decent shoes or boots were common targets for theft, since they were chronically difficult to acquire. So the refugees froze in Warsaw, while elsewhere in Poland their clothing and footwear protected the thieves. Even in the Jewish hospital at Czyste, patients developed frostbite. The heating system had never been repaired after the bomb damage in September 1939.[15] One of Dr. Janusz Korczak's charges from the orphanage returned from the hospital after having a leg amputated because of frostbite.[16]

PRELIMINARIES TO THE GHETTO: OCTOBER 1939 to NOVEMBER 1940

On 4 November 1939, the victorious Germans first revealed their conviction that it would be necessary to create a ghetto. The lack of cohesion among the German conquerors was such that the order was issued by the SS in the name of the *Wehrmacht* military commander of the city, General von Neumann-Neurode. He was visited by three members of the newly created *Judenrat*, Adam Czerniakow, Maksymilian Apolinary Hartglas, and Henryk Szoszkies, who wanted to discuss the order. Neumann seemed surprised and denied it.[17] The order was set aside at that time.[18] However, the basic idea was retained, and planning proceeded in at least some German offices.

Although the ghetto existed in the literal sense only from 15 November 1940, the concept of Jewish isolation from the rest of Warsaw began much earlier. A series of administrative actions by the Nazis, dating from autumn 1939, makes it clear where the future lay—at least in retrospect. As early as October 1939 the first barbed wire appeared, enclosing some of the main streets having particularly dense concentrations of Jews.[19] The creation of the *Judenrat* was a crucial step, perhaps the most important. But there were many others.

At least one reason for setting up a ghetto was propagandistic. As Hirszfeld described it, a repulsive picture had to be presented to the world, a picture that said: "here are the dirty, lice-infested, rejected and starving parasites, still fighting for their miserable lives."[20] Thus on 18 November 1939, Adam Czerniakow noted in his diary that the *Judenrat* had been ordered to place at its borders signs stating *Achtung Seuchengefahr Eintritt verboten* (Attention: Epidemic Area—Entry Forbidden).

Czerniakow went on to say that the takeover by the *Judenrat* of the hospital, the orphanages, and the various old people's homes had been postponed until the end of the year.[21] The "borders" referred to were those of the so-called Jewish quarter, but this area contained tens of thousands of Poles and was, besides, not precisely defined. Where *were* the signs put? The area included all the space in what became the ghetto and about half again as much territory.

This area was referred to by the Germans as the *Seuchensperregebeit* or "quarantined area,"[22] so that the concept of isolating the Jews on medical grounds was firmly established in 1939. In June 1940, German officials told Czerniakow that whether or not schools could open in the *Seuchensperregebeit* was a decision to be made by Dr. Kurt Schrempf, the German physician in charge of public health: that is, the decision was to be medical (or quasi-medical), not political.[23] The schools were not permitted to open.

Another step toward establishing a ghetto was taken in the autumn of 1939. The first duty assigned to the *Judenrat* was to undertake a statistical census of the Jews, which even in 1939 was understood by the Jews to be information required for setting up a ghetto in Warsaw.[24]

By March 1940, the Nazi rationale for ghettoization centered on their stated

Figure 3.1. Gate into Warsaw ghetto, late 1940 or early 1941 (probably at Leszno Street).

conviction that the Jews were especially susceptible to typhus and that they must therefore be confined in order to prevent the general spread of this much-feared disease.[25] However, on 8 March the plan to create a ghetto was postponed yet again.[26] Even so, on 1 April 1940, Jews were forced to begin digging ditches in preparation for the construction of walls.[27]

The construction of the ghetto wall began long before the plan for a functional ghetto was verified to the Jews. Initially, short, unconnected segments were erected. The subcontractor was the Lichtenbaum Company, representing a prominent and unloved Jewish family. The father was a member of the *Judenrat* and later the successor to Czerniakow as chairman after the latter committed suicide.[28] At the time the Jews were sealed off in November 1940, the wall remained incomplete. The final work, including alterations to accommodate later German reductions in the space, continued into 1942. The cost, which predictably was to be paid by the Jews themselves through the *Judenrat*, was immense. The statement of account of 7 July 1942 indicates a grand total of 1,309,559.71 zloty, about $260,000.[29] Needless to say, the Germans profited enormously from this construction, particularly the German contractor, Schmidt and Munstermann, Tiefbaugesellschaft.[30]

Although a few ghettos had been set up elsewhere in occupied Poland, ghettoization was by no means a general policy. Where ghettos were set up, it was originally thought that they would be short-term holding and concentrating areas while arrangements were made to ship the Jews elsewhere.[31] For some months, a favored site was Madagascar. Thus, when Frank was trying to prevent a further influx of displaced Jews into the *Generalgouvernement* in the late spring of 1940, he was delighted to hear that Himmler had found a colony in Africa for the Jews.[32] This plan was widely known at the time. On 1 July 1940, SS Sgt. Gerhard Mende declared to Czerniakow that the war would be over in a month, "and that we would all leave for Madagascar."[33] The *Umsiedlung* (resettlement) division of the Nazi government in Poland apparently dropped a plan to set up ghettos in two suburban areas of Warsaw when word was received "that Hitler wants to ship all of the European Jews to Madagascar 'after the war.' "[34]

The phrase "after the war" identified the basic defect of the plan, aside from its fundamental logistical impossibility. It was dependent upon the Nazis' winning the war. In the summer of 1940, they had just rolled through much of Western Europe and Norway and had confidently begun the "invasion" of Britain by initiating a softening-up program based on destruction from the air. However, the Nazis lost the Battle of Britain, thus failing to end the war or eliminate British sea power, vital factors preventing them from sending Jews to Madagascar.[35] The idea died, and another huge step was made toward the extermination "solution."[36] Nevertheless, for the Polish Jews, Madagascar remained a hopeful prospect, and after the ghetto was created and life deteriorated, the African island must have come to seem a potentially idyllic alternative. The Nazis may have abandoned the idea, but the Jews were not certain of that. According to Dr. Wilhelm Hagen, German public health officer, sometime during the ghetto period Dr. Izrael Milejkowski, head of the *Judenrat's* health department, requested his consent for the *Judenrat* health department to present a series of seminars on tropical diseases. He wanted the Jewish physicians to be prepared for conditions they might encounter on Madagascar.[37]

The Nazis had a penchant for arranging both apocalyptic announcements and catastrophic events to occur on Jewish holidays. This happened often enough that it seems unlikely to be coincidence. For example, in September 1939, the High Holidays for the Jews were celebrated by the Nazis in their own way; they concentrated heavy bombing raids on the Jewish quarter of Warsaw. Whether this practice represented sheer malevolence or a calculated decision to make announcements of significant import at times when most of the population would be available and sure to hear them cannot be certainly decided. But it is a fact that Warsaw's Jews learned officially that they would be confined within a ghetto on 12 October 1940, which was Yom Kippur, the Day of Atonement, the most solemn Jewish holiday.[38]

The German governor of the Warsaw District, Dr. Ludwig Fischer, issued an order on 2 October establishing the boundaries of the ghetto and calling for its institution by 31 October.[39] This date was extended twice, but by 15 November 1940 the ghetto existed. At least 80,000 Polish gentiles had been moved out of the area and around 140,000 Jews forced in.[40] On the morning of 16 November 1940, Jews preparing to go to work outside the ghetto found all exits blocked by German and Polish police.[41] The ghetto was sealed, thus demonstrating to the Jews that their future was going to be difficult. But few suspected just how difficult it would be or foresaw the catastrophe that loomed ahead.

At this same time, November 1940, the cynical process of reassuring the world that the Jews were in no danger continued. Two American representatives of a relief organization known as the Commission for Polish Relief were entertained at lunch in Warsaw. They discussed many aspects of relief at a conference and lunch with Governor General Dr. Frank. "During that very informal meeting, Dr. Frank assured us that there was absolutely no discrimination between Christians and Jews in the distribution of supplies from foreign relief organizations. Dr. Frank furthermore stated that no line was drawn either in the distribution of relief through governmental agencies."[42] Presumably the Americans were given no opportunity to discuss this question with the Jews of Warsaw.

The exact location of the ghetto—and there were running battles between the Nazi administration and the *Judenrat* with regard to streets to be omitted (the usual German demand) or retained (as Czerniakow fought for as much space as possible)—was in general terms the site of the unofficial Jewish quarter before the German occupation. That is, it was an area with a high concentration of Jews; but many Poles lived there also, and many Jews lived in other parts of the city, including some of the wealthiest Warsaw suburbs. Now, by Nazi edict, all Poles were to leave the ghetto area and all Jews were to move in. Where possible, simple trading of dwellings was encouraged, but this could actually be done infrequently, and, if done, rarely was the trade equitable.

The experiences of several of the interviewees illustrate the problems implicit in such forced moves. Best off were those who already lived in the ghetto area, since they could remain in their own homes with their own belongings. The Borman sisters were fortunate in this regard, living at Pawia 38, just across from the notorious Pawiak Prison.[43] Another interviewee, a Catholic Pole, had to move out of the area with her parents, and they moved to a former Jewish home in a suburb.[44] And Eugenia Pernal and her family had to abandon their home outside the ghetto and move in with an aunt at Panska 39. They considered themselves very lucky to have a relative to join, rather than moving into cramped quarters with strangers. The apartment consisted of five rooms plus a kitchen and was occupied by five families, fortunately small, a total of 13 people.[45]

CONTROL OF THE JEWS BY THE JEWS

In essence, the Germans ruled the ghetto from outside the walls, using as their chief agent the *Judenrat* inside. Over the four-year period between the occupation of Warsaw by the Nazis at the end of September 1939 and the final deportations and destruction of the ghetto in May 1943, there were many changes in German administrative structure. These changes were summarized at the beginning of this chapter.

The *Judenrat* remained in control inside the ghetto, in a very limited sense of the word "control," until early in 1943. At that time a de facto change occurred, the *Judenrat* losing its moral leadership to the Jewish fighting organizations within what remained of the ghetto. This arrangement was unofficial, dramatically representing the alteration from ghetto as producer, with hope for survival, to ghetto as resistance point, with hope for survival gone. Of course, this last switch took place without approval by the Germans or by the *Judenrat*.

There were two fighting groups. It is symptomatic of the strength of the internal political factions among the Jews that even at the end, when there was not only acceptance of the need to resist but even a certain nervous enthusiasm, that the Jews could not find unity. Two politically separate groups fought against the Nazis in April and May 1943. They often cooperated tactically, but they were separate. One leader of the smaller group, the Betarists, has offered an explanation: Dr. Wdowinski believed that many of the Jewish leaders who had been reared in the spirit of the Russian Revolution thought that they could translate the ideas of the class struggle into Zionist terms. This attitude "so numbed the minds of its adherents that even in the last year of the Ghetto it paralyzed any unified action against the Germans."[46] This is, however, criticism from a political opponent. But it is a fact that the two fighting groups within the ghetto in 1943, ŻOB (Żydowska Organizacja Bojowa) and ŻZW (Żydowski Związek Wojskowy), remained unintegrated,[47] though they were jointly commanded by Mordechai Anielewicz, the commander during the ghetto uprising.

ORDNUNGSDIENST, or JEWISH ORDER POLICE

On broad departmental lines at least, the structure of the *Judenrat* within the ghetto was the same as that created under enormous pressure when the *Judenrat* was first organized in the autumn of 1939. The *Ordnungsdienst,* or Jewish Order Service (also known as the "Jewish police" and, in Polish, as *Służba Porządkowa* or the SP) is important to any examination of the medical aspects of life in the ghetto. Its members were sometimes involved in specifically medical activities such as participating in the work of the public health antiepidemic brigades. They also played a distinct if sometimes negative role in terms of their anti-smuggling responsibilities.

Professionals unable to obtain work in their usual fields in the ghetto flocked to join the *Ordnungsdienst,* especially lawyers. It eventually included more than 2000 members, offering a haven for otherwise unemployed intellectuals. But it was also penetrated by hoodlums of many kinds. The *Ordnungsdienst* included a women's unit headed by Mrs. Horowitz, a lawyer from Lodz.[48]

The relationship between the *Ordnungsdienst* and the ghetto population was uneasy at best. An unknown but apparently very large percentage of the police took bribes, which were frequently paid in efforts to avoid punishment if caught smuggling, attempting to leave the ghetto, and for a variety of other offenses. One *Ordnungsdienst* official claimed that only the honest policemen took bribes; the dishonest ones simply stole everything they wanted.[49] By the time of the deportations, which were carried out with the active participation of most of those in the force, they were despised by their fellow Jews of the ghetto.

Nominally, the Polish police was responsible for prosecuting common offenses. But this seems to have been true only in theory. "In practice, the law of the jungle prevailed in the ghetto with very few exceptions. Neither the Polish Police, nor the Public Prosecutor's Office, and not even the Polish Tribunals, intervened in our lives."[50]

The *Ordnungsdienst* had a jail within the ghetto that it used for incarcerating Jews charged with or convicted of intraghetto offenses, as well as for the "crime" of leaving the ghetto illegally. This prison was known as "Gęsiówka" because it was located on Gęsia Street.

PSYCHOLOGICAL CONDITIONS

One weapon used most effectively against the Jews, not just in Warsaw but generally, was humiliation. This was the case before the ghetto was created and also within the ghetto. The Nazis seemed to delight in cutting or tearing out the side curls of a Hasid, or forcing Jewish women to use their underwear to clean streets, or pushing elderly Jews to exhaustion with calisthenics. Scenes of this nature were repeated numberless times and often were photographed by the Germans. Dr. Henryk Makower was punched in the face by a 20-year-old Nazi for failing to remove his hat while passing the soldier.[51] Examples of callous brutality were multiplied hundreds of times.

A curfew was established early on. Jews were forbidden to be on the streets between 9 P.M. and 5 A.M.[52]

THE WARSAW GHETTO

> The ghetto was a malignant tumor of humanity. Every single one of those crammed into it understood it as such and felt himself to be the sick cell of an organism, which, objectively, he really was.[53]

The area of the ghetto initially was 425 acres, of which 375 acres was residential space, so that 30 percent of the population of Warsaw was crowded into 2.4 percent of the city's living area. Of 1800 streets in Warsaw, 73 were in the ghetto. The wall was about 18 kilometers (11 miles) long, 3 meters (10 feet) high, and topped with broken glass and, in places, barbed wire.[54] In places where the physical wall itself was unfinished in November 1940, barbed wire barricades were substituted until the wall could be built (see Figure 3.2).

Trunk has made the following calculations: Warsaw as a whole encompassed 14,150 hectares, the ghetto 340 (which included 29 for the cemetery and 4 for a field intended to be incorporated into the cemetery); Warsaw had 284,912 dwelling units, of which 61,295 were in the ghetto. The number of residents per hectare in Warsaw was 96.5, in the ghetto 1308.8. Residents per room in Warsaw, numbered 4.8; in the ghetto, 7.2.[55]

These figures show clearly how crowded the ghetto was even at the beginning, when the population was about 390,000.[56] Six months later, as refugees from outlying areas poured into Warsaw and into the ghetto, the population reached a peak of perhaps 460,000.[57] After that, the accelerating death rate outran the influx of refugees and the numbers fell (see Figure 3.3).

In November 1940, when roughly 10 percent of the total ghetto population was permitted to work outside the walls, with appropriate passes, there were 22 gates. By July 1942, as the organized exterminations began, only four gates remained functional.[58] In addition to gates, there was at least one other semiofficial access to the ghetto; the court building at Leszno 56, on the border of the ghetto, permitted some direct access to Poles, who entered from Biała Street.[59] Sufficiently Aryan-looking Jews could remove their armbands and risk going out into Warsaw as Poles. Many did so. More often, though, this site provided an opportunity for conveying important papers back and forth and for exchanging valuables for cash.

The ghetto was always crowded; crowds are etched indelibly on the memories of survivors. One of these was Jan Karski, a Christian Pole, who visited the ghetto so that he could describe it firsthand; he was about to set out on a perilous trip to

Figure 3.2. Outline map showing approximate position of the Warsaw ghetto within the city of Warsaw; the size is slightly larger than to scale. Between one-quarter and one-third of the total population of the city was forced to live within this small area.

England to report to the Polish government-in-exile. He was horrified at what he saw. At the end of his visit he began to run towards a gate:

> It is hard to explain why I ran. There was no occasion for speed and, if anything, our haste could have aroused suspicion. But I ran, I think, simply to get a breath of clean air and a drink of water. Everything there seemed polluted by death, the stench of rotting corpses, filth and decay. I was careful to avoid touching a wall or a human being. I would have refused a drink of water in that city of death if I had been dying of thirst. I believe I even held my breath as much as I could in order to breathe in less of the contaminated air.[60]

This was the reaction by an outsider to one quick visit. The Jews had to live in this atmosphere of death and decay. But it struck them the same way. When one man returned to the ghetto after some months in a labor camp, he felt as if he were a tourist in a foreign land. He was appalled at the crowds, the dirt, the noise, and the hordes of tattered beggars.[61]

And yet, despite this noisome, cramped existence, there were a few oases. One of these was a small garden at the Hospital of the Holy Ghost. The hospital had been heavily damaged in September 1939, but one wing was functioning. Two young doctors, later to be married, enjoyed occasional quiet moments there, escaping from their work to lie on the grass and feel the sun on their bodies: "It was a real treat. In spite of the ruins we forgot the war and did not think of the dark, dreaded future."[62]

The physical size of the ghetto changed between November 1940 and July 1942, when the massive deportations to Treblinka began. In October 1941, for example, Czerniakow and the *Judenrat* struggled to adapt to one of many compressions. "The area we are to lose," he complained to his diary, "contains 43,530 residents; we are getting space for 8,100."[63] This particular change affected Czerniakow directly. He lived at Chłodna 20, on a section of the street that was one of the relatively well-to-do areas of the ghetto.[64] The Nazis appropriated it, so that he himself had to look for a new home. His dilemma sparked one of Dr. Janusz Korczak's acerbic reactions. Sardonically, as Czerniakow recorded the moment, "Korczak has inquired if I secured a place to live. He added that if I didn't, he could give me the name of an official in the Community [i.e., one of Czerniakow's subordinates in the *Judenrat*] who, for a bribe, will give me an apartment."[65] Both men knew that the joke hid a bitter truth. There was much bribery, much under-the-table dealing, in the *Judenrat*.

By January 1942, the ghetto's size had been reduced to only 300 hectares and was inhabited by about 400,000 Jews. This meant a remarkable concentration of 1330 per hectare, or 85,000 per square mile.[66] It was at this time that the Chłodna

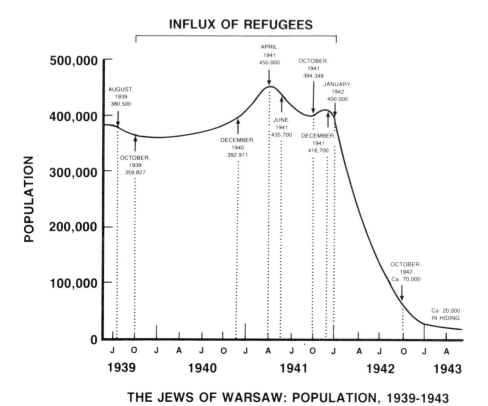

Figure 3.3. Population figures for the Warsaw ghetto, based on statistics collected by the *Judenrat* and approximations from other sources for the dates shown. Although the death rate was high during these years, the population figure remained relatively stable because of the periodic influxes of refugees, mostly from other sites in Poland.

Street overpass was built,[67] a structure that figures prominently in collections of photographs of the ghetto.[68]

As in any city of nearly half a million persons, the Warsaw ghetto had internal dissensions, arguments, political and religious confrontations, and occasionally physical brawls, though these seldom. Outside pressures of the most fundamental nature exacerbated the difficulties that would have occurred normally.

But within the ghetto there was one element that has no genuine parallel in most similar groupings of human beings. The Germans created the problem by applying Hitler's racial laws strictly. The consequence was that an abrasive, vocal, well-educated minority was forced into daily contact with the ordinary Jews of Warsaw and of rural Poland. These were the converts, the baptized Jews.

People abandon their family religion for many reasons. In Poland at the end of the nineteenth and the first decades of the twentieth centuries, one of the chief reasons for a Jew to convert was to cease being a Jew. For some, it was an attempt to escape from violent antisemitism; for others, a calculated move designed to find a way into areas of employment not open to avowed Jews. Some had a more philosophical background to their conversion, believing that a good, patriotic Pole was one who fitted the major definitions of Polishness: speaking Polish as a first language, educated in Polish schools, and adhering to the Catholic religion. For at least some converts, abandoning their faith was a necessary step to cut themselves off from a way of life and a people they found repugnant: the prototypical poor, often dirty, uneducated, distinctively "Jewish" masses. Marcus believes that most converts continued to consider themselves Jews, few sustained any connection with their new church, and "virtually all continued to donate to Jewish religious charities."[69]

There was, of course, a middle ground. This was the position held by the so-called assimilationists. Many of these Jews also took this position because they considered themselves good Poles—perhaps Poles first and Jews second. They retained their Jewish religion but promoted education for their children in Polish schools in the Polish language. For some this was protective covering for their Jewishness, for others a position of sincere Polish patriotism. Janusz Korczak was an assimilationist, as revealed by his insistence that the orphans in his institution learn Polish—if not instead of Yiddish, certainly just as well as Yiddish.[70] Gutman assessed Adam Czerniakow, chairman of the *Judenrat*, as "essentially an assimilated Jew who lacked confidence in the ability of the Jews to behave as a disciplined community,"[71] and Czerniakow's colleague, Apolinary Hartglas, recalled him as an apolitical student and later a declared assimilationist.[72]

Many in the hierarchy that ran the ghetto were assimilationists. A large number were converts. Because of the reasons that drove converts away from Judaism, and also because they tended to be better educated, better dressed, and better housed than the mass of Jews, the converts tended to consider themselves superior. Their religious attitudes often were held with deep conviction, and this determination and self-righteousness help to explain many of the human problems that beset the administration of the ghetto.

For example, Dr. Izrael Milejkowski was an assimilated Jew. He had a sharp aversion to Prof. Ludwig Hirszfeld, who was a convert, and once referred to Hirszfeld with disgust as a "turncoat."[73] Yet these were two of the key figures in the medical world of the ghetto, and a good working relationship between them might have benefited many ghetto dwellers. It is easy to oversimplify, and Milejkowski may have had other reasons to dislike Hirszfeld and vice versa. But the religious/cultural separation certainly played some role.

To the incredulous baptized Jew, forced into the ghetto, his lot probably seemed especially difficult. Not only did he share the common misfortune, but he bore the burden unfairly, or so he might think. Many had been baptized a generation earlier or longer. The ordinary Jew could be thought of as having expected some such treatment as ghettoization. This was the lot of the Jew in Eastern Europe. But someone who had been a practicing and believing Catholic for decades understandably felt devastated by inclusion in the Nazi trap.

Of course, the converts lost a great deal by entering the ghetto. They were rightly indignant in complaining of beautiful homes, paintings, furniture, and clothing abandoned.[74] Yet all Jews forced into the ghetto lost most of their belongings, and the converted Jews seemed to be among the fortunate minority who had managed to secrete diamonds and gold coins. Most Jews had never seen a diamond.

There were fewer than 1600 Christian converts in the ghetto,[75] including some very odd characters indeed. Many were notoriously antisemitic, one of the worst of these being the infamous agitator and writer, Susanna Rabska.[76] Most, however, had no such stigma. But a number rapidly acquired bad reputations in the ghetto because of the remarkable ease with which they gained positions of influence and prestige, in the *Judenrat* and elsewhere. Adler itemized the converts who achieved prominence in medical matters: these included Prof. Ludwig Hirszfeld; Col. Dr. Moritz Kon, director of the Health Department; Maj. Tadeusz Ganz, commissar in the battle against typhus; Dr. Jerzy Landau, director and a physician at the Health Centers; Dr. Josef Stein, director of Czyste Hospital; and Dr. Wilhelm Szenwic, head of a department at Czyste.[77] Of course, most or all of these may have been the best people for the job.

There were other reasons for dissension too. Most of the converts lived well on Sienna Street. There, in September 1941, they scandalized the community at large because many of the women paraded the street in elegant high leather boots, said to cost 450 zloty[78]—more than many Jews made in a month. Dissensions could center on money, on language (many converts knew nothing of Yiddish, the common language of the ghetto), on religion, or on unadulterated envy.

Inevitably, any kind of ostentation caused criticism. Lewin was infuriated at seeing some young women on the streets wearing new outfits with "wavy peroxide hair, beautifully styled, their brightly powdered cheeks [*sic*] and their purple-red lips," and so on, a display of "sickly elegance."[79]

An example of the basically pointless but painful scrimmaging that went on was an exchange involving four powerful leaders within the ghetto. They were Dr. Henryk Sikorski, a Pole and, in 1940, the administrator of Czyste Hospital; Dr. Josef Stein, a convert and the director of Czyste; and Adam Czerniakow and Dr. Izrael Milejkowski, assimilationists. The details were recorded by Czerniakow in his diary. On 8 June 1940, a Saturday and therefore the Jewish sabbath, Sikorski and Stein visited Czerniakow on business; Czerniakow worked almost every day.

Stein wanted to light a cigarette and was scolded by Czerniakow, who "pointed out that smoking was forbidden. At the same time I assured Sikorski that this rule did not apply to him. On his way out, Sikorski saw Dr. Milejkowski with a lit cigarette in the corridor, and shouted, 'Smoking is forbidden here.' "[80] This was merely childish bickering, but it hid deep feelings.

Among the advantages enjoyed by the converts was the assistance of Caritas, the Catholic charity organization that provided assistance to converts in the ghetto. But it did not aid Jews, no matter how needy. Some Jews committed apostasy for the pragmatic reason that if they converted to Catholicism, they and their children might be fed by Caritas.[81] For someone who was starving and not strongly Orthodox, the decision may have been relatively easy, though there is no evidence that many Jews followed this course.

The converts were outnumbered in the ghetto by about 250 to 1. To many Jews they seemed like alien creatures. Not only did the Jews walk over to Sienna Street to stare at the women in their fancy boots, they also gathered in front of the Christian churches on Sunday to take in the spectacle of the converts attending mass. At Easter in 1942, the crowd of watchers was so large at the church on Leszno Street that the *Ordnungsdienst* stationed a special squad there to maintain order.[82] There was often ill will on both sides in these matters. But not all converts behaved disruptively. Stanislas Waller, a Jewish physician at Czyste who criticized converted physicians, nevertheless concluded his remarks by saying that, in general, the converts were honest persons. "They did not steal and they were true to ethical values."[83] A guarded endorsement.

Michael Zylberberg, an observant Jew, has made perhaps the most balanced and compassionate evaluation:

> The tragedy of the converts in the ghetto was perhaps even greater than ours. They suffered as Jews and finally died as Jews, unable to resolve the terrible dichotomy created by their religious and philosophical conflicts. Their suffering took on a different quality. For us it was an inevitable adjunct of our heritage; for them it was an additional burden, an unrelieved trauma.[84]

The ghetto was not the home solely of Jews. Although the vast majority of the inmates were, of course, Jewish, there were Gypsies there too, at least briefly. The first substantial group of Gypsies seems to have arrived in April 1942, at Gęsiówka, the Jewish-run prison on Gęsia Street. The Nazis rounded up large numbers of Gypsy and Polish beggars off the streets and confined them to the prison—already desperately overcrowded with Jewish offenders, most of whom were accused of smuggling or leaving the ghetto without a pass. On 25 April 1942, Heinz Auerswald, the Commissar of the ghetto, ordered Czerniakow to have the beggars deloused and then released into the ghetto.[85] On behalf of the *Judenrat* Czerniakow protested, and two days later Auerswald relented and said that the Poles could leave the ghetto; the Gypsies remained.[86]

Like the Jews, the Gypsies were required to wear armbands. Theirs were to be white, bearing a red Z (for *Zigeuner* or "Gypsy").[87] At least one observer felt that the Gypsies disappeared quickly from the ghetto, and that therefore they may have escaped.[88] But the order for them to wear their armbands was dated 16 June 1942, just five weeks before the deportations began, and it seems more likely that as beggars they would have been among the earliest to be rounded up by the *Ordnungs-dienst* and sent via the freight cars from the *Umschlagplatz* to Treblinka.

From autumn 1939, when it was first announced that the Jews must wear arm-bands proclaiming their Jewishness, the system was continually elaborated. The Gypsies, as noted above, wore bands that were white with a red Z. The regular bands were white with a blue Star of David. Members of the various health services had permission to wear armbands that were white with a red Star of David, presumably as a means to indicate their life-supporting activities, particularly in times of med-ical emergency. The *Ordnungsdienst* wore yellow armbands. When "The 13" (dis-cussed in Chapter 4) began their so-called antiracketeering activities they were granted the right to wear green armbands, and Gancwajch's Emergency Service (an offshoot of The 13) wore checkered armbands.[89] According to Gutman, rag collec-tors also had distinctive bands.[90] All of these bands were to be worn in addition to the standard one. This profusion of labels continued until the time of the deporta-tions, when all special privileges were withdrawn and only the original white and blue armband was acceptable.

The need to wear an armband created its own business. Janina David found street sellers everywhere, perched on the curbs or in the gutters. They sold every imaginable object, calling out their prices, "plucking at passing sleeves and thrust-ing their wares into our faces. Armband sellers multiplied daily. They showed a great variety of products. There were cheap paper armbands, practical celluloid ones that could be washed and the luxury satin bands with the star embroidered in deep blue silk. One could almost tell a person's income and status by the armband he wore."[91]

The Germans seemed obsessed with photographic records. One occurrence late in the life of the ghetto was the arrival of a German cinema team to make a movie of the Jews in their ghetto. This was not to be a documentary—or, at least, not a documentary much concerned with verisimilitude. The Germans did not try to show what was going on in the ghetto, but rather what they wanted German citizens and the world to believe was going on. Many ghetto dwellers were seized, or pro-vided by the *Judenrat*, to appear in this epic. Lewin cites the experience of Dr. Nathan Eck, who saw the filming of a staged funeral, and also describes a friend who was forced into a restaurant and made to stuff himself with food for the cam-eras, while emaciated Jews were filmed watching hungrily.[92]

Another survivor observed this particular bit of movie making, carried out at Schultz's Restaurant at the corner of Karmelicka and Nowolipki streets. The res-taurant had been closed since early in the war, but the Nazis "opened" it especially for their mock gluttony scenes. "The 'guests' had to push the beggars away from the tables and the 'waiters' had to complete the act by throwing the beggars out of the restaurant."[93] Of course, there was some accuracy to the message they were trying to portray, even if they were staging the event for the screen. Many survivors have commented on the indecent contrast of shops with windows filled with delicacies, while on the street in front there might be a dead body leaning against the wall and a tattered child begging for food.[94]

This experience provides an example of how events can be perceived differently. Czerniakow, in one of his typical terse, factual diary entries, notes on 12 May 1942 that the German propaganda film (by then, in the making for several days) would have a scene at the *mikvah*, or ritual bath, on Dzielna Street. The *Judenrat* had been ordered to provide, the following day, 20 Orthodox Jews with earlocks and 20 upper-class women.[95] He does not say how acceptable subjects were found and filmed. Lewin, referring to the same event in his diary entry for 13 May 1942, states that the Nazis commandeered a group of Jewish men and women of all ages, took them to the bathhouse at Dzielna 38, and forced them to strip and have sex—or simulate sex—while 200 Germans watched and a film was made.[96] There is nothing in the German treatment of the Jews that makes Lewin's account improbable. But why was there no indication of the degrading sexual insult in Czerniakow's diary? Perhaps he was being circumspect in not recording it. If it occurred he must have known, as the Jews were anything but reluctant to seek him out and complain vigorously about such matters.

Circumcision intrigued the Germans, and more than once the ghetto physicians were required to stage an operation for the edification of groups of officers. Having been circumcised was a lethal condition in some circumstances;[97] perhaps the Gestapo wished to be certain exactly what they were supposed to be able to identify. Czerniakow noted on the same day he discussed the bathhouse scene that a baby was to be provided for the filming of a circumcision and expressed some doubt that the tiny actor would survive to be operated on, since he weighed only 4.4 pounds.[98] A year earlier, Dr. Milejkowski arranged for a ritual circumcision to be carried out for a Gestapo physician and some others. An adult male Jew's circumcision was displayed."Later the displaying of an adult."[99]

ECONOMICS

Neither the Warsaw ghetto nor any aspect of life within the ghetto was exempt from economic pressures. The Nazi principles for the economics of oppression were revealed early and blatantly: theft, blackmail, extortion, and chicanery were the operative techniques. Individual Germans, from the highest official to the humblest soldier, seemed determined to make the most of the financial opportunities that presented themselves. Extortion was common. To give a single example, a large group of refugees from Pruszkow were confined in the quarantine station at Leszno 109 just outside the Warsaw ghetto. The manager expressed "regret" that he had to obey the authorities and force them to remain in a frozen, unhygienic building for the full 14 days. After negotiation, for 10,000 zloty the group was permitted to move into the ghetto after experiencing a single painful night in January 1941 during which the temperature fell to −25° C (−15° F).[100]

Extortion of the community as a whole was so common that it almost seems to have been a matter of policy on the part of the Germans. The technique was simple and direct. In September 1940 the *Judenrat* was suddenly notified that it must pay a fine of 100,000 zloty ($20,000) immediately. When Czerniakow investigated the reasons, he found that not long before, a demented Jewish woman had attacked a German nurse, member of a welfare organization.[101] The fine was a sort of racial penalty; while a portion of the fine may have gone to the aggrieved nurse, there is every likelihood that it also helped pay for a chalet in the Schwarzwald for some Nazi officer.

Attacks on the Jewish economy were introduced by the Germans long before the ghetto was created. By November 1939 all Jewish deposits and bank accounts were blocked. A Jew was permitted to withdraw no more than 250 zloty (ca. $50) weekly, and all Jews were required to deposit all cash reserves in excess of 2000 zloty (ca. $400).[102] Thus no Jew was permitted to have more than 2000 zloty in cash.[103] For those thousands of Jews forced to move into the ghetto from other parts of Warsaw, only a few belongings could be taken. The remainder, and all business assets as well, were appropriated by the conquerors, either without compensation or with payment so low as to guarantee poverty for the formerly well-to-do.

Of the tens of thousands of Jews who were forcibly moved from outlying towns to Warsaw, the vast majority arrived almost destitute. Those who had the means and the opportunity brought whatever gold, jewelry, and other valuables they were able to preserve through searches by various guards en route; all of these could be sold to help support the family. Most Jews had little or nothing of this kind.

Refugees had other problems as well, depending upon their background. The Warsaw ghetto was a Yiddish enclave, at least as far as daily conversation in the street was concerned. If you didn't speak Yiddish, you were seriously handicapped. Frank Stiffel found this out; he arrived in the city in March 1942 speaking no Yiddish. He considered this problem "one of the most serious obstacles to my ever becoming a regular Ghettoan." He understood that to survive there, one had to become a hustler, "and how do you hustle without a knowledge of the native idiom?"[104]

The *Judenrat*, the chief administrative institution for Jews both before there was a ghetto and within the ghetto, was placed in an economically untenable position from the beginning. The *Judenrat* officials were not only expected but required to operate all of the various departments necessary to maintain a city of half a million persons. This included arrangements so that the Jews could clothe, house, and feed themselves. The *Judenrat* also had to provide health, sanitary, post office, police, and other services, all without a viable base of income.

The budget of the *Judenrat* for 1940 illustrates the problem and reveals at least some of the methods by which the *Judenrat* tried to salvage the situation. The entire budget amounted to 10,680,000 zloty, of which 3,811,000 zloty was spent on wages for forced laborers, 3,059,000 for hospitals, 920,000 for welfare, and 113,000 for vocational courses. Income came from burials, 1,193,000 zloty; from fees for exemption from forced labor, 2,603,000; 634,000 from a community tax; 541,000 from a hospital tax; 423,000 in registration fees; and 325,000 in fees for food cards. Adding up the figures for income gives a total of 5,719,000 zloty—a shortfall from expenses of just less than 5,000,000 zloty, or almost half of the total expenses.[105]

Providing forced labor was obviously an important part of the *Judenrat*'s function. It was one that they had taken on voluntarily in an attempt to make life easier for their constituents. The Nazis had a direct approach to finding laborers. They would drive into the Jewish quarter, before it was walled in, and simply commandeer the desired number of workers from among whoever happened to be found in the streets. This method was so disruptive and terrifying that the *Judenrat* volunteered to provide Jews on demand. This probably was a better system, though inevitably it led to other kinds of abuse. Working conditions were terrible. Between 5000 and 8000 laborers were required by the Germans daily. In any month, a Jewish man (within certain age limits) might be required to work for six to nine days. The abuses arose because the well-to-do hired the poor to substitute for them. Even though the poor needed the tiny sums they earned, they resented the fact that the others didn't work. Also, the need to find substitutes led to graft, as foremen saw an opportunity for bribes to supplement their own incomes.[106]

As is evident from the figures above, the *Judenrat* also depended on fees it earned by granting exceptions. An official in that organization described an incident in which a man suffering from general paralysis of the insane, a late manifestation of advanced syphilis, who had a speech disorder, and who was completely unable to stand or walk was examined for forced labor. He was, of course, exempted by the medical board for three months after having "covered the cost" of the medical examination.[107] So even the incurably and obviously ill had to pay the *Judenrat* recurrently for exemptions.

Difficult and unpleasant as it was to be forced to clean up bombed-out areas of Warsaw or dig ditches, the Jews doing this sort of work soon found that these were relatively privileged jobs. Far worse were the labor camp assignments. Beginning in August 1940, young Jews began to be shipped to distant locations to work.[108] Conditions were truly appalling at these camps, and only a minority of workers survived to return home.

The *Judenrat* used various schemes to attempt to get around its fiscal problem, in general without success. They tried to persuade the Nazis to give them access to frozen Jewish bank accounts, and they attempted to borrow, sometimes successfully. And, inevitably, they introduced more and more taxes. The only potentially effective method to create employment was by importing industry, often German owned, to manufacture various products. Most were intended for use by the *Wehrmacht*. By June 1942, income began to balance outflow, and it appeared that the ghetto could become self-sufficient.[109] But then the extermination phase began that wiped out most of Warsaw's Jews, workers as well as babies and the elderly, and the question of solvency became irrelevant.

The *Judenrat* established a postal service that functioned at least until after the massive deportations occurred. The post office was located at Zamenhof 19, at the corner of Gęsia and Zamenhof streets.[110] The building had once been a nobleman's palace, later a prison when the Russians held Poland.[111] There was a greater connection with the world outside the ghetto than might at first be supposed. For example, in June 1941, 113,006 parcels were delivered to ghetto residents, and for the first six months of 1942, before the deportations, between 10,000 and 13,000 letters per month were sent out of the ghetto.[112]

Though the post office seemed to work, the telephone did not. Service was maintained in Aryan Warsaw, but within the ghetto only doctors and druggists had free use of the telephone. There were connections between the ghetto and the outer city, but it seemed highly likely that the Germans tapped the lines to overhear conversations.[113]

Another problem was transportation. Before the ghetto was established, the Warsaw train system crisscrossed this area. The ghetto walls, when they were constructed, would have disrupted service on some of the main lines. So the Germans ordered gates sited so that most trains continued to cross the ghetto, but they were not permitted to pick up or discharge passengers. Jews could not use these trains, but Poles traveled through the ghetto regularly and could see the state of the Jews, the bodies lying covered with newspapers, and the crowded streets.[114] Inside the ghetto, a few trains were permitted to function. These didn't leave the ghetto; they were plainly marked with large Stars of David. The last ghetto train, operating from Żelazna to Dzika streets via Leszno and Karmelicka, finally ceased running on 15 August 1942.[115] Horse-drawn buses also carried passengers within the ghetto. They held up to 30 passengers, who paid a fare of 60 groszen. There were 25 of these buses in operation,[116] part of the short-lived business empire of Kohn and Heller.

Jews who left the ghetto temporarily without passes, always at great risk, some- times were helped by kindly train conductors who, recognizing that they were Jews without papers, might let them ride to the ghetto gate.[117] More often, these men reported the illegal Jews to the authorities, as required by German edict.

The Nazis prohibited the importation into the ghetto of food other than the approved and grossly insufficient rations. Thus smuggling became a major occu- pation for many (see Figure 3.4), even though it was an activity repeatedly proven to have lethal consequences. These realities sent prices soaring, so that the available zloty bought less and less (see Chapter 6 for a more detailed analysis).

Trading became a common occupation, hundreds of little stalls springing up to further crowd the already bloated streets. On Gesia Street a bazaar offered every imaginable item from Jewish Warsaw. Many Poles smuggled or bribed their way into the ghetto to buy at bargain prices.[118]

Except for work details initiated by the Germans, all Jews eventually were restricted to the ghetto on pain of death.[119] Inside, the potential employers were,

Figure 3.4. Germans searching a Jew suspected of smuggling, Warsaw ghetto.

with a few notable exceptions, almost entirely their fellow Jews. Though the population probably averaged, over the period from 1940 to July 1942, about 450,000 (deaths were more than balanced by periodic influxes of refugees from other Jewish communities in occupied Europe), there were only so many jobs that needed to be done, and there were fewer and fewer individuals or companies capable of paying others for their work. Moreover, by German edict, Jews working outside the ghetto received only 80 percent of the wages paid for the same job to gentile workers, and all their benefits were canceled—limitation of working hours, overtime pay, and vacations.[120]

Shops inside the ghetto had trouble getting new supplies of raw materials, human needs became increasingly pitched at the level of survival, and prices continued to rise. Services also were affected by these trends. Moreover, being thrifty could create problems for those who lived by providing service. The well-to-do mother of one of the interviewees, like many of her friends, ceased having her hair done after the Germans took over the city. It seemed a frivolous expense, though normal during peacetime. But when they discovered that hairdressers were starving, she and her friends went back to being stylish, at least for a few months more.[121]

Some Jews, particularly large-scale smugglers, became temporarily rich, and some Jews had been rich before the war and remained better off than most. The first group seems to have done little or nothing to provide charity or social aid, though there are differing opinions on this point. The second group did less than they might have if contemporary writers were accurate in their criticisms.[122] Rabbi Yitzhak Katz, at a conference of ZTOS, the Jewish Social Self-Help, on 6 January 1942, charged that too few Jews were acquitting themselves "of the elementary duty of commiseration. In the streets we see people dying of hunger, starving, stumbling and falling in the street, without anyone showing compassion for them."[123]

Given the relentless pressure of economic disaster and the frightening specter of starvation and epidemics, it may be that some Jews lived according to Adler's axiom: "In our jungle, everyone had to be the guardian of his own health and his own pocket."[124] But many inhabitants of the ghetto were incapable of this utopian self-sufficiency. Without outside aid they would go under.

PUBLIC WELFARE

By November 1941, a survey suggested that 80 percent of the 100,000 children then in the ghetto required public aid and care.[125] Yet the means of funding such care were shrinking daily. The work of mutual aid, or "self-help," as it was commonly called, occupied much effort on the part of many people. It is a record of selfless dedication in the face of difficulties and discouragements of daunting dimensions, always clouded over by the shadow of imminent doom. Fortunately, the Jews had a long heritage of welfare activity and, when war came, and then the ghetto, the community could call on a comprehensive agglomeration of existing welfare groups, including CENTOS, TOZ, and ORT (*Obshchestvo Razpostranienia Truda*, the Institute for Vocational Guidance and Training). Throughout the existence of the ghetto, Joint provided major financial support to all efforts at self-help.[126] All of these organizations are discussed in more detail in Chapter 4.

Aid also came from both businesses and individuals within the ghetto. Particularly in the case of the latter, however, the ability of most potential donors shrank steadily. Moreover, the demands were so endless that they became overwhelming. Janusz Korczak described the mental process involved:

> At first you gave willingly, then without enthusiasm; first from a sense of duty, then according to the law of inertia, by force of habit and without feeling; and then, finally, unwillingly, with anger, in despair.[127]

Korczak saw this process from both sides. He himself undoubtedly gave, but much of his energy in the ghetto was devoted to making personal appeals for funds or supplies for his orphanage.

Support for the Jews from the Poles collectively was, according to Gutman, nonexistent. The sole exception was Caritas, a Roman Catholic aid society, which provided support for Christians forced into the ghetto by Nazi racial laws—people such as Prof. Ludwig Hirszfeld, Dr. Josef Stein, and hundreds of others.[128] Some individual Poles did aid old friends and colleagues inside the ghetto, supplying food and clothing, loaning money, and helping to plan escapes, all at considerable risk to themselves.

When the ghetto was created, a Jewish section of the Polish Red Cross was set up there, with many distinguished physicians and others offering their patronage. Those Jews who still had substantial means, and there were many, contributed funds. The Nazis then ordered the Jewish section dissolved, presumably retaining the funds.[129]

With greater resources, the self-help organizations could have done much more. But they accomplished a great deal, and the fact that ultimately all their efforts seem to have been wasted by the massacres at Treblinka and elsewhere should not blind us to the real contribution they made. Relief was provided regardless of social class, and as a consequence, artists, historians, religious leaders, and professionals of many kinds were helped, as well as the chronically poor.[130] Children were major recipients of aid, and one of the workers in this field believes that "[t]he aid given to these children became one of the greatest achievements of the dismal life of the ghetto."[131]

Although almost 100,000 Jews died of all causes in Warsaw from September 1939 to July 1942, it is estimated that another 100,000 or more survived that long *only* because of the various self-help enterprises that operated in the ghetto.[132] One measure of the scope of aid provided is the number of ration cards that the *Judenrat* exempted from payment; that is, the recipients were sufficiently destitute to receive free rations. Table 3.1 displays the proportions and the change with time.

Nor was relief available only within the ghetto. Despite the enormous need there, self-help activities were also carried on for the benefit of others. For example, in November 1941 a trainload of German Jews passed through Warsaw en route to Minsk. *Judenrat* representatives took bread and water to the train station to feed them.[134]

The deportations ended most relief work. By the end of July 1942, the only vol-

Table 3.1. Self-Help, 1941[133]

Date	Ration Cards	Cards Exempt from Paying	% Exempt
April 1941	443,583	127,518	28.8
August 1941	420,116	127,263	30.3
October 1941	394,348	139,348	35.3

unteer organization still in existence and offering relief in the ghetto was ŻTOS, located at Nowolipki 25.[135] However, ŻTOS had absorbed TOZ as its medical division and CENTOS as its child-care division, and these functions were maintained as well as they could be under the circumstances. The *Judenrat* also carried on its efforts.

One additional activity of the relief organizations that constituted a different kind of self-help was their clandestine activity. Several of these groups actively supported the underground, including the fighting organizations that came to prominence late in the life of the ghetto.[136]

The whole social structure of Jewish life was twisted, particularly in the period of the ghetto—November 1940 through July 1942. New social practices sprang up in many aspects of life. Irena Bakowska, both of whose parents were dentists, remembers patients coming in to have gold inlays or caps removed so that they could sell the gold and buy food and shelter.[137] Halina Berg survived the war, at least partly because she had the good fortune to manage to contract an arranged marriage. After 22 July 1942, single women without jobs were being transported to Treblinka, but married women had a chance to remain in the ghetto. Berg was married to a man older than her father, a legal marriage though not an actual one. Shortly afterward, her new husband was able to save her from the *Umschlagplatz* at a crucial time.[138] Similarly, Dr. Egon Tramer, while in Sosnowice, married a woman to save her from going to a camp.[139] And Stiffel mentions a man who married his own mother with the same motive.[140] Such arranged marriages were a common device, though in retrospect we know that the chances of either the bride or groom surviving were negligible.

Nor were such "war marriages" necessarily part of the struggle to escape deportation. Much more often, they were simply a means for lonely people to find companionship. Men and women became unattached by death or separation and, quite naturally, they came together, an act that was often "not licentiousness, but the need for someone close, whom one could turn and talk to in tragic moments."[141] There was a deep need to be with someone in the ghetto, so that as long as a person continued to survive, "he had to stick to some other living human being."[142] In many cases, when deportations loomed, these informal couples would rush to find a rabbi who would marry them, so that they could go to the *Umschlagplatz* as husband and wife.

The extreme and increasingly lethal pressures on the ghetto inhabitants had the varied effects one would find in any group of half a million people exposed to similar worries and unresolvable frustrations. Many rose above the dismal, grinding circumstances to become highly moral, self-sacrificing leaders. Many went in the other direction, finding ghetto life an opportunity to exploit others or to abandon moral standards. As death became imminent, these effects grew more widespread.

Czerniakow's diary mentions many of the difficult people, as well as happier notes on the generous and the helpful. His patience was noticeably wearing thin as 1942 presented ever more serious problems. He refers to his ongoing struggle with "that repulsive witch" popularly known as "Miss Ghetto," actually one Regina Judt.[143] And contemplating the activities of several troublemakers, Czerniakow notes tiredly: "Watching some people I come to the conclusion that life is too short to enable them to reveal the whole gamut of their stupidity and malice."[144]

REFUGEES

In the streets the naked hands of people swollen by hunger, whose bodies were covered in rags or a bit of a blanket, stretched out toward the crowds passing by, sometimes in silent reproach, sometimes with screams and howls.[145]

Some reference already has been made to refugees. Their arrival in Warsaw signaled another component of the German solution to the "Jewish question," making the areas of Poland outside the cities *Judenrein*—free of Jews. The majority of the refugees who came to Warsaw were from the towns and villages of Poland. Beginning in early 1942, German Jews also began to appear there.

Although refugees were part of the population of Jews in Warsaw by the end of 1939, the major influx began in the last half of 1940. On 31 December 1940, the newly opened ghetto contained at least 78,625 refugees from 73 locations.[146] These people registered with the *Judenrat*, but others failed to register, so the actual number was higher. All movement was into the ghetto. Until the ghetto was closed, there was at least the theoretical possibility for Jews to emigrate. However, this possibility vanished on 23 November 1940; ostensibly the reason was that few countries would accept Jewish immigrants, so the Germans gave preference to German Jews who wished to emigrate.[147] The Polish Jews would remain in their ghettos.

The refugees often lived in appalling conditions. The *Judenrat* set up shelters at various locations throughout the ghetto, but space was severely limited, as were the fiscal resources of both the community and the refugees. Trunk visited one such center in March 1941. In one room he found 3 windows, 70 people, and 25 cots. The refugees were filthy and lice-ridden and hadn't undressed for four weeks.[148] In the refugee center at Smocza 47, between February and May 1941, there were 68 deaths in a population of 456 (15.5 percent), while at Stawki 15, 207 deaths occurred among 673 refugees between March and July 1941 (30.8 percent).[149]

There was another refugee center at Stawki 9. In January 1942 there were 1100 inhabitants existing in 170 rooms, most of which were not heated. There was no running water, and the toilets did not function. Of the 1100, 280 (25 percent) died that month, of whom 58 were 10 years old or younger.[150] In that same month, a house at Ostrowska 14 was found in which only women and children remained. All the men had died, partly because they had done extremely difficult forced labor.[151]

The mortality was so high in these centers or "points" (*punkts* in Polish, for hostels), as they were called, that housing for the successive waves arriving at the gates was recurrently available despite the general overcrowding in the ghetto.[152] Other mortality statistics for refugees were cited by a newspaper published by the Union for Armed Resistance in Warsaw: At Miła 46, inhabited by 500 people, 233 died; in the house at Miła 51, with 578 inhabitants, 250 died. At Pawia 63, with 794 residents, 430 died, 200 of them in the previous three months. The record in these wretched statistics was held by the house at Krochmalna 21, inhabited by 400 people, where the same number of people died. In 17 refugee centers, 710 out of approximately 780 rooms had no heat at all during the winter of 1941–42.[153]

The same Polish report gave more information about the Krochmalna 21 site. During the first three months of 1942, 126 Jews had died there, 64 of typhus and the rest of starvation. A total of 365 people had contracted typhus, about 100 had nutritional edema, 45 families were displaced, and there were 28 families in the building, with a total of 140 persons who, reportedly, owned absolutely nothing.[154]

In April 1941, the number of refugees in the ghetto was about 150,000—one-third of the population. And in the winter of 1941–42, nearly 70,000 additional refugees arrived from the western region of the Warsaw district.[155] Conditions were so bad that in poorer families the entire family might die and their loss go unnoticed until their bodies began to decompose and the smell became oppressive. Some corpses were found gnawed by rats.[156]

In March 1942, German Jews began to be seen in Warsaw. Unlike the Polish refugees, the Germans generally arrived well dressed, well fed, and with money in their pockets. This situation did not last long, and they soon began dying off just like their destitute cousins. As well as being susceptible to disease, the German Jews had to cope with a major dislocation, being a small minority among strangers who found their Yiddish accents (those few who even spoke Yiddish) difficult to understand, and whose customs were quite different. Accentuating these problems was the all-pervading fear about the future.

As it turned out, the German Jews had little opportunity to fit in, since most of them were in the ghetto only three or four months before the deportations began. They often arrived at night, unexpectedly, and were dumped at the gate by their guards from Germany. On 25 March 1942, for example, a group of more than 400 found themselves at the ghetto gate at Leszno and Zelazna. The guards wouldn't let them in, so they spent the night at the quarantine building at Leszno 109, outside the ghetto.[157] Presumably they were allowed in the next day and became the responsibility of the *Judenrat*. A few days later, 1000 Berlin Jews arrived at midnight. They were sent to the quarantine building, to be joined the next morning by another shipment of 1000 Berliners.[158] On 5 April there were 2019 Jews in the quarantine building at Leszno 109, and more were arriving.[159] The building never emptied, new arrivals taking the place of those admitted to the ghetto.

Dr. Wilhelm Hagen, then the German head of the public health system in Warsaw, points out that in the winter of 1941–42 the Germans were acutely uncomfortable and the Poles barely survived, and in the ghetto conditions were appalling. Water and sewage systems were frozen solid. "Cascades of frozen refuse were spread through backyards, hung from windows, and in the dwelling caves straw and rags were frozen solid."[160] Coal was expensive and scarce even if one had money. Families often were forced to huddle together day and night, thus increasing the likelihood of transmitting lice and disease. The problem was especially acute for the starving Jews because an emaciated body requires a warm environment and is very susceptible to frostbite.[161]

Compounding the problem was the frequent absence of electricity.[162] Some people used candles, but the common replacement for electricity for lighting was the carbide lamp. These were found throughout the ghetto. The lamps looked like soup cans. Solid carbide was placed inside, the lamp sealed, water poured in through a tube, and gas released. When this gas was lit it burned brightly, but the lamps gave off a characteristic unpleasant odor.[163] (A kind of ersatz vodka called "bimber" could be made from carbide, but it was a dangerous replacement for the real thing, causing blindness in some.[164])

Even more serious than the lack of electricity was the difficulty with water supply and sewage disposal—the most dramatic manifestations of the latter being those described by Hagen. Often it was necessary to line up at street pumps to get water, and families soon became adept at having several members bathe in the same water and then using the dirty water to flush toilets.[165] But most homes in the ghetto didn't have flush toilets. Even the streets became cloacal at times; one ghetto inhabitant noted that in December 1941, walking from Leszno to Śliska streets, one had to step carefully to avoid the streams of water and excrement.[166] Naturally, inadequate cleansing led to poor sanitation and disease, as summed up by a physician in the ghetto:

> The hospital population is usually very poor and also very dirty as a result of the terrible sanitary conditions in the ghetto. The skin is infested with parasites such as lice, scabies, and crusted ringworm, and dermatoses, furunculosis, subdermal abscesses, and diffuse phlegmons are very common. Lice and dermatoses cause itching and the scratched skin is excoriated and traumatized.[167]

By the middle of 1942, as conditions worsened rapidly, the ghetto became an especially grotesque place, a caricature of normality. There were bizarre sights that continue to haunt the memory of survivors, pathetic examples of people coping as best as they could in the face of unprecedented disaster. Stiffel remembers the Silent Family and their

> dignified, ghastly appearance. The barefoot man, his huge torso nude, pushed a baby carriage from which his wife, a little atrophied body with a big head, showed to the world around her an ever-smiling row of teeth. Their three naked children walked silently behind them. As they disappeared into the distance they left behind them shudder[ing] and uneasiness.[168]

It seems unlikely that there would be two such families in the ghetto, using the same mode of transport, but perhaps there were. Janusz Korczak was moved on seeing a cantor, who "slowly pushed a pram in which his paralyzed wife was lying. . . ." In contrast to the Silent Family, the cantor sang loudly, appealing to his god with the words, "The soul is Thine, and the body is Thy work; have pity on Thy labor."[169]

RELIGION

> On the First Day of the Year it is inscribed, And on the Day of Atonement the decree is sealed, How many shall pass away and how many shall be born, Who shall live and who shall die. . . .[170]

The religious observance of many Jews was an occasional rather than a regular thing. But there was a large body of deeply religious Jews who sought to perform the rituals and enjoy the comfort of Judaism. Initially, observance of Shabbat, the sabbath, from sundown Friday to sundown Saturday, had to be a clandestine affair. In December 1939, prayer in synagogues was forbidden.[171]

Gradually, the authorities permitted more and more open observance, and in early 1941 the *Gazeta Żydowska* printed an announcement over Czerniakow's name designating the Shabbat, Rosh Hashanah, Yom Kippur, Sukkot (four days), Passover (four days), and Shavuot (two days) as the official days of rest in the ghetto. This followed an order by Frank on 4 March 1941, which permitted the holding of religious services in homes, synagogues, and houses of study during these holidays. During Shavuot in the autumn of 1941, services were held in the Great Synagogue on Tlomackie Street.[172] Nevertheless, many small synagogues were abandoned; some were later used as living quarters for refugees (see Figure 3.5).

The rabbinate suffered excessively in Warsaw. According to Trunk, of all the rabbis in the Warsaw ghetto, only one survived the war.[173] Occasionally, however, a small victory was achieved. One of these took place in the Warsaw ghetto. It was in 1944, long after all the Jews had been deported or driven into hiding. The Nazis set up a small concentration camp on Gęsia Street and filled it with Jews assigned to clean up the ravages made by the almost total destruction carried out by the Ger-

Figure 3.5. Interior of a synagogue in the Warsaw ghetto. Note its use as a shelter, probably for Jews forced into the ghetto from outside Warsaw. The sign in Hebrew is a brief passage from the Torah (courtesy of the late Dr. Karolina Bein).

mans. During a severe Russian air raid, a German officer suddenly asked if there was a rabbi among the prisoners. Ezekiel Ruttner stepped forward and was astonished to hear the German order him to pray for their survival. "And so, by German request, traditional Jewish prayers were offered among the ruins of destroyed Jewish Warsaw. The bombs kept falling but the German SS men were relaxed, confident that the young rabbi's ancient Hebrew chant had drawn around them a magic circle."[174] Whether the officer simply craved any kind of spiritual aid, or whether he was a crypto-Jew coming out of the closet under pressure, as it were, we do not know.

BURYING THE DEAD

> I looked at them all with wide eyes and my mind shut. I refused to think of what
> I was seeing, and even more resolutely I forbade myself to feel.[175]

This was the response of a young Jewish girl to the spectacle of dead bodies lying in the streets of the ghetto. Every ghetto resident had to devise a way to deal with this macabre, unnatural, but increasingly common sight. Ringelblum notes that most of these corpses were anonymous, lacking any means of identification. Rarely did a family member come to identify a body. If he did, the purpose was to claim the corpse's shirt.[176] But most corpses in the street had been placed there deliberately by the relatives, who usually removed all clothing as well as identification papers.

The chief undertaker in the ghetto was the firm of Pinkiert. Its carts traveled the streets of the ghetto all day, collecting the bodies and taking them to a mortuary on the cemetery grounds. Before the war, religious Jews would take the bodies of deceased family members directly to the mortuary at the entrance to the cemetery. The body would be taken without a coffin, to be washed and then buried wrapped in sheets (*tachrichim*).

During the war, that procedure was followed less and less often. Most families had no money for such ceremonies. By 1941 bodies were being buried naked because linen shrouds were unobtainable and one couldn't even get paper to substitute for the linen.[177]

The Jewish cemetery in Warsaw, on Okopowa Street, still exists. It is a depressing place, all except a few sections a chaos of tilted, broken headstones twisted by the roots of a forest of 40- to 50-year-old trees permitted by neglect to grow uncontrolled. The neglect reflects the current tiny number of Jews remaining in Warsaw. The cemetery covers 75 acres, surrounded by a brick wall that varies from 8 to 20 feet in height. It must have been an impressive place when there was a large population to provide for its upkeep and to lavish attention on the individual gravesites. Despite decades of neglect, the Jewish cemetery is perhaps the only place in Warsaw where one can still get some impression of the size of the Jewish population of the city before World War II.

Okopowa Street was not in the ghetto. There was a single gate at the corner of Okopowa and Gęsia through which Jews, alive and dead, had to pass to enter. Through this gate, between 1939 and 1942, tens of thousands of Jews went to their uneasy rest. At one point, planners at the *Judenrat* proposed that an overpass be

Figure 3.6. Taking a child's corpse to the Jewish cemetery, Warsaw (Bundesarchiv, Koblenz).

built across Okopowa Street to the cemetery, thus making it unnecessary to present papers to guards, bare one's head, and risk a beating. However, before the scheme proceeded very far, someone pointed out that it would be almost impossible to carry the dead up and down the steps of this overpass, and the idea was discarded.[178]

The number of burials escalated rapidly. During 1940, 8981 were recorded, of which 2757 were paid for, the remaining 6224 not (70 percent). In the first two months of 1941, 1110 Jews were buried; of these, over 90 percent had to be buried at the expense of the community, a commentary on the declining fortunes of the ghetto inhabitants.[179]

Communal graves were in use by the beginning of 1941.[180] By March 1941, most of the dead from Czyste Hospital were buried in mass graves, naked.[181] Families would never be able to identify exactly where a loved one began his or her last rest. Indeed, this happened even in 1939. During the massive German bombardment of Warsaw, the grandmother of Karolina Borman and Irena Bakowska died of natural causes. The bombing was so heavy that the family had to entrust her burial to men who were strangers to the family. Afterward they were shown a grave in the cemetery as that of the grandmother, but something in the manner of the men convinced the family that the deceased had been simply abandoned somewhere out of sight.[182]

A special trial for Jewish families attempting to mourn their dead was the fact that the Germans used the cemetery as a bizarre amusement park. Off-duty soldiers seemed to be constantly there. They snapped photographs of the procession, the coffin, the relatives; they even took snapshots of the bodies laid out in the mortuary.

"The Nazis were particularly active in this respect on Sundays, when they would visit the cemetery with their girl friends."[183]

Nor were the Germans the only ones who dishonored the dead. In a macabre preview of what would happen in the death camps, gold teeth were removed from the mouths of the corpses. Czerniakow, Ringelblum, and Adler were all inmates of the ghetto. All held positions in which they were likely to know what was going on. All kept diaries or wrote memoirs about what was happening to the Jewish people. All wrote about this revolting practice, and all three identified a different culprit or group of culprits.

According to Ringelblum, it was the Jewish police, the *Ordnungsdienst*, who desecrated the graves. Some members of the force were found, in September 1941, to be digging up bodies recently buried at night, extracting gold teeth and stealing shrouds.[184]

Adler, an *Ordnungsdienst* official, accused the grave diggers themselves. Apparently some were guilty, because they expressed surprise that their actions were considered inappropriate. They claimed that taking gold from corpses did not harm anybody, while at the same time it contributed to the improved balance of payments in the ghetto.[185] These "cemetery dentists" were arrested and tried before a disciplinary tribunal inside the ghetto. Adler does not indicate the outcome.

Czerniakow is less specific. On 9 November 1941 he penned a terse note in his diary to the effect that the *Ordnungsdienst* had reported about "cases of graves being dug up by some gang to extract gold teeth from the dead."[186]

Figure 3.7. Burying a body wrapped in a shroud, Warsaw Jewish cemetery (Bundesarchiv, Koblenz).

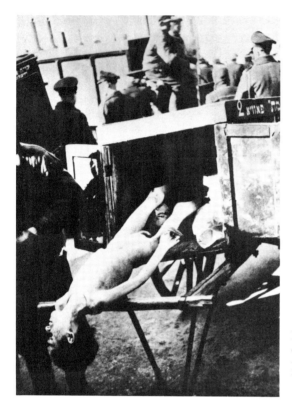

Figure 3.8. Bodies at the Jewish cemetery, Warsaw (from Anonymous, *The Warsaw Ghetto,* Warsaw: Interpress Publishers, 1988).

SEXUALITY

Sexuality was commonly affected negatively by ghetto life. Sex is central to the thoughts, desires, and well-being of most of us. It is also an activity likely to have been disrupted by the severe physical and psychological pressures of life under Nazi rule. But attitudes toward sexuality were ambivalent. Henry Fenigstein was in his twenties, recently married and living with his wife in their own tiny room in the Czyste Hospital. He might be assumed to have had an active sex life, with morality not a question. But his memory is otherwise. In fact, he remembers little about the subject at all, guessing only that there was probably less activity in the ghetto than there would have been before that time.[187] Like most Jews in the ghetto, the Fenigsteins did not want to start a family, the totally unpropitious nature of the times seeming to make childbirth a mockery.[188]

The Fenigsteins had one boon that was unavailable to most ghetto dwellers: They had their own private room for many months. Most Jews had to share living space; in some cases this affected sexual mores. As one physician pointed out, when six or seven people shared a room continuously, the customary avoidance of sexual intercourse in the presence of others was no longer possible.[189]

While doubts about the wisdom of raising a family were common, many found

sexuality itself as intriguing as always. Although the grossly inadequate ration probably had an antiaphrodisiac effect, and certainly caused some impotence as well as
lack of interest—a phenomenon much commented upon in prisoner-of-war
camps, though there the disinclination was usually reinforced by a total absence of
women[190]—again one must keep in mind the differences among the ghetto population. At any given time, while many were starving and perhaps were indifferent
to sexuality, many others, better fed, felt the usual physiological urges. Moreover,
these urges may have been felt at an earlier age, or indulged in earlier, than had been
the case before the war. A teacher in the clandestine schools was convinced that the
students he saw, aged 11 or 12 "devoted a major part of their leisure hours to activities of a sexual nature."[191]

For many, the atmosphere late in the ghetto's existence must have strongly suggested the desirability of experiencing at least some of life's mysteries before it was
too late. Apathy and hedonism coexisted in many of the Jews.[192] Many so-called
nice girls, who would never have engaged in sexual relations out of wedlock before
the war, did so in the ghetto. "Nobody liked to admit it seriously, but the atmosphere there was one of anxious expectation of the ultimate fate, and sex seemed a
way to become immortal."[193] This same phenomenon was also observed in smaller
towns such as Hrubieszów. Everyone knew they were living on borrowed time,
"and the girls were eager to make love so that when the time came to die, they would
have experienced one of life's most talked-about pleasures."[194] Moreover, the risk
of unwanted pregnancy was somewhat lessened because many women did not
menstruate for lengthy periods. Nevertheless, some survivors believed that disso-
lution of morals was restrained by the lessening of sexual capacity due to mental
trauma, a condition that often was diagnosed by physicians.[195]

That sexual activity continued at some level is shown by the ongoing need for
contraceptives. A record exists indicating that Jewish ingenuity had found a way to
make condoms out of baby pacifiers,[196] the latter being little in demand for their
designed use.

Sensual experimentation by young people increasingly aware that their lives
were likely to be short was only one aspect of ghetto sexuality. Another was prostitution. North American readers in particular may not know or recall that prostitution was an ordinary, accepted, and common part of urban life in Europe, a fact
with a very long history. There was nothing especially Jewish about this activity—
or anything explicitly non-Jewish—though Jewish prostitutes were relatively few in
number. But prostitution was a fact.

Thus we find Chaim Rumkowski, head of the Łódź ghetto, in one of his earliest
official communications with the local Nazi government, pressing for an adequate
hospital, one that would permit separate wards for surgery, internal medicine, children, expectant mothers, and a special division for prostitutes.[197] Warsaw had its
own Jewish as well as Christian prostitutes. Early in the German occupation, a year
before the ghetto came into being, the Nazis ordered all Jewish prostitutes into the
Czyste Hospital; the interviewee who observed this could suggest no motivation,
since the women were not ill.[198] Perhaps this was simply another form of humiliation, to fill the only Jewish hospital with streetwalkers, but they did not remain there
for long.

In 1940 one of the Nazi health officials sought to ensure that Jewish prostitutes wore armbands, since otherwise German soldiers looking for company would be unable to distinguish the Polish from the Jewish prostitutes. "It was pointed out to him that the ladies in question would not wear armbands anyway."[199]

The cruel economic realities of the ghetto contributed to the incidence of prostitution. As long as men were willing and able to pay, the trade offered a means of earning bread, and perhaps feeding a family. Emmanuel Ringelblum noted in his diary, just two months after the ghetto was established, that he had been accosted in the street and propositioned by a very respectable-looking woman who, he implied, had no background in that business.[200] For those who had, there were brothels, which were active at least until the massive deportations began in July 1942. One of these was located at Dzielna 17.[201]

Edelman has reported that two or three prostitutes shared a bunker with some of the men in the Jewish Fighting Organization (ZOB) during the April 1943 uprising. They were "good, clever, resourceful girls."[202] He refused to let one of the prostitutes attempt to escape with them through the sewers, though he cannot say why.

NIGHT LIFE AND CRIME

Where there are brothels, nearby will be bars, taverns, restaurants, and nightclubs. Even in the Warsaw ghetto, such places existed in bizarre and frenetic abundance. Attendees were no longer the affluent and near-affluent of Warsaw society, but the new leaders, the nouveau riches of Warsaw's underworld—in this case, mainly the smugglers who regularly risked their lives in the most literal sense, and who eased the tension, and any guilt, in the customary way. They ate too well, drank too much, and thought as little as possible about tomorrow.

One of these establishments was the Hotel Britannia, in the basement of Nowolipie 18. The Thirteen not only frequented the place, they owned and operated it, on the sound economic principle that one may as well profit from one's own and others' weaknesses. The Britannia didn't close its doors until 7 A.M., and one could buy a kilo of wine for 25 zloty ($5).[203] And a gambling house existed at Chłodna 16 (almost next door to the home of the *Judenrat* chairman, Czerniakow), operated by a *Judenrat* official, Henryk Czerwinski.[204]

Among the restaurants that functioned well into the ghetto period, Adler especially mentions two as having notoriously impressive menus despite the circumstances: A La Fourchette, at Leszno and Solna, and the Adas, at Leszno 14. Both were patronized largely by black marketeers.[205] Another anachronism in the starving ghetto was Gogolewski's cake shop, mentioned in a frank and unashamedly existential account by a former black marketeer:

> I sold my goods at exorbitant prices, ate cakes from Gogolewski's cake shop, and dispensed charity. Was it unfair? I lived as best I could in the hell which they had created. I was holding my own, all of us were trying to hold our own.[206]

The ghetto leaders were distressed, though not surprised and rarely outraged, at the evidence of dissipation around them. Only a minority participated, probably a tiny minority. But every Jew had to find his or her own way of coping with what might be seen as a fundamental tenet of life in the ghetto: "The demoralization and corruption in the Ghetto result from the fact that everything is forbidden to Jews. A Jew, that is to say every Jew, is therefore compelled to break the law."[207] This truism was not the self-serving excuse of a libertine or a criminal, but rather the observation of a member of the *Judenrat*, the head of the Labor Division, Henryk Rosen.

If every Jew did break the law, in most instances it was German law that had been devised expressly to humiliate, to distress, to starve. Of true crime in the customary "civilized" sense of that word, remarkably little was perpetrated by the Jews, though a notable exception was the theft that commonly seemed to be part of the disinfection process, about which more will be said in discussing epidemics, particularly typhus, in Chapter 7. Adler, an *Ordnungsdienst* official, claimed that despite the appalling misery of the ghetto, manslaughter, aggravated assault, and other serious crimes did not occur. There was no general increase in criminality.[208]

When rape occurred, it was Jewish women who were the victims; most often the rapists were Germans,[209] sometimes Poles.[210] However, Rubinlicht claims that members of the Jewish *Ordnungsdienst* either raped young Jewish girls or extorted sexual favors from them at the *Umschlagplatz*. Young women caught up in an *Aktion* and desperate to escape would allow anything "in order to be promised release from that hell. Of course, they were never released. But the guards had their way with them."[211] And Edelman witnessed six or eight Ukrainian guards raping a Jewish girl in a large room in the former hospital at Stawki 6–8:

> They waited in line and then raped her. After the line was finished, this girl left the niche and she walked across the whole gym, stumbling against the reclining people. She was very pale, naked, and bleeding, and she slouched down into a corner. The crowd saw everything, and nobody said a word. Nobody so much as moved, and the silence continued.[212]

An unpleasant aspect of Czerniakow's personality invests a diary entry about rape in which he manages to combine lack of empathy, crudity, and male chauvinism. He describes how "An old hag who had been raped appeared today, coiffured, with her lips painted, etc. Rejuvenated at least 20 years."[213]

There was a Jewish prison operated by the *Ordnungsdienst* or Jewish police, located on Gęsia Street and known as Gęsiówka. Its inhabitants were Jews, and there were sometimes as many as 1600 inmates in an institution built to hold 150.[214] One physician imprisoned there, a Dr. Beiles, saw several inmates die every day. In some instances, the cells were so crowded that people suffocated and died.[215] At any time the population was about half male and half female, many extremely young.[216] They were there almost without exception for offenses against German arbitrary ghetto-related laws such as smuggling food or leaving the ghetto. So many were children—in May 1942, 500 of the 1300 then incarcerated[217]—because smuggling became largely an occupation of the youth of the ghetto.

As for the ultimate crime of murder, historically this was never a Jewish crime, and that remained true in the Warsaw ghetto. Murder of a Jew by a Jew was almost unheard of. Up to July 1942 there had not been one case, according to Gutman,[218] who describes what he claims to be the sole case as occurring just before the end of 1942 when there was a falling out among a group of Jewish smugglers, who killed one of their own number.[219] Lewin finds the record slightly worse, declaring on 11

June 1942 that there had been two murders in the ghetto up to that date, though he gives no details.[220]

The Jews in the ghetto were kept largely in the dark about German plans for their future. This was, of course, the case in terms of the ultimate fate, once that decision was made late in 1941. But there were decisions on a less global scale going on around them that they learned about only as events unfolded. One of these was of crucial importance, at least in the short term. This concerned the basic attitude of the local Germans toward the fate of the Jews and to their possible contribution to the war effort. Many observers have commented on the fact that the Jews became an object of rivalry among various German groups, of which the most obvious were the Gestapo, the SS, and Frank's largely civilian government.[221] There is some evidence to show that the civilian administration—Auerswald and his colleagues—sometimes responded humanely and rationally toward the Jews. The SS, the police, and the Gestapo almost never did so.[222]

Browning has pointed out that for the first 20 months of the German occupation, a school of thought predominated that he calls "attritionist."[223] That is, the attitude of the Nazis who then held power in the *Generalgouvernement* was not only not sympathetic to the Jews—few Germans were, and fewer took the risk of making their feelings known—but also uninterested in any attempt to maintain their potential productivity for the Third Reich. But by about May 1941 that group had lost power, to be replaced by the "productionists."[224] This group saw a need to keep at least the customarily healthy, vigorous young men and women adequately fed and employed at work designed to aid Germany in its increasingly costly war. With this group holding the reins, the introduction of "shops" into the ghetto was pursued actively.

After this, the shop system expanded rapidly. German firms came in to tap the reservoir of skilled labor available at minimal cost. The Walter Többens shop was involved mostly with tailoring, Schultz U. and Company with furs and shoemaking; K. G. Schultz concentrated on knitted goods, based on the Jewish factory of Brown and Rowinski.[225]

Yet despite all this activity, most Jews were unemployed. When Gutman declares that "the overwhelming majority of the Jews did not engage in any productive work or wage-paying labor,"[226] he does not mean that they were lazy or shirking. There was nothing for most of the Jews to do.

Thus the seeds of disaster not only were planted, they sprouted vigorously. The ghetto was a place of hunger, cold, exposure to infectious diseases, and especially fear. Starvation not only created its own victims, it prepared an endless crop of Jews for the ravages of disease. For everyone in the ghetto, the burgeoning concern for the future exacerbated all the problems they struggled with. Now it is necessary to describe more explicitly how these conditions pushed the Jews of the Warsaw ghetto closer and closer to extinction even before the full horror of the Holocaust overtook them.

This brings the general story of the ghetto through stage 3, the ghetto existence to July 1942. A more detailed look at the strictly medical side of ghetto life during the period up to July 1942 is presented in the next several chapters.

4

Structure of the Medical
System in the Ghetto

The Warsaw ghetto was forced to become a self-contained city with a peak population of almost half a million. This is more people than currently live in Edinburgh, Ottawa, or Cincinnati, and approximately the same number as in Nagasaki; or Ventura, California; or the entire county of Gloucestershire, England.

The medical and medically related needs were immense, and the attempts to meet these needs complicated and ultimately unsuccessful. The *Judenrat* had to create a health department to fulfill many of the roles previously played by the Warsaw city department.

The *Judenrat* as an institution has received a great deal of negative comment since the war, as well as understandably acerbic criticism from the inhabitants of Poland's various ghettos during the war. Certainly the *Judenraten* had an unenviable and fundamentally impossible task. The membership was sometimes dishonest and often undistinguished because in some communities the traditional leaders had fled just before or at the beginning of the war. Fortunately for the Jews of Warsaw, the head of the health department was both honest and competent. He was Dr. Izrael Milejkowski, described by a medical colleague in the ghetto as "one of the few decent and honest members" of the *Judenrat*.[1] The most awesome responsibility in his jurisdiction was public health, for the public whose health was to be attended to consisted of far too many people in far too little space provided with inadequate food, electricity, coal, water, and sewage facilities, and ultimately with half or more of the population requiring regular welfare support simply to maintain their semistarved existence.

Dr. Milejkowski did not work in a vacuum, of course. Most directly, he was responsible to the *Judenrat* as a whole and to Adam Czerniakow, its chairman. Among the Germans there were, as always, many bosses, but throughout the period of ghettoization his most direct contact was the German physician Wilhelm Hagen, who was appointed health officer for the civilian population of Warsaw in November 1940, just as the ghetto was created.[2] He arrived in Warsaw and replaced Dr. Kurt Schrempf early in 1941.

His responsibilities and lofty contacts conferred little prestige on Milejkowski, at least in German eyes. In April 1940, despite bearing an impeccable German *Ausweis* and other documents, Dr. Milejkowski was caught on the street and forced to spend the day carrying bricks in a downfall of rain.[3]

There were many preexisting institutions to be run, as well as new institutions to be created and set to work. These included clinics and hospitals: general, pedi-

atric, psychiatric, tuberculosis, and some small private hospitals. Trunk has summarized the various institutions:

> The health department established six health centers staffed by specialists in
> hygiene care and sanitary personnel. Chief physicians were in charge. The depart-
> ment supervised the activities of the two hospitals (operating . . . in six buildings),
> three outpatient clinics, a sanitary commission of physicians, eight disinfection
> units (as of September 1941), four bathhouses, three places of quarantine, and var-
> ious institutions of public welfare.[4]

This was the situation at a particular point in time. But circumstances altered
these arrangements. There was, for example, a surgical clinic at Pańska 43[5] in the
Small Ghetto not far from the Berson and Bauman Hospital. But in mid-1941 an
especially brutal German guard nicknamed "Frankenstein" was assigned to the
gate at Żelazna and Leszno in the Large Ghetto. This man delighted in shooting
Jews, and injured so many that it became necessary to open a surgical emergency
clinic in a former public school building directly across from the Collegium where
the *Arbeitsamt* and the medical school were located. At this clinic, victims of Frankenstein received initial treatment before being sent on to the surgical wing of Czyste
at Leszno 1.[6] The ghetto hospitals are discussed in Chapter 5.

There was a bacteriological institute, where, among others, Prof. Ludwig Hirszfeld (see Figure 4.1) spent much of his time.[7] There were pharmacies. And there
were large groups of professionals—physicians, nurses, dentists, pharmacists, and
so on. For all these institutions and groups of professionals, some direction was
required.

Figure 4.1. Dr. Ludwik
Hirszfeld.

From the beginning there were numerous problems. Some were inherent in the life ghetto dwellers were doomed to live. Others, unfortunately, were created by individuals who might have been less selfish. One example was the reaction to efforts of a group of physicians who proposed to supply free medical care to members of the *Ordnungsdienst* in their consulting rooms. This offer was extended in December 1940, just after the ghetto had been set up, and at a time when the *Ordnungsdienst* still had an unsullied character and, moreover, some sympathy because their jobs were essentially unpaid. But the offer was rejected by a Dr. Fajncyn, a venereal disease specialist who was also director of the Communal Outpatients Clinic. If implemented, the new proposal would have taken money out of the pockets of Fajncyn and his coworkers. So the *Ordnungsdienst* had to attend the clinics and pay a 2-zloty fee, which in turn was supplied by the *Judenrat*. Adler was indignant at this action:

> I admit to not understanding at all why it was against the ethics of the medical profession to extend entirely free assistance to hosts of functionaries who are receiving no pay, while it was in conformity with these same ethics to charge fees for that service to the Jewish Council that itself was unable to extend adequate aid for the poorest, for lack of funds.[8]

The *Judenrat* did maintain two outpatient clinics for a time before the ghetto was created. One was on Grzybowska Street, which was inside what became the ghetto, and it continued operation. The other was on Nowiniarska Street. This street was not included in the ghetto, and somehow Dr. Fajncyn (not one of Adler's favorite people) prevented its reopening inside the ghetto; Adler says this was done for personal gain.[9]

In addition to the visible and permitted institutions, there were organizations of which the Germans knew nothing, or at least let on that they knew nothing, though they had spies everywhere. Among these groups was an association of block physicians under the aegis of Professor Hirszfeld,[10] an underground medical school headed by Dr. Juliusz Zweibaum (see Chapter 10),[11] and a major research project investigating the physiological and pathological effects of profound, long-term starvation (see Chapter 6).[12]

The provision of social welfare became a matter of desperate urgency within the ghetto. The *Judenrat* organized some efforts in this area, but their work became suspect because of the general contempt in which they came to be held. Fortunately, the Jewish tradition of self-help was deeply ingrained. Assistance came both from the population at large, in the form of unorganized alms giving and, more important, through the labors of social welfare organizations. Some of these sprang up during the ghetto years; others had existed before the war.

TOZ

Perhaps the most important of the latter was the group known as TOZ. The letters are an acronym derived from the first three words of the name *Towarzystwo Ochrony Zdrowia Ludności Żydowskiej*, the Society to Protect the Health of the Jewish

Population. TOZ had been created in 1922 by a group of Jewish physicians and laymen,[13] taking over work previously done by the American Jewish Joint Distribution Committee (AJDC or Joint). TOZ was located at Gęsia 43 throughout the war.[14] The TOZ soup kitchen was at Lubeckiego 2.[15]

TOZ was in parallel with the *Judenrat* with respect to medical work; sometimes it was in competition. Like the *Judenrat*, TOZ found itself coping with many new problems under Nazi rule. Some of these included hospitals, maternity clinics, and bathhouses.[16] They fed refugees and were even driven to creating a clothing factory. There, early in 1940, 51 persons were employed, remodeling old clothing into new articles of clothing to distribute among the needy.[17] The new responsibilities seem to have been taken on because institutions would otherwise have been forced to close. Early in 1940 the budget of TOZ had risen to about 1 million zloty monthly (ca. $20,000). Much of this money came from the Joint, which from the start provided the major financial support for Jewish self-help activities.[18]

The work was draining. The Warsaw officials representing the AJDC managed to get to Amsterdam for a meeting early in 1940. One of their colleagues reported that although they "had obviously suffered a great deal and were in such a mental state that they found it difficult to discuss the work coherently, it was clear that they had organized a comprehensive program for emergency aid."[19]

That program included Medem, the tuberculosis sanatorium in Otwock, with an average of 150 patients; the insane asylum Zofiowka, also at Otwock, with more than 300 patients; the nursing school at Czyste Hospital; Czyste Hospital itself and the attached research institute; and the only children's hospital in Warsaw, Berson and Bauman.[20] And, of course, there was TOZ itself and its many endeavors. TOZ did not operate these institutions on its own. The *Judenrat* also was involved in them all. Budgeted funds for TOZ for 1940 included 6.5 million zloty for additional feeding, 1.5 million for the various health-related activities, 1.3 million for CENTOS, and some smaller projects, for a total expenditure of 10.5 million zloty.[21]

Nor was Poland the only country in need. Joint conducted programs around the world. Every country felt its demands to be especially pressing, and Joint officials spent much time reminding desperate supplicants that this was the case and telling them that everything depended on how much money American Jews contributed.[22] The response from Warsaw was to reiterate the urgency of the need:

> Since early morning big crowds of people besiege our gates for tickets to our institution. We cannot satisfy all the needs as we lack the necessary means and personnel, and even the personnel we have staggers [*sic*] from exhaustion and sheer lack of food.[23]

In the spring of 1940, TOZ reportedly employed almost 200 doctors, more than 100 nurses, 65 pharmacists, 14 dentists, and 8 laboratory workers. Since the war began, TOZ had acquired two surgical institutions, three maternity hospitals, and four establishments for infants, as well as the Otwock hospitals and several establishments for sanitary and disinfection duties.[24]

By the end of 1940 the workload had become impossibly heavy, yet TOZ officials reacted with indignation when they learned on 4 December 1940 that all TOZ children's kitchens were to be transferred to CENTOS, and that in the future only

CENTOS and ŻTOS would operate such kitchens.[25] Eventually this "arbitrary decision" was explained. Jewish children were not allowed to attend school, but CENTOS had obtained permission from the Germans to give "oral instruction" to the children before and after feeding periods. Because only CENTOS had such permission, and to allow as many children as possible to benefit from at least this minimal teaching, the change was made. Instruction was provided by male and female teachers who spent the entire day with the children in the CENTOS homes.[26] This answer probably did not placate TOZ, for they took their responsibilities seriously, but they obeyed orders.

CENTOS, or *Centrala Opieki nad Sierotami* (Society for the Care of Orphans), was perhaps equally influential though in a narrower field, its efforts being devoted solely to children.[27] In the ghetto its headquarters was at Leszno 2, a 15-room building near the great Tłomackie Synagogue.[28]

Although Joint was a major contributor to self-help, distributing American funds as generously as its means permitted, money was also received from many other sources.

SELF-HELP

In September 1939, Warsaw had created a network of civil defense tenement committees. These were called the OPL, for *Obrona Przeciwlotznica* or antiaircraft defense, because the original responsibility was to oversee a number of crucial activities relating to protection from aircraft and bombing. These included enforcing blackout precautions, organizing firefighting squads, providing shelter for tenement occupants, and administering first aid. By extension, in Jewish neighborhoods the OPL also set up services for those who had been bombed out and for other refugees, services involving food distribution and health and welfare assistance. In the beginning, the tenement committees operated independently, but they soon came under the aegis of a Coordinating Commission (KK), formed on 14 September, 1939 "at the initiative of the JDC, with the participation of the leading Jewish welfare organizations of prewar Poland."[29]

The KK was associated initially with the Polish social welfare organization.[30] But in January 1940 the Nazis ordered the Jewish division to become independent. The new group then called itself ŻSS, *Żydowska Samopomoc Społeczna* (Jewish Communal Self-Help).[31] The ŻSS had its headquarters in Kraków, where it was headed by Michal Weichert. It operated across the entire *Generalgouvernement*.[32] Somewhat remarkably, ŻSS-ŻTOS received financial support from the budget of the *Generalgouvernement* until the time of the deportations in 1942.[33] It was the only official Nazi-controlled channel through which assistance flowed to Jews. The actual amounts involved were small, and the Germans may have tolerated the operation for its propaganda value.

ŻSS had branches throughout the *Generalgouvernement*, of which the largest was, of course, the one in Warsaw. In October 1940, the Warsaw branch was renamed ŻTOS (*Żydowskie Towarzystwo Opieki Społecznej*, the Jewish Society for Social Welfare).[34] ŻTOS represented the cooperative actions of Joint in both the

Zionist and non-Zionists camps.[35] Among their many activities was the creation of public kitchens—141 in all—that served passable soup at nominal prices, as well as providing the poor with raw food and old clothing.[36]

Finally, at about the end of 1941, both TOZ and CENTOS officially disappeared, the former becoming the medical department of the Jewish Social Self-Help, the latter the child-care department of the same organization.[37] In mid-1942 the Nazis dissolved ŻSS; ŻTOS vanished along with the Jews of Warsaw. However, the Nazis later reconstituted ŻSS as the JUS (*Judische Unterstutzungstelle* or Jewish Relief Office).[38]

These arrangements for the provision of social welfare, including many aspects of health care, have been described in some detail. The system in the Warsaw ghetto was a pastiche of several systems. The *Judenrat* was the official government within the ghetto, put in place by the Germans for that purpose. It had both a medical department and a variety of social welfare operations. Independently, and sometimes competitively, were the prewar groups such as TOZ and CENTOS, their position greatly strengthened by their long relationship with the Joint and by their familiarity to the Jews. Because of this relationship, they had financial backing that was substantial, even if not as great as either the Warsaw agencies or the AJDC would have wished.

The third layer of organization was the OPL-KK-ZSS-ZTOS chain. TOZ and CENTOS cooperated closely with these groups but were nevertheless independent until forced, a few months before the deportations began, to become departments within ŻTOS. Because of its small but real financial backing from the *Generalgouvernement*, the ŻSS/ŻTOS had a major advantage over the *Judenrat*. "As one ŻSS official put it, it appeared that the Judenrate took from the Jews to give to the Germans, whereas the ŻSS took from the Germans to give to the Jews."[39]

Nevertheless, ŻTOS was not without its critics among the Jews. Kaplan, for example, in relating the death of the distinguished Judaic scholar Joseph David Bornstejn, on 8 March 1942, has bitter words for Self-Help. According to Kaplan, Bornstejn was far too modest and unassuming to get help from Self-Help, despite his deserving character. "The dignitaries of the Jewish Self-Aid entertain no special affection for unaggressive paupers. Anyone who can talk big, no matter how ignorant, is welcomed and given assistance."[40] So Bornstejn died of neglect and starvation.

Nor were these all the agencies and activities, though they were among the most important. The tenement committees, also known as "house committees," have been mentioned. They were "the first, most fundamental cell in the ramified network of organized social welfare organs."[41] At the time of the creation of the ghetto there were nearly 2000 house committees in Warsaw; after the ghetto was set up the number fell to 1108, since far fewer buildings were available to the Jews. The ghetto was divided into six precincts, as were the house committees.[42]

The main function of these house committees was seen by them, and by the ŻTOS of which they were so important a constituent, as the provision of social welfare assistance to the tenants of the various buildings. They supported communal kitchens, arranged for clothing pools, set up cultural activities, and attempted to extend their aid even outside their own buildings. Thus one building cooked a special kettle of soup for the Berson and Bauman Hospital for children every Friday.[43] The activities at one house committee meeting are presented dramatically by Lifton in her biography of Janusz Korczak.[44]

The *Judenrat* saw the house committees as a useful tool. They tried to involve them in various administrative and regulatory functions, such as tax collection. But both the committees and ŻTOS fought this effort. They knew that if the committees began to do unpopular tasks such as collecting taxes, they would lose all the good will they had built up among their tenants. So in this and many other ways, the *Judenrat* and the main social welfare agencies were in conflict.

There was one other group of importance in this area: the refugee committee. There were about 60 *landsmanshaftn*, associations of fellow townsmen, each representing a single town or village, among the refugees who were driven into Warsaw. From the *landsmanshaftn*, many of whose members had been in the *Judenraten* of their previous homes and therefore were experienced in communal affairs, a central committee was set up.[45] This committee cooperated with ŻTOS, TOZ, and other groups, which in turn were trying to aid the large numbers of refugees in the city.

Some of the organizations in the ghetto were unequivocally political. To give a single example, the Betarist (right-wing Zionist) group set up the revisionist Jewish Military Union, or ŻZW (*Żydowski Związek Wojskowy*), as a paramilitary organization in parallel with the ŻOB, or Jewish Fighting Organization (*Żydowska Organizacja Bojowa*).[46] ŻZW had a medical department, headed by Dr. Josef Celmaister. Its medical activities included stockpiling and distributing medical supplies to the fighting units, arranging first aid training, and providing poison (cyanide) to those members of the ŻZW who were most at risk of falling into German hands when the fighting began.[47]

There were also organizations that did not help, though their cooperation might have been expected. One of these was the Polish Red Cross, which by February 1941 ceased all activities in the ghetto,[48] many of the inhabitants of which had presumably supported the group financially in the past.

PHYSICIANS IN THE WARSAW GHETTO

At the beginning of the ghetto, there were more physicians per capita inside the walls than outside; no precise census exists, but there were about 800 doctors in the ghetto.[49] All of these, or the vast majority, belonged to a Jewish medical association, of which Milejkowski said he was the head.[50] There were two medical societies, one for hospital physicians and one for block physicians.[51] The latter group included most of the medical practitioners in the ghetto who were not working in hospitals. Each was assigned a certain number of blocks or buildings that constituted his or her working area. For example, Dr. Noemi Wigdorowicz had responsibility for several blocks on Nowolipki Street.[52]

In all, the number of Jews involved in health-related activities was very large. Rosen estimates that in July 1942, just before the deportations to Treblinka began, there were about 46,500 Jews, men and women, working in the various areas required to run the ghetto services. Of these, about 4000 held jobs in some aspect of health and hygiene, including physicians, nurses, dentists, and pharmacists.[53]

The actual numbers varied uncontrollably. Physicians failed to keep appointments, and a few days later it was discovered that they had been killed.[54] The event often was totally capricious. Katzenelson recalls passing a well-dressed man in the ghetto and, shortly afterward, hearing a shot. He turned back and learned that the Germans had kicked the man and, as he turned toward them, they shot and killed him. For sport. He was a Jewish doctor.[55] Sometimes people disappeared because, when laborers were needed, the Germans rounded up as many people as they needed off the street, without regard for occupation or the possession of passes.

PRIVATE PRACTICE IN THE GHETTO

During the war, the attrition in professional personnel in Poland generally, and among the Jews in particular, was immense. Zablotniak estimates that 800 Polish physicians registered in Poland in 1939 had died of natural causes by 1945; an additional 550 died in combat, were executed, or died in jails or camps, and 350 had emigrated, most of the latter presumably in 1939 or early 1940. Those figures do not include any calculation of those who would normally have graduated from medical schools in Poland or abroad during the six years of the war but who did not because of the war. Zablotniak further states that 2500 dentists, 1300 pharmacists, and 3000 other medical professionals died between 1939 and 1945, the vast majority before their natural time.[56] These figures refer to Poland as a whole, however, not to Jews in Poland.

In November 1940, about 750 physicians were included in the ghetto's population of about 460,000.[57] Many of these men and women worked in the various hospitals and institutions, such as the separated divisions of Czyste Hospital, the Berson and Bauman Hospital, and TOZ, which employed almost 200 doctors by the summer of 1940.[58] But the majority had been in private practice and remained in that work as best they could throughout the life of the ghetto. What kind of life did these practitioners have? How did they conduct their practices? Who were they?

No study of private practice among the Jews in wartime Warsaw seems to have been made, either at the time or subsequently. But some idea of this aspect of medical life can be obtained from documents and memoirs.

Many medical practitioners were out of work. Dr. Michael Temchin returned from a labor camp early in 1941. He could find no medical work to do and lived the life of a beggar.[59] Some doctors had been established in suburban areas with large numbers of non-Jewish patients; now they found themselves forced to move into a ghetto and forbidden to continue to treat these patients. Some were newcomers to Warsaw, refugees from Lwów or Łódź, or one of the rural towns, forced to abandon everything when they left. The practitioners who had been looking after the Jews of central Warsaw continued to do so. Often the newly arrived physicians found themselves both poor and jobless. They needed assistance, and the various arms of the self-help apparatus moved to aid them. Teachers, engineers, and lawyers were perhaps in an even worse situation, but needy members of all professional groups received food supplies, while the Joint tried to devise methods of retraining.[60] Many refugee doctors and nurses were immediately engaged as sanitary personnel in the receiving stations for the refugees.[61]

Some efforts were made to carry on the usual scientific endeavors. Czyste Hospital continued its regular medical meetings, at which community physicians probably were attendees (see Chapter 5). Moreover, Prof. Ludwik Hirszfeld took advantage of one loophole in the German edict forbidding any gathering of large numbers of Jews; the Nazis permitted block physicians—those with professional responsibilities for a particular apartment building—to meet without needing preliminary approval. Hirszfeld gave his first lectures inside the ghetto to this group, early in 1941, and soon met with them regularly, two sessions a week of two hours each, "under the pretext of combating the epidemic."[62]

From the beginning of the Nazi occupation, Jewish physicians came in for special attention by the conquerors. They suffered in being heavily represented in the various roundups of intellectuals. For example, Adam Czerniakow struggled in January and February 1940 for the release of a group of several dozen such men, arrested and held for unspecified reasons early in the new year. On 22 January, when he called on the SS to inquire about the status of his petition for their release, the Nazis told him that 100 had already been shot and that more executions were likely.[63] A few days later, caught as always between the Jewish population and the Germans, Czerniakow found himself assailed by the distraught families of the physicians, who accused him of turning the men over to the Germans.[64]

German arrests, usually arbitrary or based on patently contrived grounds, constantly harassed Jewish medical activities, just as they did essentially every other aspect of life. For example, in July 1940, Czerniakow was forced to write to the SS requesting the release of Drs. Typograf and Rubinstein, who were in custody for no apparent reason, and whose services were badly needed in the *Judenrat* clinics where they customarily worked.[65]

Doctors were regularly requisitioned for various jobs. Early in 1940, a large number were needed for an enormous task—the physical examination of all males in the ghetto between the ages of 14 and 60. There would have been perhaps 150,000 men in this category. Dr. Lenski served on one of the boards of doctors set up to conduct the exams and record their findings. Although all the documents have been lost, Lenski's recollection is that "we did not find among the Jewish population symptoms of extensive infection from serious diseases, such as tuberculosis, etc."[66] This was, it should be noted, early in the war; no similar findings could have been reported two years later. Chairman Czerniakow recorded in his diary in February 1940 that he had drafted 53 Jewish physicians "for a limited period of time" to conduct medical examinations during the registration of 35,000 Jews between the ages of 16 and 25. These young men and women were required to perform forced labor for the Germans.[67]

The scenes at these mass examinations were chaotic. One *Judenrat* member described his observations sometime during 1940. The medical commission conducting the examinations had set up its offices in the Merchants' Association building on Solna Street, from the front doors of which a queue of those awaiting examination, or seeking exemption, extended several hundred meters along the street, often as far as Twarda Street.[68]

Violent death was the ultimate reality for all the Jews of Poland, including medical practitioners. But there were many other problems that occupied their lives before they either died or, less likely, escaped. Physicians were regularly commandeered for various assignments. Ludwik Stabholz, a survivor, was drafted to go to Belzec as a physician to a labor battalion there in the autumn of 1940. He was selected because he was unmarried. The term of work was to have been one month, after which he and his colleague would be replaced by two other doctors from Warsaw. But the German commandant at the camp refused to let them leave. Conditions in the camp were brutal, and the physicians knew they would not survive long there. So they escaped, and Stabholz succeeded in returning to Warsaw in time to be forced into the ghetto and ultimately to carry out his teaching of anatomy in the clandestine medical school.[69]

The camp at Belzec was a particularly brutal introduction to German treatment of the Jews. The first contingent of laborers left Warsaw on 16 August 1940.[70] Immediately, word began to drift back to Warsaw that conditions were bad. Czerniakow wrote in his diary on 25 August that the *Judenrat* would send four physicians, as well as instruments and drugs. But on the 27th he noted that it was impossible to persuade any doctors to go.[71] By 3 September, Lambrecht, German chief of the health subdivision of the Interior Division of the German district administration in Warsaw, was demanding 20 physicians for the labor camps.[72] Probably in despair by this time, Czerniakow reported six days later that only one physician had volunteered, and this man was from a public clinic, so that sending him did not increase the number of doctors in the public service.[73]

In lieu of wages for the laborers, the Nazis had promised that they would supply food, shelter, clothing, and medical services. None of these promises was honored. Food was insufficient and was limited to bread, coffee, potatoes, and a few scraps of meat. Workers had only rags to wear, they worked seven days a week, and the only medical care "provided" by the Germans was to order the *Judenrat* to supply the care.[74] Naturally, no one wished to go there if he could avoid the responsibility.

Until the ghetto was closed, separating most of the Jews from the rest of Warsaw, there was a constant danger of being involved in one of the incidents of public humiliation that so many Germans—and many Poles as well—apparently found amusing. Izrael Milejkowski, at the time he became head of the health department in the *Judenrat*, was assaulted in October 1939. He was wearing a Red Cross armband and going about his medical duties but was seized, beaten severely, and ordered to sing and dance on the spot. In a lugubrious conversation, re-created from memory by Szoszkies, a fellow member of the *Judenrat*, Milejkowski recounted that not only did he wish to live a little longer, but he also had patients who depended on him: He danced.[75] Another doctor, also wearing a Red Cross armband that had overlapped his Jewish Star of David armband, was beaten in the street and fined.[76] Dr. Henryk Makower was punched in the face for not removing his hat to a *Wehrmacht* private.[77] A few months later, after the ghetto was established but while Czyste Hospital was still outside the walls, a group of physicians riding the street car on a Sunday were made to get off and perform calisthenics before an audience of German soldiers and passersby.[78] One official points out the paradox that faced Jewish doctors: For example, they had special privileges, such as the right to ignore the curfew in making their professional calls; but this right carried a lethal danger, since some Nazi guards followed the principle of shooting a curfew breaker first and investigating the circumstances afterward.[79]

Adam Czerniakow was seen by the Nazis as just another Jew, receiving no special consideration as chairman of the *Judenrat*. On 4 November 1940 German soldiers broke into the *Judenrat* building, assaulting many of those present. Czerniakow was severely beaten and ended up in Pawiak prison, sharing a crowded cell with five others, one of whom had constant diarrhea. He was released the next day, and that evening was "examined by 3 doctors and a paramedic. They patched me up with bandages on my head, both legs, and one arm. I can hardly walk."[80] The cause of this attack was that a German officer's wife thought that she had been insulted by some unidentified Jew, and her husband was taking his personal revenge for her hurt dignity.

Another problem that existed from October 1939 until the establishment of the ghetto related to Jewish dwelling places in Warsaw, where the central core consisted almost entirely of large, multistory apartment buildings. In September 1940, as the move into the ghetto loomed, Czerniakow noted that there "has been a deluge of reports about confiscation of homes and furniture. Today Dr. B. was thrown out in a matter of minutes."[81] A Dr. Typograf was forced to leave his apartment by a landlord and move up to a less desirable one on the fourth floor.[82] These buildings had no elevators. A private practitioner used his home as his office, so a forced move to the fourth floor would almost certainly discourage some of the physician's patients from making the effort. But doctors' homes were better than average and thus more desirable, so the doctors and their families moved out.

ECONOMICS OF PRACTICE

Medical practice in Eastern Europe at the time of the Second World War was, with the exception of the Soviet Union, largely a matter of payment for service (sometimes through insurance companies), with free clinics provided for the poor. Depending upon the location, there were sometimes sufficient clinics for the poor, though often not. Clinic physicians were usually dedicated, idealistic individuals who labored for low salaries. Private practitioners were often high-minded men and women whose major concern was providing good medical care, but some were primarily interested in personal enrichment. In private practice, the so-called Robin Hood principle was a common denominator, the rich and the well-to-do paying more for medical services than the struggling laborers and small shopkeepers.

This schema of medical care, though presented simplistically here, was generally true not only in Europe but also in North America. It was the case regardless of a physician's ethnic or religious affiliation. It was the predominant system.

Thus one should not be surprised to find the same system in effect in the small city that constituted the Warsaw ghetto. And since the system had flaws and the potential for injustice, the same weaknesses existed in the ghetto.

As has already been described (see Chapter 3), the ghetto was an economic nightmare. Only a tiny percentage of the Jews had failed to be seriously affected economically by the Nazi occupation and the creation of the ghetto. These few were the Jews who were previously well off, who had lived in what became the ghetto before the war and thus were able to retain their homes and possessions, and who had substantial proportions of their wealth readily available in the form of gold or jewelry, not in a bank vault but in their homes, since bank vaults were frozen early on. Not many Jews in Warsaw met these criteria. So the majority of the ghetto occupants needed daily income to enable them to live and to feed and clothe their families. This was true of physicians, just as it was of every other occupational group, though, of course, doctors began the Nazi occupation better off than most of the population. And doctors were considered for at least a few special concessions; when all furs in the ghetto were requisitioned in December 1941 because German soldiers were beginning to freeze to death in large numbers on the Russian front, Czerniakow sought to have doctors exempted, as well as members of the *Ordnungsdienst*.[83] Presumably the reason was that doctors had to be out on their rounds day and night, as were the police. The Germans refused his request. Six months later, they withdrew one of the last privileges permitted Jewish physicians; along with several other groups (including dentists and *Judenrat* officials), doctors had been able to wear a special armband, in addition to their mandatory Star of David band, but all these signs of special status were eliminated. No one was allowed any visible status except that of Jew.[84]

As early as January 1940, physicians began to feel the economic pinch that later became a remorseless squeeze. Before the war, some had made as much as 1000 zloty a day, though this was unusually high. But now fewer and fewer of their patients had money to pay medical or any other bills.[85] As a consequence, there were poor doctors in the ghetto, as well as a very few rich ones. Docent Sterling, a faculty member of the underground medical school, was approached by a society of merchants and offered an honorary diploma of some sort. They then requested a donation for "impoverished merchants." Refusing, he pointed out that the merchants didn't offer to help the impoverished physicians, of whom there were many. The merchants took back the diploma.[86]

Even the self-help organizations collected whatever fees they could from individuals they assisted. For example, TOZ reported that in the six-month period from April to October 1941, they were able to collect 228,581 zloty from private patients—25 percent of their income for the period.[87] So private payment was still a significant factor this late in the life of the ghetto.

A few doctors undoubtedly overcharged. But Adler, who as a member of the *Ordnungsdienst* may have possessed accurate information, claimed that in the ghetto, physicians, "except for the fashionable ones," charged nearly the same as they had before the war.[88] On the other hand, one who certainly overcharged was a certain Dr. Fajncyn, who amassed a huge personal fortune before and during the war. While proceeding toward the *Umschlagplatz* and Treblinka, he lost a suitcase that contained jewelry supposedly worth 7 million zloty.[89] Adler disapproved of Fajncyn and felt even more strongly about a Dr. Mejlachowicz. This man was a venereal disease specialist and "a prominent dandy." He was also "a dangerous ruffian," a leader among the small coterie of practitioners who associated themselves with Abraham Gancwajch and the other unsavory members of The 13.[90]

Many physicians died with their professional boots on, in the best tradition of centuries of service. Zylberberg paints a sympathetic portrait of a Dr. Korman, a Warsaw pediatrician, who labored to help the poor Jews in the ghetto and then accepted a call to go to a camp and provide medical care. He took his family to a labor camp at Zaklikow, where he died of typhus within a few weeks.[91]

Ignominious death was too often the fate of Warsaw's Jewish physicians. One refugee, a formerly "fashionable internist" from Łodż, Dr. Goldblat, had a severe chest affliction. During the deportations he attempted to hide in the attic of a house on Nowolipie Street. He was found by Ukrainian soldiers and shot on the spot. "The thugs cured him now, radically and forever."[92]

Ultimately, the effect of these various realities and pressures emphasized a division within the profession that exists everywhere. There were the majority, who did their best to be good, honest practitioners in the ghetto, as they had been before, and there were those who reacted by becoming corrupt. This latter group presumably was not large, but their activities were well known and were the source of much sarcastic or bitter comment at the time.

This situation will be alluded to in discussing the weaknesses of the disinfection system (Chapter 7), one of which was that physicians could be bribed to issue certificates of disinfection to the nondisinfected. Similarly, rich men quickly found that they could be exempted from forced labor by bribing susceptible doctors during physical examinations. In this case the corruption was nondenominational, since a gentile physician had to sign each exemption certificate as well as a Jewish one, so two bribes were necessary.[93] Eventually, an ordinary Jew who wanted to get a medical examination had to wait daily for two or three days, often joining the lineup at 5 A.M. But again, for a bribe of 5 or 10 zloty, one could enter a side door immediately.[94]

Medical practice carried all of the worries and uncertainties that it does elsewhere, as well as many that were expressly related to life in a Nazi ghetto. There have always been untreatable patients, but physicians in the ghetto had the added burden of being unable to treat patients not just because they had conditions for which no effective treatment existed, but also and increasingly because the appropriate remedies were unavailable for otherwise treatable diseases.

The reality of misunderstandings in connection with medical practice sometimes invests our insights into disease in the ghetto and the difficulties involved in caring for patients in the ghetto. A letter has survived, written during 1943 by Franciszka Rubinlicht. She complains about her health and about her physician, who, though a "noble Person," wasn't a very good doctor, "if one is permitted to say bad things about the dead. Dr. Felix Praskier was murdered, together with his family, on July 16, 1942."[95] Six months after writing the letter, Mrs. Rubinlicht died of stomach cancer, so the failure of her doctor to cure her in the ghetto can be understood, and perhaps he wasn't such a "bad" doctor.[96] Moreover, there were problem patients of all kinds. One example is the addicted physician; Dr. Wdowinski relates his struggle to care for one such person until the unhappy man lost his addiction and his life at Treblinka.[97]

A chronic worry for doctors was the problem of obtaining medications for one's patients. Very few were available,[98] less and less so as the summer of 1942 approached. By April 1941, the shortages were so severe that representations were made to the *Transferstelle*, the German office through which all authorized shipments came into the ghetto. But the appeal for increased supplies of both drugs and disinfectants achieved nothing.[99] Some drugs were available in limited amounts, but writing prescriptions for them was not without its hazards. The *Judenrat*, in one of their many tax-collecting efforts instituted in a desperate attempt to remain solvent, collected 40 percent of the cost of medications as a tax, a cost that certainly would have had to be passed on to the purchaser, thus making it painfully expensive to be treated with drugs for any illness.[100]

Always a contentious problem for practitioners is the question of abortion. For orthodox Jews, abortion ordinarily was not a readily available procedure. But the Jews proved adaptable to the realities of their situation. In Kaunas, for example, a rabbi ruled that abortion was permissible without any medical indication. The reason was that the Nazis had declared the death sentence for any woman flouting their order forbidding pregnancy.[101] However, this law was never in effect in Warsaw, so this rabbinical dispensation presumably was not needed. Few women in the Warsaw ghetto got pregnant. When they did, at least some Jewish doctors took into consideration the realities of the life they all were living, and they performed abortions without compunction.[102]

The Jewish physicians of the Warsaw ghetto ended their practices the same way other Jews concluded their businesses and professions and work. Many died in the ghetto, many more died at Treblinka or in other camps, and a few escaped.[103] Most of the dead had no obituary notice of any kind; a few had a terse statement of fact, a flash of recollection in a survivor's memoir. For example, Lewin notes that Dr. Zygmunt Steinkalk, a pediatrician, was murdered on 21 July 1942, the day before the massive deportations began.[104] He had no other memorial. Some disappeared without a trace; Dr. Julian Lewinson was medical officer to the *Ordnungsdienst*,[105] and his name comes up repeatedly in Adler's memoirs.[106] But during the uprising in April 1943 he presumably was killed or deported. The record is blank.

After 22 July 1942, the losses became massive. On 26 August 1942, Jews were rounded up from several blocks of Pawia and Zamenhof streets, including 15 doctors from Pawia 14,[107] which must have contained a large number of medical families. Three days later, two more doctors from Pawia 14 who were working outside the ghetto failed to return home, and their families and friends had to assume they had been seized.[108]

By November 1942, the Nazis had made Lublin *Judenrein*; then, having emptied the city of Jews, they found a need to establish a large tailoring establishment there—undoubtedly another instance of the competition that went on regularly between those Germans who wanted every Jew killed immediately and those who saw the desperate need Germany faced for manpower and wanted to use Jewish labor. Thousands of Jews were still left in Warsaw, so the Germans sought tailors there. Not surprisingly, with the great summer deportations just over, tailors found no enthusiasm for any other "emigration" scheme. Eventually, to get their tailors, the Nazis had to collect them forcibly. A roundup was conducted, and among the "tailors" sent to Lublin were "physicians . . . taken out of ambulances [and] bakers straight out of bakeries."[109]

The urge to practice one's profession could have fatal results. Early in 1943, a cousin who had previously escaped into non-Jewish Warsaw began to make arrangements to find a secure hiding place there for a Dr. Zyf and his wife and young daughter. A place was found, and all signs seemed propitious: The Zyfs had "good faces," they had some money, and they spoke excellent Polish. But Zyf still had patients in the pitiful remnant of the ghetto that remained after the January deportations to Treblinka. He kept putting off the date of departure so that he could look after his patients. Was his motive high ethical standards? A desire to make more money? (The cost of survival was astronomically high.) Or was this some type of subconscious suicide? Finally, a definite date was set for the fateful rendezvous to escape: 20 April. On 19 April the ghetto uprising and the final destruction of the ghetto began. The Zyfs were never heard from again.[110]

At this time, private practice was ending in the ghetto. Almost all Jewish practitioners had been deported, had died of disease or been murdered by the Nazis, or had made a risky "escape" into Aryan Warsaw. Medical education had ceased. No hospitals existed; their former patients and staff were dead. Medicine as a profession had disappeared from Jewish Warsaw. The few doctors who survived would attempt to pick up the thread of their professional lives in Israel, Sweden, Canada, the United States, or elsewhere.

AMBULANCE SERVICE

In a society ravaged by so much severe disease, and always at risk of beatings and bullet wounds, an ambulance service was mandatory. This need was emphasized pragmatically early in the German occupation. A man was injured by being beaten, and bystanders tried to find help but discovered that there was no quick medical service available.[111] There had been a citywide service before the war, *Pogotowie Ratunkowe*, located at Leszno 56. Under the Nazis, however, no assistance was given to Jews, and the main operation moved to another location.[112]

An ambulance was also needed to transport patients to institutions outside Warsaw. This was true in particular for Zofiowka, the mental hospital in Otwock, a town about 15 miles southeast of the city. For some months the ambulances of Dr. Nick and Dr. Julian Lewinson performed that task. Then the Germans prohibited their use. The city's first-aid ambulances replaced them. This was the Leszno Street operation, which would not provide first-aid or emergency service but did transport Jewish patients to and from Zofiowka and other institutions in Otwock. Indeed, for many months it was the only reasonably safe way to travel between Warsaw and Otwock.[113] But when the ghetto was sealed off in November 1940, this method could no longer be used.[114]

When he arrived in Warsaw early in 1941, Wilhelm Hagen found that there was only a single motorized ambulance for the 500,000 people in the ghetto, and it rarely operated because there was no fuel.[115] A few horse- and man-driven carriages were added,[116] but these were already decrepit and soon broke down.[117] However, at least one new ambulance did find its way to the ghetto, presumably a horse-drawn type. On 7 June 1941 there was an official ceremony on Ceglana Street, presided over by Czerniakow, marking the presentation of an ambulance to Czyste.[118]

The provision of an ambulance service brings us to one of the sinister aspects of life in the Warsaw ghetto—the underworld. One Avraham Gancwajch established the Control Office for Combatting the Black Market and Profiteering. The group's title designated a noble purpose, but it lacked the sanction of the *Judenrat*. It came to be known to all as "The Thirteen" (*Trzynastka*) because it was located at Leszno 13. The true power behind Gancwajch's throne was the Gestapo.[119] Certainly their approach to controlling the black market and profiteering seemed to consist of trying to corner these rackets for themselves. For example, they taxed clandestine bakers, but the tax became income for The Thirteen. They did nothing to eliminate the bakers, who passed the tax along to their unfortunate but starving customers. So the hard-pressed residents of the ghetto were further oppressed by their fellow Jews. According to one survivor, The Thirteen was an open and suppurating abscess.[120] Another technique: A man from The Thirteen entered a shop and bought some coffee, a luxury almost beyond price in the ghetto. Shortly afterward he returned, confiscated 10 kilos of coffee, and arrested the owner. But for 1000 zloty he released him.[121]

The Thirteen established an ambulance service, possibly as a public relations gesture to offset some of the negative aspects of their image. The attendants had special uniforms consisting of blue-striped caps with red Stars of David[122] and special checkered armbands worn on the right forearm.[123]

The ambulance had a "festive inauguration," in the words of a Gestapo informer, that took place in the afternoon of the first day of Passover, 2 April 1942, at Elektoralna 32. Representatives of the *Judenrat*, the *Ordnungsdienst*, and various social agencies attended. Gancwajch and his colleagues "solemnly declared that they had always desired to cooperate with the social organizations of the *Judenrat*, and that they were still willing at any time to become integrated into these organizations."[124] The occasion included hymns by Cantor Sirota and a male choir directed by one Zaks.

The supposed task of this ambulance was to care for people taken ill in the street, giving assistance, distributing bread and bitter tea, and, if necessary, taking the sick to the hospital. Eventually the only visible activity of the ambulance service was transporting sick people.[125] However, it seems that the ambulance rarely dealt with an emergency case, being tied up in the important business of smuggling,[126] until it vanished along with The Thirteen in July or August 1942. According to Adler, who as an *Ordnungsdienst* member would likely have been hostile to The Thirteen, they established dispensaries and outpatient clinics that never opened their doors. The best they could do was to institute two-man patrols theoretically empowered to help the sick: "But in fact, they ran away (and this is authentic!) when they encountered somebody in need of assistance, since they had neither experience nor training in rescue operations; their coffee flasks and bread containers were empty, and their emergency kits contained only iodine."[127]

A year earlier, Czerniakow had managed to have that part of the organization doing police work dissolved.[128] The victory was perhaps pyrrhic, however, as the members of the group were to be incorporated into the *Ordnungsdienst*, though at least not as a separate unit.

Children's Aid Commission

Before leaving The Thirteen, let me mention another of their activities. Though The Thirteen were recognized as self-seeking scoundrels by many, some people either disagreed or were fooled. Gancwajch called a conference of about 60 local VIPs. Many declined, but among those who came was Dr. Janusz Korczak, and a consequence of the meeting was that Gancwajch set up a children's aid commission, with Korczak at the head.[129] What it accomplished is unknown, but Korczak's approach was forthright, as always; he would take help from anyone if there was a chance to aid his children, not excepting the arguably collaborationist and certainly racketeering members of The Thirteen.[130]

HEALTH COMMISSION AND HEALTH COUNCIL

The Health Commission was attached to Milejkowski's department in the *Judenrat*. It was chaired by Dr. Anna Braude-Heller; Dr. Henryk Makower was the secretary; and members included Drs. Akiwa Akibz Uryson, Aleksander Wertheim (Wertajm), and Margolis. Makower reports that it discussed all the weak points in the approach to health problems in the ghetto.[131] Whether it had any executive power is uncertain, but it is unlikely.

The Jewish Health Council succeeded the Commission. It was created in 1941 in a reaction by Ludwig Hirszfeld and others to the destructive disinfection methods being forced on them by the Nazis in connection with the typhus epidemics. Hirszfeld takes the major credit for creating the Council,[132] and his role has not been challenged by others. Makower labeled the Council inefficient,[133] perhaps reflecting the opinions and attitudes of his superior, Milejkowski, for whom he had great admiration. Apparently when Hirszfeld offered his services in the fight against typhus, Milejkowski called him a turncoat and an antisemite and refused the offer. From then on, relationships between the two were cool.[134] However, Milejkowski did serve on the Health Council along with Hirszfeld.

The Council was broadly based in the ghetto's medical community, consisting of the following members: Hirszfeld himself, Dr. (formerly Colonel) Mieczyslaw Kon, Szymon Wyszewianski (*Judenrat*), Dr. Chaim (Committee for Aid to Jews), Dr. Josef Stein (Czyste hospital), Dr. Anna Braude-Heller (Berson and Bauman Hospital), Waclaw Brockman and Michal Friedberg (hospital curators), Dr. Owsiej Bielenki, Dr. (formerly Major) Tadeusz Ganc (administrative chief of the Health Division of the *Judenrat*,[135] in charge of antiepidemic measures), and Dr. Izrael Milejkowski.[136]

The Council met weekly for the many months that it existed. Because of the realities of life in the ghetto at that time, much of its effort was devoted to attempts to curb the typhus epidemics, though this was by no means its only responsibility. In Hirszfeld's opinion, its major contribution was to regularize typhus control measures—that is, to take over more and more aspects of disinfection so that the retrogressive steps forced upon them by the Nazis could be replaced by more productive steps.[137] The problems associated with typhus control are elaborated in Chapter 7. The Council also organized a typhus exhibition for the public as part of their effort to improve public understanding of the disease; Hirszfeld believed the exhibit would have been helpful, but it never opened. As with so many Jews, it was killed by the deportations.[138]

The genuine accomplishments of the Council are debatable. Hirszfeld thought that positive steps were being taken. Others were less sanguine; Fenigstein believed that the actions of the Council may have made lice more prevalent and the incidence of typhus higher.[139] To put Hirszfeld's enthusiasm into perspective, here is his own general conclusion about antityphus activities by the medical profession within the ghetto: "all our Health Councils, vaccinations, and conferences were only mental hygiene for ourselves."[140]

BLOOD BANK

Appropriately, because of his important observations on blood grouping, Hirszfeld became involved in the efforts to set up a blood bank. The Jews of Warsaw, however, had no tradition of donating blood. Hirszfeld thought that the group most likely to agree to become blood donors was the *Ordnungsdienst*. They were sometimes injured in their police work, and many had required blood transfusions in the past; who would more likely be sympathetic to the need? But the scheme failed. These men would not donate; they invented excuses, refused to donate, or fainted when the time came. Finally, Hirszfeld gave them up in disgust, concluding that the *Ordnungsdienst* was "made of poor stuff."[141] Then he appealed to the medical and other students. Large numbers donated willingly.

BACTERIOLOGY LABORATORY

When Hirszfeld came into the ghetto, he found that the only laboratory work being done in Czyste Hospital, setting aside the pathology department's microscopic studies, was urinalysis plus some hematological and blood chemistry studies. Since there was no bacteriology laboratory, an obvious requirement when there is much contagious disease, Hirszfeld set one up.[142] At the same time, he obtained facilities at the Stawki site of Czyste—five small rooms.[143] Some practitioners brought their own microscopes to the laboratory, and Abraham Gepner, a member of the *Judenrat*, donated money so that Hirszfeld could buy a good microscope.[144] When Czerniakow inspected this institute in 1942, he was sufficiently impressed to offer 5000 zlotys to help purchase equipment.[145]

MEDICAL LIBRARY

There seems to have been only one medical library in the ghetto, associated with Czyste Hospital. The organizer was Mrs. Juliusz Zweibaum, the wife of the anatomist who founded the underground medical school. She obtained books as best she could. Some were remnants of the original Czyste Hospital library; others were donated by practitioners or were smuggled into the ghetto. One of the interviewees, Marek Balin, assisted her in this task.[146]

The library was located in one room of the largely burned-out Hospital of the Holy Ghost. Dr. Szwatzowa was in charge, but the library usually was closed. Dr. Makower found that it contained only medical news magazines and old books. Apparently the new books that had been in the library at Czyste Hospital outside the ghetto were stolen or destroyed at the time of the move inside the walls.[147]

PHARMACIES

Jewish pharmacies were closed down by the Nazis in December 1939 as part of their general campaign against Jewish businesses and professions.[148] In March 1941, Ringelblum noted that the nine pharmacies inside the ghetto owned by gentile Poles were to be purchased by the *Judenrat*. To do this, the ghetto Jews somehow had to raise 300,000 zloty.[149] Apparently they did so, because two months later 14 pharmacies were operating, employing 150 pharmacists and about 120 others. By August 1941 there were 19 pharmacies, one of them giving medicines to the poor without charge.[150]

The names of those who operated the pharmacies have not come to light, but they would have been forced to deal with Kohn and Heller. These men, refugees from Lodz, were for a time associates of Gancwajch and The Thirteen. Later they separated, strengthened their Gestapo contacts, and extended their entrepreneurial activities to include operating the horse-drawn wooden trolleys that replaced the Warsaw trains in providing transportation throughout the ghetto.[151] They also had a monopoly on bringing drugs legally into the ghetto.[152] Trunk, however, questions this mechanism, stating that medicines were bought by the Purveyance Office of the *Judenrat* in the Aryan part of Warsaw, using the *Transferstelle* as an intermediary.[153]

What is known definitely is that the *Judenrat*, always desperate for funds, taxed drugs. In 1942, each prescription filled was taxed 40 percent, the money being used for the benefit of the *Judenrat*'s treasury,[154] which was chronically in the red. In 1940 the *Judenrat* spent 3,059,000 zloty for health care, 28.6 percent of the entire budget. Income from the hospital tax amounted to 541,000 zloty, so the operating deficit in health care was 2,518,000 zloty,[155] an enormous sum.

Some drugs did reach the ghetto from relief agencies outside Poland, though the amounts must have been small compared with the need. Dr. B. Tschlenoff, in Switzerland, was one who labored to assist the TOZ in providing some necessary medicines for the ghetto. By late 1941 he was finally successful. More than one shipment got through. The International Red Cross had to intercede with the German Red Cross in Berlin so that part of a shipment could be directed expressly to TOZ in Warsaw. Finally, Tschlenoff was able to report, with joy and quite legitimate pride, that the authorization had come and the drugs and serum had been shipped.[156] Even after the ghetto had been destroyed, some of Warsaw's Jews may have benefited from unspecified shipments of medicines, bandages, and foodstuffs received from abroad. Dr. Michal Weichert, of the Jewish Relief Agency of the *Generalgouverne-ment*, stated that between 2 May 1943 and 15 July 1943, 56 shipments of medical material received in gift parcels from abroad had been sent to 29 labor camps, ghettos, and factories employing Jews.[157] Although technically this might have been seen as a contribution to the German war effort, since the Jews were all working at war-related jobs, by this stage in the destruction of Jewry such quibbles must have seemed irrelevant.

JEWISH MEDICAL INSTITUTIONS
OUTSIDE THE GHETTO

Although theoretically all Jews in the Warsaw area were to be confined to the ghetto inside that city, in fact there were exceptions, some of which existed until about the time of the deportations in the summer of 1942. The exempt medical institutions were located in Otwock, a suburb of Warsaw. One was Brijus, a sanatorium for patients suffering from tuberculosis;[158] the other was Zofiowka, an institution for "adult lunatics and children."[159] When the inmates were deported in 1942 or killed on the spot, many doctors and staff committed suicide there.[160]

THE NAZI MEDICAL ORGANIZATION

This organization was complex, and was characterized by the divisiveness and territorial struggles that seem so routinely a part of the modus operandi of the Third Reich. But the office having the most direct impact on the ghetto and on medical conditions there was the Warsaw public health office, of which the two heads during the period 1939 to 1943 were Dr. Kurt Schrempf (1939 to 10 February 1941) and Dr. Wilhelm Hagen (10 February 1941 to 1943).[161] Hagen claimed that he had no executive power,[162] which was probably true. Their relationships with the medical establishment in the ghetto are mentioned in several of the following chapters. The impact of Nazi medicine on the residents of the ghetto was felt most directly in connection with the epidemics of typhus (Chapter 7).

NURSING

No history of medicine, no examination of health and disease in the Warsaw ghetto, can be considered complete without some discussion of its nursing services and education. Unfortunately, there is scanty information on the topic.

Czyste Hospital had operated a nursing school since 1922.[163] From its inception the school received funding from the AJDC, and by 1939 had been given grants totaling approximately $140,000.[164] When reporting for 1937, the school's director stated that it had graduated 245 nurses. Of these, 79 (32 percent) were nursing on the wards of Czyste; 49 (20 percent) were in private practice; 39 (16 percent) had emigrated, chiefly to Palestine, where they almost certainly were working; 18 had left nursing (7.4 percent); and the remainder were employed in various institutions, including the children's hospital, the city orphanage, and public health centers.[165]

The school was located on the upper story of Czyste Hospital. In 1939 it applied for a large grant to permit the admission of more students[166] and the provision of more ample dormitory space.[167] There was a library containing 608 books.[168] The 1707 hours of teaching during the school year included 1169 lectures, 412 demonstrations, 70 hours in the laboratory, and 56 hours in the dietetic kitchen.[169] The average number of patients in the Jewish hospital nursed daily by the students was 74.5.[170] Students had 694 sick days from complaints including "angina, influenza, bronchitis, appendicitis, polyarthritis, furunculosis, colitis, cystitis, one case of erysipelas and general ill-health."[171] This report was signed by Nina Lubowska, director.

In the summer of 1940, the AJDC in New York received a direct account of the school. Miss Nina Lubowska, here listed as associate director of the nursing school, had managed to leave Poland and was in New York on official business. She presented a letter from the school that she had received via the International Committee of the Red Cross in Switzerland. At that time there were only 35 student nurses in the training school, a number considered entirely inadequate to service the hospital, in view of the tremendously increased number of patients. But the hospital was unable to add to the staff because "they have not sufficient food to provide even for the present number. . . . the patients, as well as the staff, are starving."[172]

One of the best-known names in Jewish nursing circles was that of Luba Bielicka-Blum, who succeeded Nina Lubowska as director of the Czyste nursing school. She continued that work in the ghetto, even through the days of the first deportations in the summer of 1942 and into 1943. Her students were so determined to excel in her eyes that one of them is reported to have given alcohol back rubs to several dead patients, put out in the corridor at night before being removed in the morning.[173] At the end of 1942 she was still to be seen in the hospital or walking back and forth to her home on Gęsia Street, the final site of Czyste Hospital.[174] Wearing her white uniform,[175] she carried on until the hospital was finally destroyed. Luba Bielicka-Blum survived the war and ultimately was awarded the Florence Nightingale medal for her courageous work in maintaining nursing education.[176] She was the wife of Abrasza Blum, a leader in the Jewish uprisings of 1943.[177] He died later that year.

Teaching continued throughout the life of the Warsaw Jews. By July 1940 the nursing school was the only institution of post–grammar school teaching officially permitted to the Jews, with the curious exception of a professional dancing school operating out of the "Melody Palace."[178] Sometime before the end of 1940, with its move inside the ghetto, the nursing school became established in the former offices

of the Sick Benefit Fund on Wolynska Street.[179] Some time later, according to the
recollection of an interviewee, the school was located on Mariańska Street.[180]

Eugenia Pernal, a wartime student in the Czyste nursing school in the ghetto,
recalls that there was a very compact course, with the customary three years of training compressed into a single year.[181] The monthly fee paid by students attending
there was 50 zloty.[182] Late in the life of the ghetto, beginning at the end of September
1942, the school was located at Gęsia 31.[183]

Czyste had, in fact, two nursing schools operating during the ghetto period. One
was its regular school, which continued its prewar teaching activities. The second
offered a course to 250 girls combining nursing school, perhaps in a type of nurse's
aide program, with daily work in the hospital.[184]

Although graduate nurses wore white uniforms, including caps, the students
predominantly wore pink. One mother described her daughter's uniform as consisting of a pink striped dress, long white apron, kerchief, and blue cape.[185] With
their starched white caps, the students looked like a flock of white birds.[186]

According to Marek Edelman, when the time came to issue "life tickets" during
the Kettle or Cauldron selection at the first deportations in September 1942, the
nursing school received five tickets. There were 60 students. The head of the school,
Luba Bielicka-Blum, decided that these priceless tickets should go to the best students. She set them a one-question examination, with a life-or-death sentence rest-
ing on the results: "Describe the appropriate nursing care for a patient during the
first days following a heart attack." The five students with the best answers received
the tickets.[187]

This is a sad but appealing story, and one can only hope that it is accurate.
Another source gives a totally different account: There were 20 life tickets and not
even that many students left in the school. "Mrs. Bielicka, the head of the school,
had two children: a girl of 11 and a boy of 4. They were in the list."[188] Perhaps these
stories refer to different episodes. Certainly the Nazis made selections repeatedly
between July 1942 and April 1943.

The practice of nursing went on at a particularly urgent pace throughout this
time. The head nurse at Czyste, Miss Frid,[189] had awesome responsibilities. The
strains on all practicing nurses, as on physicians, must have been intense. Eugenia
Pernal was taken to the *Umschlagplatz* despite being in her nursing uniform and
carrying complete and correct papers. She managed to extricate herself.[190] Millie
Eisen, who trained in Vilna but came to Warsaw in 1938 and remained there after
being licensed, worked at Czyste, at all of its locations, until she escaped from the
ghetto in October 1942.[191] Two particularly trenchant memories from the ghetto
period relate to her work as a nurse. On one occasion she was assigned to nurse a
Dr. Alfred Nossig, a notorious figure whom she believed to have been a collabora-
tor.[192] She refused to nurse him, avoiding the assignment by assuring him that she
had scabies.[193] On another occasion, she remembers being so exhausted that she
moved a dying patient off a stretcher, lay down, and slept—an action of which
she remained deeply ashamed more than 40 years later.[194]

Not all memories of these times are bad, of course. An interviewee who was a
medical student recalls a time-honored aspect of medical education around the
world: occasional informal parties with the nurses when a few spare moments permitted.[195]

Sabina Gurfinkiel-Glocerowa, a nurse, survived the war, and her short memoir is a helpful indication of the realities of nursing in the ghetto. In January 1943, in response to general warnings of a Nazi *Aktion*, the medical staff of the tiny, vestigial Czyste Hospital went into hiding with as many ambulatory patients as possible. When Gurfinkiel-Glocerowa returned to her ward three days later, she found the beds either empty or occupied by the bodies of patients who had been unable to move and had been murdered by the Germans.[196] A month later, a final incarnation of Czyste having taken place, she found an opportunity to escape. She toured the wards, saying sad farewells to the few patients and staff, most of whom she never saw again. Even at this stage she was consumed with guilt at leaving her charges, but she had been given a chance to save her young daughter as well as herself, and felt she must try.[197] Unhappily, her child was killed later.

Another nurse recalled with great respect was Mira Braude. Adolf Berman, a high official in the children's aid organization, CENTOS, pays tribute to this woman, who headed the sanitary department of CENTOS "under conditions of raging plagues," and did so with determination and great talent.[198]

The discouraging, enervating struggles against hunger, contagious disease, and injury consumed the residents of the ghetto every day of its existence. The professional services available to support them were grossly inadequate, hampered by lack of money and supplies, by obdurate rulers, and by internal dissension. Definitive remedies were known but unavailable and forbidden. But the efforts went on. Medical practitioners labored; committees met; welfare agencies stretched their resources painfully thin; and nurses, pharmacists, and others worked at their posts. The impossibility of their task will be clearly demonstrated in the following chapters.

5

Hospitals and Other Medical Institutions

The central institution and the main focus of the Jewish medical world in Warsaw, from long before the war until its final liquidation in 1943, was the Jewish Hospital. This hospital was referred to throughout its existence as the Czyste Hospital because of its prewar location in a district of Warsaw called Czyste, a Polish word meaning, appropriately enough for a hospital area, *clean*. It was the largest hospital in Poland in 1939, a superior institution well equipped and staffed, with 1490 beds, 147 physicians, 119 nurses, and six pharmacists.[1] Czyste occupied several buildings on Dobra and adjacent streets.[2]

Before the war, Czyste Hospital had a fine reputation, not just among the Jews but among the Poles as well. The staff was Jewish, since the hospital had been created to provide a workplace for Jewish nurses and doctors. Jewish physicians in Poland found other hospitals closed to them or their use restricted, so that if patients were hospitalized, their physicians could not look after them. Jewish hospitals were thus set up in many Polish cities, of which Czyste was the preeminent example. The majority of patients in the hospital before the war were Jews, but many non-Jews also came there for treatment, sometimes through attendance at a clinic run by the hospital, more often because they were in the care of a Jewish medical practitioner and these doctors could admit patients who required hospitalization only to Czyste.

The Germans, while making the Jews operate the hospital, totally controlled its supplies, thus maintaining ultimate control. The Jews had the responsibility of caring for their patients without the means to do so effectively. But even before the war, pressure was being applied by the Poles. According to an article published in France in July 1939, the municipal authorities of Warsaw were beginning to attempt to take control. "Gradually the medical and administrative personnel of the institution is replaced by a non-Jewish personnel. To obtain hospitalization thus the Jewish sick people meet with great difficulties."[3]

The director of the hospital when the Germans invaded Poland in September 1939 was Dr. Henryk Stabholz, a noted surgeon in Warsaw.[4] During the German campaign in Poland, which lasted until 27 September, the city of Warsaw was seriously damaged, first by heavy bombing raids, later by artillery fire. To the Varsovians there seemed a special malevolence in the fact that essentially all of the city's hospitals received substantial damage. Every permanent hospital was damaged by bombs or shells, frequently by both. In addition, the bombardment had been heavy enough so that electricity, water and sewerage services, and telephones were out of operation all over Warsaw, producing major problems for hospitals trying to care for hordes of patients.[5]

In Czyste Hospital, the operating rooms were destroyed by bombs,[6] and many other departments were damaged as well. Appropriately enough, the first operation done in Czyste after the Nazis attacked was the amputation of the leg of a patient injured in the bombing of the city on 1 September 1939.[7] As the influx of wounded Poles, Jewish and non-Jewish, accelerated, the hospital staff sent home as many pre-war patients as they could to make space. Essentially, the whole hospital became a surgical ward. There was no electricity, gas, running water, or sewage system. Surgical instruments had to be sterilized in the laundry area, where it was still possible to make steam.[8]

One example of the chaos that characterized the operation of Czyste in that painful autumn of 1939 was the change of administration that occurred. In mid-September the government asked all able-bodied men to leave the city and head east, hoping to reorganize the army there and continue fighting the Germans. Many staff physicians at Czyste responded, including Dr. Stabholz.[9] At this time an older man, Dr. Rotsztadt,[10] was named director. However, he was unable to cope with the chaotic, constantly changing crisis situation, and after a few days he was succeeded by Dr. Adam Zamenhof on 26 September 1939.[11] The Nazis occupied Warsaw on 28 September, and shortly afterward, Dr. Zamenhof was taken away, never to return—caught up in an orgy of imprisonment and death indulged in by the Germans as they removed Poland's leaders from their positions.[12]

Dr. Zamenhof was followed by Dr. Julian Rotstadt, appointed by direction of the Germans. He had a longer reign, lasting until 15 December 1939. On that date, Dr. Kurt Schrempf,[13] the Nazi official with overall responsibility for health in Warsaw, inspected a newly established quarantine facility within Czyste, created to help deal with the increasing incidence of typhus. Schrempf found the facility incomplete and, on the spot, had Dr. Rotstadt and several colleagues arrested and removed from the hospital.[14] On another occasion the hospital pharmacy was late in opening. According to an eyewitness, Schrempf ordered both the hospital director and the chief pharmacist to be arrested.[15]

After the removal of Rotstadt, some stability was achieved when Dr. Josef Stein became director. Before the war, Stein had been deputy head of the pathology department at the Hospital of the Holy Ghost.[16] He might seem to have been an unlikely selection, for Stein was a Christian convert who, reputedly, had changed his religion "not for the sake of a career but rather to sever ties with Jews, who always used to annoy him."[17] To Hitler and the Nazis, of course, Stein's choice of religion was irrelevant; he and thousands like him were decreed to be Jews still, and forced to live and die as Jews. Stein, despite his feelings about the Jews of Warsaw, served them honorably and well for the remaining three years of his life. According to one of his professional colleagues, who recorded his opinions during the war, Stein was intensely concerned with the lot of his patients, insisted on painstaking care of all the sick in the hospital, and paid great attention to the ethical standards of his staff.[18] By great good luck, as the Jews of Warsaw approached their time of greatest—and, for most, last—suffering, they had a man of high character at the head of Czyste Hospital.[19] There is a contrary view, however. Dr. Stanislaw Waller was a Czyste staff member; he believed that Stein had informers among the staff, and that he favored fellow converts both in ordinary hospital activities and during the emotion-laden distribution of life tickets.[20]

Dr. Stein needed every good quality he could muster, for the situation of the hospital deteriorated steadily. Before he took over the directorship, the absolute nature of German authority had been established immediately and unequivocally, an authority made concrete when arbitrary shifts in administration were carried out by the Nazis. The Germans were equally arbitrary about assigning the hospital the role it was to play in the new Warsaw, though their orders were as capricious as they were absolute. Early in the autumn the hospital was declared to be a military hospital, so all civilian patients were taken elsewhere and military patients concentrated at Czyste. Soon afterward, that order was rescinded, and it was designated a hospital for Germans and *Volkesdeutsche* in Warsaw and the surrounding area. Then that order was also canceled, and Czyste resumed being what it was to be to the tragic end three years later—a hospital for the Jews of Warsaw and, soon, of the Warsaw ghetto.[21]

The Nazis made other capricious moves, at least some of which seem totally unexplainable. A nurse who was at Czyste from 1938 on remembers that in the fall of 1939, the Germans rounded up all the Jewish prostitutes of Warsaw and installed them at Czyste—not for the purpose of prostitution, or because they were ill, or for any other reason that has survived.[22] Possibly they planned to screen out those with disease in the hope of protecting the men of the *Wehrmacht*.

On 5 December 1939, Adam Czerniakow was ordered to establish a 500-bed hospital, for which the *Judenrat* was to have full fiscal responsibility; the budget was to be 150,000 to 200,000 zloty per month plus the cost of repairs.[23] Precisely what and where this hospital was to be is uncertain. What actually happened was that the *Judenrat* took over fiscal responsibility for Czyste Hospital, the formal transfer of responsibility occurring on 1 January 1940.[24] To prepare, Czerniakow set up a Department of Hospitals, with Ignacy Fliederbaum, former superintendent of Czyste, as departmental chief.[25] In this way the *Judenrat* began one of its most onerous struggles: trying to operate a hospital in the midst of an increasing medical disaster, with very limited financial means and little possibility of raising money except by taxing the Jews, who were increasingly unable to pay. They did, however, receive one major boost in February 1940 when the German mayor of Warsaw, Oskar Dengel, directed that all the securities held by Jews in Warsaw banks were to be converted to cash, which was to be used by the *Judenrat* to finance Czyste Hospital.[26]

The hospital for which the *Judenrat* assumed responsibility in December 1939 was struggling to cope with a major medical crisis. Both typhoid fever and the dreaded typhus had flared up in Warsaw that fall. The wards at Czyste began to fill up with patients with these diseases, especially typhoid fever. In a move that they said would contain the outbreak of typhus, the Nazis instituted a total quarantine of the hospital on 19 December 1939.[27] No one was permitted to enter or leave, staff or patients, except that new typhus patients were pushed in. Some of the staff had living quarters in the hospital, so while they were inconvenienced, the situation was not intolerable. Marek Balin, a student, was one of those who lived in the hospital, where he learned to do intravenous injections during the epidemic. He also recalls helping with autopsies before Henry Fenigstein arrived, these postmortem examinations being demanded by the Nazis in order to document the cause or causes of the epidemic.[28] Other staff members had a serious domestic problem, since many of the nurses, for example, had young children at home who would be uncared for without their mothers. Some of the staff devised ingenious and dangerous methods to evade the quarantine. One subterfuge involved switching out of nursing uniforms into civilian clothing, hiding the identifying Star of David armband, and pretending to be a Pole trying to recover money the hospital owed her.[29] Other schemes were equally risky, but they usually worked and mothers managed to care for their children. Fortunately, after about three weeks the quarantine was lifted.

What we know about conditions in the hospital indicates that even as early as the end of 1939, it was far from being a model institution. Largely, if not entirely, this was because of the extremely onerous general situation forced upon their Jews of Warsaw by the Nazis. Czyste Hospital shared all the difficulties and hazards. When food was short—and it was always short—Czyste and its patients suffered as much as everyone else; on the priority list maintained and enforced by the *Judenrat*, workers had number one priority to get food and the hospitals were only number three.[30] A further burden for the administrators was created by some of the rabbis, who protested against the provision of nonkosher hospital food.[31]

Even before the war, the institution was in financial difficulty. It received only slight support from the city of Warsaw even though Varsovians, Jew and Christian alike, made up the patient population. At the beginning of the war, the Jewish community, through the *Kehilla*, contributed about 35 percent of the costs, municipal aid of various kinds accounted for perhaps 5 percent, and the remaining 60 percent had to come directly from the patients.[32]

Finding enough staff was difficult at first, as so many men had fled the city and ended up in the hands of the Russians. Medical students were pressed into service. Marek Balin was a medical student in Paris trapped in his native Warsaw when the war began. Since he had completed his basic studies and had done a little clinical work, he was welcomed at Czyste and became part of its "house staff," the equivalent in responsibility of interns and residents in contemporary hospitals.[33] He was one of 13 or 14 who joined the hospital in 1939, but this number increased to perhaps 50 during 1940.[34] These men and women were an important part of the staff and also continued their own education. At times, the hospitals were so shortstaffed that medical students headed entire wards, at least briefly.[35] Tadeusz Stabholz was an example of the latecomers in this group; he and his father returned to Warsaw in March 1940 after being released by the Russians. Tadeusz also joined the house staff; his father, who had been director, took on the responsibilities of chief of surgery.[36]

The somewhat makeshift nature of Czyste Hospital's existence is also shown by the way staff was acquired and used. Fenigstein, for example, wanted to study surgery when he joined the hospital in the spring of 1940, having recovered from his combat wound the previous fall. No posts were available, but Dr. Stein was now head of the hospital; he was a pathologist and offered his old student a post in the pathology department. This put a trusted junior colleague in a position of responsibility, enabling Stein to devote more time to the spirit-breaking realities of administration under the prevailing conditions. For Fenigstein, there was a position, a modest wage, room and board, and permission for his soon-to-be wife to move in and to work at something appropriate to her background in pharmacy.[37]

Further illustrating this casual approach was the appointment, two years later, of Frank Stiffel to the same department. It was March 1942. Stiffel was a medical student who needed work badly; with members of his family he had just escaped from Lwów, where the Jews were being liquidated. In Warsaw he became an assistant in the pathology department, working under Henry Fenigstein, whom he remembers repeating, all day long, "like a sad litany, the cause of death: 'Atrophy of liver; atrophy of heart.'"[38] The job lasted less than four months, ending with the disruption of the hospital in July.

MOVING CZYSTE INTO THE GHETTO

The second distinct phase in Czyste's last years was the move into the ghetto in early 1941. The ghetto was established in mid-November 1940; its existence immediately created major new problems for the hospital. These new hazards affected both staff and patients. Simply getting from the ghetto to the hospital and back was complicated and often dangerous. The total staff consisted of nearly 1000 persons. Many lived within the institution, though this number remained a minority of the total. The others had already been forced to live in the ghetto; now they had to go back and forth to work.

On the first two days of the ghetto's existence, 16 and 17 November, no Jewish physician was permitted to leave the ghetto for any reason.[39] After that, passes were needed for safe passage through the gates and into non-Jewish Warsaw. The Germans issued a total of 75 passes at first, though that number later was increased to 200.[40] Their distribution was left in the hands of the *Judenrat*, which, always desperate for ways to raise operating funds, taxed them at 5 zloty each.[41] For those fortunate few who received a pass, life was reasonably simple: one presented one's pass at the gate nearest the hospital and, barring new regulations or unanticipated and arbitrary refusal by one of the guards, one could proceed to the hospital—always mindful of the possibility of being attacked without warning or specific reason by Polish antisemites looking for someone wearing the conveniently identifying armband. For those without passes there was a new regulation: All members of this large group had to gather at the gate at Twarda 6 at 7 A.M. There they were formed into a column and marched to the hospital.[42] At night, the reverse procedure was followed.

The ultimate location of the hospital was not decided for some time, though the fact that it would be moved, and that its modern buildings would be used by the Germans as they saw fit, was clear. In September 1940, Dr. Konrad Orzechowski, head of the Hospitals Department for the city of Warsaw, visited Czyste; Czerniakow noted glumly that he had an impression that the hospital would be taken away.[43] A few days later, a group of Nazi officials touring the ghetto made a special detour to the court building on Leszno Street, where, the *Judenrat* had been informed, Czyste Hospital would be transferred.[44] The swap with the court building was confirmed by Schrempf on 15 October.[45] But typifying the confusion of the times and of the Germans, the day before, a different official had announced that the court building would be outside the boundaries of the ghetto and therefore probably not usable by Czyste.[46] But on 2 December, Czerniakow noted that any new location *could* be outside the actual ghetto walls, so long as it was on the periphery of the ghetto. A suitable building still had to be found, however.[47]

By January 1941 this anomalous situation ended when Czyste Hospital, the last substantial Jewish presence in Warsaw outside the ghetto, was ordered to move. All patients were to be transferred, but only minor and portable equipment. Everything attached to walls, floors, or ceilings was to remain, as well as everything large—for example, operating tables, sterilizers, and the hospital beds themselves. Also interdicted was the removal of the numberless items of equipment required for surgery and other forms of treatment in the twentieth century—all objects that the Nazis planned to put to their own use. One survivor has estimated that at least three-quarters of the hospital's equipment was lost by being left behind.[48]

Had Nazi orders been followed to the letter, the hospital in its new locations would scarcely have deserved that name. Fortunately, much ingenuity came into play and large quantities of *verboten* items such as operating room instruments were smuggled out. One nurse recalls piling instruments under pillows and insisting that her patients put up with these awkward and uncomfortable lumps under their heads while they were being transferred. When German soldiers entered the ambulances to search for contraband, they were sent quickly on their way by the magic words "Epidemic disease!"[49] Marek Balin and Tadeusz Stabholz became integral parts of the caravan that came into being when the hospital was forced into the ghetto. They and their colleagues smuggled as much equipment as possible.[50]

The original Czyste had been a modern hospital of the 1930s, consisting of spacious buildings grouped together as a planned functional unit. In 1941, that situation changed irrevocably. For the two painful years that were left, Czyste was a shifting entity, with departments located in various buildings all over the ghetto, none of them designed for that use, and with units and departments changing location as the exigencies of ghetto life demanded. In return for their modern buildings outside the walls, the Jews received several totally inappropriate municipal buildings, former schools, and other even less suitable structures.[51]

The first locations, into which they moved with their caravans of patients, bedding, staff, smuggled instruments, drugs, and other paraphernalia, were allocated by types of patients or conditions to be cared for (see Figure 5.1). All surgery plus the x-ray department went to Leszno 1, into a building formerly housing the Polish State Tobacco Monopoly.[52] Obstetrics and gynecology moved into what had been Dr. Frischman's clinic at Tłomackie 5 (a reasonably appropriate site had the patient population been a small fraction of what it actually was). Infectious disease patients were housed in former schools (teaching was forbidden) at Stawki 6–8 (see Figure 5.2) plus a temporary location at Żelazna 80. And the pharmacy, plus the sterilization and disinfection units, were placed in the only surviving wing of the heavily bombed and shelled Hospital of the Holy Ghost at Elektoralna 12.[53] Later in the life of the ghetto, this site also housed some of the Czyste staff.[54]

Stawki 21 was also used as part of the infectious diseases unit, set up across the

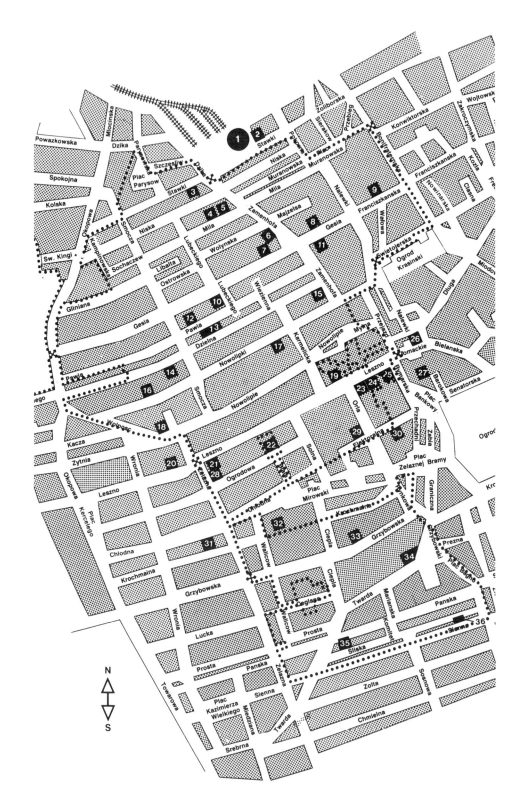

Figure 5.1. *(facing)* Map outlining the major portion of the Warsaw ghetto in mid-1942, just before the deportations to Treblinka began in July.
KEY: **1.** *Umschlagplatz.* **2.** Czyste Hospital, Stawki 6-8 (infectious diseases, internal medicine). **3.** Czyste Hospital, Stawki 21. **4.** Miła 18, site of headquarters bunker of ŻOB *(Żydowska Organizacja Bojowa),*, the Jewish underground military organization, organized in August 1942, that led the 1943 battles against the Germans. **5.** Marek Balin's last home in ghetto, Mila 4, with bunker underneath. **6.** Post Office; a pharmacy was located here also. **7.** *Judenrat* (second location, late in ghetto life), and *Judenrat* prison *(Gęsiówka).* **8.** Czyste Hospital, Gęsia Street, September 1942 to January 1943: last hospital functioning in the ghetto. **9.** *Transferstelle* or Supply Authority. **10.** TOZ headquarters (*Towarzystwo Ochrony Zdrowia,* Society for the Preservation of Health). **11.** Bunker where Tadeusz Stabholz lived until captured 6 May 1943; connected by tunnel to #8. **12.** Borman/Bakowska home, Pawia 38. **13.** Pawiak Prison, Dzielna 24/26. **14.** Home for Destitute Children, Dzielna 39. **15.** Moriah Synagogue. **16.** Oneg Shabbat, Emanuel Ringelblum's underground archives. **17.** CENTOS (*Centrala Opieki nad Sierotami,* National Society for the Care of Orphans). **18.** *Befehlstelle* (deportation office), Żelazna 103. **19.** Emanuel Ringelblum's home, Leszno 18. **20.** *Arbetisamt* (labor office); also site of lecture rooms, underground medical school, April 1941-July 1942. **21.** Czyste Hospital, Leszno Street site of infectious disease wards. **22.** Law courts; readiest clandestine access to and from the ghetto. **23.** HQ for "The 13," Avraham Gancwajch's extortionate organization, a Gestapo branch, Leszno 13. **24.** Hospital. **25.** Czyste Hospital, Leszno 1 (surgery); site of former Polish State Tobacco and Alcohol Monopoly. Marek Balin, Tadeusz Stabholz, and Karolina Borman worked here. **26.** Czyste Hospital, Tłomackie 5 (obstetrics and gynecology, formerly Dr. Fryszman's clinic building). **27.** Tłomackie Synagogue. **28.** Többens shop. **29.** Izrael Milejkowski home, Orla 5. **30.** Czyste Hospital, Elektoralna 12 (in wing of bombed-out Hospital of the Holy Ghost; pharmacy, disinfection, sterilization, etc.). Survived the war. **31.** Original site of Janusz Korczak orphanage, Krochmalna 92. Survived the war outside the ghetto. **32.** Headquarters, *Ordnungsdienst* (Jewish Order Service—ie Jewish police). **33.** Judenrat (first location, until about September, 1942), Grzybowska 26. **34.** Nozyk Synagogue. Survived the war. **35.** Berson and Baumann Hospital, Śliska 52. Survived the war. **36.** Janusz Korczak orphanage, Sienna 16 and Śliska 9 (former Merchant's Club)

(This map is derived from one published by the author in *Medical History* in 1989, reproduced here by permission of the editors of that journal.) It is derived from numerous sources, including several of the personal interviews, and the following books: Isaiah Trunk, *Judenrat: The Jewish Councils in Eastern Europe Under Nazi Occupation* (New York: The Macmillan Co., 1972); Yisrael Gutman, trans. Ina Friedman, *The Jews of Warsaw, 1939–1943: Ghetto, Underground, Revolt* (Bloomington: Indiana University Press, 1982; R. Hilberg, S. Staron, and J. Kermisz (editors), *The Warsaw Diary of Adam Czerniakow: Prelude to Doom* (New York, Stein and Day, 1982); Joseph Kermish (edit.), *To Live With Honor and Die With Honor: Selected Documents from the Warsaw Ghetto Underground Archives, "O.S." (Oneg Shabbath)* (Jerusalem: Yad Vashem, 1986); Julian E. Kulski, *Dying, We Live* (New York: Holt, Rinehart and Winston, 1979); Louis Falstein (edit.), *The Martyrdom of Jewish Physicians in Poland* (New York: Exposition Press, 1963); Jacob Sloan (edit. & trans.), *Notes from the Warsaw Ghetto: The Journal of Emmanuel Ringelblum* (New York: Schochen Books, 1974); Leonard Tushnet, *The Uses of Adversity* (New York: Thomas Yoseloff, 1966); Stanislaw Adler, *In the Warsaw Ghetto, 1940–1943: An Account of a Witness* (Jerusalem: Yad Vashem, 1982).

Figure 5.2. *Umschlagplatz* monument and Stawki 6–8, Warsaw (photo by C. G. Roland, 1990).

street from what became the *Umschlagplatz* 18 months later.[55] The Stawki Street complex encompassed the infectious disease wards, internal medicine generally, laboratories for biochemistry and bacteriology, and the pathology institute. The pathology laboratory where the youthful Henry Fenigstein was to do approximately 3000 autopsies in the next few months[56] was in the basement of Stawki 8.[57]

The Polish State Tobacco Monopoly building was initially unsatisfactory, but after much hard work its operating room came to seem a model. Dr. Noemi Wigdorowicz, who operated there during the war, considered it the most attractive operating room in Warsaw: "It was a beautiful room painted snow white, spotlessly clean, with shining linoleum floors, metal containers with surgical supplies, cupboards filled with instruments, the whiteness of the enamel sinks and the blazing light coming from the lamp hanging over the operating table."[58]

As time passed and infectious diseases became the dominant theme of acute medical practice in the ghetto, the Stawki premises could not contain the large numbers of patients that crowded in. Wards initially set aside for internal medicine other than infectious diseases gradually were taken over by the myriad patients with typhus, typhoid fever, acute tuberculosis, diphtheria, and many other such diseases. Even that did not suffice, and eventually the children's epidemic ward was separated and transferred to a building at Żelazna and Leszno, which had been in use as a hospital for convalescents and those suspected of having infectious diseases as early as December 1939.[59] The adult epidemic wards took over the entire complex on Stawki Street.[60]

The location at Stawki 6–8 was the final formal one for Czyste Hospital, this being a site at the edge of the *Umschlagplatz*, from which the bulk of the population was transported to Treblinka and other concentration camps. A children's hospital was located on Śliska Street.[61] Additional small hospitals, clinics, and other health-related institutions also carried on medical work, but the divisions of Czyste Hospital were the main arenas for this activity. Student work in anatomy, and in all laboratory and clinical subjects, was carried out in numerous makeshift hospitals and clinics in the ghetto.

When the move into the ghetto took place, the hospital beds themselves had to be left behind, creating an immediate crisis. The chief supplier in meeting this urgent need was the firm of Balbinder, located at Twarda 8. Because of the almost total lack of materials, the beds were constructed from scrap metal pipes.[62] Equally difficult to obtain were the drugs and medicines needed, and many expedients were used to try to solve this problem—none of them satisfactory, though all were helpful. Smuggling was the most common method, but efforts were also made to supply at least some needs from within. For example, TOPOROL, the Society for Promoting Agriculture among the Jews, sowed a number of small plots within the ghetto with camomile for use by the hospital.[63] Though camomile is no wonder drug, infusions of it are often used as a tonic. One of the everyday routines of hospital care, administering large quantities of fluids intravenously to very sick patients, was made irksome because no apparatus was available. Medical students had to give such fluids by repeated and tedious injections, 40 milliliters at a time.[64]

Food for the patients presented special problems. No supplements were permitted by the Germans for the succor of those who had needs related to illness, such as patients with ulcers, those recuperating after surgery, or those fighting their way back after surviving typhus. Worse, on at least a few occasions, the Nazis confiscated food allotted to the hospital. The scattered nature of the various units was another constant difficulty. The food was prepared at a central depot at the Stawki Street site, from which it was sent to the various branches by whatever conveyance was available[65]—never a motorized vehicle, for the only ones permitted within the ghetto belonged to or were under the direct control of the Nazis.

There was an underground medical school that functioned at this time, and clinical teaching was necessarily carried out in the hospitals and clinics of the ghetto. Like everything else in that compressed, strangling world, the hospital system of the Warsaw ghetto was a complex, patched together, inefficient, and over-strained entity.

As a consequence, no hospital could be looked upon as a place offering relief and sustenance for the starving. Indeed, Dr. Izrael Milejkowski, the head of the medical department of the *Judenrat*, considered the hospitals "places of execution" where patients were as likely to die from hunger as from disease.[66]

The lack of almost everything made it impossible to run the hospital as a twentieth-century institution. Czerniakow wrote of visiting the hospitals and finding corpses in the corridors and three patients in each bed.[67] There was rarely running water, so toilets would not flush, and washing the patients, the instruments, or the floors, was extremely difficult. Tragedies occurred. In April 1941, Dr. Henryk Stabholz, former director of Czyste, died from a wound infection when he cut himself during an operation.[68] In those preantibiotic days this happened occasionally in any hospital, but this instance might have been avoided if instruments could have been sterilized properly.

The wards were lice-ridden. Patients routinely were placed two in a bed, one with his or her head at the top, the other at the end of the bed (see Figure 5.3). Sometimes three patients shared a bed; one survivor wrote that often "3 to 4 people were thrown into the same bed like dirty rags, typhoid cases and noninfectious ones stayed together for days."[69] Not surprisingly, various epidemic diseases ran unchecked through wards of every kind, surgical as well as medical. Supplies were almost nonexistent. Often there were no hospital garments for patients to wear. They lay in their own usually dirty clothes, on wet mattresses without sheets, often shivering with cold because there was no functioning heating system. A new patient might be put on the dirty mattress just vacated by a discharged or dead patient.[70]

On one occasion an operation was underway in the Leszno Street building. Officials from the electrical company arrived to cut off the power because the hospital was far behind in its payments; the company, of course, was outside the ghetto and under German control. Dr. Borkowski requested five minutes of electricity so that he could sew up the patient's incision. The response was reported to be "It doesn't matter. So there'll be one less Jew." And the power was turned off.[71]

The atmosphere was not designed to inspire confidence in patients or the staff. Nurses were in short supply, so students often found themselves doing work that ordinarily would have been done by others. Irena Piszczek, for example, while a student in the underground medical school, first worked as a technician in histology and bacteriology and then helped patients in lieu of a nurse.[72] Other "nurses" had no training of any kind but were simply young women brought into the hospital for their protection—from roundups in general or from molestation or rape because they were young and attractive—and who, in return, did what they could to assist.[73] Later there was much volunteer labor from the students in the underground medical school; those in the higher years were on the wards as part of their studies, and at the same time found themselves doing much work that might ordinarily have been done by others. The students in the first two years of the course took classes only in the early evening, and those who were still able to be supported by their parents devoted much time during the day to hospital work. For example, Karolina Borman learned to do autopsies in the prosectorium and achieved some skill.[74]

Unhappily, solidarity within Czyste was incomplete. A chief source of dissension centered on some of the converted Jews, who were forced into the ghetto by a German edict that certified their Jewishness on the basis of the religion of their parents or grandparents, regardless of their own baptism into Christianity. Some of these converts worked selflessly and loyally for the community; among the physicians, Dr. Josef Stein is a prominent example. But there were others at the opposite extreme, converts who behaved miserably in Czyste. Ringelblum noted in his diary that a Dr. Szenicer, a baptized Jew, was loud in his anger at the "filthy Jews" in the hospital. And a Dr. Werthajm was so hostile to the Jews that, rumor had it, this was the chief reason that he eventually was given significant responsibilities in the administration of Czyste by the Germans.[75]

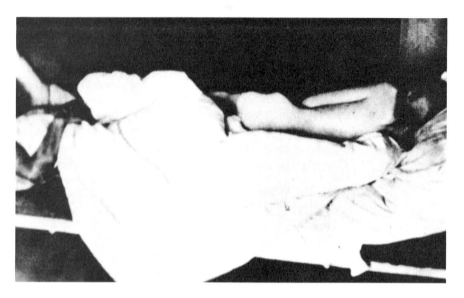

Figure 5.3. Two patients to a bed, Warsaw ghetto, 1941–42 (courtesy of Dr. Marek Balin).

Nor was that the only problem involving the staff at Czyste, or at least some members of the staff. Trunk cites an unnamed contemporary source who claimed that inefficiency worsened the hardships of patients. Moreover, friends of staff members allegedly received preferential treatment, and there were further allegations of misappropriation and even thievery. A group of physicians headed by a Dr. Jakub Munwes, along with communal leaders, appealed to the chairman of the *Judenrat*, probably in the second half of 1941, to clear up the situation.[76] There is ample evidence that many physicians and nurses—probably most of them—gave their professional and personal best during these anguished times. A few, however, apparently succumbed to the extreme pressures of ghetto existence. Although many doctors and nurses labored selflessly and upheld the traditional ethical nature of medicine, enough did not so that the atmosphere was unpleasant and abuses occurred. Trunk refers to the prevalence of an unsocial atmosphere in Czyste that "made it possible for abuses to develop such as graft, exploitation and plain thievery."[77] People were under astonishing strain. Some rose to the challenge; others failed in the face of nameless horror and unrelieved, ceaseless fear. The Nazis were doing their job efficiently and effectively.

Nevertheless, the hospital functioned. Efforts were made to continue the practices of peacetime. Staff members such as Dr. Fenigstein presented reports on patients' diseases at scientific staff meetings.[78] These began after initial wartime interruptions in December 1940 and continued regularly for 20 months[79]—that is, until the deportations of the summer of 1942. The majority of the physicians associated with the hospital participated. Adam Czerniakow reported attending such a meeting where Hirszfeld gave a lecture about blood and race. Subsequently Dr. Stein performed an autopsy on a 30-year-old woman, a mother of five children who had died of starvation.[80] So efforts were made to continue to use the hospital as a place of learning as well as a place of succor.

For the administrators of the hospital and for the *Judenrat*, daily existence became a crushing experience. Czyste was a constant financial drain on the *Judenrat*, which had had to accept total responsibility for the institution. The diaries of Adam Czerniakow return again and again to the problem: In January 1940 he had to borrow 50,000 zloty from the Joint to support the hospital.[81] As late as 2 March 1940 he attended a conference about the hospital, which was purchasing food jointly with the Joint for Czyste, and at which the payment of hospital salaries for the previous December was arranged.[82] Implicit but unstated here is the probability that this all came about because of another loan from the Joint. On 19 March 1940, Czerniakow complained that the hospitals "are eating up our resources," and on 19 July 1941 he noted the necessity of borrowing 120,000 zloty ($22,000) from the Labor Battalion and the Provisioning Authority to have funds to pay hospital employees.[83]

The question of paying the hospital physicians, nurses, technicians, and other employees was a major and chronic worry for Czerniakow, Dr. Milejkowski, and, of course, the staff. Hospital employees made up a major sector of the *Judenrat* budget; in February 1940, out of a total of 773 on the *Judenrat* payroll, 496 worked at Czyste and 32 in the quarantine hospitals (68 percent).[84] For most, salaries were all they had to purchase food and clothing. A few physicians may have been sufficiently well off to feel less pressure, but this would have been an exceptional situation.

In June 1940 the *Judenrat* was threatened by a possible strike at Czyste, so desperate were the nurses, orderlies, doctors, and other workers for some income. After a "stormy session" with a hospital delegation on 21 June,[85] Czerniakow tried to find a way to collect more money from the hospital patients,[86] and by 1 July was able to record the fact that the hospital tax had made it possible to pay the salaries.[87] His optimism was premature; on 7 July the hospital staff was threatening a hunger strike, despite the fact that the *Judenrat* was by then paying between 2000 and 3000 zloty daily in salaries there.[88]

A year later, the problem continued; a raucous delegation of hospital workers appeared at the *Judenrat* demanding their back pay and bearing a letter from Dr. Milejkowski stating that he was being held hostage pending the payment.[89] And in November 1941, Czerniakow records yet another threatened strike by hospital staff, "although I borrowed 100,000 zlotys for them yesterday."[90] The workers do not seem to have fulfilled their threat to strike at any time.

Some physicians apparently were not paid at all. One survivor recalls that doctors who were attached to the hospital but were not full-time staff members received nothing.[91] Ludwig Stabholz, who taught anatomy in the underground medical school, has no recollection of receiving a salary.[92] Perhaps, like Henry Fenigstein, he received only board and room.

Regardless of shortages of supplies and despite difficulties among the staff, the patients poured in. One estimate is that 1400 patients were treated daily.[93] The pressing demands for space meant that patients were discharged from the hospital much more quickly than would have been ideal,[94]

As time went on, the shortage of hospital supplies became severe and the *Judenrat* was forced to create a special department to raise funds for Czyste. The department was headed by a Mr. Ekerman; to deal with recalcitrant taxpayers, he was empowered to confiscate bedding and linen for the hospital.[95]

Among the myriad problems darkening the days of those trying to make Czyste function was the enormous difficulty of feeding the patients. The shortages of food will be described in Chapter 6. The end result was an extremely high mortality rate. The worst month may have been June 1941, when of 1419 patients admitted, 346 (24.9 percent) died.[96]

CZYSTE AND THE DEPORTATIONS
OF JULY-SEPTEMBER 1942

On 22 July 1942, the massive deportations to Treblinka began. Though the destination and fate of the Jews were kept secret from them, it soon became known that "relocation" meant death. One of the few survivors who brought the grim news back to the ghetto was Elie Linder, a Czyste employee removed by the Nazis and sent to Treblinka with his family. All perished except Linder himself.[97] The news he brought would have been persuasive to his fellow workers, who may have been more inclined to believe him than they would a stranger. Belief was difficult in the beginning.

Czyste was one of the first ghetto institutions affected by the deportations. On 21 July the staff was ordered to vacate the Stawki Street premises immediately; though they did not know it then, the hospital site was destined to provide the only shelter for Jews held at the *Umschlagplatz* awaiting the cattle cars running to Treblinka. The staff discharged as many patients as possible, perhaps as many as 750.[98] Some simply fled, regardless of their medical condition. The remainder were carried to buildings at Leszno 80 and Dzika 3; the pathology laboratories and as much research material as could be saved went to Leszno 1.[99]

Czyste Staff Members

Hundreds of individuals worked at Czyste in various capacities during World War II. No detailed list exists, but some names have come down to us and should, perhaps, be recorded. Partial lists appear in the works of Gurfinkiel-Glocerowa[100] and Fenigstein.[101] Not many of these persons survived, but a few did, including Dr. Emil Apfelbaum, head of internal medicine; Dr. David Wdowinski, head of the Department of Psychiatry; Dr. Stanislaw Waller, a staff physician; Dr. Henry Fenigstein; in charge of the prosectorium in the Department of Pathology; and Mrs. Sabina Gurfinkiel-Glocerowa, a ward head nurse in Czyste. A great deal of what we know about the hospital comes from their postwar accounts.[102] In addition, Prof. Ludwig Hirszfeld's biography[103] contains additional information, though his connection with Czyste was largely tangential.

A further vitally important source of information is the archival collection made during the years 1939 through 1943 by historian Emmanuel Ringelblum and his colleagues in "Oneg Shabbat," the code name for the underground archival operation. Fortunately, a large proportion of its papers—half or more—was retrieved from the underground hiding place after the war and now makes up a substantial part of the archives at Yad Vashem in Jerusalem. The staff of that archive has translated and published in English a major portion of the material.[104] Other survivors' memoirs flesh out the story, including several of the interviews that are the backbone of this book.[105] Some other authors have recorded the names of former colleagues: Dr. Aharon Solowiejczyk was head of a surgical department at Czyste until he died in the ghetto in October 1942.[106] Dr. Maurice (Marcus) Plonskier, a pathologist, headed the laboratory in Czyste Hospital; he was posthumously an author in the hunger disease research.[107] Dr. Julian Rotstadt was in charge of the Physiotherapy Department at Czyste.[108]

RELOCATION OF CZYSTE HOSPITAL, SEPTEMBER 1942

On 5 September 1942, Dr. Stein received an order from the Germans stating that all Czyste sites in the ghetto were to be vacated within 24 hours.[109] What this meant in human terms is difficult to comprehend. By that time, no motorized ambulance existed within the rapidly constricting Jewish world. Hundreds of sick persons would have to be transported somehow, and quickly. Those who could walk did so, a limping, bandaged stream toiling toward Stawki Street and the *Umschlagplatz*. The building at Stawki 6–8 was their destination.[110]

The patients at Leszno 1 had to wend their way, or be carried or driven on rickshas, along Leszno and then up Karmelicka and Zamenhofa streets; similarly, those at Leszno 1 and at Elektoralna 12 had to make the painful trip, fully aware of the consequences of not obeying the Nazi order.

The staff knew even more pointedly what would happen to those who failed to move. They labored frantically for the next 24 hours, struggling to comply with an order that was brutal and unreasonable. But for the Nazis, it was a rational directive as they prepared for what came to be known as the "kettle" or "cauldron" in the immediate future.

Sabina Gurfinkiel-Glocerowa, a nurse, was with her patients on Leszno Street when the order came. She describes the panic that ensued, the desperate struggle to organize means to move the bedridden, and the straggling groups of the walking wounded and the least ill. On the morning of 6 September, some trucks (presumably supplied by the Germans) did move the last of her patients. But she and her nursing companions were not permitted to accompany them. Nor were the doctors. Fearing the worst, they carried their scanty possessions to Zamenhof 19,[111] a block away from the new hospital site to which the patients had been directed. This was to be their home for the immediate future, sharing space with the members of the *Judenrat* and their families. But what of the patients?

Late in the day, some of the medical staff found a way to get to Stawki Street, though this was forbidden. There they found the sickest patients lying in the street in front of the building that was to be turned into a hospital. The patients lay in the mud where the trucks had left them, helpless and without help.[112] Many had open wounds, severe infections, limbs in traction. But they lay in the mud until the medical staff began the painful task of moving them into the filthy building that had been allotted to them: the latest incarnation of the Czyste Hospital.

During these few days, while the cauldron selections went on, conditions at Czyste, back at the edge of the *Umschlagplatz*, were appalling. In the few streets within which all the remaining Jews were confined, a seething mass of humanity, the Nazis beat men, women, and children brutally. Many were shot. In the hospital the surgical staff labored ceaselessly to remove bullets, sew up wounds, sometimes save a life. So heavy was the load that one surgeon, Dr. Amsterdamski, reached a state of total exhaustion. He could not carry on.[113] But the injured continued to pour in.

The selection of patients went on continually at this time. From the ghetto, the deportations continued at what had become the customary rate, about 6000 a day. The majority of Jews went to Treblinka and died there, most of them less than a day after leaving the ghetto. Sick Jews were in a category that the Nazis particularly wanted to include in the deportations, and so it was done. But with characteristic barbarity, the medical staff was ordered to make the selection: 10 percent to stay, 90 percent to be relocated in the east. Long before September, the Jews of Warsaw knew precisely what relocation meant—death at Treblinka. A few had escaped and made the perilous journey back to Warsaw and into the ghetto again. They had seen the system at work at Treblinka: the fake railway station, the tree-lined road to the gas chambers and eternity.[114]

And the Nazis told the doctors to choose. Balin has described the terrible feelings, the appalling burden of being thus forced, as a medical student, to say: This patient will live; all those must die. He was forced to select but managed to slip away after an hour or so, incapable of continuing.[115]

Unhappily, Balin's superiors could not avoid the same dilemma. The staff had to undergo selections, just as did the patients. The Czyste director, Dr. Stein, and the chief administrator selected those who would live a little longer on their staff, and therefore who would not. The Germans had given them a certain number of supposedly inviolate passes to distribute, so-called life tickets. But the number was far fewer than the total number on the staff. Again, German inventive cruelty put Jews in the awful position of having to choose among their own people. At least one surviving staff member believed they chose as fairly as was possible and did everything in their power to increase the number, hiding people, creating jobs, inflating the importance of some positions to justify extra passes, and so on; the testimony of this survivor acquires added weight because she was *not* among those chosen.[116] Others were less charitable, suggesting that Stein chose preferentially from among his fellow converts.[117]

The cauldron finally ceased to bubble on 12 September 1942, and after almost two months of unprecedented terror the deportations slowed to a trickle. The final act, like the first, involved Czyste directly. The patients and all the staff except the minority who had received the precious life tickets were transported to Treblinka, approximately 900 patients and 50 or more staff members. The remainder of the original staff included those with life tickets, those previously sent to Treblinka, and a large group who attempted to survive by going into hiding or trying to escape into Christian Warsaw.[118] Any remaining patients were shot in their beds.[119]

Few of the remaining ghetto inhabitants can have doubted that the deportations would resume sometime, though they continued to hope against hope. Life did not return to normal. There was no normality in the Warsaw ghetto. Casual murder remained a daily event. The 35,000 Jews who had passes permitting them to be in the ghetto found existence increasingly difficult. Most worked in one of the shops that produced goods for the *Wehrmacht*, and these survivors found themselves forbidden to move about in the ghetto.[120] That much-constricted area now had only empty streets and eerie silences,[121] contrasting strongly with its previous noisy vibrancy.

The *Umschlagplatz* continued to function. One of the final deportations of the summer *Aktion* of 1942 comprised the patients and staff of Czyste. But intermittent selections continued to be made. On 17 September, an outpatient clinic was opened on Stawki. This was a two-room makeshift arrangement, but it provided the sick at least the comfort of seeming to be cared for; the staff lacked everything but compassion. This site, adjacent to the *Umschlagplatz*, was convenient for the patients and also allowed the staff the opportunity, occasionally, of smuggling someone out of that fearsome place.[122] According to one source, another small clinic was set up at Pawia 6. This temporary sick bay had 12 beds and a room for minor surgery. It also began functioning on 17 September.[123]

A complete hospital could no longer exist on Stawki Street, and another site was needed. There were no truly satisfactory sites left, but a building at Gęsia 6–8, a former textile warehouse,[124] was somehow transformed into a 400-bed hospital. The children's ward comprised three small rooms on the first floor.[125] A small part of the building became living quarters for some of the medical staff, with others living nearby at Franciszkańska 24[126] and Gęsia 48.[127] Ludwig Hirszfeld's laboratory was transferred to the children's infectious hospital, a division of the old Czyste, on Żelazna and Leszno streets, but it was not set up[128] and never functioned again.

DEPORTATION FROM THE GESIA STREET HOSPITAL

After September 1942, the sole hospital in the ghetto was the final incarnation of Czyste at Gęsia 6–8. There the doctors and nurses united with the few remaining staff from the Berson and Bauman Hospital (see below).[129] The staff lived where they could. Henry and Ala Fenigstein had a room on the third floor that they shared with two women.[130] Tadeusz Stabholz, his fiancée, and five others shared two small rooms near the hospital.[131]

The building was a shambles, and the first task was to clean the filthy, heavily plundered site. Once this was done, the staff created as many departments as they could, depending to some degree on the qualifications of the survivors.[132] They also began to build bunkers in the basement and on the second floor for patients and staff,[133] an activity that was going on all over the ghetto by this stage.

Typhus reappeared in the constricted ghetto by late October.[134] On November 15 there were 289 patients in the hospital, 10 of them with typhus; two weeks later things were much worse, with 371 patients needing care, 14 with typhus.[135]

The problem of staffing was serious, since nurses, orderlies, technicians, and others had largely disappeared into the *Umschlagplatz* and the gas chambers at Treblinka. The solution was to replace them with the wives of physicians in the hope of saving some of them from the next selection. Workloads were heavy, with a night nurse perhaps having 90 patients and no assistance at all.[136]

On 18 January 1943, a new round of deportations began. This episode was destined to be of short duration, since the Germans unexpectedly found themselves facing armed Jews fighting for their lives. But one easy target was the hospital, and it suffered heavily. The Gestapo forced the medical staff to carry bedridden patients down to the street; those who could walk were ordered to go into the street immediately without being given time to dress.[137] About 400 patients were taken to the *Umschlagplatz*[138] and to Treblinka, any who could not leave their beds being shot there.[139] The Nazis then set fire to the building; one books cites an eyewitness who had "seen them dash out the brains of newborn babies against the walls, rip open the bellies of pregnant women, and throw casualties into the flames. He'd seen them."[140] The murder of hospital patients was not an event unique to Warsaw. If not a matter of explicit policy, the practice was certainly a routine one for Germans, at least when dealing with Jews. Among the many places where this occurred were the ghetto at Brody, where the hospital was burned down with its full complement of patients and staff,[141] and the Kraków ghetto hospital, where the patients too ill to flee were murdered in their beds.[142]

Jack Eisner saw the murders at Gęsia Street. A teenager who had survived by smuggling, in January 1943 he was a member of ŻZW, the Betarist fighting organization. On 20 January he and some comrades heard peculiar noises while moving along Kupiecka Street. They climbed to the roof of Kupiecka 11 and found themselves overlooking the backyards at Gęsia 6–8. "Before our eyes, the SS soldiers were tossing screaming patients out of the second-, third-, and fourth-floor windows, and on the ground the loading squad was piling the bodies on the platforms. The continuous screams were horrifying."[143] They had only pistols, and the range was too long to be effective. One of their number ran to get the only Schmeisser machine gun the unit had. Before he returned, they saw more sickening scenes. When the gun arrived, they killed several of the Nazis before being forced to flee themselves.

Those who survived were the few who had the good fortune to be able to reach a hiding place before the *Aktion* began. The Fenigsteins managed to get into a hiding place on the second floor of the hospital building and were undetected.[144] Gurfinkiel-Glocerowa was in a bunker in the basement, where a group were preserved largely by the courage of the hospital accountant, who stayed out of the bunker and warned those inside whenever Germans approached, so that they would be completely quiet. After two days the Germans left the area, and those remaining were temporarily safe.[145]

BERSON AND BAUMAN HOSPITAL

Czyste Hospital was by no means the only institution in the ghetto where doctors and nurses struggled to offset the pitiless effects of starvation, filth, disease, and despair. Another, smaller but well-known in its own right long before World War Two, was the Berson and Bauman Hospital for children (see Figure 5.4). This hospital, headed in the war years by Dr. Anna Braude-Hellerowa, had one substantial advantage over Czyste when the ghetto was created: Berson and Bauman Hospital did not have to move into the ghetto, since it was located at Sienna 60 and Śliska 51,[146] within the boundaries laid down by the Germans in 1940. Thus they had a purpose-built building, constructed in 1923,[147] and, at the beginning, reasonable facilities and supplies.

But even in the summer of 1940, before the ghetto phase began, Czerniakow noted that Berson and Bauman, as well as the tuberculosis sanatorium known as Brijus, and Zofiowka, a mental asylum, were appealing to the *Judenrat* for help because they had no financial support.[148] Berson and Bauman had first experienced serious fiscal problems in January 1940. At that time the number of patients suffering from infectious diseases was so large that the children's hospital had to be converted temporarily into an infectious disease hospital. This action eliminated a crucial portion of its income, which had been derived from fees paid by private patients. Municipal sources had also vanished, and the *Judenrat* had not yet evolved even a partially functioning economic policy. In this situation, it was necessary for TOZ (and thus, indirectly, the Joint) to grant Berson and Bauman Hospital financial aid.[149]

By early 1942, when some of the staff of this institution were participating in the investigations of disease due to hunger, even the minimal equipment available to the researchers at Czyste could not be duplicated at Berson and Bauman.[150] What could be duplicated was dedicated leadership. Dr. Anna Braude-Heller (in the Polish style, Braude-Hellerowa) was widely respected. Professor Hirszfeld referred to her as "a splendid human being," and in his postwar memoir he was quick to criticize when he thought it was deserved.[151] Dr. Braude-Heller came from a wealthy family, graduated in medicine from a Swiss university, and returned to Poland in 1914. There she organized a home for orphaned and abandoned children. She also helped to set up the Medem tuberculosis sanatorium and became medical director of the Berson and Bauman Hospital for children on Śliska Street. Szwajger describes her as a "short, black-haired lady who spoke in a deep alto voice and moved with surprising agility considering her weight."[152] She always wore black, in perpetual mourning for a son tragically dead of undiagnosed appendicitis.

After the July–September deportations of 1942 finally ended the existence of Berson and Bauman, Dr. Braude-Heller helped organized the new Czyste general hospital. When asked if she would attempt to escape, she declined: "I am not going.

Figure 5.4. Sienna 60, former Berson and Bauman Hospital (photo by C. G. Roland, 1990).

I have agreed to send my son and his wife and child. As long as there are Jews in the ghetto I am needed here, and here I will stay."[153] In April 1943, Jewish patrols found her body in the courtyard of her last post, the Gęsia Street hospital, where she had died after a lifetime of service.[154]

Other administrative and staff personnel of the hospital included its president, the lawyer Maksymilian Schoenbach, whom an *Ordnungsdienst* official remembers as "one of the most noble and righteous men" in the ghetto.[155] Another important person in the Berson and Bauman hierarchy was the trustee administrator, Dr. Waclaw Skonieczny. He was particularly remembered for heading a delegation that attempted to persuade the Nazis to increase the food allotment for the hospitals of the ghetto. Unhappily, they failed; Dr. Hagen informed them that there was no food.[156] Dr. Henryk Makower was head of the section of infectious diseases in the children's hospital during the war years,[157] Dr. Inka Schwieger (Szwajger) was a pediatrician, and we even know that Bronka Feinmesser had been the telephone operator there.[158] All these people, and the many others who made up the staff, had a special mode of identification for the Nazis and the Polish police; as well as the standard white armband with a blue Star of David, they wore a white band with a red Star and the word *Kinderkrankenhaus*, meaning children's hospital.[159]

They were swamped with sick and dying children. By March 1941, when the ghetto had been in existence for four months, it was routine to have at least two children in a crib or pediatric bed, often three.[160] Everything was in short supply except sick children. Diapers were nonexistent, so the staff tore up sheets to make substitutes as long as the sheets lasted.[161] In cold weather the children shivered and sometimes froze because there was no coal.[162] Early in their occupation, the Germans took all ether supplies away from the operating rooms, because the anesthetic was almost impossible to obtain. When the staff entreated them to leave at least a minimal supply for emergency operations, the doctors were arrested as punishment for their insolence.[163]

As everywhere in the ghetto, food was completely inadequate. Nor were special supplies or supplements available, as one might have expected because Berson and Bauman was a children's hospital. One three-year-old child in a crib was found to weigh 4 kilograms (ca. 9 pounds), about what a two-month-old baby should weigh.[164] What food existed was of poor quality. The patients became so hungry that the older ones were found to be stealing from those who were younger and smaller.[165] Not surprisingly, Dr. Braude-Heller and other staff members at Berson and Bauman were participating in the research into hunger disease.[166] Perhaps something beneficial could come from all the suffering and misery.

But even being well-fed was no guarantee of well-being. The staff noted that when the German Jews arrived in the ghetto, still more than adequately nourished, the children turned up in Berson and Bauman discouragingly soon, often sick with dysentery, and they seemed to die just as quickly as the local children.[167]

Illness combined with severe starvation created unusual patterns of disease, patterns that further hindered the medical care of these youthful patients. For example, Dr. Braude-Heller recorded one case history of an 11-year-old boy who, at autopsy, was found to have tuberculosis throughout the body even though all tests had been negative.[168] And if the physicians couldn't determine that a patient had tuberculosis, they couldn't treat him for it, though in the circumstances nothing could have helped this patient anyway.

The other general problem, in the ghetto and in every institution within it, even those we think of as traditionally and somehow innately clean, such as hospitals, was filth and its natural accompaniment, vermin. Children arrived at Berson and Bauman swarming with lice. Despite the best efforts of the staff, these lice, fleas, and other vermin could not be eradicated. Many children had bed sores, commonly found to be swarming with maggots. Picking a child up, for example to take him or her to the operating room, might reveal a mattress seething with worms, and the children's scalps were alive with lice.[169] Eugenia Pernal worked as a nurse in the Berson and Bauman Hospital in 1941 and 1942. There dysentery and bed sores were among the more common clinical problems.[170] While nursing at Czyste Hospital, she remembers a typhus patient who fell out of bed while delirious, hitting his head. His wound was bandaged, and when the dressings were checked a few days later, the wound was found to be full of maggots.[171]

The combined operation of all these forces, totally negative, produced the predictable result. Children died in the hospital at a staggering rate. According to one report, during the last quarter of 1941, 24 percent of the 724 children confined to the hospital died there.[172]

On a completely different level, the children's hospital was a terminus in operations by the Polish underground in cooperation with the ŻZW, the Jewish Military Organization. The latter, from its creation in late 1939,[173] and particularly within the ghetto, had been heavily involved in supplying food to some of the refugee cen-ters.[174] They were also deeply committed to smuggling medical supplies, flour, rice, and other foods to Berson and Bauman Hospital.[175] Serious efforts to resist by force were finally being planned.

But when the fighting began, it coincided with the end of Jewish hospitals in Warsaw. Though efforts to aid the sick and injured continued after January 1943, no true hospital existed. The distinguished humanitarian traditions of Czyste and of Berson and Bauman were only memories.

6

Nutrition,
Malnutrition,
and Starvation

Death from long lasting hunger is like a candle burning out slowly.[1]

Hunger was the fundamental problem to be coped with in the Warsaw ghetto. It was one that almost every Jew came to know well and to struggle with at length, a gnawing, endless torment only worsened by remembering happier times or by encountering those more fortunate. Beginning about 1940, large numbers of Jews began to starve to death; after the ghetto was walled in, the pace accelerated uncontrollably. Official statistics indicate that 4 Jews starved to death in the last part of 1939 and 91 during 1940.[2] Though official, these figures seem unrealistically low. In 1941 the number increased manyfold. Dr. Wilhelm Hagen believed that 58,000 Jews died of starvation in Warsaw.[3] The doctors of the ghetto collected data indicating that more than 98,000 Jews died in the ghetto, but identified only 18,320 deaths as being due to hunger.[4] But they were unable to assign specific causes of death in 77,000 of these cases. Many of the 77,000 must also have died of starvation. Although the Jews struggled to cope, every circumstance was against them.

SCENES OF HUNGER AND STARVATION

Anecdotal evidence attesting to this desperate situation is voluminous and will only be sampled. Before things became too difficult, it was possible to joke about the shortage of food, as was the case with the previously plump middle-aged women who laughed about no longer needing to diet.[5] The ghetto slang for food coupons was *Bona*—bone—a play on the idea of throwing a dog a bone.[6] Another bit of ghetto slang was the phrase "to surrender [ration] coupons" as a euphemism for "to die."[7] A poem has survived titled *Fun Letztn Hurbn*, "The Ration Card," which ends: "To part with you is very hard/ I won't give up my darling card."[8] And another anonymous rhymer wrote:

> When we have nothing to eat,
> They gave us a turnip, they gave us a beet.
> Here have some grub, have some fleas,
> Have some typhus, die of disease.[9]

Obviously, it was easier to rhyme "disease" with "fleas" than with "lice," the true culprit in typhus.

One of the interviewees remembers her mother stretching the noon meal of soup, the main meal of the day, further and further. The neighbors and others who had no food were invited in, so more water was added to the soup.[10] There came a time for most families when they had to stop inviting others to share a meal. One's own family had to come first. Another survivor, a girl at the time, recalls how upset she was that her mother wouldn't let her give food to beggars, not understanding that her own family was short of food and her mother sick with apprehension.[11] A young man, recently married, recalls the delight they felt when his wife could afford to buy a pound of horsemeat to make a feast.[12] Later, even horsemeat was unavailable, and some ghetto residents were reduced to eating coagulated horse blood mixed with salt and pepper and spread on bread.[13] Dr. Jakob Penson collected the blood from cows secretly slaughtered in the ghetto, mixed it with onions and a small amount of fat, and fed it to patients swollen with hunger edema. He hoped to increase their blood proteins this way and reduce the swelling, but it didn't seem to help.[14]

In the spring of 1941, shop workers were fainting from hunger,[15] and the ghetto inmates had become blasé about seeing dead bodies lying in the streets[16] although recollections of the bloated corpses of children remain vivid 45 years later.[17] The chief historian of the ghetto, Emmanuel Ringelblum, recorded the case of a six-year-old beggar boy who lay in front of Muranowska 24 one night in August 1941, too weak to roll over to a piece of bread thrown down to him from a window.[18] A similar painful account is that of a family of four, starving, who were given some soup and four rolls. The two children ate their rolls, as did the father; the mother saved hers until the next day. During the night her husband, driven by uncontrollable hunger, crawled to her bed, stole the roll from under her pillow, and then fell over dead, still clutching his shameful prize.[19] In an apartment in the house where Emmanuel Ringelblum lived, a father, mother, and their son all died of starvation on the same day in March 1941.[20]

An unidentified inhabitant of the ghetto recorded seeing a boy, walking down Grzybowska Street, bend over to sweep something up out of the dirt and eat it; there was some ersatz coffee made of roasted wheat mixed in the mud.[21] One waif tried to make a meal of a package of starched collars.[22] But nothing describes more nauseatingly the state of many of Warsaw's Jews than the incident of a young girl walking to the doctor's office, carrying a jar with a sample of her sick mother's feces; the jar was snatched from her on the street and the contents gulped down by a starving man.[23] Another version of this story, or a separate but similar occurrence, was related by Henryk Rubinlicht. His sister, a trained bacteriologist, was visiting a sick friend. She had some human excrement samples with her, en route to the laboratory, when they were snatched out of her hands. Since he is discussing the extremes of hunger at this point, we can assume that the samples were eaten, though he is not explicit on that point.[24]

When a woman committed suicide by jumping from the fifth floor of their building into the courtyard, she landed on a large cooking pot in which fish were being prepared. The pot collapsed and she lay dead, her head badly smashed. Pieces of brain lay mixed with the bloody fish. "Suddenly, small children crawled out of every nook and cranny; they headed for the scene like crawling ants. They grabbed the pieces of fish covered with brain and blood and shoved them into their mouths. I can never forget this scene."[25]

People of all ages died in the streets, in shelters, in homes, and in hospitals. As Adler observed, "Natural death in the street from hunger, exhaustion, exposure, heart attack, or infectious disease had become the rule."[26] Wdowinski used to walk about 1 kilometer from his home to Czyste Hospital, and often saw 6 to 10 bodies lying in the street each day.[27] Nighttime created a special hazard because

> even the most courageous or insensitive lost their nerve when, in the darkness of
> the night, they happened to accidentally step on some soft object that turned out
> to be a cadaver. On those occasions, invariably, hysterical screams rang out.[28]

Those found dead on the street usually had not died there. The family commonly transferred the body from their home to the street after removing all evidence of its identity. That way, they might be able to use the extra ration card for a few days; if the family attended the funeral at the cemetery, they were sure to stand well out of the way so as not to be recognized and risk having the card taken away.[29]

Similarly in the refugee shelters, mothers hid dead children under beds for days in order to receive a larger food ration.[30] An official *Ordnungsdienst* report for 22 July 1941 records the investigation conducted when the decomposed body of six-year-old Moszek Borensztajn was found in front of Krochmalna 16. His mother, Chudesa, was found living in No. 14. She stated that the *Judenrat* refused to bury anyone without payment. Her child had died and she would soon die also, precisely because she had no money. The boy had starved to death. Another body was found in the courtyard and a third in the apartment where the Borensztajns lived.[31]

In desperation, starving mothers left their babies where pedestrian traffic in the ghetto was heaviest, or near a district *Ordnungsdienst* office, hoping that a passerby would take pity on the child, or that the Jewish police would take it to an orphanage or another institution. Abandonments such as this happened almost daily.[32]

Conditions were especially bad in prison. In Gęsiówka, the prison on Gęsia Street run by the *Ordnungsdienst*, there were 1600 prisoners in May 1942, about half men, half women. There was no sick bay or hospital, and many died from hunger. There were frequent cases of starvation diarrhea, which had been found to be a sign that death is imminent. "In such cases people are not let out at all. They dirty themselves until they die."[33]

There is some evidence that TOZ may have been providing food both to Pawiak Prison and to Gęsiówka. Dr. Leon Wulman, who had escaped from Warsaw to the United States some months after the war broke out, reported in a letter to the Joint that in one month in 1941, TOZ had supplied 7652 meals to two houses, one at Gęsia 24, the other at Dzielna 61. Wulman made a point of mentioning this otherwise banal fact because he knew that Gęsiówka and Pawiak prisons were located on these streets at the numbers given. He concluded that TOZ had been compelled to take over the feeding of the inmates of these institutions.[34]

An infuriating contrast based on food partially explains the hatred aroused by the *Ordnungsdienst* among the ordinary Jews of the ghetto. Amid scenes of starving beggars and emaciated corpses there were a few Jews such as Szerynski, the head of the *Ordnungsdienst*, and his deputy, Stanislaw Czaplinski. Because of their positions, these men had unlimited though illicit access to food. Adler, a deputy in the *Ordnungsdienst*, has described the effect: "On the hunger-stricken streets of the Jewish Quarter, the sight of Szerynski and Czaplinski, those two obese men rolling along, produced a tragi-comic effect."[35]

Another highly visible victim of his own gluttony was the lawyer who headed the tribunal set up by The Thirteen. Aleksander Bramson had been corpulent before the war; with his new position and the resulting easy access to black market food and drink, this morbidly obese man grew even fatter. "He presented a fantastic and almost unbelievable sight with his insatiable appetite when he sat stuffing food into himself at a loaded table in the Adas restaurant where the 'court's' clientele gathered to drink and to make deals."[36]

STARVATION AS POLICY

After they occupied Poland, the Nazis laid down a table of rations for all who resided there. Hans Frank, the governor of the *Generalgouvernement*, predicted unequivocally that the Nazis had condemned 1,200,000 Jews to death by starvation.[37] The provision of food in the *Generalgouvernement* was difficult from the beginning. The Germans prohibited the importation of food from the Reich, including those parts of Poland that had been incorporated into the Reich as soon as the surrender took place in 1939. Thus Warsaw effectively was cut off from its usual source of supply, the farms of western Poland.[38]

At first there was no differentiation between the food allowances for Poles and for Jews, but as the Nazi machine revealed its increasingly restrictive and destructive policies against the Jews, they were deprived even more than were gentile Poles. And the Nazis were quite capable of biased distribution of food relief even in the beginning. According to the leaders of the Joint in Warsaw, Lejb Neustadt and David Guzik, when the Germans entered the city, they brought motorized kitchens with them. These traveled throughout Warsaw and fed large numbers of Poles, "but Jews were not permitted to receive any food through this source. It was obvious that this caravan feeding was conducted as propaganda to curry favor with the Poles."[39] This discriminatory relief was confirmed by William McDonald, an American Quaker official of the Commission for Polish Relief, who visited Warsaw early in October 1939. He described an automobile procession of 142 cars, three miles long, distributing 250,000 meals daily. None of these meals was served to Jews. When he returned to Berlin, he was informed by the National Socialist Welfare Organization (a propaganda arm of the Nazis) that "the word Pole does not under any circumstance include Jews."[40]

Rationing began in December 1939, though the fact that an item was rationed did not mean that one necessarily could buy it.[41] In May 1940, the bread ration was cut from 500 grams daily to 200 grams for Jews, though Poles continued to receive 570 grams. Moreover, from this time on, Jews were allowed essentially no sugar. Poles could obtain limited amounts.[42]

Thus, although the non-Jewish Poles were hungry too, their situation was not nearly as bad as it was in the ghetto. Various estimates show that Christian Poles received about 500 calories officially.[43] The allotment for patients in general hospitals was increased from 1000 to 1400 calories during 1942. Despite this change, hospitals were hardly idyllic places with respect to rations.

One Jewish woman who had taken a Christian identity in Warsaw told of looking after a friend who had a baby in a Warsaw hospital. She had to struggle to find food to take to her friend, since the hospital was woefully lacking.[44] Dr. Hagen admitted that in health institutions outside the ghetto, such as orphanages and nursing homes, the ration remained at 500 calories, the standard Polish daily caloric supply.[45] Because of steadily diminishing resources, the caloric value of self-help meals provided in Christian Warsaw fell from 460 calories in December 1940 to 153 calories in July 1941.[46]

By 1941, the official ration provided 2613 calories per day for Germans in Poland (including the *Volkdeutsch*), 699 calories for Poles, and 184 calories for Jews in the ghetto.[47] Gutman states rather naively that there was "little chance" of surviving on the official ration alone.[48] Actually, there was not the slightest chance for Poles or Jews to survive on the official ration.

Gutman also makes the important observation that at no time during the existence of the ghetto did the entire public find itself in the same situation.[49] It is tempting to simplify the facts and to think that hunger was slight in 1940 and severe in 1942. But one's dietary status depended on whether one was a native Varsovian or a refugee, and on whether one had money or valuables, or was working regularly, or had neither money nor a job. Refugees arrived in successive waves. People used up their money or lost their jobs, and these events took place at different times. Thus the population was never homogeneous with respect to its position on any imaginary scale between well-being and death by starvation.

Trunk has provided a graphic representation of the insolubility of the money/food equation in June 1941, midway through the existence of the ghetto. He presents a monthly budget, for a family of four Jews, to purchase from the black market only those staples not supplied in the Nazi ration—that is, what the family needed to survive, over and above what was officially permitted. The family needed to buy food that added up to a total monthly expenditure for staple foods alone of 1114.16 zloty. A skilled carpenter, if able to work at all, and working 10–11 hours daily, might earn about 1000 zloty ($200) a month.[50] And few Jews were skilled carpenters, one of the better-paid trades; most Jews could not find any type of paid work. Both within the ghetto and in the rest of Warsaw, the increase in prices far exceeded any alterations in wages. Indeed, wages for the Jews probably decreased somewhat for those who could obtain work, while in gentile Warsaw wages doubled but prices increased 20 times.[51] The Nazis forbade raises and then claimed that there was no inflation, only high prices. Inside the ghetto, food prices increased 27 times.[52]

By comparison with the food supply in the ghetto, prisoners of war from the Western nations averaged perhaps 1700 calories from German supplies,[53] though one estimate suggested a range of only 128 to 684 calories a day. The remainder needed to sustain health came from the highly esteemed Red Cross parcels.[54] Fortunately for the prisoners, Red Cross supplements usually were available. French civilians in northern France during the war averaged 1200 calories during 1941.[55]

For an ordinary-sized adult performing only sedentary activities, the minimum caloric intake needed simply to sustain the status quo is between 2000 and 2400 calories daily. This figure is the same whether one is German or Polish, Christian or Jewish.

Yet German policy depended upon who was interpreting it. While Hans Frank calmly observed the Jews starving to death on 200 calories daily, Dr. Wilhelm Hagen protested that the food supply in the ghetto needed to be improved up to the bare subsistence level (*einer Aufbesserung bis zum nackten Existenzminimum*),[56] which would have meant providing at least 2000 calories daily. Even if Hagen was sincere, the likelihood of being able to do this was small. And, of course, it did not happen. On 19 August 1941, Heinz Auerswald told Czerniakow that the Krakow administration of the *Generalgouvernement* "is also inclined not to starve out the ghetto Jews. However, the ration cannot be increased at this point because the newly captured territories [in the USSR] absorb a lot of food."[57] That is, the Nazis would permit nothing to benefit the Jews if it was at the expense of any other group.[58]

Germany itself had a serious shortage of food. Even in the capital city, Berlin, the heart of the Third Reich, food was scarce as early as the end of 1940. There, on 11 November 1940, "Missie" Vassiltchikov saw a dead donkey being carried in the back door of her butcher shop.[59]

Nevertheless, had the Nazis wanted to do so, the rations to the Jews probably could have been increased at least to the level of bare subsistence. But we know now, unequivocally, that by late 1941 or early 1942, the Final Solution had as its avowed endpoint the extermination of the Jews. Thus increasing their rations could not have become policy.

The midday meal in the ghetto varied, depending upon who you were and what your resources were. Lewin has summarized the various alternatives for those who were able to afford to pay anything at all for their food.[60] For a large majority, the noon meal was a dish of watery soup for which they paid 90 groschen. For the small minority who could afford it, however, a lunch could be purchased that included nourishing soup, a large portion of meat, vegetables, and dessert, for up to 20 zloty. This was apparently outside Lewin's means, since he outlined the meal "as it was described to me." Yehoshua Perle left an account of the daily food available to a "permitted" person in the shrunken, broken-up ghetto that remained after the major deportations of the summer of 1942. By then, everyone was merely a number:

> My number receives one quarter of a loaf of loamy bread a day, a tasteful stew, consisting of cooked water, a potato that has been stolen earlier from the pot by someone or other, and also two or three grains of groats which swim around eternally chasing one another and, alas, never catch up. Moreover, from time to time they allot to my number an egg of yesteryear with a drop of blood in it, sometimes a lick of honey, and once in a century also a tiny lump of ancient meat which, crush it into as many pieces as you wish, will never have the taste of vintage wine.[61]

With a prescribed ration of about 200 calories daily, how did the Jews survive for almost two years in the ghetto? Many attempts were made to increase the daily ration. All efforts to have the German supplies increased proved to be dead ends.

But other routes were more effective. These included the provision of food to the poor by the *Judenrat* and by several social welfare agencies, direct smuggling of food by hungry Jews, increased production of food, and, most commonly, purchase on the black market of smuggled food.

Before the war, estimates had suggested that a laborer required 2380 calories per day. The official ration actually received in the ghetto in January 1941 was 219 calories (9.2 percent of normal), and in August 1941, 177 calories (7 percent).[62] Yet more calories actually were received, thanks to the various clandestine methods mentioned. In December 1941, the actual caloric intake was estimated to be 784 calories for beggars and 1125 calories for the general population, with a select few receiving as many as 1665 calories daily.[63] These figures include food from all sources.

What did the actual 800-calorie diet for refugees contain? Researchers in the ghetto estimated that there were 3 grams of fat and 20 to 30 grams of vegetable protein: "It consisted of dark bread, rye flour, kasha, potatoes, traces of butter, lard, oil, sugar, and a plateful of soup. It contained mostly carbohydrates and was grossly deficient in vitamins."[64] The consequence was predictable. Trunk estimated the percentage of refugees swollen with starvation edema in four centers: at Stawki 9, 49 percent; at Dzika 3, 62 percent; at Grzybowska 48, 63 percent; and at Żelazna 64, a remarkable 73 percent.[65] In May–June 1941 there were about 20,000 refugees living in the centers; 609 died of hunger and only 4 from typhus.[66]

One startling observation emphasizes the severity of the hunger even before the ghetto was set up. In May 1940 the public kitchens had to be closed for 10 days, and by the end of this time a large number of cases of starvation edema were diagnosed.[67] The Jews being fed from these kitchens were chronically and severely undernourished despite the feedings. Otherwise, edema would not have appeared so quickly.

In hospitals in the ghetto, starving children, often bloated with the edema that accompanies hunger, were given half a powdered egg and one vitamin C tablet daily, in addition to whatever daily ration of food was available. The supplement had to be distributed by the doctors because the ward attendant, himself swollen with hunger, "cannot handle the torture of the distribution." Only doctors and nurses received special rations: 500 grams of soup and 60 grams of bread. Other hospital employees did not get this ration, so the doctors and nurses had a meeting and agreed that everyone in the hospital would share, each therefore getting the same amount: 300 grams of soup and 40 grams of bread daily per person.[68]

THE *JUDENRAT* AND THE SUPPLY OF FOOD

Two departments played a central role in determining the food supply to the ghetto. One, part of the Nazi bureaucracy, was the *Transferstelle*, or Transfer Authority. This office had official control over the flow of goods, including food, into the ghetto, and that of goods and manufactured products out of the ghetto. The second department was within the *Judenrat*, the *Zakład Zaopatrywania*, or Supply Authority. Having responsibility for distributing ration cards, obtaining and storing food, and obtaining other essential supplies such as coal, the crucial importance of the Supply Authority needs no emphasis.[69] It became involved in some tangential activities such as making jam and synthetic honey; grinding grain into flour; and providing food for orphanages, hospitals, soup kitchens, and refugee centers. Throughout the ghetto period, the office was headed by Abraham Gepner, fortunately one of the handful of *Judenrat* officials of unquestioned talent and wide respect.

The German office, the *Transferstelle*, was charged with carrying out official policy with respect to provisioning the ghetto. It was headed first by Alexander Palfinger. He had had experience with the ghetto at Łódż and attempted to transfer the rigid approach used there to Warsaw. This was not found acceptable by the Nazi hierarchy, who wanted Warsaw's ghetto to be economically productive, so Palfinger was replaced by Max Bischoff, who held this responsibility until the ghetto disappeared in 1943. In Gutman's opinion, Bischoff tried to have the food rations for the Jews increased. One gets the impression that his actions were motivated "more by rational thinking than by blind ideological hatred."[70] Though it is small consolation, it seems that the ghetto might have been worse served had someone else been in charge of the *Transferstelle*.

Nevertheless, Gepner and his Jewish Supply Authority faced a heartbreaking and ultimately hopeless task. The rations were simply grossly insufficient, and no efforts at persuasion influenced the Germans to make significant changes. The Supply Authority could not be involved in smuggling food and could react to needs within the ghetto only in terms of what the Germans permitted to come in.

Nor was what entered the ghetto necessarily of high quality. Between July and December 1941, the chemical and bacteriological institute of the Health Department examined various specimens of imported food and found one-third to be unsatisfactory.[71] This finding merely quantified what every Jew knew already from personal experience.

Among religiously observant Jews, many rules govern foods that are permitted and their preparation—*kashrut*. Except for the exceptionally devout, observances of *kashrut* lapsed during these trying times. *Sh'hita*, the ritual slaughter of animals, was forbidden by the Nazis, and in at least one case clandestine practitioners paid with their lives.[72] Cows were occasionally smuggled in and butchered to provide kosher meat.[73] But the issue was not a problem for much of the time because meat was almost nonexistent in the ghetto.[74] Nevertheless, kosher lunches were available at least as late as 1941; refugees given free lunch privileges could have their applications stamped "kosher" and then be assigned to a kitchen where the dietary laws were observed.[75] These kitchens were located at Nalewki 37, Zamenhof 11, 22, and 44, Ciepla 10, and Nowolipie 15, among others.[76] There was, inevitably, a committee to look after the interests of those matters, and one of its activities was to promote the observance of these dietary laws, reminding the refugees that forbidden foods "decay the soul and body, the Jewish heart, the Jew's entire being."[77] But in the harsh reality of the Warsaw ghetto, fewer and fewer Jews felt able to follow the rules of *kashrut*.

COLLECTIVE AID FOR THE STARVING

Aid was required from September 1939 on. In October it was reported that of all the prewar Jewish welfare organizations, only the Joint has been able to continue its relief efforts.[78] Gradually, the others resumed their work. But the need was enormous. The directors of the Joint in Warsaw assumed in November that 75 percent of the Jewish population needed immediate assistance.[79] In December the Joint provided 50,000 dinners for adults and 25,000 breakfasts, as well as meals for uncounted thousands of children. The cost for the month was 905,000 zloty.[80]

By June 1940, the Center for Refugees at Spokojna 13 was overflowing. As a consequence, infectious diseases broke out and the center was periodically quarantined. This put yet another pressure on TOZ, which provided food to the quarantined refugees.[81] But the problem was by no means just a question of the inflow of refugees. The Joint found that because of the destruction of 30 percent of the Jewish homes in Warsaw, the number of those requesting aid grew rapidly. About 25,000 Jewish families (125,000 persons) became homeless, and "these were mostly people who had never asked for help but always helped the poor."[82] The pool of needy Jews had been much enlarged.

In January 1940, 70 kitchens under the subvention of the Joint provided 87,000 lunches to Jews in Warsaw. That number fell to 73,500 in February. Food packages were delivered to about 10,000 Jews.[83] By September 1940, the number of kitchens was only 50 and the number of meals served had fallen to 29,600. However, one should not conclude from this that there was more food and less hunger. The decrease occurred entirely involuntarily because of the diminishing funds of the Joint.[84]

In mid-1941, an observer estimated that of the 500,000 Jews in the Warsaw ghetto, 250,000 would be classified as being poor enough to need social aid, though the available food permitted the community to serve only 120,000 soup rations a day (see Figure 6.1).[85] By comparison, outside the ghetto, the Polish self-help organization was providing at its peak, in May 1941, 133,000 lunches[86]—not many more than were going to the Jewish population, though the number of gentile Poles was more than twice the number of Jews. The increasing need within the ghetto is displayed by the fact that on 19 June 1941, 102,000 lunches were served and, two weeks later, the figure had risen to 117,481.[87] Some idea of what such a "lunch" contributed to the recipient's nutrition is conveyed by Czerniakow's rueful assessment: "I write verse occasionally. A vivid imagination is needed for that, but never did I have the imagination to refer to the soup that we are doling out to the public as lunch."[88] Even less poetic is the scientific information that soup at the public kitchens varied between 170 and 227 calories per serving.[89] And for many, the noon lunch of soup was the main meal for the day.

A worker's ration a year later was a quarter of a loaf of bread daily plus some watery cabbage soup; "Who can be spurred to work with this kind of food?"[90] But the need far exceeded the means that could be found, not only privately but also in the community.

Even in the hospitals, no respite was possible. The daily food ration authorized by the Germans for each patient was estimated by an internist there as supplying,

Figure 6.1. Kitchen for Orthodox Jews at 21 Nalewki; coming for supper (reproduced by permission of Yad Vashem Archives, Jerusalem: YVA FA 36-2128).

at the most, 800 calories. Death from starvation was, therefore, as common in the hospital as in the street or at home.[91] Here, just one example among thousands, is how the last few moments in the life of a Jewish child were spent. This boy is not lying in a gutter somewhere; he is in a hospital in the Warsaw ghetto:

> In the entrance hall lies a boy of five, swollen with hunger. He is in the last stage, his life ending because of hunger. He came to the hospital yesterday. Eyes swollen, hands and feet puffed up like balloons. Every possible analysis is being made; maybe kidneys, perhaps heart. No, neither this nor that. The child still moves his lips, he begs for some bread. I try to feed him something, hoping he could take something down. Alas, the throat is swollen shut, nothing passes down, too late. The doctor asks him "did you get anything to eat at home?" "No." "Would you like to eat now?" "Yes!" Some few minutes later he utters for the last time "a piece of bread," and with this expression he sinks in sleep. Dead for a piece of bread.[92]

This was March 1941, only five months after the ghetto was created. A year before, things must have slightly better; a nurse recorded that in March 1940 one of her patients suffering from tuberculosis was fed five times a day.[93] Probably the quantities were small. He asked the nurse if she could take some of his food to his mother, who was in a refugee center and had nothing.

In August of the same year, a handbill soliciting aid for the Jewish Welfare Society (*Yiddishe Geselshaft far Aleinhilf*) refers to "[s]hocking cases of death from star-

Figure 6.2. Child, probably with hunger edema, Warsaw ghetto, 1941 or 1942 (Anonymous, *The Warsaw Ghetto,* Warsaw: Interpress Publishers, 1988).

vation among our intelligentsia,"[94] who presumably had no salable skills that would have permitted them to earn wages and thus supplement their food supplies. On the street one day, a child snatched a parcel that contained a paraffin candle and began to eat it. Crying, he apologized, saying he did it because he was hungry.[95] Meanwhile the rich, as everywhere, could get whatever they wanted, "from white pastries to the best fish, and the poor are dying on the streets from hunger."[96]

Throughout the ghetto, efforts were made to feed the hungry. House collectives tried to provide food for the poor among them; charitable and political groups created kitchens, orphanages, and children's shelters; and various other centers arose.[97] Besides the obvious vital function of kitchens, these places became centers for a number of activities quite unrelated to food. The Germans had forbidden mass assemblies; the Jews substituted the gatherings at kitchens as places to disseminate news, organize political activities, educate children, and recruit for the fighting organizations.[98]

Aid was also received from outside Poland. Jewish organizations inside Poland, particularly CENTOS and TOZ, had for years received a substantial portion of their funding from the Joint in the United States. That practice continued during the war, though the process became exceedingly complicated because the Joint was absolutely determined not to flout American wartime legislation designed to ensure that neither financial nor material aid should go to the German war machine.

One way out of the problem of getting money to Poland was provided by coop-

eration with the *Reichsvereinigung der Juden in Deutschland* (RJD). This organization existed to promote emigration of Jews from Germany. The arrangement
with the Joint was simplicity itself once the mechanics were worked out. German
Jews leaving the country were not permitted to take money with them aside from
a token sum. They gave German Reichsmarks to the RJD equivalent to what would
be needed to purchase their boat and train fares. The Joint purchased these tickets
in unoccupied Europe or North America with its money. The RJD then had money
in its bank account that could be forwarded to the Polish Joint to sustain their
efforts.[99] The *Generalgouvernement* was part of the Third Reich, so the Germans
permitted the transactions. Joint money was not supporting the war effort; just the
contrary—not only were they helping to rescue Jews, but they also were depriving
the Nazi government of Jewish funds that it might otherwise have confiscated.

Unfortunately, this scheme foundered when Jewish emigration from Germany
was stopped. But it does show the ingenuity that went into attempts to get relief to
Jews in occupied Poland.

Some of the difficulties with which outside agencies contended are outlined in
the report of a meeting between a Joint official and a representative of the Polish
government-in-exile held in Paris early in 1940. At this meeting the problems were

Figure 6.3. Baby dead of starvation, Warsaw ghetto, ca 1941–42
(reproduced by permission of
Yad Vashem Archives, Jerusalem: YVA 43-D-03).

summarized: First, the British would permit relief supplies to pass through their naval blockade only if distribution could be supervised to ensure that the supplies went to needy Poles. The German government wouldn't agree to any such proposal for outside control and also seemed to be deliberately stalling. Up to that date, the Joint had stayed out of the discussions, since it was believed that negotiations might more likely be fruitful if the discussants were nonsectarian; the proponents were the Quakers and the American Red Cross. Finally, food was increasingly difficult to obtain in bulk either in Poland itself or in the neighboring countries.[100] In December 1940, for example, a Joint Committee reluctantly decided that it could not support requests from Poland that food be imported there from Slovakia. That territory was "virtually under German control," and the Joint could not justify sending American dollars there even to feed the Jews of Poland.[101] These and other hurdles hindered all progress, no matter how determined the efforts.

Supplying aid to Poland was extremely complicated even when the aid was for Poles in general. The Commission for Polish Relief (CPR), was set up in the United States on 25 September 1939. It was nonsectarian, "a strictly neutral, entirely humanitarian undertaking."[102] The CPR was patterned on the relief operations administered by Herbert Hoover after World War I.

For the next 15 months the CPR labored to raise money, to find a way through bureaucratic jungles on both sides of the Atlantic, and to get food and clothing to Poland. They succeeded in many ways. In June 1940, the CPR sent a large shipment of food from the United States and Norway (cod liver oil) to their distributing centers in Warsaw, Radom, and Lublin.[103] The food included 540,000 pounds of evaporated milk and 1,260,000 pounds of rye flour. About one-quarter of their shipments went to Jewish children, and there were arrangements for the replacement of bacon and pork for these children, with herring from Norway.[104] Moreover, a CPR official accompanied the shipment and ultimately reported that he saw materials distributed to Jews as well as to gentiles.[105] But despite these extremely helpful successes, ultimately the CPR failed. In December 1940, the group announced that because of lack of funds, it was winding up its work in Poland.[106]

All efforts of these high-minded organizations were only of short-term value. Lives were sustained for a few days or hours. But the dying went on; Czerniakow reported to the Nazis that 1700 Jews had died in the first half of May 1941 "due to the insufficient food allocation (13 groszy [2.5 cents], on the average, per day for a Jew—35 groszy for a Pole)."[107] Eight months later, a delegation from the welfare shelters called on Czerniakow to inform him that 20 percent of their charges had died of starvation.[108] In February 1941, it was estimated that the Jews of Łodź were being fed on 23 pfennigs daily, less than half what was being spent by the German administration on feeding common prisoners in jail.[109]

SMUGGLING

Smuggled food preserved life in the ghetto for many months longer than the Jews could have existed on the official ration alone. The leaders of the *Judenrat* understood perfectly well how dependent the ghetto was on this illegal and clandestine source. Adam Czerniakow estimated that 80 percent of the food entering the ghetto was smuggled in,[110] and Dr. Milejkowski stated unequivocally that "smuggling food from the Aryan part of Warsaw curtailed the prevalence of hunger, its spread, its tempo, and its irreversibility."[111]

Nor was the existence of smuggling any secret to the Germans. The guards at the gates observed it daily, sometimes only confiscating the food but, all too often, jailing or killing the smuggler. On 13 June 1941, Auerswald told Czerniakow that the German authorities were "looking the other way" as far as smuggling was concerned.[112] When Dr. Wilhelm Hagen, who had succeeded Schrempf as chief of the German medical service in Warsaw, was asked to supply milk for babies, he refused on the basis that the Jews could get it on the black market, a response that drew from Ringelblum the dismayed comment that his attitude had been a generally humane one up to then.[113] Hagen claimed that by the summer of 1941, the milk supply to Warsaw was only 2 percent of normal.[114] Because of disruption of farming, exportation to Germany, and problems of transportation, the amount available had dropped from a prewar level of 300,000 liters a day to only 6000 liters. Thus, for 50,000 infants under 18 months of age, who needed it most acutely, almost nothing could be provided.[115] And the 50,000 children referred to by Hagen were Poles, not Jews. For Jewish children there was no fresh milk. As has been mentioned, some evaporated milk reached Jewish children via the CPR. In 1941, the Joint succeeded in having a shipment of Nestle's milk sent to the Warsaw ghetto— 7000 cans.[116] This was, of course, only a tiny fraction of what was required.

Smuggling was carried out at two levels. There were the amateur smugglers, working alone or in small groups, and there were the professionals, bringing in bulk quantities of supplies and protecting themselves by bribing German, Polish, and Jewish gate guards, as well as higher German officials.

Among the amateurs, children were perhaps the most effective. Memoirs of the ghetto abound with stories of these children, often the sole support of their parents, who went out into Aryan Warsaw day after day, begging for food and bringing home to their families a few potatoes, some kasha, or a loaf of bread. Some risked traveling through the gates, counting on their small size and the supposed German weakness for children to protect them. This might work for days or weeks, but often enough they would creep home bruised and battered, their treasures taken away from them. And many died at the gates, shot by a German or Polish guard whose antisemitism made Jewish children unlovable.

Another route for individual smugglers was the wall. Though it was 10 feet high and topped by broken glass, it was not impregnable. In places it was lower, or the glass had been crushed and flattened, or enough bricks had been removed in some out-of-the-way corner so that a small gap existed—the smallness being another reason for the preeminence of children in this dangerous trade. These routes were more dangerous than the gates. An unlucky child, leaping down from the wall or emerging through a hole in the view of a guard, was unquestionably doing something illegal; shots or severe beatings, often resulting in death, were a frequent result.

Christian Poles also participated actively in this work. For much of the life of the ghetto, streetcars ran through it connecting the adjacent non-Jewish sections. These streetcars could be used only by the Poles and did not stop in the ghetto, but some enterprising Poles bribed the conductors so that the cars slowed down at some point and the Poles leaped off, bearing sacks of food for sale at black market prices.[117]

Many Poles did try to help, at least to the extent of giving food to the Jewish beggar children who approached them. Kindly street sweepers were known to "sweep" objects such as parcels of food or clothing into the rain culverts, where the Jewish children could crawl in and retrieve them.[118]

Other techniques for smuggling existed. One required a confederate inside the wall at an agreed-upon place and time; objects would be thrown over the wall, to be retrieved and quickly hidden. The chief risk here was that while the thrower could bide his or her time until it seemed safe to throw, there was no way to know if conditions were safe for the recipient. Often they were not, so that at best the goods were lost. On 26 February 1942, for example, a parcel sailed over the wall and over the head of Heinz Auerswald, Nazi *Kommissar* of the ghetto, just as he was getting out of his car at the Housing Office on Nowolipie Street. He was not amused.[119]

The Jewish cemetery on Okopowa Street was a particularly favored site for smuggling.[120] Hearses entered the cemetery bearing their accustomed burdens but might return laden with bread and flour.[121] When the deportations began, the smuggling reversed its direction, and many Jews were able to slip into Warsaw and, in some cases, to safety over the cemetery walls.

These efforts, valuable as they were to a few, could not have made a major difference to the lives of the Jews as a whole. For this, the professionals deserve the chief credit. And their efforts were prodigious, though at least as self-serving as they were altruistic. The potential for profit was immense, though paralleled by the risk. Ringelblum noted in his diary in September 1941 that the month before, the price of bread in gentile Warsaw was higher than it was in the ghetto, reflecting the fact that so much bread had been smuggled into the ghetto in August that supplies outside were grossly deficient.[122]

Rubinlicht worked the black market during the war. One of his deals was a transaction for *dupniki*, which he identified as "not a very nice Polish word" meaning rectum. It comes from the Polish slang word *dupa* for behind/rump/ass/butt. Before the war, slaughterhouses discarded the rectums of cattle, but now they washed them and put them in large barrels. Rubinlicht was able to arrange a deal, finding butchers in the ghetto who were happy to buy these barrels. They entered the ghetto hidden under piles of refuse. The butchers washed the rectums, passed them through their grinders, and sold the product—*dupniki*—as ground meat. "This was the meat—a delicacy if you could find it—of the ghetto!"[123]

AGRICULTURE AND MANUFACTURE

The Hospital of the Holy Ghost, largely destroyed by German bombing in September 1939, lay within the ghetto walls. In June 1941, the grounds had become a field planted with vegetables.[124] TOPOROL, the Society for Promoting Agriculture among the Jews, played an active role in the Warsaw ghetto. Under their aegis and with their help, vegetables and flowers were planted in about 200 yards.[125]

A farm functioned in the suburb of Czerniakow, near Warsaw, from the beginning of the war until the deportations began. This was a working farm operated by Jews who were members of Dror He-Halutz, part of the radical youth movement.[126] In 1942, more than 140 youths were on the farm.[127] It supplied some food to the ghetto, and in addition it was a cover for underground activities. The Germans disbanded the farm on 10 December 1942, and the 83 remaining members joined the fighting organization inside the walls.[128] For many months it had helped to feed the ghetto, though only in a small way.

CANNIBALISM

In all situations in which food for human beings is severely limited, the consumption of human flesh can occur as a dietary necessity, as a matter of survival. Though such a practice is found repugnant by most in the late twentieth century, there is abundant proof that this is the case. Cannibalism occurred in the jungles of New Guinea and Leyte among Japanese troops during the Second World War. It seems to have taken place among the citizens of Leningrad late in the German siege and blockade of that city.[129] In the concentration camp called Dora, according to an eyewitness to at least the punishment, starving prisoners broke into the morgue and cut meat from the corpses. When caught, they were forced by the Germans to devour the testicles and then were hanged.[130]

Three cases of cannibalism are documented in the Warsaw ghetto. At least a few more must have occurred, given the large number of people dying of starvation and the all too ready availability of corpses. In all three documented cases, the situation was that of a mother eating portions of a dead child. One took place at Śliska 53, on 15 December 1941; another at Solna 30, date unknown;[131] and the third at Krochmalna 18, apartment 20, on 19 February 1942.[132] One of these sad events involved a mother who was probably insane, since she was observed at her awful task over a period of time by many passersby in the streets. These included a nurse; the interviewee, Eugenia Pernal;[133] and Professor Ludwig Hirszfeld, who described seeing a mother with "insane eyes" biting the dead body of her child.[134] Possibly the persons they observed were the unfortunate woman and child at Śliska 53, since Pernal was a nurse working at the Berson and Bauman Hospital, located very close to that address.

Some details of the episode at Krochmalna Street are recorded in the memoir by Adler. According to him, this event took place in mid-1941, but almost certainly this is the same episode dated precisely by Czerniakow in his diary as occurring on 19 February 1942. Adler was a member of the *Ordnungsdienst* and cited an official report. A 12-year-old boy was found dead in a cellar apartment: "His buttocks had been cut off, and his own mother was eating the flesh. In another hole, occupied by an old beggar-woman, five decomposed corpses were found."[135]

Errors occur in many of the accounts written about cannibalism in the ghetto. For example, Trunk refers to the cases as instances where three mothers ate parts of the bodies of their "babies,"[136] though we know that at least one victim was a 12-year-old boy, not a baby. Tannahill, in her book on cannibalism, gives a quite inaccurate account of this event; she cites a report of 21 March 1942 by the Warsaw propaganda division of the *Generalgouvernement* to the effect that this episode was the first noted in the ghetto, though it was at least the third, and also stating that the guilty mother had died about two days afterward.[137] But Turkow gives the name of the victim as Berek Urman,[138] and he has detailed knowledge that Berek's mother did not die two days later. While a prisoner in Gęsiówka, the *Ordnungsdienst* jail on Gęsia Street, Turkow saw Mrs. Urman, who was a prisoner there in the women's section. "She was a short, thin woman, with a numb, bloodless face, and dull, expressionless eyes."[139] The woman was not destined to enjoy freedom again. In order to avoid a trial that would have brought the whole story to public knowledge, she was held in the prison hospital as insane. When the liquidation of the Warsaw ghetto began, she and the other inmates of the prison were among the first groups to be sent to Treblinka. So she died five months after being discovered eating her dead son.

Janusz Korczak recorded an incident of relevance here, though not too much should be read into it. He was shopping one day and purchased 50 grams of smoked sausage (for which he paid 20 zloty and noted that it used to be 80 groschen). Korczak had a mordant wit, and asked the clerk if the sausage was made of human flesh because it was too cheap to be horsemeat. He was bemused by the fact that she answered quite matter-of-factly: she didn't know because she hadn't been there when the sausage was made. But she didn't acknowledge recognizing a joke, or being dismayed or horrified at the possibility that it *might* be human meat.[140]

Late in 1942, when only a small fraction of the Jews remained alive in Warsaw, both the gentile Poles and the Jews were given cans of preserved meat. The rumor spread in Christian Warsaw that the meat had been made from the flesh of murdered Jews, and the Poles, revolted, refused to eat it.[141]

SCIENTIFIC STUDY OF HUNGER AND STARVATION

So widespread was hunger that it became the topic for a major scientific study carried out clandestinely by the medical profession within the ghetto, on the practical principle that starvation was the one thing they had in unfailing abundance.[142] The results of the study, recording work done by many scientists and physicians, were smuggled out of the ghetto and hidden by sympathetic colleagues until after the war, when they were published in French[143] and Polish[144] and, more recently, in a condensed version in English.[145] Many of the contributors also were members of the faculty of the underground medical school. For the majority, the research on hunger disease was their last scientific work.

Dr. Milejkowski, one of the originators of the hunger disease project along with Czerniakow, Abraham Gepner, and David Guzik (of the Joint Distribution Committee),[146] indicated in his Introduction how the research study came to be and how it was pursued:

> Hunger was the most important factor of everyday life within the wall of the Warsaw ghetto. Its symptoms consisted of crowds of beggars and corpses often lying in the streets covered with newspapers. Mortality data on hunger and its two com-

panions, tuberculosis and typhus, were collected from orphanages and refugee centers and from specific hospital material.[147]

The work began in February 1942. It was done clandestinely. The attitude of the Germans to work of this sort was described by Dr. Emil Apfelbaum, one of the chief researchers into hunger disease and an internist at Czyste. He saw groups of SS and Gestapo searching the hospital for scientific records, "threatening repeatedly that Jews have no right to scientific work."[148]

The research carried out and preserved justified the effort and supported the determination of the Jewish physicians and scientists to attempt to benefit from their adversity. Before World War II, no systematic medical research had been done into the effects of long-term, generalized starvation on large numbers of human beings. During the war, two major studies were carried out, each of which advanced medical science. One was the extensive research of Prof. Ancel Keys and a large group of collaborators in Minnesota, studying volunteers, mostly university students, who undertook long periods of carefully monitored starvation or deprivation, and whose body functions were studied in great detail.[149] The other study was the one carried out in the Warsaw ghetto.

Of the work done between February and July 1942 in Warsaw, perhaps half of the studies were completed and were preserved until after the war. These portions survived and have come down to us. A detailed exposition of the findings would not be appropriate here, but a summary will give an indication of what was accomplished and a hint of what has been lost.

The book in English has seven chapters. Two are general descriptions of what effects hunger disease had on adults and children. The third chapter examines the effect of hunger disease on the human metabolism, the fourth the alterations in the heart and blood vessels, the fifth the effects on the blood and bone marrow, the sixth diseases affecting the eye, and the seventh and final chapter the alterations caused by hunger disease as seen by gross and microscopic examinations of the body after death.

General Changes in Adults

Julian Fliederbaum and his fellow researchers observed that the first signs of hunger disease in adults were constant thirst and a substantial increase in the amount of urine passed, signs that occurred after even a short period of hunger.[150] As hunger continued, these symptoms decreased but were replaced by profound weakness and the inability to sustain even the smallest physical effort,[151] and the patients became unwilling to work. They felt chilled, depressed, and uninterested in everything around them until they saw food; then they sometimes became aggressive, stuffing themselves regardless of circumstances.

Seen in the hospital wards or in homes and refugee shelters, the sufferers from hunger disease lay curled in the fetal position, always sleepy and always cold, so that they covered themselves with whatever they could find, even in warm weather. Zylberberg described someone in this condition:

> I noticed in the crowd an old friend of mine, Gershon Fraenkel. Just before the war he had completed his Oriental studies in Belgium; now, he was hardly recognizable.

His normally corpulent frame was emaciated; he was wearing two suits and a heavy winter top coat, not realizing, apparently, that this was the heat of late summer. The perspiration was pouring down his face.[152]

On admission to the hospital the patients were pale and bluish-looking, had very faint pulses, and were in a state of collapse. Unlike normal persons, they had little reaction in blood pressure to physical stress. Their lungs did not seem to function normally, and they often had symptoms of bowel inflammation: noisy bowels, drum-belly appearance, and copious bowel movements that accentuated the swelling of the feet and legs and hastened death.

The hospitalized patients weighed between 30 and 40 kilograms, which was 20 to 50 percent below normal for age and sex in the prewar Jewish population. Fliederbaum recorded data on one 30-year-old woman who was 152 centimeters (5 feet 8 inches) tall and weighed 24 kilograms (53 pounds). In the final stages of hunger, all patients, but especially the women, looked far older than their years.

General Changes in Children

In children,[153] the earliest changes were in their behavior. They were apathetic, stopped playing, lost their sense of humor, and simply slowed down all their activities. They became quarrelsome and irritable, and in some cases their intellectual level became so low that they seemed retarded, though they were known not to be.

Those children not swollen with edema looked like skeletons covered with skin. They had all the signs just mentioned for adults, of which the diarrhea was particularly pronounced. One effect seen more often in children than in adults was the formation of contractures, so that the arms or legs became fixed in a drawn-up or curled-up position and could not be straightened. Even a child fortunate enough to be caught in time and to recover on a temporarily adequate diet retained these disfiguring contractures long after other signs had disappeared. Of course, they prevented the child from walking.

A characteristic and dramatic feature in these children was their unusual reaction to other diseases. When children with hunger disease simultaneously developed an infectious disease such as measles, diphtheria, tuberculosis, or chickenpox, they did not show the usual symptoms of these diseases. Instead of having high temperatures, they had little fever. The diagnostic skin eruptions were less than those in nonstarved children. But the children with hunger disease and infection grew sicker and died of their infection despite the lack of symptoms.

The immune systems in these children had become deficient under the stress of starvation. The Jewish physicians in the Warsaw ghetto recognized the existence of an immune deficiency. Immunity is a complex phenomenon, and most of what we know in the 1990s has been discovered since World War II. We know now that there are two immune systems. The system involved with the reaction to infection was damaged in these children, but the other system was not, or less so; thus the ghetto children would have responded normally or nearly normally to artificial immunization (had vaccines been available) even though they were much more at risk once they became infected.[154]

Metabolic Changes

The metabolism was affected significantly in hunger disease.[155] According to the editors, this chapter represents the most sophisticated research attempted by the ghetto physicians:

> [T]he decision to undertake this kind of investigation under the conditions that were prevalent in the ghetto must have been made with full awareness of the odds against getting any really meaningful results. In spite of this, the studies were initiated and carried out meticulously and have given us extraordinary data that have stood the test of time.[156]

The researchers studied various aspects of hunger disease relating to temperature regulation, the adaptation of the heart and blood vessels, regulation of hormones, and adaptation to hunger by tissues and cells. In broad summary, they found dramatic evidence of the capacity of the human body to adapt to even so profound a challenge as lengthy and serious underfeeding. Starvation precipitated the clinical deficiency of several hormones. In hunger disease there were no findings that permitted the researchers to state which vitamin deficiencies were most pronounced, and "no therapy with a single vitamin or with a vitamin complex is able to reverse the clinical and biochemical symptoms of hunger disease."[157]

The Circulatory System in Hunger Disease

According to the authors of Chapter Four,[158] "the motor of life stops not because of a dissociation between particular parts but because of a lack of fuel."[159] The evidence suggested that the body manages its energy balance differently in hunger disease, the demands of that state resembling those of animals hibernating in the winter. The systolic blood pressure is unnaturally low, though the diastolic pressure is more or less normal. Because loss of body weight outruns decreasing blood volume, there is relatively more blood in the body than during health, and this presents a major and sometimes fatal load for the heart to pump, since the poorly nourished cardiac muscle has to work much harder than in a normal individual.[160]

Changes in the Eyes

According to the editors, the research on eye changes describe at least three observations that were new in the 1940s. Patients suffering from hunger disease developed cloudy lenses, the pressure within the eyeball decreased compared to normal, and the whites of the eye took on an unusual bluish hue.[161]

Pathological Changes in the Body

In the prosectorium, or autopsy room, pathologists and students labored over the painstaking examinations of hundreds of bodies.[162] Up to the time of the destruction of Czyste Hospital and the end of pathological work there in September 1942, 3658 autopsies were done, of which 3282 were complete; 491 of these (15 percent) were done on patients who had died of hunger disease.[163] Indeed, during the first six months of 1942 only limited pathological studies were done on patients dying from other diseases, so that more time could be devoted to the studies of hunger disease.[164]

The difficulties of the entire research program on hunger disease are summed up by Stein and Fenigstein, who point out that

> the poor nutrition and poor general living conditions in the ghetto created a very difficult climate for scientific work. The lack of libraries, the lack of instruments and reagents, and the low morale associated with the constant fear of losing one's life were ever present for all. [In September 1942] . . . the hospital, its institutes, laboratories, autopsy rooms, and library were completely destroyed, making any further work impossible. . . . Organs preserved in formalin were completely destroyed.[165]

Nevertheless, much important work was done, requiring the cooperation of many workers.[166] With the exception of microscopic observations on six patients dying of hunger disease, published in the French and Polish volumes but omitted from the English one,[167] none of the microscopic research has come down to us.[168] This is unfortunate because the microscopist, a German Jew named Gilde, was well trained and conscientious.[169] He was probably deported to Treblinka before completing his manuscript.

The gross examinations revealed much of value. In the 491 starvation victims on whose bodies autopsies were performed, nutrition was graded as "poor" in 34 (6.9 percent), "very poor" in 173 (35.2 percent), and "terrible" in 284 (57.9 percent).[170] The weight of the brain remained approximately normal, but the heart, liver, kidneys, and spleen were much lighter than normal.[171] Changes were also found in the intestines. Clinically, it seemed that the patients had dysentery,[172] but bacteriological and serological tests proved that this was not the case.[173] Finally, in those patients who had edema at the time of death, this was found chiefly in the torso in 18, the arms in 21, and the legs in 157; 33 percent of these patients had generalized edema at autopsy.[174]

The investigators presented their findings at least once at a scientific meeting held at Czyste Hospital on 6 July 1942. Adam Czerniakow attended the presentations; he recorded that the session was chaired by Dr. Milejkowski and that papers were read by Drs. Apfelbaum, Stein, Fliederbaum, and Drein[175] (the last evidently being one of those whose work did not survive, though Fenigstein does not recall anyone by this name doing medical research). Sixteen days later, the massive deportations to Treblinka began, Czerniakow committed suicide in despair, and all scientific work ceased except for the efforts of survivors to complete and preserve their manuscripts.

In October 1942, with three-quarters of Warsaw's Jews murdered, Dr. Milejkowski was completing his editorial work on the hunger disease manuscript. Wryly, he mentioned that he was actually doing this work "in one of the undestroyed rooms of the cemetery buildings. This is the symbol of our living and working environment."[176] Other survivors who labored on, intent on preserving some scientific contribution from their ordeal, were Henry and Ala Fenigstein, who prepared the statistics for the pathological section of the report, the chief author of which was Dr. Josef Stein.[177]

Winick has paid tribute to the Jewish physicians and scientists who performed these investigations:

> These were not investigators who came in, did their tests, and went home. These were physicians, dealing with the easiest disease to cure, and helpless to effect that cure. They cared for their patients in whatever manner they had available, and at the same time carefully noted their deterioration. Afflicted with the same disease, knowing that their time was limited, they persevered.[178]

The efforts to supply Poland's Jews with food from outside the country continued into 1943. Early in that year, the Board of Deputies of British Jews supplied the Polish Committee of the Joint with a list of 12,559 specific names and addresses of Jews in Poland. The Committee sent individual parcels of figs (the only permitted item) to each individual on the list, with a request for acknowledgment. By July, only 925 had been acknowledged, and of those, only 76 personally. The others were receipted by the *Judenrat* of the town of the addressee. Of the 76 personal acknowledgments, 22 were from Warsaw addresses[179]—this from a city that had had 400,000 Jewish residents before the war. The evidence was unequivocal. Hunger was no longer a problem. Warsaw's Jews were almost all dead, and the Warsaw ghetto was completely destroyed.

7

Typhus, the Terror
of the Ghetto

Typhus is a central theme in the existence of the Warsaw ghetto. Memoirs invariably mention the disease, some at great length and with deep emotion. For this reason alone, no historian can neglect mentioning typhus fever. But there are at least two additional reasons for giving the disease a major emphasis in this book. First, from the beginning of the war, typhus became the great whipping boy for the Nazis, the rationalization of their ghetto policy: a "scientific" explanation for the forced isolation of the Jews and a justification for a long list of edicts and impositions. Typhus also requires careful attention for the paradoxical reason that it was, in strictly medical terms, *less* important than the memoirs would have us believe. In retrospect, typhus may not have been the most serious disease affecting the residents of the Warsaw ghetto. That possibility is explored in Chapter 8.

THE WORD "TYPHUS"

There is a problem in the terminology of typhus that can be a source of misunderstanding. The confusion arises because typhus is called *Fleckfieber* in German (see Figure 7.1), but typhoid fever, a totally different disease, is called *Typhus*. And in at least one Polish-English dictionary, both typhoid and typhus are translated as *tyfusowy*, typhoid also being referred to as *tyfus* and *dur brzuszny*.[1] Additional Polish synonyms include *dur plamisty*, *dur wysypkowy*, and *osutkowy*. This confusion in terminology must be kept in mind when reading articles,[2] books,[3] transcripts of interviews with survivors of these times (who often use the words interchangeably),[4] and translations from European languages made by translators who are unaware of the problem.[5] But it was *typhus* that ravaged the ghetto, and it was *typhus* that the Germans claimed had a special affinity for Jews.

A SHORT HISTORY OF TYPHUS FEVER

Typhus fever seems to have arrived in western Europe from Asia about five centuries ago,[6] but there is no reason to suppose that the disease has not existed somewhere in the world for countless millennia. However, earlier diseases identified by the name "typhus" seem quite different clinically from the disease we see in the twentieth century. For example, there are descriptions of a disease named typhus in the writings of the Hippocratic School (ca. 450 B.C.) entitled "Internal Affec-

Figure 7.1. Typhus quarantine in Warsaw ghetto (Bundesarchiv, Koblenz).

tions." Most of these references are to disorders that seem largely abdominal in their main effects, and in none is a rash mentioned.[7] Typhus in the modern sense has been identified clearly only since the mid-1500s, when Jerome Cardan, an Italian physician, wrote about a disease characterized by a rash that looked like the bites of fleas.[8] From his clinical description there seems no doubt that he was seeing typhus, though he called the disease *morbus pulicaris* (from *pulex*, the Latin word for flea). Because the book in which this observation was published was a contentious manual pointing out to Cardan's fellow physicians the mistakes they were making in diagnosis and treatment, it seems obvious that typhus was common in Italy then.

Just a few years later, Fracastorius, also Italian, similarly noted the resemblance of the rash to flea bites, probably not a difficult diagnostic feat since fleas and other vermin were every day visitors among all classes of European society at the time. Fracastorius advanced our knowledge of the disease a step further by noting that typhus was contagious, but not rapidly and only by handling the sick.[9] He was correct, but how handling the sick conveyed the disease would not be proven until early in the twentieth century. In the context of studying typhus in the Warsaw ghetto, it is interesting to note that Fracastorius specified that in Verona "almost none of the Jews perished."[10]

One of the earliest medical contributions from North America concerned typhus. In 1570, Francisco Bravo, a Spaniard, published in Mexico City his description of the disease, emphasizing the severe headache, lassitude, intense fever, and often dizziness or symptoms of coma and delirium.[11] Tobias Cober, an Austrian, seemingly was the first to mention lice explicitly in conjunction with typhus in 1606. He did not suggest any causative relationship, though he noted with feeling the ubiquity of lice in army camps of the day. He had thought that he could avoid these pests "by always dressing with fresh linen, but this I have proved of itself attracts many of them, much less destroying them."[12]

Thomas Willis carried Cober's observation a step further. During the English Civil War, he noted that when the troops were billeted in very close quarters in a healthy town and "had filled all things with filthiness and unwholesome nastiness, and stinking odors," they began to fall sick with typhus; so did the families with whom they were billeted, and then the neighbors, and so on.[13] A century later, James Lind, the great British naval surgeon, reported that whatever caused the disease (and he admitted that he did not know what that was), it could be destroyed by great heat "like that of an oven."[14]

Finally, in 1909, Charles Nicolle published his Nobel Prizewinning research showing why lice were commonly found in times of epidemics and why heat could eliminate the cause. He discovered that typhus is transmitted by lice, and of course, lice can be killed by sufficiently high temperatures.[15]

Typhus is caused by a *Rickettsia* (a microorganism or germ smaller than bacteria but larger than viruses); actually, typhus is a closely related family of diseases caused by various *Rickettsia* organisms. Classical epidemic typhus, which is the variety that terrorized the Germans and killed so many Jews, is a product of the organism *Rickettsia prowazeki* and requires the human body louse, *Pediculis humanis*, to incubate the organism and to convey it from human to human.

Typhus occurs sporadically in most parts of the world. Probably some humans are typhus carriers. They retain the germ in their system, from which it can, when conditions are right, be conveyed to others, though they themselves are not ill with the disease. Alternatively, mild forms of typhus may occur that become more serious epidemic typhus when conditions are bad. In North America, so-called Brill's disease may be an example from the second category,[16] though the transformation into epidemic disease has never occurred.

The social conditions that predispose to epidemic typhus are overcrowding, inadequate sanitation, and general dislocation of life. These conditions prevail regularly in wartime and were especially likely to be seen in the ghettos of Poland in the early 1940s, among other places. They also characterize existence in the jails and aboard the crowded, slow sailing vessels of earlier times, thus explaining the common lay terms for typhus before the twentieth century: "jail fever" and "ship's fever."

Although the rat plays a crucial role in transmitting some types of typhus, in epidemic typhus it seems unimportant, the reservoir of disease being man himself, so that the chain is simply man–louse–man. The role of the louse is crucial. Zinsser outlines the position of the louse with unusual sympathy, criticizing as he does the egocentricity of human descriptions of disease:

... the host [human] may survive; but the ill-starred louse that sticks his haustellum through an infected skin, and imbibes the loathsome virus with his nourishment, is doomed beyond succor. In eight days he sickens, in ten days he is *in extremis*, on the eleventh or twelfth his tiny body turns red with blood extravasated from his bowel, and he gives up his little ghost.[17]

Zinsser spoke from personal experience with typhus and therefore with lice. Another admirer of the louse was Janusz Korczak. One day in the ghetto he killed a louse on his body "with a dexterous squeeze of my fingernail." But he felt remorseful, commenting that if he had time he would write an apology to the louse. Our attitude "toward this lovely insect is unjust and shameful."[18] But the apology was never written.

Most of us have difficulty mustering that much empathy for lice. But their role certainly is fundamental. Since lice revel in situations where humans do not or cannot bathe, it is obvious how close the interrelationships are among dirtiness, infestation with lice, and typhus.

The clinical picture of the disease may vary, but there are typical characteristics of epidemic typhus.[19] It begins with a rapid rise in temperature, chills, a feeling of impending doom, weakness, pains in the limbs, and severe headache. On about the fourth or fifth day a rash appears on the skin, usually on the shoulders, chest, and back. It then spreads to the arms and legs, the backs of the hands and feet, and sometimes the soles; rarely does it appear on the face. This characteristic rash can be diagnostic. It begins as pink spots, fading on pressure, which later become purple, brown red, and finally light brown. Delirium is common in severe cases.

Since early in this century, a diagnostic blood test has been possible, though often neither available nor needed during true epidemics, when the diagnosis usually is obvious. This test is known as the "Weil-Felix reaction." At least once in Poland during World War II, shrewd Polish practitioners used the test to convince the Nazis that their towns were typhus-ridden, thus saving their residents from forced labor for the Third Reich.[20]

The information about the cause and clinical picture of typhus was universally available to the medical profession in the 1930s. Yet German physicians played a leading role in forcing the Jews to live in conditions guaranteed to ensure the presence and epidemic spread of typhus. As will be seen, the problem was not one of scientific ignorance on the part of Nazi physicians in Poland; rather, it was one of making science subservient to ideology.

ILLEGAL TYPHUS EXPERIMENTATION

In considering typhus in the sphere of Nazi control during the Second World War, one especially unsavory aspect of the subject cannot be ignored. This is the criminal experimentation performed on forced subjects in the concentration camps at Buchenwald, Natzweiler, Auschwitz, and other sites.

In Buchenwald, SS Hauptsturmführer (Captain) Ding-Schuler carried out experiments on 39 prisoners,[21] assessing the efficacy of acridine and rutenol for I.G. Farbenindustrie (Höchst).[22] In another experiment, 90 patients were deliberately infected with typhus organisms. These virulent organisms were deliberately "farmed" by Ding-Schuler; he kept one prisoner near at hand, a human stockpile that Ding-Schuler created to maintain a constant supply of typhus germs. When one human farm died, he infected a new prisoner, who would then become the source of germs for experiments for a few days—and so on.[23] He found that the same proportion of infected patients who were given the drugs died as in a smaller group of typhus patients who were without special therapy. The drugs were useless.

In a much larger experiment, 392 individuals were given one or another of 12 different vaccines against typhus and then were deliberately infected with the bacteria; 66 died, and no significant conclusion could be reached. The results of these experiments were published in a German medical journal in 1943.[24]

At Natzweiler, in Alsace, experiments were made by Dr. Eugen Haagen, professor of hygiene at the Reich University of Strassburg. Little is known of what went on in these experiments, which were not as widely publicized as those of Ding-Schuler. Dr. Haagen is on record as having complained about the poor quality of research subjects (concentration camp inmates) that were sent to him. He needed subjects who were healthy and well fed to simulate the average Nazi soldier. Such subjects were scarce in the concentration camp world of the 1940s; presumably Haagen made do with the poor-quality human beings available to him.

At Auschwitz also, experimentation was done on typhus, though not as extensively as at the other sites.[25] But some patients on the infectious disease ward at Auschwitz did receive rutenol—perhaps as many as 50 individuals—with results as unsatisfactory as those achieved elsewhere.[26]

There may seem to be little direct relationship between these so-called experiments and the Warsaw ghetto, but the latter could be seen as a sort of gigantic criminal experiment in itself. In addition, involuntary experimentation may have been carried on in Czyste Hospital early in the war. Isaiah Trunk has written that the Nazi public health authorities in Warsaw forced the Czyste medical staff to use a drug called Uliron in treating typhus. Luba Bielicka-Blum, head of the nurses' training school at Czyste at the time, said that the staff was threatened with penalties if they did not use Uliron.[27] The agent was toxic. Patients often became blue and cold, and some died. The Germans made films of some of the patients.[28] As well as being toxic, Uliron, a recently discovered sulfonamide drug, seemed useless against typhus.

TYPHUS AS IDEOLOGY

By the late 1930s, German medical science had constructed an elaborate world view equating mental infirmity, moral depravity, criminality, and racial impurity. This complex of identifications was then used to justify the destruction of the Jews on medical, moral, criminological, and anthropological grounds. To be Jewish was to be both sick and criminal; Nazi medical science and policy united to help "solve" this problem.[29]

The ghettoization of Poland's Jews was a direct and logical endpoint of such a world view. The subsequent annihilation of almost all the Jews was equally "logical" (in terms of Nazi ideology), though somewhat less direct.

After the *Wehrmacht* conquered Poland in September 1939 and Germany divided the country with Soviet Russia, this concept of the Jews as a collective personification of disease was applied in practice. Hitler's oft-repeated threats against the Jews were given explicit reality when the Nazis implemented the policy of ghettoization. A chief reason given for enforcing this practice was that Jews had a particular affinity for and propensity to spread major infectious diseases, of which the pre-eminent and most feared example was typhus fever. Thousands of Jews in Poland and elsewhere died of typhus during these years, largely because conditions in the ghettos provided an ideal breeding ground for the disease.

German medical scientists, world leaders from the mid-1800s through the First World War, played a significant role in pursuing the investigations into typhus fever. The international nature of such findings ensured that German practitioners knew as much about typhus as did any other segment of the medical profession. Thus they would have known that there was nothing "Jewish" about the disease, but that ghetto conditions would almost guarantee epidemics in any population. Yet the policy of ghettoization and its justification as a public health measure aroused little or no objection from German physicians. Indeed, it had the energetic support of many. Why was this so?

Answering this question is a particularly difficult necessity in considering questions concerning the Holocaust in general and the Warsaw ghetto in particular. It is tempting to view events such as the creation of the Warsaw ghetto as unique aberrations, perhaps explainable as a manifestation of madness on the part of Hitler or of some underling. This is not the case. The Nazi policy that ended in the extermination of millions of Jews, Gypsies, and others was deliberate, organized, ideological, and fully participated in by millions of Germans. Nevertheless, it was not a unified policy, nor was the ultimate end of extermination either apparent or even agreed upon from the beginning. This lack of unity explains some of the apparent contradictions and confusions that invest the study of the Holocaust and, explicitly, the story of the Warsaw ghetto.

When we look at the question of typhus and the ghetto, for example, we do not discover some Nazi monster malevolently forcing his destructive will not only on half a million Jews but also on the Germans and *Volksdeutsche* around him who themselves held positions of power in and influence over the ghetto. On the contrary, we find that the fate of the Jews was determined prosaically, through a series of typically bureaucratic decisions, by consensus at meetings of the German officials in charge of various aspects of life in occupied Warsaw. And those Nazi officials were, in turn, influenced by events taking place far from Poland.

One of the German propaganda activities undertaken early in the war was to spread their unscientific but politicized ideas of disease transmission. Articles appeared in the Polish press stating that Jews carried germs that did not infect them; therefore, the Jews ought to be avoided as a prudent measure of public health.[30] Thus the Germans worked "to widen the breach between Jews and non-Jews."[31]

Nor was German propaganda delivered only to the Poles. The *Volksdeutsche*, the ethnically German citizens in Poland, needed to be reassured that their health and that of their sons and husbands serving with the *Wehrmacht* was being looked after. A typical instance of the propaganda line was a newspaper article from Krakow stating that it had been proven possible to keep the rest of the population of

Warsaw almost free of typhus fever "spread by the Jews. Careful watching over the traffic between the Jewish dwelling section and other sections of the city should in the future reduce to a minimum the impairment of the population's health" resulting from the presence of half a million Jews among a million Poles and Germans.[32] From this comforting report no reader could discern the true nature of "the Jewish dwelling place" or the brutal excesses that constituted "careful watching" over traffic.

Browning has studied the process of ghettoization in Poland. He concludes that in Warsaw, with the largest Jewish community in Europe, the German doctors "played a decisive role in ghettoization, and that this then set the pattern that was followed in the rest of the General Government."[33] The first approach to forming the Warsaw ghetto took place in November 1939. Actually creating a ghetto was logistically impossible at that time. Moreover, the Nazi hierarchy was still planning to put all Jews in a massive "reservation" near Lublin, so there seemed no need for a ghetto in Warsaw. However, the Lublin scheme collapsed because of logistical impossibilities.

But the Jewish quarter, meaning the area of central Warsaw containing the bulk of the poorer Jews, which became roughly the area later enclosed as the ghetto, was declared to be *Seuchensperregebeit*—that is, a quarantined area—and was put out of bounds to the German military. So even at this early time, the concept of special risk to Germans from infected or infective Jews was emphasized in Warsaw. Within a few months, the public health department declared that the construction of walls around the quarter was absolutely essential because the Jews allegedly had not complied with various public health regulations.[34] At the same time, these German public health officials found the whole city of Warsaw deficient in delousing facilities in 1939; but by September 1940, 22 delousing stations were functioning.[35]

Browning cites a German publication that appeared in 1941, though the articles seem largely to predate the ghetto. The authors were Dr. Jost Walbaum, head of the Division of Public Health in the *Generalgouvernement*, which included Warsaw, and several of his colleagues there. Walbaum's department saw its role as ensuring the health of the Germans and *Volksdeutsche* in the area. What they soon realized was that to do so, they would also have to protect the health of the despised Poles, since there was no choice but to live among them.[36] Thus the Poles were able to obtain immunization against typhus.[37] With the Jews, on the other hand, there was a choice. By isolating them, the Germans considered that there was no need to provide immunization to prevent disease or treatment if it occurred: "in German self-interest the Poles were to be protected from epidemics, but in contrast the Jews were to be locked up with the diseases they allegedly carried."[38] Locked up without much possibility of immunization.

One or two of the German physicians involved in public health affairs in the *Generalgouvernement* proposed combining ghettoization with other, medically sound concepts. For example, Dr. Wilhelm Hagen, who arrived in Warsaw in January 1941, fully supported the enforced isolation of the Jews. But he also advanced the somewhat radical idea that they might be given more food than they were currently receiving.[39] However, Dr. Walbaum replied that although "Naturally it would be best and simplest to give the people sufficient provisions," that could not be done because, he claimed, there was no extra food available.[40] Hans Frank found the idea of increasing the food supplies to the Jews "utterly inconceivable."[41] And according to Hagen, Heinz Auerswald, the *Kommissar* of the ghetto from the spring of 1941 until the time of the deportations, "tied the hands" of the health officer (Hagen himself) by refusing to supply the hospitals or increase food rations.[42]

Walbaum was also in the psychologically dangerous position of being openly committed to the ghettoization decision. He had played a significant role in persuading Frank that it must be done. The two men met in early September 1940 in Krakow. Walbaum had statistics that, he claimed, showed that typhus was being spread from the Jewish quarter. Ghettos, especially in Warsaw, had to be set up as quickly as possible.[43] Walbaum's "statistics" came from SS Obersturmführer Dr. Arnold Lambrecht, who had found that in August 1940 there had been 18 cases of typhus in Warsaw and 50 outside the city. His report of 3 September 1940 concluded that the figures "make the outbreak of spotted fever in numerous places in the district in the coming of the winter months an absolute certainty."[44] Lambrecht had just arrived in Warsaw, so he can hardly be seen as an expert on conditions there, but even with such a small number of cases he was absolutely certain.

Yet the figures are revealing. Lambrecht claimed that the existence of 68 cases in one month in the *Generalgouvernement* signified the imminence of an epidemic. In 1936, a year not considered an epidemic year, there were more than 4500 cases of typhus in all of Poland. If we assume that what became the *Generalgouvernement* was one-third of Poland, then in that third of the country in 1936 there might have been 1500 cases of typhus. In a nonepidemic year. And 1500 cases for the year meant an average of 125 cases per month. But Lambrecht asserted firmly that 68 cases in a month meant that an epidemic definitely was coming. This conclusion seems patently false and self-serving.

There is at least some evidence that Hagen genuinely sought to have the food supply increased in 1941 and 1942. True, the evidence is cited by Hagen himself, but he quotes a document attested to in 1947 by Knud Ahlborn, who was at the meeting described:

> During a large training course for medical officers on spotted fever Hagen gave a truthful account of the desperate situation of the Jewry confined in the ghetto. . . . Hagen protested fearlessly against the totally inadequate food supply and absence of medical care which actually promoted the further spread of spotted fever.[45]

Hagen alludes to charges made regarding the failure of communicable disease control measures in the ghetto. He suggests that at least with regard to the "systematic process of pauperization" and especially to starvation, the charges are justified. "I have shown that I protested with all my resources."[46] Hagen noted the need not only for bread, but also for coal and soap.[47] The absence of coal was important because without it the Jewish delousing stations could not function.[48]

Dr. Hagen was not the only occupation official to understand the implications of inadequate soap, coal, and food. One public health official protested that epidemics were being promoted by "artificial famine."[49] In the Radom district, a Dr. Waisenegger observed that typhus was largely confined to the Jews. But his explanation did not depend on Nazi medical ideology. The reasons, he said, were insufficient coal and soap; excessive room density resulting in the multiplication of lice; and lack of food, which lowered, resistance to disease generally.[50]

Such rationality had little influence on those who held power. They "knew" that Jews were the focus of typhus. Thus they knew that their quarantine policy was the correct one. Even those who doubted this were nevertheless bolstered in maintaining the official position by their knowledge that supplies of food, coal, and soap were extremely limited. What there was would go first to the Germans and *Volksdeutsche*, the Poles then getting limited amounts as required for bare subsistence. There would be little or nothing left for Jews.

Perhaps these German physicians truly believed that there were medical reasons for ghettoization. Browning suggests that Nazi doctors " accepted as a medical premise that the Jews—by nature and culture—were the particular carriers of spotted fever. They threw the weight of their medical prestige and authority behind ghettoization as the appropriate response."[51] A survivor of the ghetto years, a pathologist, has pointed out that the staff at Czyste was required by the Nazis to perform autopsies on Jews who died in the ghetto. This was largely because the Nazis wanted to verify the number of cases of typhus in order to prove that the Jews were the source of typhus and were spreading the disease.[52] At any rate, statistics derived from that activity would provide a patina of "science."

Probably the German public health physicians would have been offended had anyone suggested to them that what they were doing was antihumanitarian, inhumane, and cruel. For at least some of these men, and thousands like them, the fundamental defect was the years of intensive conditioning of the German people by the Nazis. One consequence of this conditioning was to persuade them that any obligation to behave humanely toward Jews was removed. Conditioning had gone on in Germany since 1933; the medical schools were subjected to it,[53] as were all other faculties, as well as the public and the high schools. A basic premise of this ideological propaganda was that the Jews were a "diseased race" and that the "Jewish question" must, therefore, be solved by medical means.[54] The Nazi program to eliminate so-called "useless lives" by eradicating the populations of mental hospitals[55] was advanced by claiming that more Jews had mental disease than did the German population at large. Once this medical approach was accepted, the belief that Jews might also be more susceptible to typhus, for example, could more easily be sustained.

This ideological approach was carried to great lengths. For example, in Vilna, an epidemic of typhus began in the non-Jewish population outside the ghetto. The Jewish physicians within the ghetto offered to care for the sick, but the Gestapo prohibited any efforts by them to cure the Aryan patients.[56] The logic was pursued repeatedly in Nazi-occupied Poland. The Nazis forbade communal prayers among the Jews of Warsaw because they claimed that epidemics could be spread in such gatherings.[57] Jews were forbidden to ride trains for the same reason.[58] Later in the life of the ghetto, similar edicts affected Jewish industry and, therefore, the German war effort. German manufacturers were warned not to send raw materials into the ghetto for the production of articles for the *Wehrmacht*. "Were it not for the fear of spreading infectious diseases," the *Volkischer Beobachter* said, "about 40% of the Jewish population in occupied Poland could be used as qualified laborers."[59]

The fear of spreading disease justified murder as well. A German auxiliary policeman at Kutno received a glowing citation for his diligence in observing five Jews leaving the ghetto, chasing them nearly a mile, and then shooting them. "Because of the vigilance, resolution, and good shooting of auxiliary policeman Schultz, the great danger of a spread of spotted fever and other epidemics to the German population was removed."[60]

Some Germans were unalterably terrorized by typhus. These reactions were observed and commented on widely at the time. This fear often influenced their actions. At the hospital at Stawki 6–8 in 1941, a medical student noted that the Germans did not come there very often. "Nobody could come there because they declared it so-called quarantine because of the typhus fever, so the Germans were scared to come there. . . . So it was relatively peaceful."[61] With a little *chutzpah*, the Nazis' fear could be turned to a Jew's advantage; on the street in November 1940, Germans threatened to confiscate a man's winter fur coat. He said that of course they could have it, but that he had just been discharged from the typhus ward in Czyste. He kept his coat.[62] This fear could be useful to the Jews in many ways. For Ludwig Stabholz and his family, it was parlayed into a means of escaping the ghetto. He knew that the Germans were afraid of epidemics, and there was then an epidemic of exanthematous typhus in the ghetto. So the Germans allowed a car to leave the ghetto to collect necessary materials to fight the disease. It was via this car that Stabholz and his family were able to escape.[63]

Nor was this fear directed solely against the Jews. At the prisoner-of-war (POW) camp at Hammerstein, 2000 Russian POWs were ill with typhus. The Germans killed every one of them over a three-day period, thus ending the epidemic.[64] The same course was pursued within the concentration camps, where a diagnosis of typhus—or, indeed, any serious disease—automatically meant that one was "selected" for death, usually by injection of poison or in the gas chamber.[65] At a voluntary work camp at Osowa, near Chelm, where there were about 50 Jews, they were forced to dig their own graves when typhus broke out, and the SS shot them.[66]

Fear of typhus was by no means limited to the Germans, of course. Many Jews quite legitimately shared this emotion, for they were the ones literally living amid the epidemics. Adler provides graphic evidence of how he felt when, in January 1943, he shared a crowded bunker on Miła Street:

> From time to time somebody passing by brushes against me. I am horrified because so many people are infested with lice and, even worse, some people [in the bunker] are sick with spotted typhus. The danger of that infection terrifies me. Only yesterday, Dr. Regelman of the Health Service promised to inoculate me against typhus. Now the unfortunate Dr. Regelman is lying in the street, hit by two revolver bullets. Evidently the "race-purifiers" did not like the conspicuous hump on the back of this excellent public health physician.[67]

Nazi physicians were well aware that not only Jews, but also Russian POWs and others were severely afflicted with typhus; what they did not care to do was to make the obvious extrapolation: Jews in ghettos and Russian POWs shared one common characteristic. They were forced to exist in conditions of squalid filth and starvation. Therefore they developed typhus and other epidemics. And the filth and starvation were the direct result of Nazi policy.

Is it possible that there actually is some fundamental biological difference in the way Jews react to typhus compared to the rest of mankind? Good scientific evidence exists that racial and ethnic differences do occur with respect to some human disorders. Tay-Sachs disease is well known to affect chiefly Jewish children; however, this disease is a hereditary defect of lipid metabolism and a specific disorder. Gastric cancer has a particular predilection for the Japanese. Sickle cell anemia occurs almost exclusively in blacks and is genetically determined. These and other diseases do have a racial idiosyncrasy of incidence. But there is no suggestion anywhere in the literature that Jews are more likely to have typhus, or to harbor typhus, than any other racial or ethnic group (Nazi ideological claims aside, of course). Indeed, one German source that the Nazis seem to have ignored, perhaps because it was published in a Jewish journal, is Silvagni's article in the *Jüdisches Volksblatt* in which he claimed that Jews had more nervous disorders, gallstones, and other disorders, but less syphilis, alcoholism, and typhus, than did non-Jewish Germans.[68] And in 1941, when typhus began to afflict the Konskowola labor camp, the medical attendant observed that "Luckily, as it turned out, most of our inmates, Polish Jews, were quite resistant to the disease and had a good chance of recovery."[69]

None of the racially determined disorders mentioned is an infectious disease such as typhus. Where differences in the incidence of infectious diseases occur, these seem most often related to climate or other geophysical factors. So-called tropical diseases largely affect persons who live between the tropics; but the high incidence of these same diseases in temperate zone dwellers who move to the tropics shows that the differences relate to location, not genes. Smallpox decimated Canadian Indians in the seventeenth century, and that fact might seem to indicate a racially influenced phenomenon. But instead, this and other historical epidemics are seen to be examples of the absence of group immunity.[70] Once the disease has existed in a population for a sufficient number of generations, the survivors come to a state where they are no more seriously affected than are those who live in the more immune population that introduced the disease.

No scientific evidence exists to indicate that typhus attacks Jews preferentially compared with any other group of humans in the same state of nutrition and sanitation. Nor can Jews be shown to have any increased likelihood of conveying the disease to others while themselves remaining immune.[71] Indeed, examination of these two claims shows them to be logically inconsistent. If the Jews were immune, they could not be especially afflicted; if especially afflicted, they could not be immune.

MEDICAL CONDITIONS FOR WARSAW'S JEWS

Inside the ghetto, in a space of less than 1000 acres, the Germans forced between 400,000 and 500,000 Jews to live, so that over 30 percent of the population of Warsaw was living in 5 percent of its area.[72] As mentioned earlier, one of the reasons used by the Germans to justify establishing the ghetto was the existence of epidemics, particularly of typhus, among the Jews.[73] There is little evidence that such epidemics existed to any serious degree before the ghetto was created and no evidence that Jews were any more likely to suffer from, or to transmit, typhus than any other group. By setting up the ghetto and forcing so many people to live there, the Germans made their contention self-fulfilling: Typhus did indeed ravage the Jews of the Warsaw ghetto. Nevertheless, according to one physician who was there, "until the sealing off of the Ghetto, hunger and exanthematic typhus did not particularly affect the Jewish population."[74] As we shall see, this may be too optimistic a viewpoint.

The water supply was reduced progressively by the Germans and, as more and more penniless refugees from other parts of Poland and occupied Europe were forced into the ghetto, proper sanitation became impossible and lice ubiquitous. Not even the well-to-do could escape them; one interviewee describes with some amusement now, how her well-to-do parents purchased silk underwear for her on the premise that lice would find the material too slippery and would not attach themselves.[75] No efforts at prevention seemed to work or were available in sufficient volume to work. Even keeping your own home scrupulously clean, and remaining inside to avoid contact with less fastidious people, could be futile. Lazar describes the despair of such careful Jews who, soon after scrubbing their walls, found swarms of lice crawling everywhere.[76]

Within the hospitals inside the ghetto, conditions were deplorable. Nurses and other staff were in short supply to begin with, and the staffing situation became almost impossible because individuals vanished without a trace from one day to the next, caught up in the Nazi destructive process.

CLINICAL ASPECTS OF TYPHUS

There was ample opportunity for the medical profession to observe the clinical course of typhus, though the disease would not have been new to practitioners in that time and place. Only a minority of patients were admitted to the hospital, but Czyste was nevertheless swamped; eventually, during the second epidemic, in 1941, most internal medicine wards were converted into infectious disease wards.[77] The wards were desperately overcrowded, with two and even three patients in a bed.[78]

Both Eugenia Pernal and her brother contracted typhus, the latter probably as a result of working in a disinfection brigade.[79] Eugenia had the characteristic body rash and a very high temperature, exceeding 40°C, and was unconscious for two weeks. She was so ill that when she finally began to convalesce, a girlfriend had to teach her to walk all over again, as she had entirely lost the ability.[80] The main recollection of one survivor of the disease in the ghetto was the weird hallucinations he experienced, the high fever, and then profound exhaustion.[81]

Typhus often failed to be typical. Researchers noted, for example, that when starved patients had typhus, the characteristic high fever did not occur, thus complicating the diagnosis.[82] Some patients had abdominal pain when first seen by a physician, and there were some mistaken diagnoses of appendicitis.[83] Dr. Wisniewski was startled the first time he found that he couldn't hear the heart sounds in a patient with typhus. He soon became familiar with the phenomenon, caused apparently by the disease's attacking the heart itself.[84]

SPECIFIC EPIDEMICS OF TYPHUS

When one studies the available statistics, there seem to have been two epidemics of typhus between 1939 and 1943 (see Figure 7.2). The first took place before the ghetto was created; it was not a major epidemic, but its very existence played a role in the German decision to set up the ghetto. The second occurred in the last half of 1941.

Although the Nazis placed primary responsibility for combating the epidemics on the Jews, they were nevertheless heavily involved. The public health officers, successively Drs. Schrempf (during the first epidemic) and Hagen (during the second), were on the scene constantly. Hagen mentioned having daily meetings with Drs. Milejkowski, Stein, and Hirszfeld during the worst months of 1941.[85] Another German imposition on the ghetto medical staff was in the form of a commission set up to combat the epidemics and headed by Joachim Koblinski, a Pole from Posen. Koblinski's chief activity seems to have been extorting large sums of money. After the war, he was tried in a Polish court and sentenced to five years' imprisonment.[86]

The First Epidemic

This epidemic occurred in the first few months of 1940, the highest incidence being in March, April, and May. Several factors contributed to its occurrence, a chief one being the continuing influx of refugees from towns and villages in the *Generalgouvernement*. To experienced public health personnel, the implications of overcrowding, which began in the Jewish quarter long before the ghetto was opened, were obvious. Epidemics would result. Gentile Polish physicians in Warsaw warned the Germans that these displacements of population could only lead to outbreaks of typhus. According to Hirszfeld, the answer they received only proved the Germans' tremendous ignorance: "Where Germans rule," they proclaimed arrogantly, "there is no typhus."[87]

There had been typhus in Warsaw throughout the fall of 1939,[88] though the number of cases was relatively small.[89] According to Wulman, there were 14,000 cases of typhoid fever (1120 deaths) and 750 cases of typhus (83 deaths) from late 1939 to 1 April 1940.[90] This is certainly a significant number of cases of typhus, but it is obvious that the major problem that winter was typhoid.

However, there were enough typhus cases in Czyste Hospital to produce a major reaction from Dr. Schrempf. At a meeting at the hospital he discharged the director on the spot because one typhus patient had not been included in the daily statistics. Schrempf then put the hospital under total quarantine, no movement of personnel in or out being possible for several weeks.[91] The Jewish quarter was posted as an epidemic area as early as November 1939.[92] Nazi antisemitic policy was fanning

---

Figure 7.2. *(facing)* Graph of deaths in the Warsaw ghetto and incidence of reported cases of typhus, 1939–42 (figures derived from Myron Winick, ed., *Hunger Disease: Studies by the Jewish Physicians in the Warsaw Ghetto,* trans. Martha Osnos, New York, Chichester, Brisbane, and Toronto: John Wiley & Sons, 1979, Table 1).

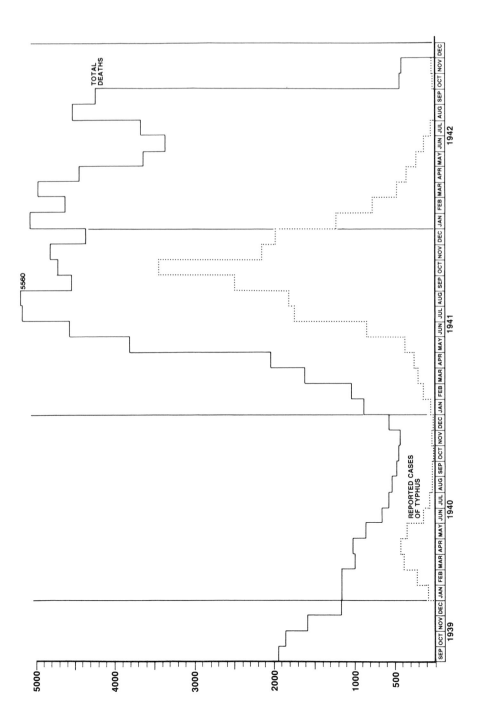

TOTAL DEATHS

5560

REPORTED CASES OF TYPHUS

5000 4000 3000 2000 1000 500

SEP | OCT | NOV | DEC | JAN | FEB | MAR | APR | MAY | JUN | JUL | AUG | SEP | OCT | NOV | DEC | JAN | FEB | MAR | APR | MAY | JUN | JUL | AUG | SEP | OCT | NOV | DEC | JAN | FEB | MAR | APR | MAY | JUN | JUL | AUG | SEP | OCT | NOV | DEC

1939   1940   1941   1942

Polish antipathy toward the Jews, as well as their fear of disease, by placing crude signs all over Warsaw coupling the slogan "Jew—Louse—Typhus" with a repulsive caricature of a Jew.[93]

The Jewish community made vigorous efforts to combat typhus from the appearance of the first case. At least in the beginning, their concern was less for the Nazi rhetoric than for the specter of serious disease. TOZ, bolstered financially by the Joint, began a program that included free vaccinations, free distribution of medications, and the establishment of bathhouses, disinfection centers, delousing places, and homes for evacuees.[94]

By February the number of cases was growing and the fear of a quarantine loomed.[95] In March the Jewish quarter was formally designated *Seuchensperrgebeit*, a plague-infested district, and the *Judenrat* was ordered to begin building a wall around the "infected area."[96] So, medical-ideological theories were beginning to be translated into physical responses; when the wall approached completion, it became the wall intended to seal all the Jews in and everyone else out.

Meanwhile, the disease spread. In the Leszno Street quarantine station, as Czerniakow pointed out wryly, "there must be lice, since they have just had a case of typhus."[97] A TOZ report gives a good summary of the efforts carried out:

> The epidemic of spotted fever (typhus) was attacked by bringing the victims into the hospitals and clinics. The immediate families of the patient were held in quarantine or placed in isolation camps and were bathed and their clothes freed from lice. Besides, with the help of the sanitary brigades the entire population was subjected to a campaign to rid them of lice. Both Jewish and City and district bathhouses, 70 in all, were made use of for this purpose. The greatest difficulty lay in the scarcity of good disinfecting apparatus. We were compelled to limit ourselves to what we found on hand. There was also an insufficient amount of soap, disinfectants, clothes and underwear for the poor.[98]

Late in May, 15 cases of typhus were found in a house on Muranow Street but the house was not quarantined because, Ringelblum said, a doctor was getting 800 zloty daily as a payoff to suppress the information.[99] At the other end of the ghetto, at Śliska Street, typhus resulted in quarantine.[100]

Cases were first reported in December 1939, the final ones in August 1940, when there were 18 cases. The peak month was April, with 407 cases added to the records. All told, 1842 cases were reported.[101] How many actually occurred we will never know. But despite the lack of vaccine for any mass program of immunization, despite the regular, uncontrolled intermingling of the Jewish and Christian populations, and despite the serious overcrowding in the Jewish quarter, the epidemic disappeared.

For whatever reasons, the epidemic had waned by the late summer of 1940. The first epidemic was over. The ghetto did not yet exist, though the epidemic would be a potent excuse for setting it up.

The Second Epidemic

By the end of 1940, typhus was widespread in gentile Warsaw, so the Germans checked all Jewish apartments in the newly created ghetto for hidden cases, assuming that this was the source of the epidemic. They found none.[102] Nevertheless, typhus was never totally absent from the ghetto, and soon after its creation the incidence of death from typhus began to rise slowly. In May 1941 the pace quickened, and by July a major epidemic was underway. It began to subside in November and fell to relatively inconsequential levels only after February 1942.

From August through December 1940, very few new cases of typhus were reported. In January 1941, Hagen arrived in Warsaw to replace Schrempf. He noted that "The danger of spotted fever had just been overcome," and for that reason, he said, he protested against the plan to introduce into the already crowded ghetto large numbers of Jews from outlying areas. He was sure that this would cause an increase in typhus. He was right, but his advice was ignored.[103]

One writer has suggested that the transfer of Czyste Hospital from outside the ghetto to its new locations inside, in January 1941, contributed to the epidemic.[104] But Favel's claim that there were 3000 cases of typhus in the hospital in January 1941 seems exaggerated (according to official statistics, there were only 57 cases among the residents of the ghetto in January 1941), and his contention that all the typhus cases in Warsaw—Jew and gentile—were in Czyste, and thus forced into the ghetto, does not fit the known facts. Czyste had been an all-Jewish institution for many months before the move to the ghetto. In the first quarter of 1941, Hagen reported an epidemic of 77 cases of typhus among the prisoners of the (gentile) Mokotow prison in Warsaw, so the disease was not restricted to Jews.[105] He also claimed that the chief cause of the epidemic was the resettlement of Jews from outside Warsaw. The public health officials had drawn up plans to disinfect 500 arriving refugees a day but found themselves inundated with 1000 or more. The system could not function.[106]

By the late spring of 1941, cases were accumulating with frightening speed. The number of new cases exceeded 800 in June and 2000 by September. The *Judenrat* established Sanitary House Committees to ensure that apartments and houses were clean. According to Trunk, these committees and the building superintendents were made jointly responsible for hiding the sick.[107]

In May, one observer noted that death in the streets had become "a mass phenomenon," and Pawia 65 alone had seen 25 typhus patients, of whom 15 died.[108] In June, 280 houses were closed because of the epidemic.[109] On 5 June 1941 there were 229 new cases in the ghetto, on 12 June 278 new cases,[110] and on 28 July, 70 new cases.[111] Czerniakow states that this number of cases was reported on each date. But it seems likely that the figures are actually weekly cumulations; June 5 and June 12 are one week apart. Given that in all of June 841 cases were reported, the likelihood that 507 of these would begin on only two days of the month is slight, but 507 would be a reasonable two-week total. And weekly reporting fits bureaucratic routine.

The lack of sanitation among masses of the population was startling. Nurses working with TOZ found complete nests of lice under bandages when they dressed wounds among the poor.[112] Sometimes children's hair was so filled with masses of lice that the resulting mass was like a helmet.[113] Pitiful cases abounded. One physician remembers an instance when a policeman brought a boy to the hospital in a ricksha. The boy had multitudes of head lice in the hair and inside the ears. He was "practically eaten alive by lice, and looked more like a corpse than a human being. I didn't even find out if he had typhus. He died before being moved to the ward."[114]

By August 1941, a historian in the ghetto observed that "Next to hunger, typhus is the question that is most generally absorbing for the Jewish populace.... The graph line of typhus cases keeps climbing."[115] At this time there were, on any day, about 900 typhus patients in the hospital and more than 6000 ill at home. Monthly mortality rates had risen from 900 in January 1941 to more than 5500 in August.[116] And these figures relate only to reported cases; many instances are known where, for a variety of reasons, the existence of typhus was hidden.[117] Lenski estimates that 100,000 Jews suffered from typhus during the year and a half that the ghetto existed before the massive deportations began,[118] yet the official figure was about 20,000. That enormous discrepancy and other statistical matters related to typhus and other diseases are discussed in Chapter 12.

The first death from typhus in the *Ordnungsdienst* occurred in May 1941. Given their constant contact with their fellow Jews in the crowded streets and the likelihood that their homes suffered from the common difficulties in doing proper cleaning, this late appearance of the disease seems remarkable. But it was at about this time that a contingent of the *Ordnungsdienst* began to be used directly in combating typhus. From this time on, large numbers of the policemen suffered typhus and many died, including Berenson, the head of Section I, the group assigned to help fight epidemics by assisting the sanitary columns of the Health Department of the *Judenrat*.[119]

By this time, Hagen had decided that some Jewish doctors and other staff, as well as the Polish workers, were not assiduous in their antiepidemic efforts.[120] Auerswald insisted that Czerniakow fire Milejkowski on the principle that the problem of epidemics was his responsibility and the worsening situation showed that he was incompetent. Czerniakow "set his mind at ease by promising to mobilize the whole population for the struggle."[121] One action taken was the appointment of Dr. Tadeusz Ganc, a former major in the Polish Army Medical Corps and a converted Jew, as administrative head of the *Judenrat* Health Division, with the responsibility of heading the antiepidemic activities in the ghetto. To ensure that he had authority and muscle, Ganc was given the use of 200 members of the *Ordnungsdienst* to carry out his orders.[122]

Another aspect of Czerniakow's "mobilization" was raising taxes to pay for whatever was done. The *Judenrat* was frequently forced to create special taxes for specific purposes. For example, it placed a 2-zloty tax on the bread ration,[123] an especially unpopular approach. Moreover, various departments in the *Judenrat* created their own taxes to underwrite operations. Collecting these taxes was arduous, but the departments hit upon the device of threatening the reluctant with being forced to take in refugees, a fate much dreaded because of the shortage of space and the related fear of importing lice and disease. The Resettlement Commission became so sophisticated in its independent tax collection techniques that it used a hired corps of simulated "refugees" who would move in to an apartment, looking fearsomely filthy, until the levy was paid, at which point they moved on to threaten someone else.[124]

At Czyste Hospital, all wards except surgery and gynecology discontinued their work and gave the space to typhus cases, yet there were still too few beds.[125] Although treating patients in their homes defied the Nazi edict, it was not necessarily a bad, or a medically unsound, thing to do. One surviving physician has pointed out that conditions in the hospital often were so bad that it was better for the patient to be treated at home.[126] Of course, this method ignored the epidemiological aspects of the epidemic.

The incidence of typhus increased rapidly every month through October 1941. In August, Ringelblum estimated that there were 9000 typhus patients in the ghetto hospitals and at least 7000 being treated at home.[127] The official number of cases in the ghetto was 1805. By November, perhaps 15 percent of the Jews in the ghetto had had typhus.[128] The incidence then began to drop rapidly, an unusual order of events since typhus customarily becomes more common in winter.[129]

Nevertheless, although the prevalence of typhus was abating by the late fall, the disease seemed to be more virulent than ever.[130] Fenigstein thought that the death rate increased, though the percentage of the population infected was lower.[131] According to one source citing "official German figures," there were 17,800 cases of typhus in Warsaw during 1941, of which 15,449 occurred in the ghetto.[132] The official German figures were no more or less than what the *Judenrat* gave them. The research by Jewish doctors on hunger cites the same number of typhus deaths, 15,449,[133] and Trunk mentions precisely the same number.[134]

The Krochmalna Street Aktionen

Krochmalna Street was a sore spot in the ghetto. It was in the so-called Small Ghetto, a street of very shabby dwellings, extremely crowded, dirty, and poor. It had been the core of the old Jewish quarter, a hangout for the shady characters of prewar Warsaw. Isaac Bashevis Singer wrote a pungent recollection of Krochmalna Street. First, one detected the stench, "a blend of burned oil, rotten fruit, and chimney smoke." Then one saw the dirty, rough cobbled streets, deep gutters, and washing hanging from every balcony.[135] The whores' district was in the area.[136] Krochmalna Street did not improve by becoming part of the ghetto.

During both epidemics, the festering sore of Krochmalna Street came under special attack in the battle to control typhus. The first indication that this street would receive particular attention came in March 1940, when the first physical separation of Jews from other Varsovians was beginning. Wooden fences were set up at nine places in Warsaw, especially at Krochmalna Street, which the Germans already considered a focal point, the chief source of typhus for the whole city.[137] At this stage, Krochmalna Street was the home of both poor Jews and poor gentiles.

By May, the first, smaller epidemic was already beginning to burn out. However, the health officials were unaware of this, early in the month, and decided to have an *Aktion* to root out what were suspected to be unreported masses of patients.

On 7 May 1940, Krochmalna Street was sealed off. In the rigidly quarantined area, 30 new cases of typhus were identified; moreover, major areas of filth were found, since apparently two landlords had not removed garbage for nine months.[138] But the cost was high. Twenty buildings with about 20,000 inhabitants were roped off and isolated for 23 days, during which time no one was allowed in or out. The people who lived on Krochmalna Street could not survive for 23 days without food, and only vigorous smuggling behind the backs of bribed guards saved their lives.[139] These same actions negated much of the effect of the quarantine.

The second *Aktion* occurred in late August 1941 in the depth of the second typhus epidemic. Had the inhabitants given the matter any thought, they might have predicted that they would again be singled out for special attention. The crowding and sanitation were worse than they had been 15 months earlier, before the ghetto was established.

Hagen states that the decision to isolate and delouse Krochmalna Street on this occasion was taken jointly by himself, Dr. Milejkowski, Dr. Stein, and Dr. Laski, head of the Warsaw public health system. The *Aktion* was to last a single day, people being bathed and homes disinfected simultaneously. Sixty unreported cases of typhus were found during the activities on 28 and 29 August, but the confusion, fright, thievery, and other undesirable side effects were so bad that the experiment was never repeated.[140] As Czerniakow put it, "Unfortunately, the neighborhood scum used this opportunity to steal many articles from the residents."[141] They had little they could afford to lose.

Though the Nazis rarely entered the ghetto except to conduct prisoners to and from Pawiak Prison and along a few other regular routes,[142] this *Aktion* on Krochmalna Street was a notable exception. The raid involved the physicians of the *Judenrat* health department, Polish physicians, and German officials of Hagen's public health office.[143] The report of the *Ordnungsdienst* has survived, and from it we learn just what a raid of this sort meant to those raided.[144] The whole of Krochmalna Street, from Ciepła Street to Rynkowa Street, was to be disinfected and its inhabitants bathed. The residents were assembled and marched to public baths, chiefly the bath outside the ghetto on Spokojna Street, many long blocks northward across the entire Large Ghetto. The ill and the crippled traveled by ricksha or hand carts. Patients found to have typhus were taken to the hospital.

By evening, those who had been bathed were able to return home and assess the damage caused by the disinfection procedures. But a group of 800 had not been bathed, the facilities being overtaxed. They were herded into the Janasz Market Hall, where officials tried to find a way to feed them and get them through the night, for the baths would not reopen until morning and the unbathed could not be permitted to mingle with those who had been deloused. A 5-year-old boy was taken dead from the arms of his mother, and the corpse of a 20-year-old girl was found in the hall. Women carrying babies or young children in their arms had to walk around all night, because the only place to lie down was the asphalt floor.[145]

The first issue of food was made at about 4 A.M., when soup was distributed. There were no bowls, and ravenous people took the soup in caps, in handkerchiefs, even in their cupped hands. They had not eaten for nearly 24 hours. Corpses that could not be identified were transported away. A general issue of food was attempted in the morning, but only 3000 portions were available. The street housed perhaps 18,000 Jews, and the result was chaos. So ended the second, and last, Krochmalna Street *Aktion*. Within a year, essentially all the survivors of typhus and its treatment were dead at Treblinka.

DISINFECTION AND DISEASE CONTROL

Perhaps the most significant medical debate that took place within the ghetto involved disinfection as an approach to preventing or stopping epidemics of typhus. The German position was that the Jews were filthy and lice-ridden and, since lice were known to be the crucial link in the spread of typhus, the attack must be on filth in general and lice in particular. They therefore set up a system whereby, when typhus broke out in a building, a series of steps must be taken: The patient, his or her family, any other occupants of the apartment, and often of the adjoining apartments, were strictly quarantined for a period of weeks; all other inhabitants of the building were required to go to the bathhouses for personal disinfection and delousing of their garments; all apartments in the building were to be deloused while the people were at the baths (see Figures 7.3 and 7.4).

One of the interviewees, Marek Balin, then a medical student, remembers how the Germans applied their system. "They would say that the Jews are filthy, the Jews have lice in their hair, lice which are responsible for the exanthematic fever [typhus] and they don't wash and they are not clean. They should be disinfected." They would block the house off and then send groups of sanitary personnel to dis-

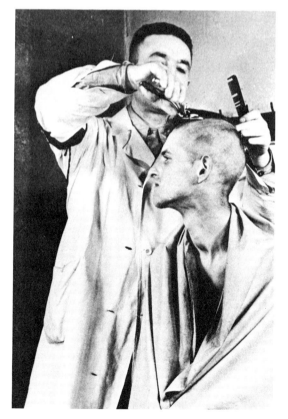

Figure 7.3. Haircut for disinfection purposes, Warsaw ghetto, ca. 1941 (reproduced by permission of Yad Vashem Archives, Jerusalem: YVA 24-C-06).

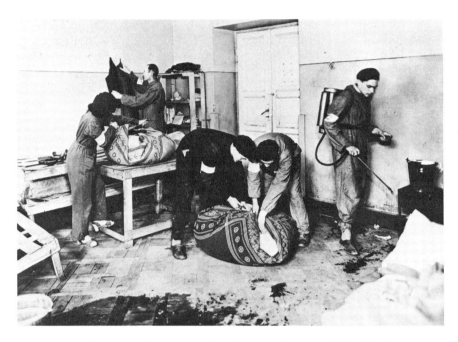

Figure 7.4. Disinfection of luggage and bedding by a Jewish self-help disinfection squad (reproduced by permission of Yad Vashem Archives FA 35-1984) [1341]

infect it. The whole house was closed. They would inspect the apartments, and from these apartments they would often pull out "innocent young girls but they would say that they have lice on them. They would close off those apartments. They would send those people from the apartments."

Balin saw the residents being sent to bathhouses, where they went through delousing and showering. Many groups came back with their hair cut off. In the houses there was "sanitary disinfection." The public health staff would make bundles of pillows or blankets in one room, and then they would seal the doors and windows hermetically with paper strips. "And they would burn sulfur to get the sulfur dioxide that was supposed to kill the lice and whatever insects would be there." In other apartments, they would spray everything with creosote and lysol.

Sometimes a house was closed all day until the whole block was disinfected. This probably produced more disease than it prevented, because people would have to stay out in the cold. They could not get into their apartments and therefore were deprived of food. "And those people going around from apartment to apartment could steal everything. . . . So I remember people complaining very much about this disinfection."[146]

These procedures created major and often catastrophic problems for the individuals involved, and for the *Judenrat*, which was required to oversee or carry out the various steps. The Jews became expert at avoiding the mandated procedures. A variety of reasons underlay their intransigence. These included simple sloth, irrational fear of the disease, a desire to avoid doing anything the Nazis ordered them to do, greed in the face of opportunities for graft, realization of the potentially disastrous consequences of complying, and genuine scientific disagreement about what constituted effective action when typhus became epidemic. As Lenski has explained, "the Jews concealed the majority of cases and treated them at home, without informing the Nazi authorities, because every case of exanthematic typhus served the authorities as a pretext for penalizing and inflicting suffering on the Ghetto Jews."[147]

Ludwig Hirszfeld was particularly scathing in denouncing this entire disease control procedure. He claimed that the German orders regarding disease control were literally death dealing in themselves. At the request of Josef Jaszunski, a member of the *Judenrat*, Hirszfeld prepared a detailed memorandum criticizing the German theories about the epidemiology of typhus.[148] In it he is said to have shown logically how nonsensical the Nazi medico-political approach was, the thesis apparently having been established only "to cover up a new barbaric act," namely, ghettoization. "Did not sealing houses for 3 weeks mean death by starvation for most people? And the disinfection was carried out in such a way that it destroyed everything. Did that not mean complete ruin?"[149] For reasons of self-preservation, Hirszfeld refused to attach his name to the document,[150] an act that was understandable but that probably eliminated any impact it might have had. Probably it would have been ignored by the Nazis under any circumstance.

How accurate was Hirszfeld's claim?

Quarantine

The Nazi authorities proclaimed that all the residents of any house that contained a typhus patient were to be isolated for two weeks. The entrance was to be locked and a policeman posted there constantly to prevent anyone from leaving or entering the house (see Figure 7.5). Moreover, no one could bring food to the barricaded residents, so even the healthy residents were condemned to starve for at least the two-week period. Few families were able to store substantial supplies of food. If the ones quarantined were starving already, the two-week period could well push them from this world to the next. This result was irrelevant to the Nazis, but as a public health procedure it had absolutely nothing to recommend it, as Hirszfeld insisted.

Remarkable efforts were made to avoid quarantine. Ringelblum, the historian, relates the elaborate steps taken in his own building at Leszno 18. A man came down with typhus. The residents took away all his identification, put the patient in a ricksha, bribed a Polish policeman, and sent the "unconscious" patient to Czyste.[151] He died there. The house avoided an onerous and dangerous quarantine. The other residents in the building apparently escaped typhus.

Sometimes quarantine was carried out in quarantine stations rather than in the patients' homes. Although entire families had to undergo this period of isolation,[152] the system offered the obvious advantage that those in quarantine had the chance to get food from the staff in the stations, rather than risking starvation if blockaded in their apartments. The capacity of these stations was about 1400 persons, not nearly enough.[153] The largest was located at Leszno 109, outside the ghetto. This

Figure 7.5. Quarantine for typhus, Warsaw ghetto; enforced by *Ordnungsdienst* officer (Bundesarchiv, Koblenz).

building was used particularly as a quarantine station for refugees in the hope of discovering and treating any diseases they might have before they entered the ghetto. Dr. Pawel Lipsztat was in charge.[154]

The quarantine stations were predictably unpopular with those forced into them. Their attitude was expressed graphically, if inelegantly, when in February 1942 Gustav Wielikowski, a lawyer and member of the *Judenrat*, was conducting a group to inspect the quarantine station on Stawki Street. As he stood in the street in front of the station extolling the cultural life maintained in these quarantine centers, "a large round rear end was stuck out of one of the windows."[155]

All patients suffering from typhus were to be reported, the reason being to ensure that disinfection of premises was carried out, as well as the quarantine of contacts. The quarantine system was in effect until the summer of 1941. Then house-by-house quarantine was stopped because the baths could no longer keep up with the huge number of persons being sent for delousing. The need was for about 8000 baths per day, but the existing baths had a maximum capacity of about 2000.[156]

Hospitalization

Although the Germans decreed that all patients with typhus should be quarantined in their homes, they also said that patients should be treated in the hospital. Orders often were contradictory as well as arbitrary. When the epidemic was in full flood,

Czyste was jammed with patients, so much so that Hagen proposed to take over half of the buildings on Prosta Street for quarantine beds. This idea not only was turned down, but the ghetto was shrunk even further and Prosta Street was no longer included.[157]

Because of the potentially disastrous effect of these measures, many ways around the system were devised. One was the private hospital. Ringelblum[158] and Hagen[159] both mention such secret and illegal institutions, though it is possible that they refer to the same one. Ringelblum reported that a secret typhus hospital was found in early March 1941; it was in a house with no water pipes. There were eight patients, and two doctors and a male nurse were implicated.[160] This may have been the same hospital discovered by Milejkowski, who in turn told Hagen about it, claiming that it was the source of more than 30 additional cases.[161] There is no indication of how this could be ascertained.

Because the Nazis insisted upon their draconian measures for disease control, backing up their edicts with threats of severe penalties,[162] in the eyes of some Jews it became patriotic to flout the regulations. Lenski declared that nurses and doctors who cared for concealed patients also took part in the passive resistance.[163] Yehuda Bauer claimed that the act of "keeping body and soul together" under the circumstances of starvation, disease, and terror should be seen as a form of resistance to the Nazis.[164] Since many ghetto physicians genuinely believed that the German-imposed methods of typhus control were wrong, and that they knew better ways, their clandestine defiance must also qualify as resistance. Whether physicians were therefore justified in forcing patients to be treated by them, as was the case with at least some block physicians who diagnosed typhus,[165] is a different question contaminated by the likelihood of self-interest.

Disinfection by Bathing

Possibly the most destructive policy involved the mandatory use of bathhouses for infectious disease control. Not only the residents of the infected home, but also their neighbors on either side, were required to attend these bathhouses. Conditions there were extremely dangerous, especially in winter. The number of baths was insufficient, and the facilities became grossly overcrowded. Both before and after the bath, waiting people were forced to line up outside or in a cold, drafty hall, sometimes naked. The groups were divided by sex. But everyone—old people, children, pregnant women, the bedridden sick—was supposed to undergo this humiliating, unhealthy, and potentially dangerous ordeal.

Many became ill after going there. "More than once," Lenski remembered, "I was called to persons dying after their return from the bath house. . . . the Nazi authorities threatened to deport to the Auschwitz annihilation camp any doctor who failed to report a case of typhus."[166] As early as April 1940, Adam Czerniakow recorded a racket that he believed was voiding the potential utility of disinfection centers. "A new industry: a woman who, for money, will take the place of another person at a disinfection steambath."[167]

The certificates, *Entlausungsscheine*, were considered mandatory by the Nazis, who once arrested Czerniakow because some Jews had not reported for delousing.

The *Judenrat* had to pay a fine of 6600 zloty to bail him out.[168] One technique to ensure that people got a certificate was to enact an edict that no one could travel by train without a delousing certificate.[169] To complicate the issue further, the certificates were valid only for 10 days. Reportedly, some Jews paid as much as 7000 zloty to obtain a certificate without going through the bathhouse.[170] The fee was divided among the bathhouse physician, the *Ordnungsdienst*, and the bathhouse personnel.[171]

The process of disinfective bathing was known as *parówka*, or "steaming," and it has been described as a mockery of the most elementary principles of prophylaxis.[172] There were only four bathhouses in the ghetto, including the famous ritual bathhouse, or *mikvah*, at Dzielna 38[173] and those at Gęsia 43 and at Solna 4, a new institution opened on 17 March 1940 by TOZ. In the last two months of March 1940, 6202 persons received baths in the Gęsia and Solna bathhouses.[174] There had also been a facility on Spokojna Street, but that had to be abandoned in November 1940 because it was outside the ghetto walls. There is, however, some evidence that the Spokojna site was used periodically by the Jews, marched in groups outside the walls for that purpose. Yet every Jew in a house where there was a pile of refuse in the yard,[175] and every Jew in a home infected with typhus, plus the neighboring homes, was required to be deloused at a bathhouse. Specific additional groups were included as the Germans saw fit. For example, in February 1940 a louse was found on a nurse's jacket at Czyste, and the entire nursing staff had to be deloused.[176]

Sometimes bribery could save the inhabitants. At Leszno 32, a fee of 1200 zloty allowed them to escape the baths.[177] And reportedly, 2000 zloty exchanged hands during an *Aktion* at Dzielna 32, in January 1942, so that some of the 3000 persons who lived there were able to save themselves from standing naked in the bitter cold.[178] Hirszfeld considered the bribery not a bad but a useful, lifesaving act that "effectively counteracted the stupidity of orders issued by Dr. Schrempf."[179] Certainly some physicians who illegally treated patients at home, thus bypassing all the unpleasantnesses and dangers of quarantine and disinfection, were making their fortunes,[180] though these did them little good.

For those lacking either the means or the inclination to attempt bribery, bathing was the only alternative. And large numbers were bathed, or at least the numbers given to the Germans were large. Hagen stated that in the first quarter of 1941, 283,947 persons were bathed and deloused (more than half the population); 500 buildings were closed temporarily, one-third of those in the ghetto,[181] and 57,000 rooms fumigated.[182]

One woman has written about her experience at the baths. She was very proud of her hair, so she ran to be among the first 50 let in; she knew that if she saw the doctor early—the first step in the process—she could probably avoid having her head shaved. Later in the day, niceties began to be abandoned as the staff became overwhelmed by sheer numbers. When she finally was finished with the *parówka*, she had to hurry home to be in her courtyard before curfew. The bath had taken the entire day.[183] This woman obviously was not single or, if married, was not an Orthodox Jewess, since she did not wear a wig; one interviewee who worked in a bathhouse commented on the lice she saw in the wigs of Jewish women.[184]

Much of the day this woman would have spent standing in line. Some of that time the queue was dressed, some of it naked. The prospective bathers were almost certainly passing lice back and forth, the premises being extremely crowded. Lines often extended up the street and, in winter, people suffered severely from the cold; even inside, cold was a serious hazard, since by this stage the people were naked and no ghetto building was heated adequately. And after all this, the evidence was that only about 60 percent of those enduring the *parowka* were actually free of lice immediately afterwards while the other 40 percent were still lousy.[185] One survivor considered it useless to submit to the indignities of quarantine and disinfection when "the first person who jostled one in the street would probably shake off some of his lice onto the newly fumigated clothes."[186]

Disease prevention could be done differently. Hirszfeld and his colleagues tried an innovative approach. They persuaded some house managers to install local showers, and introduced the ironing of linen and underwear as a replacement for the mockery of sulfur "disinfection." This method seemed to be well accepted and might have provided a viable alternative if the Nazis had allowed its general use.[187]

Disinfection of Premises and Belongings

There were other problems too. When family members absented themselves for the necessary number of hours to attend the baths, it was not uncommon for their possessions to be rifled and stolen while they were gone. This was particularly likely to occur in the early days in the ghetto, when German-appointed Polish workers from outside the ghetto, often persons who were hostile to the Jews and who accepted the job with a prospect to looting, were detailed to fumigate the premises.

Hirszfeld believed that the methods the Jews used to bypass disinfection procedures saved lives because the "preventive medicine" prescribed by the Nazis would have been lethal if followed according to instructions.[188] As he put it, "The disease offered one an 80 percent chance of survival, while the delousing could destroy all one's possessions."[189]

Dr. Schrempf put pressure on the *Judenrat* from the earliest days, forcing them to arrange for the construction of disinfection chambers.[190] Of course, all costs were to be borne by the Jews,[191] and the costs were high; Czerniakow estimated that the new quarantine facility demanded in January 1940 would cost 100,000 zloty.[192]

At least some of the disinfection brigades rapidly acquired a sinister reputation. Their approach to the process of disinfection seemed to encompass one or the other of two extremes. If the householder or janitor was willing to offer a bribe, and the bribe was acceptable, no disinfection at all might be done. If a bribe was not offered, the disinfection process was so thorough that furniture was destroyed, clothing and linen torn, and the better items stolen.

The system seems to have been rotten throughout. Trunk blames the bad effects of the quarantine system on the brigades, which at first contained both Polish and Jewish workers; on the *Ordnungsdienst*, or Jewish police; on some Jewish physicians and health commissioners; and on the *Judenrat* Health Department.[193]

Six disinfection brigades were set up in April 1940, though this number later was reduced to two as a cost-saving measure. In the autumn of 1940, 50 Jews took a special course at the State Institute of Hygiene that was taught by well-known

Polish physicians.[194] As typhus became more common, the number of brigades was increased to 12 by September 1941, which was the worst time of the typhus epidemic. By this time, any volunteer was accepted, trained or not. The brigades continued to be mixed Polish and Jewish until this time, when all the Poles were released. They had been found to be particularly brutal and excessively venal.[195] Czerniakow noted a complaint made by a German engineer about the conduct of one brigade. The workers broke cupboards and walls, beat women who refused their invitations to bribery, and stole silver spoons.[196] The daily take was about 20 zloty ($4) per apartment, and a semiofficial scale existed for "equitable" division of the spoils: Based on a point system, all proceeds were split into 25 shares, of which the physician received 4, the head of the brigade 3, the section leader 1½, and each worker 1 point.[197] Ringelblum reported that the Polish police were especially greedy, demanding 5 zloty for every bundle exempted from disinfection.[198] For 2000 zloty an entire building could be exempted; of this total, the physician who had to sign the disinfection certificate received 220 zloty.[199] The members of the *Ordnungsdienst* found their own ways to tap this source, making money by warning residents in advance that their building was scheduled for disinfection, so that bedding, linen, clothing, and so on could be removed and thus saved from destruction.[200]

Aside from the problems of corruption and robbery, there is another question that must be raised in connection with disinfection. Did it work? If the system could have been made honest, would typhus have decreased or disappeared? The answer seems to be no.

Again, Hirszfeld is a key figure. Always the scientist, he decided to make a crucial experiment. With the cooperation of an incorruptible German colleague, Hirszfeld placed matchboxes full of lice inside bundles in rooms about to be treated. The disinfection process was to spray sulfur about the rooms in an apartment and then seal them shut for a period of time judged appropriate to permit the sulfur to permeate the contents and destroy the lice. So Hirszfeld's test bundles were "disinfected." Hirszfeld observed: "If the lice died, it was from laughter. We found that all the lice in the bundles survived the treatment. . . . sulfur did not penetrate a tightly bound bundle."[201] He knew what would succeed, basing his opinion on much experience with typhus in Serbia and elsewhere during and just after World War I. To delouse a group of human beings, one must kill lice faster than they can reproduce. Disinfection columns are not needed. What is required is a modest supply of clothing: two day shirts and two nightshirts, changing them and washing them regularly. However, he concluded, German physicians prefer to fight with complex equipment, police regulations, and circulars.[202]

The Germans also lacked DDT, the wonder substance that kept the Allied armies almost totally free of lice, and therefore typhus, throughout the war. Writing long afterward, Hagen retailed the rumor that Hitler's personal physician played a key role in preventing the production of DDT by the Third Reich; he had his own invention to promote, the useless and sometimes harmful *Russlapuder*, on which he made millions.[203]

At least one German official, Hagen, was beginning to change his opinion. He claimed that Schrempf's quarantine policy was fundamentally correct but doomed when large numbers of refugees began to inundate the ghetto.[204] However, he was well aware of the general public objection to quarantine, an attitude not limited to the Warsaw ghetto or to the time of World War II.[205] But when those ill with typhus eventually had to be cared for at home, the method seemed to work, not only for individual patients but for the population. Hagen concluded that when a patient with a reported infection was nursed at home, there would be one or two associated cases, but a concealed infection led to five or six associated cases, thus substantially accelerating the epidemic and adding to the mortality toll.[206]

At any rate, the methods used in the Warsaw ghetto began to change for the better. From April 1941 on, the disinfection system was improved. One or two rooms in a house might be set aside to be used for disinfection, and only places designated by a doctor were disinfected.[207]

Of course, disinfection of clothing and bodies would suppress typhus if the methods could be applied without creating conditions that would actually negate the effects, as was the case in Warsaw. For example, after he was deported in 1943, Dr. Fenigstein ended up in a small concentration camp at Hessenthal, in Germany. An epidemic of typhus occurred there in February 1945, with 15 dying and Fenigstein himself surviving a light case.[208] Once he persuaded the camp commandant to get delousing equipment, the epidemic was aborted in 10 days.[209]

IMMUNIZATION

By 1939, it was possible to inoculate susceptible persons against typhus (see Figure 7.6). The procedure itself was simple, though the preparation of effective vaccine was not. In Poland, vaccine came either from German laboratories or from the institute under Professor Weigl (Wajgel) in Lwów. The material was expensive because its manufacture was time-consuming, each dose requiring, first, the introduction of typhus germs into the anuses of numbers of lice,[210] scarcely a simple procedure. This was followed by the extraction, by hand, of the intestines of 150 lice for each dose of vaccine.[211] In Warsaw, the value of this vaccine was understood quickly. Two rich Polish merchants traveled to Lwów and set about cornering the market for themselves; they had agents there buy up every lot of *weiglowki*, as the material was nicknamed, which they then took back to Warsaw and sold at high prices.[212]

But one of the problems in preventing typhus was that there were several vaccines on the market, some of doubtful value. Nevertheless, and not surprisingly, many people were inoculated in the hope of inducing immunity. Millie Eisen remembers having an injection before the war for this purpose; this was especially desirable for a nurse who could expect frequent contact with patients suffering from typhus.[213] Even less surprising is it to find that the chairman of the *Judenrat* sought protection. Adam Czerniakow had at least two courses of the vaccine, the first in 1939,[214] the second two years later. Then the two injections were given five months apart, the first in September 1941,[215] the second in February 1942. On that last occasion his physician took a blood test, the result of which indicated that he could still get typhus despite all these efforts at prophylaxis. Czerniakow was annoyed at what

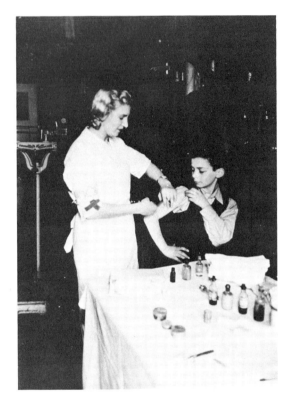

Figure 7.6. Inoculation in the ghetto (reproduced by permission of Yad Vashem Archives, Jerusalem: YVA 24-C-09).

he took to be indecisiveness on the part of the "scientists who do the blood testing and at the same time declare that neither a positive nor a negative reaction is conclusive."[216]

Weigl sent some units of vaccine to Hirszfeld. This was worth, the latter believed, up to 1000 zloty a dose on the free market, but he gave the whole shipment to the Health Council, only specifying that there should be a small charge for vaccinations.[217]

The German doctor with overall medical control over the Jews during the ghettoized period, Wilhelm Hagen, believed that the Weigl vaccine was too complicated and slow to make. He preferred the Wohlrab and Otto serum,[218] but since it came into use only in late 1942, it would have been of minimal help to Warsaw's Jews, most of whom had died in the ghetto or at Treblinka before then.

Little vaccine was available, and what was on the black market was often fraudulent and useless.[219] There was a vigorous black market activity in antityphus vaccine. According to Shoskes, Dr. Milejkowski spoke of a Dr. Deuhler, a Nazi, who sold Milejkowski typhus vaccine at high prices, even though theoretically the Germans didn't allow Jews to be inoculated.[220] Ringelblum noted in his diary that in September 1941 serum cost 500 to 600 zloty per person,[221] and one historian states that in the same year, vaccine might cost as much as 800 zloty outside the ghetto.[222] If true, that would be an unusual twist, since the price differential on essentially all items was to the disfavor of the Jews.

Referring to this period, Karolina Borman remembered suggesting to her parents that she work in a hospital, perhaps as a nurse's aid, to help the sick. Her father strongly objected to this, assuming that she would bring lice home and then contaminate the whole family. "'You can do what you want but you can't endanger our lives.' He had a point. Then we tried to fight the typhus and my father was able to get some vaccines for immunization. They came from Switzerland and were hard to get. . . but he inoculated us all."[223]

The Swiss serum may have been effective, but it was also both expensive and scarce. Because of the cost, a Swiss contact for the Joint felt obligated to pass on a veiled request for funding from the Red Cross, to underwrite at least a part of the cost. The physician added his own suggestion that a "symbolic gift" of some amount be offered.[224] The reason for the scarcity seems to have been straightforward: This serum required both dried eggs and mice for its manufacture. "Dried eggs have become a rare article in Switzerland and the mice do not get enough oats. The Red Cross has therefore cabled to the Rockefeller Institute and expects to receive from them the necessary animal preparations."[225] Whether this material was sent from the United States we do not know, but even if it was, any vaccine produced would have been too late to help the Jews of Warsaw.

Shipping American-made serum might have seemed a quicker solution, but this possibility was also fraught with difficulties. Although the American Red Cross and the United States Public Health Service were prepared to send antityphus serum to Poland, they insisted that it be used under the supervision of a Swiss doctor to ensure that the Germans did not confiscate the serum for their own use. But the International Red Cross was unable to obtain permission for this supervision from the Germans, so the American authorities refused to sanction any shipments.[226] Even if the serum had been shipped, its efficacy was uncertain. Apparently the American serum had "very doubtful value in combating the disease. The Germans themselves, as well as the Russians, claim to have had much more effective success in anti-typhus serum."[227]

Hagen wrote much about typhus and the ghetto, and it is difficult to know if his account is precise or if some self-justification occurred. He refered to the high cost of Weigl's vaccine, the fraudulence of some others in use, and said of Weigl's that "I managed to beg serum for the most important doctors" in the ghetto.[228]

Whether it was obtained via the black market or in other ways, many doctors seem to have received some sort of immunity from the vaccines used. Henry Fenigstein had typhus in the concentration camp at Hessenthal in 1945: "I remember suffering from severe headaches and fever and weakness, and I was full of these red little spots, with the typical rash."[229] But both he and his medical colleague were lucky to have had the disease in a very light form, presumably because they had had immunizing injections in the ghetto. Weigl's vaccine apparently did not confer total immunity, but rather meant that one would have only a light attack if one did get typhus.[230]

THEORIES ABOUT TYPHUS

Inevitably, theories abounded as people attempted to understand what they saw happening around them. Some observers noticed idiosyncrasies in the spread of the disease. It was obvious to all—particularly the refugees themselves—that the refugee centers or points were a focus of typhus. The sanitary conditions there were impossible.[231] And yet, at least some doctors were convinced that although there was much typhus in these centers, the mortality rate was lower than elsewhere in the ghetto.[232]

Czerniakow, Ringelblum, and Fenigstein all believed that deaths occurred more readily among the intelligentsia than among the poor. Czerniakow noted late in 1941 that friends and acquaintances were dying all around him, all of them members of the intelligentsia.[233] He gave many specific examples: The whole staff of the funeral department was ill with typhus, including Kaminer, the chairman, who died of the disease on 18 October 1941.[234] The secretary of the *Judenrat* Council, Michael Krol, died 16 June 1942.[235] Rosa Simkowicz, working for CENTOS as a social worker, died of typhus,[236] and on and on. Ringelblum thought that such a distinction could be made, well-to-do professionals dying more quickly even though they smeared oil or naphtha on their bodies, or wore vials of foul-smelling sobidilla to drive off lice.[237] And Fenigstein, with his perspective as the physician who did most of the autopsy examinations of victims, also thought that the aged died more quickly than the young.[238]

With regard to the cause of the disease, Hagen stated that the ghetto (and, by implication, the Jews) was the cause of the spread of typhus. Czerniakow believed, however, that "typhus spreads because of dire poverty and malnutrition."[239] Modern epidemiologists would agree. Hagen, of course was well aware that the typhus organism was needed, as well as a ghetto. His concern was less with typhus in the ghetto than with its spread into Aryan Warsaw, where it might affect the Poles, the *Volksdeutsche*, and, most important, the German army. He came to believe that typhus could be spread via droplets of moisture in the breath and by contaminated dust (*Über die Atemtröpfchen und infizierten Staub*).[240] This theory itself was in the air: On 29 October 1941, Czerniakow mentioned a "new theory," namely, that not only the louse is responsible but also the secretions of lice floating in the air.[241] Both Hagen and Czerniakow probably were expressing the view of the most prominent scientist in the ghetto, a man who had done much original work with typhus during and after World War I: Ludwig Hirszfeld. He wrote after his escape from the ghetto in 1943:

> I got the impression that the typhus was not transmitted just by louse bites. The disease also appeared in very rich families who lived in clean apartments with absolutely not a single louse and whose members never got in touch with the crowds because they never got out in the street. . . . Possibly the louse feces get into the street dust, and a certain percentage of infections proceeded via the lungs, nose, or eyes.[242]

After the war, one of Hirszfeld's admirers, Henry Makower, found the professor's theory unacceptable.[243] Makower was a renowned expert on infectious diseases, a consultant to the World Health Organization.[244] But recent opinion still supports Hirszfeld. An article in the *British Medical Journal* commented that Weigl had proved, in the 1930s, that dead dried lice were infective and that louse excreta remained infective for many months.[245] This was the justification for disinfection.

Certainly, if louse excreta are infective, it is easy to visualize them being wafted about the ghetto from dirty areas to those supposedly clean.

Those inhabitants of the Warsaw ghetto who recorded their opinions on the subject seemed unanimous on one point: Crowds mean danger. Inevitably, one would be infested with lice on the crowded streets, and while all streets in the ghetto were crowded (see Figure 7.7), some were especially busy: "if one has to go through Karmelicka Street, which is crowded whichever way one turns, or through the bazaar at 40 Leszno Street, or through Walicow Street, or if one has to take the streetcar, or visit the public kitchen, one is bound to become infected sooner or later."[246] The spread of lice, and therefore of typhus, was caused especially by children, who "were everywhere, running at dizzying speed through the crowds, rubbing against every pedestrian. . . . they spread it, without being aware of what they were doing."[247] The sale of old clothes was indicted as a mode for spreading lice, and therefore typhus, probably with justice.[248] Given the crowded state of most ghetto streets, it would be difficult to walk without brushing against lice-infested rags of all kinds, even if one wasn't interested in buying. For some time, two men called Kohn and Heller operated horse trolleys that connected the Small and Large ghettos, running on Leszno and Solna streets at 60 groschen a ride. These trolleys were always crowded and thus, again, ideal for disseminating lice among the riders.[249]

Figure 7.7. Street scene in the Warsaw ghetto, probably fairly early; shows many person-power *rikshas* Ulrich Keller, ed., (Bundesarchiv, Koblenz).

If brushing against old clothing carried a risk, how much greater was the danger for those working every day with the refugees? "Those lice-infested, shirtless, sore, and exhausted people who had no strength to kill even a louse"[250] brought billions of lice with them and often little else. Some came back to the ghetto from work camps. In one of these, at Belzec, a medical witness recorded that corpses might be covered with lice to a depth of 2 or 3 centimeters![251] It comes as no surprise to hear that nurses, doctors, orderlies, social workers, and others who worked with the poor had a high incidence of typhus. Fenigstein states that the medical profession suffered especially: 20 percent of the admitting staff at Czyste and 8 percent of the physicians and orderlies died of typhus.[252] Early in 1942, the danger was so great that CENTOS, whose workers spent so much time and energy helping the children of the ghetto, announced a new hiring policy for recruits: They must have had typhus in the past.[253] People were desperate for jobs, and one candidate apparently wrote that he hadn't had typhus but was quite willing to do so.[254]

Judenrat officials, at least those who did their jobs conscientiously, had to take special precautions. Czerniakow wrote about visiting a quarantine facility in 1939: "I try to be as careful as possible. Others still need my health; I need it least of all."[255] A year and a half later, he discovered a louse in his nightshirt, a "white many-footed revolting louse."[256] At about the same time, a crisis occurred in the office of ghetto *Kommissar* Auerswald: A louse crawled out of some correspondence on Jewish affairs lying on Auerswald's desk. Panic ensued, and the *Kommissar* declared that he would accept no letters from Czerniakow in the future.[257]

A group of rabbis approached the chairman of the *Judenrat* with a proposal that they believed could halt the epidemic. They proposed "as a propitiating religious rite at the cemetery, a marriage ceremony between a bachelor and a spinster, both of them poor people, immediately after the approaching Day of Atonement."[258] The quotation is a translation from the rabbis' written proposal. There is no record that the test was ever made. If it was, certainly it did not work.

RESEARCH INTO TYPHUS IN THE GHETTO

The research program initiated by Milejkowski, Stein, and others into what they called hunger disease[259] (see Chapter 6) also produced some useful observations on typhus. Many of these have been cited. The nurse, Millie Eisen, recalls doctors and medical students asking her for test tubes in which they could collect lice, and this must have been part of some research investigation.[260]

Hirszfeld did research on the topic, one aspect of which required the preparation and distribution of a questionnaire about typhus. He entrusted this task to a pediatrician, Dr. Mieczysław Szejnman, who had participated in vaccination programs for years[261] and who was also a researcher in the hunger disease project. Another aspect of Hirszfeld's studies was more typically laboratory oriented; he followed up the suggestion of another scientist and mixed the serum of typhus patients with their own urine; the reaction that he observed he found useful in separating the different strains of typhus organisms.[262]

Hirszfeld wasn't content simply to pursue his own hobby-horse, doing research in the laboratory. He and the other leaders of the medical profession in the ghetto knew how urgently the hospital physicians and the private practitioners needed up-to-date information. So Hirszfeld organized a series of weekly lectures on typhus—and, later, on other topics—which were given to physicians and students in the ghetto.[263] From this developed an association of block physicians, offering this group a way to supplement their medical knowledge.[264]

Hagen reported an interesting instance of inferential reasoning. One hundred cadavers (not hospital deaths) were examined and 8 percent had positive typhus reactions, presumably to a blood test, though this is not stated. From this finding, Hagen concluded that among the 10,000 who died in the ghetto in the first months of 1941, 1000 must have died of typhus; from that result, he decided that the number of infections with typhus would have been about 10,000, based on the assumption of a 10 percent mortality rate due to typhus. But only 1664 cases had been reported during that time. Therefore, large numbers of cases were being hidden.[265]

Finally, though this is really not research, there was the question of "typhus belts." People in the ghetto were selling belts that supposedly would protect the wearer from lice. They seemed to work, and when examined were found to be impregnated with mercury. This would kill lice but might also damage the health of the human wearing the belt, though most persons did not survive long enough for the ill effects to become apparent. The belts probably were World War I belts used by the Austrian army.[266]

The ravages of typhus fever were severe. Under the conditions prevalent in the Warsaw ghetto, perhaps no preventive or treatment methods could have changed the course of events significantly. Fear of the disease was as much a factor influencing events in the ghetto as was the disease itself. Brutal as the German-imposed methods for control were, they were introduced because the Germans feared typhus so much. And despite Jewish claims to the contrary, the methods were intended to prevent the spread of disease, not explicitly to kill Jews. Hundreds of Jews did die in the Warsaw ghetto from typhus, but there is no evidence to suggest that this was the result of any plan or conspiracy by the Nazis. Rather, the disastrous events reflected the effect of a combination of the Nazi ideological approach to disease and the extension of that ideology to Jews as a diseased people.

But while the typhus epidemics absorbed much of the attention of both Jews and Germans, other diseases were also affecting the ghetto. These will be considered in the next chapter.

8

Tuberculosis
and Other Diseases
in Jewish Warsaw

Typhus has been emphasized in this book both because it caused the illness and death of so many and because the residents of the ghetto themselves emphasized it. The amount written about that disease far exceeds what has been written on any other medical topic except starvation.

The preoccupation of the Jews with typhus is easily understandable. All serious epidemic diseases create human alarm and even panic. This is true whether the disease is smallpox, cholera, diphtheria, typhus, or AIDS. And, in the case of Warsaw's Jews, their attention was especially directed to typhus because it was literally the disease that forced them into the ghetto. Or, at least, it was the official German justification for creating the ghetto.

But the Jews in the Warsaw ghetto were afflicted by many diseases in addition to typhus. The majority of these were trivial and self-limited. They occasioned little or no comment in the documents that have survived. A few diseases did have significance in affecting the overall quality of life in the ghetto, and some of these will be described in the following pages. One of these diseases, tuberculosis, was extremely important. Tuberculosis, along with typhus and starvation, made up the three major scourges of the Warsaw ghetto. In absolute numbers of those ill and dying, tuberculosis may have exceeded typhus.

TUBERCULOSIS

Tuberculosis is an ancient disease. Signs of its effects have been found in Egyptian mummies and, perhaps, in cave paintings many millennia old. Until the 1950s, when effective drug therapy was discovered, tuberculosis was one of the greatest killers of mankind. It has two general forms: The acute disease, which can attack any body organ and which kills quickly, and the chronic form. This is the variety we are best acquainted with in the Western world. Characteristically, chronic tuberculosis is pulmonary tuberculosis, the so-called silent killer affecting the lungs of its victims. It causes the wasted bodies, the coughing up of blood, and the pale countenances that have been described not only in innumerable medical reports but also in literature and music. Tuberculosis is the theme of Thomas Mann's novel *The Magic Mountain*, as well as of the opera *La Boheme*.

But tuberculosis is not a literary creation. The disease is a major killer. It was

154

the killer of thousands of Jews in the Warsaw ghetto in the 1940s, though we have far less information on tuberculosis than we have about typhus or about starvation.

Before the War

Tuberculosis was a common disease in Poland, among both Jews and gentiles, before the war. This would have been predictable given the inadequate diet and crowded living quarters of so many of the poor (see Figure 8.1).

There were two institutions devoted to the care of tuberculous Jews near Warsaw. One was the Brijus Sanatorium in Otwock, 20 miles away; the other was the Medem Pediatric Tuberculosis Center. Some idea of the scope of the infection among the Jews comes from information about Medem, located in Międzeszyn, about 15 miles southeast of Warsaw and across the Vistula River.

Medem was the only sanatorium in Poland for Jewish children. It was founded in 1925 and, by the end of 1937, it had cared for 7500 tuberculous Jewish children. This was a significant accomplishment, but one that was dwarfed by the magnitude of the problem. In the same 12-year period, 76,000 children were entered on the books at Medem as candidates needing treatment after having been examined by physicians.[1] So only 1 child in 10 received care for his or her tuberculosis.

According to Trunk, in the period 1931–33, tuberculosis was responsible for 8.3 percent of all deaths among Polish Jews, and it was in fifth place as a cause of mor-

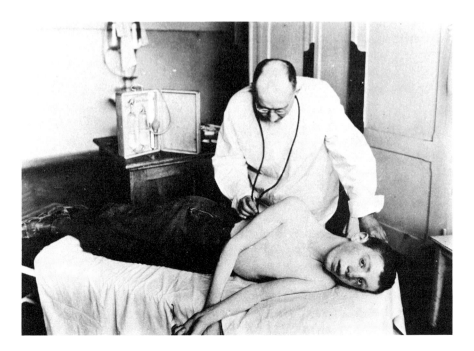

Figure 8.1. TOZ, the Society for the Health Care of the Jewish People: examination for and diagnosis of tuberculosis (reproduced by permission of Yad Vashem Archives, Jerusalem: YVA FA 35-1973).

tality. Trunk also states that 387 Jews (out of a population of about 350,000) died of tuberculosis in 1939.[2]

Tuberculosis During World War II

The existence of tuberculosis in a community is dependent on two interlocking factors. One is the presence of the tuberculosis bacterium, *Mycobacterium tuberculosis*. The second is social—chronic hunger coupled with overcrowded living conditions. Conditions in Poland under Nazi rule became ideal for ensuring that tuberculosis would increase. There, poverty plus the imposed stringent rationing guaranteed inadequate nutrition. At the same time, these conditions ensured overcrowding and consequent constant exposure of previously well persons to those who had active tuberculosis and who were producing virulent germs in their sputum and breath.

Hagen, the Nazi health officer in Warsaw from February 1941 until early in 1943,[3] believed that tuberculosis was the major health problem in Poland. He pointed out that even before the war, the death rate from tuberculosis in Poland was twice that in Germany. And he was referring to the whole of Poland, not the supposedly unhealthy Jewish portion of the population. There were 160 deaths per 100,000 population in 1937, and the rate rose to 280 in 1940.[4] By the following year tuberculosis mortality was 400/100,000, and twice as many Poles died of tuberculosis as of typhus.[5] Hagen claimed that gentile Poles were more severely affected by tuberculosis than were the Jews, and that tuberculosis in Poland generally was less a chronic disease (as it was in Germany and in North America) than an acute epidemic.[6] He himself claimed to be more worried about tuberculosis than about typhus or any other disease.[7] According to his figures, the incidence of tuberculosis tripled in the last three months of 1939.[8] He cited the statistics presented in Table 8.1.

Hagen was convinced that Jews suffered less from tuberculosis than did non-Jewish Poles. This opinion again reflects his dependence on data supplied by Milejkowski's department of the *Judenrat*. Even if correct, this should not be interpreted to mean that tuberculosis was an insignificant problem in the ghetto. The opposite was the case: Tuberculosis became a major public health concern in the Warsaw ghetto and killed thousands of Jews.

Table 8.1. Tuberculosis Mortality, 1937–41[9]

Year	Deaths per 100,000 Population	
	Warsaw	Germany
1937	148.0	63.0
1938	140.7	65.0
1939	160.0	68.0
1940	280.0	ca. 70.0
1941 (1st quarter)	400.0+	—

To the vast majority of the Jews of Warsaw, statistical data were of no interest. What they knew was that tuberculosis was one of the diseases that affected their families, often fatally. In the spring of 1940, the first typhus epidemic—the one that became the great excuse for ghettoization—was waning. But just at this time, a flurry of deaths began from starvation and tuberculosis. Mortality began to rise dramatically.[10] By February 1941, three months after the Jews had been sealed into the ghetto, an epidemic of tuberculosis threatened; it was seen clearly that because of the serious overcrowding and inadequate diet, the disease could spread catastrophically.[11]

In March 1941, TOZ officials reported that "the number of Jewish consumptives registered with it in Warsaw and Lublin reached many thousands, with 250 cases being registered during one week alone in the former city."[12]

The characteristic type of tuberculosis seen by Lenski, who had been a radiologist at Czyste Hospital, was the malignant pulmonary form[13]—that is, tuberculosis that affected the patient's lungs but attacked fiercely, often killing quickly and thus contrasting with the usual type of tuberculosis of the lungs seen in North America, which might last for years. But there was also much miliary tuberculosis, a particularly lethal form in which the tuberculosis germ is present in large quantity in the bloodstream and thus spreads throughout the entire body, overwhelming its defenses.

In 1942 the chairman of the *Judenrat* himself may have suffered from tuberculosis. Referring to his struggle to have prisoners released by the Nazis, Czerniakow said he had been spitting blood from his ceaseless but unavailing efforts to have prisoners released[14] Spitting blood most likely was a symptom of tuberculosis of the lungs, though other diagnoses are possible.

The Medem Sanatorium would have been of little help to the sick Jewish children of the Warsaw ghetto. It was small, and starved for financial support and for food and other supplies. During the fighting in September 1939, the Medem Sanatorium was appropriated and used as a Polish military hospital. Ultimately, it was completely destroyed by incendiary bombs.[15] By November 1939, the sanatorium had been reconstructed and began functioning again in the fight against tuberculosis. Financial responsibility for Medem had been taken over, partially or completely, by the Jewish Labor Committee in the United States.[16]

In Warsaw itself, tuberculous children may have been able to get treatment at the Berson and Bauman Hospital. That institution had a tuberculosis ward throughout the ghetto period. As early as the autumn of 1940, before the ghetto existed, a physician at Berson and Bauman noted that the incidence of tuberculosis was rising rapidly. Moreover, children "didn't recover from TB in those days."[17] By spring 1942, she found that tuberculosis prevailed "all powerful."[18]

After all the deportations were over and the ghetto had been destroyed, the Brijus Sanatorium at Otwock was also emptied. This institution was located among pine woods, and was intended for adult Jewish patients who had tuberculosis.[19] After the ghetto was emptied, the Nazi plan was to convert the building into an institution in the *Lebensborn* program,[20] that controversial Nazi invention that functioned as either a nursery for "Aryan" prototype babies or a brothel for the SS, or both.[21] But by then the institution had ceased to serve the Jews, and its disposition is irrelevant to our purpose.

Trunk states that the prewar mortality rate from tuberculosis among Jews in Warsaw was 8.3 percent of all deaths, whereas in 1941 tuberculosis accounted for 33.7 percent of the deaths of Jews in the Warsaw ghetto.[22] The latter figure is the only statistical or quantitative estimate I have found in any source relative to the scope of the problem of tuberculosis in the Warsaw ghetto.

Since there were at least 43,329 deaths among Jews in the Warsaw ghetto in 1941,[23] Trunk's suggested percentage would mean that he expected and predicted 14,602 deaths (33.7 percent of 43,329) from tuberculosis. One cannot prove this figure wrong because, of the 43,329 deaths, the Jewish medical profession identified specific causes in only 12,962.

Can Trunk's figure of 33.7 percent be supported? If it can, then tuberculosis will be seen to have far surpassed typhus in number of deaths in the ghetto and to rival the ravages of starvation. I suggest that it can be used as a helpful approximation, though the evidence to support this opinion is largely circumstantial.

Tuberculosis was a major killer during World War II. There are abundant data to show, for example, that the men and women who survived the war while incarcerated in concentration camps suffered heavily from the disease. At Bergen-Belsen, up to 20 percent of the inmates were found to have tuberculosis when examined by Allied medical teams.[24] Another report cites 10,000 cases of tuberculosis among 45,000 survivors at this camp, or 22 percent.[25] Tuberculosis was one of the chief diseases at Buchenwald,[26] and some physicians thought the disease to be so widespread among camp survivors generally that its recurrence would create a public health hazard in Europe for years to come.[27] One reason, though not the most important, for the existence of so much tuberculosis in some camps was the experimentation done by Nazi doctors who gave the disease to prisoners. This was true, for example, at Neuengamme KL.[28]

Tuberculosis was also common in ghettos other than Warsaw. In the Łódź ghetto, one observer commented on the unusual increase of tuberculosis among children and young people, causing the hearse to be busy "as never before."[29] This was in May 1941; three months later, the disease had continued to affect more and more Jews in the Łódź ghetto. Although a group of Jews who arrived from Warsaw complained of the situation there, still "none of them has that dreadful pasty tubercular skin seen here. The cadavers walking around the streets give the entire ghetto that pale, musty tubercular look."[30]

The evidence points to tuberculosis as being both common and fatal in incarcerated communities of Jews during the war years. Certainly there was tuberculosis in the Warsaw ghetto. Why do the statistics, collected by the Jews themselves, fail to reflect the seriousness of this disease?

The answer seems to lie in a combination of circumstances that have conspired to conceal the true impact of tuberculosis, both to the ghetto dwellers themselves and to subsequent students of ghetto life.

The reasons behind this phenomenon relate to the nature of our perception of tuberculosis itself, to varying psychological reactions to different diseases, to specific conditions within the Warsaw ghetto, and to alterations in the way the Jewish patients responded physically to infection with tuberculosis compared with their reactions in normal times. These reasons will be discussed in turn; some have been alluded to already.

1. *Perceptions of Tuberculosis*: Tuberculosis consists of two different general types. It may be chronic, undramatic, slowly affecting the body, killing over months to years, the "silent killer." Or it may be acute, quickly attacking the body and killing the patient but affecting any and all organs and simulating many diseases, so that it is possible for physicians to mistake the diagnosis and, in the absence of an autopsy, to certify that death was due to some other disorder. And autopsies were infrequently carried out in the Warsaw ghetto. At Czyste Hospital, autopsies were performed exactly 3658 times, though almost 100,000 Jews died in the ghetto.[31]

   Both forms of tuberculosis existed, and both complicated the collection of adequate statistics. In the chronic disease, the patients simply were not much noticed in comparison with the dramatic pictures presented by both starvation and typhus. In the acute forms of tuberculosis, the diagnosis often would be missed.

2. *Psychological Reaction to Disease*: Epidemic diseases that strike suddenly and dramatically, noticeably affecting many victims all at once, create fear and panic. But diseases such as tuberculosis are less fearsome. When a population is in the grip of an epidemic such as typhus, tuberculosis is even less likely to be seen as a significant problem. This is true for doctors and also for the general public, in turn affecting such mundane matters as the kind of information that is put in letters and diaries—and thus the kind of evidence that is available to historians after the event. In the various diaries and memoirs read and interviews conducted in the research for this book, tuberculosis was almost never mentioned, but references to typhus and to starvation were voluminous.

3. *Specific Conditions Inside the Ghetto*: The Jews of Warsaw had excellent doctors among them, including a number of Europe's best. But as this book shows, the conditions under which they attempted to practice were chaotic. Facilities were grossly inadequate. The volume of illness was enormous, and this affected both doctors and patients. Doctors could not devote the appropriate time to investigate obscure illness or to give unusual attention to ordinary disease. Patients tended to do without doctors, partly because they knew the doctors were overworked, partly because private physicians charged for their services, and partly because many families used home remedies.

   All of these factors combined to lessen the likelihood that diagnoses would be correctly made or that patients would be seen at all by physicians (many people died in the ghetto without medical attention). This last point will be expanded.

4. *Different Responses of Patients to Tuberculosis*: This is a crucial factor in solving the puzzle of the anonymous nature of tuberculosis in the Warsaw ghetto. The information about this aspect of tuberculosis comes largely from

the ghetto physicians who studied hunger disease. The findings must be presented in some detail.

The available firsthand information about tuberculosis derives chiefly from three sources: the research into hunger disease in 1942[32] and the papers of Trunk[33] and Lenski.[34] The latter had been a medical practitioner in the ghetto.

Hunger Disease and Tuberculosis

When the ghetto physicians designed their study of hunger, they did so in the best possible scientific manner. The first step was to avoid contaminating their experimental results by including in the study patients who had a number of diseases simultaneously. The reason for doing this is that the effects of one disease may mask or alter those of another, so that the investigator ends by being uncertain which disease has created a given change in the body.

Dr. Michal (Mieczysław) Szejnman carried out the studies on changes in the blood and bone marrow. He outlined the way patients were selected: "We considered only patients with no fever, no specific organ symptoms, negative results in tests for parasites and for blood in the feces, lack of tuberculosis bacilli, and negative X-rays."[35] This would seem a thorough and safe approach. But in fact it was not, for reasons that would have been difficult to predict in 1942.

First, there is the matter of x-rays. In patients who have tuberculosis of the lungs, examination of x-ray films of the chest is a highly effective (though not invariably accurate) way of detecting their disease. Thus one would suppose that negative x-rays would mean that the group of patients studied did not have pulmonary tuberculosis. In ordinary circumstances, that would be the case. But circumstances were not ordinary in the Warsaw ghetto.

One problem was the profound lack of medical equipment. In Chapter 5, the move of Czyste Hospital into the ghetto is described. The hospital personnel were allowed to take no large pieces of equipment such as x-ray apparatus. Most patients who had internal diseases, such as would be studied in the hunger disease research, were hospitalized in the division of Czyste Hospital at Stawki 6–8. But the only x-ray apparatus in ghetto hospitals was at Leszno 1.[36] And Dr. Szejnman goes on to say, in his description of how patients were selected, that actually taking the necessary films was a problem "because we had to transport very sick people to a different building, and often did not have the facilities to do so. Therefore not all cases were X-rayed."[37] Therefore, patients who had pulmonary tuberculosis might well have been included, unknowingly, in the patients selected for the hunger disease study.

Mordecai Lenski, himself a physician in the ghetto, wrote that there was less tuberculosis than typhus. But his perspective was perhaps a narrow one. He was a radiologist in Czyste Hospital at Leszno 1, the only place a physician could have an x-ray film made in the Czyste complex. Thus it was to his department that patients suspected of having pulmonary tuberculosis frequently could *not* be sent, according to Lenski's professional colleague, Dr. Szejnman. If they couldn't be sent there, Lenski would not know about them. Even more to the point, patients with acute tuberculosis would almost certainly not have been sent for x-rays, so Lenski also would not have known about them. They would not be sent because they were extremely ill, because their tuberculosis may have simulated some other disease, and because x-ray examination is not particularly useful even if a physician suspects the existence of acute tuberculosis. So, Lenski's remark about there being less tuberculosis than typhus should not carry too much weight.

Even so, the short paragraph Lenski wrote about tuberculosis is important. He emphasizes that he did see malignant tuberculosis. He also says that there were many cases of miliary tuberculosis.[38] So, he certainly confirms that tuberculosis was a problem in the ghetto.

Like Dr. Szejnman, Dr. Apfelbaum-Kowalski experienced difficulties in his study of the circulatory system in hunger disease. He and his colleagues tried to obtain what they called "homogeneous material and clean hunger disease patients," thus excluding those patients who were known to have other diseases. But, he goes on to say, this was "sometimes very difficult, especially with patients with anergic tuberculosis, which in cachectic patients show no symptoms."[39] That is, it was difficult to exclude tuberculosis that shows no symptoms in patients extremely emaciated from starvation: the very group they were attempting to study.

This is the crux of the explanation for the low rate of reported diagnosis of tuberculosis in the Warsaw ghetto. In starved patients, the signs of tuberculosis were minimal or absent.

We have already mentioned one of the usual diagnostic tests for tuberculosis, the chest x-ray. But even hospitalized patients attached to a scientific study were infrequently x-rayed because the inadequate x-ray equipment was housed many blocks away. If these patients weren't x-rayed, it can be assumed that other hospitalized patients were not, to say nothing of patients ill at home or in the refugee shelters.

There are other diagnostic tests for tuberculosis. One is analysis of sputum for the presence of tuberculosis bacteria. The other is a skin test. Even in a good laboratory in the 1940s, technicians could not invariably find tuberculosis bacilli in known tubercular patients. The procedure is lengthy and requires painstaking care. The laboratories of the Warsaw ghetto were poorly equipped and seriously understaffed; so the necessary stains may not have been readily available, though the point is never mentioned. If so, this test would not have been reliable when negative results were reported.

But even more important is the fact that a doctor must suspect the presence of tuberculosis before he thinks to order the tests for it. And the type of tuberculosis most common in the ghetto had hidden symptoms.

The skin test done then, known as a "Pirquet test,"[40] was reasonably reliable in detecting individuals who either have or have had tuberculosis. But again, the findings of the ghetto physicians reveal how unhelpful the test actually was. This discovery was, indeed, one of the significant scientific observations made in the hunger disease research.

Anna Braude-Heller and her colleagues, studying hunger disease in children, reported the significant observations. They mentioned that a colleague had studied the reaction of the skin to various substances, but that this manuscript had been lost. But they went on to remark on the striking clinical observation that, in severe hunger disease, the Mantoux test failed to give a positive result. Pigment reaction was usually negative, even in proven cases of tuberculosis.[41] Fliederbaum and his colleagues confirmed this observation. They found too that the skin loses its capacity for reacting to tuberculin (the material injected in the skin test).[42]

So, another of the usually reliable diagnostic aids failed to work under the conditions prevalent in the Warsaw ghetto. Chest x-rays were difficult to obtain, sputum tests were unreliable, and the skin test did not work.

There are, of course, physical signs of tuberculosis that are of great importance in making the diagnosis. One of these, perhaps the most general, is wasting of the body tissues. Patients lose fat and muscle, although continuing to eat their regular meals. Until the nineteenth century, tuberculosis was called "consumption" precisely because of this sign; patients who had tuberculosis seemed to be consumed from within. But in the Warsaw ghetto, everyone was both emaciated and hungry. So, this sign was unhelpful.

Another sign of tuberculosis is fever. But again, the presence of fever could not be relied upon. "We saw many cases of tuberculosis, some with severe symptoms, but the temperature was normal or even below normal."[43] The difficulty in making the clinical diagnosis constantly confronted the physician in the ghetto. For example, in diagnosing the cause of abnormal fluid collecting in the pleural cavity, the area between the lungs and the chest wall, caution was required. Many diseases cause this sign, including tuberculosis. "The differential diagnosis was very difficult because tuberculin tests were negative and there was no fever."[44]

Yet despite the absence or unreliability of customary signs and the failure of diagnostic tests for various reasons, tuberculosis was present. Some of it was pulmonary tuberculosis, but many other organs were also affected. It was observed in the brain and in the sex organs, a very rare complication.[45] When lymph nodes were enlarged, this usually was because of tuberculosis.[46] If edematous swelling occurred only on one side of the body, and persisted, the doctors learned to suspect the presence of a blood clot in a vein in the upper leg or the pelvis. This complication was quite common, "and autopsy would show advanced tuberculosis."[47] Another problem was "enlarged, cheesy extraperitoneal glands . . . pressing on the veins of the abdominal cavity and, as a result, a net of the dilated veins would appear in the hypogastrium [on the upper abdominal wall]."[48]

So, despite the absence of statistical evidence of its occurrence, tuberculosis affected both adults and children. Apfelbaum-Kowalski notes that tuberculosis had become very prevalent, unlike before the war, and had spread rapidly.[49] Virulent tuberculosis was extremely common.[50] Braude-Heller cites one case in which tuberculosis was not suspected, but at autopsy the child was found to have tuberculosis of the lungs, tuberculous glands in the abdomen, and tuberculous ulcers in the intestines.[51]

Thus evidence of a major epidemic of tuberculosis is found in the research into hunger disease, but without quantitative documentation. One highly significant reason that the disease was not featured more prominently in the research is directly related to the tragedy of the ghetto. Braude-Heller and colleagues, in their chapter in *Hunger Disease*, noted that a separate chapter in the book dealt with tuberculosis.[52] But they were mistaken. The modern editor has added the note "(manuscript lost)." Similarly, the specific details of the skin's failure to respond to tuberculin, research done by Dr. B. Raszkes, were also lost.[53] Had these chapters been written and had they survived the war, the place of tuberculosis in the medical history of the Warsaw ghetto would have been made explicit and undeniable.

Now we must reexamine what little we know about the statistics of tuberculosis in the ghetto. These come largely from Hagen[54] and Trunk.[55] Hagen was extremely interested in tuberculosis, and indeed, this interest led directly to his departure from Warsaw in disgrace. But his figures relate largely to Warsaw generally or to Aryan Warsaw. He states that there were twice as many deaths from tuberculosis as from typhus early in 1941.[56] This figure may include the ghetto. But when he says that tuberculosis mortality in 1942 was three times the prewar rate, he must be referring to either Warsaw or Poland generally.[57] By the end of 1942 few Jews were left in Warsaw, and no one was collecting statistical data about their illnesses.

Hagen had the audacity to write directly to Hitler about medical affairs in the *Generalgouvernement*. Soon afterward, he submitted a detailed recommendation to his superiors to provide elaborate antituberculosis care to the Poles of Warsaw. Nazi ideology permitted no interest in spending money on health care for Poles. One of SS Hauptstürmführer Pakebusch's criticisms of Hagen's proposal noted: "The planned budget for this comes to the sum of Zl. 18,000,000!!!"[58] The exclamation points were in the original. Himmler recommended that Hagen be put in a concentration camp until the end of the war.[59] This was not done. He went to the Russian front instead, and survived. Had he suggested this kind of care for Jews, his punishment would almost certainly have been more severe.

Trunk, then, offers all of the statistics we have for tuberculosis in the Warsaw ghetto. They are few enough. Tuberculosis deaths in Warsaw's Jews rose from 387 in 1939 to 649 in the first two months of 1941.[60] If we extrapolate the second figure over the entire year, this gives a total estimate of 3892 deaths from tuberculosis in 1941. Since conditions were worsening rapidly by 1941, this seems a safe minimal estimate to make. Note that according to the hunger disease researchers there were 1991 deaths from typhus that year, the year of the major epidemic.[61] This would give a ratio of deaths due to tuberculosis vis à vis typhus of about 2:1. But Trunk says that only 1580 Jews died of typhus in 1941,[62] giving a ratio of 3892 to 1580, or 8:3.

Trunk also states that in May and June 1941, 12 percent of all deaths among refugees were due to tuberculosis.[63] Since we have no isolated data on deaths among refugees, we cannot draw further conclusions from this number.

Trunk further identifies 3171 deaths from contagious diseases in 1941 among 4920 deaths in ghetto hospitals.[64] Removing the 1580 deaths that he says were due to typhus leaves a total of 1591 (3171 − 1580) other contagious deaths. Some of these 1591 deaths were due to tuberculosis, though we don't know how many; note that 1591 is 32 percent of 4920. Total deaths in the ghetto in 1941 were 43,239,[65] but apparently only 4920 patients died in the hospital. The obvious conclusion is that 38,319 (43,239 − 4920) died in the streets, in orphanages, in homes, in Gęsiówka, and in refugee centers.

We have no independent verification for Trunk's figure of 33.7 percent of all deaths in the ghetto in 1941 as being caused by tuberculosis. But given all of the circumstantial evidence just cited, I propose that the figure be accepted and extended to 1942. Moreover, I conjecture that the figure for 1940 was halfway between the prewar percentage of 8.3 and the terminal figure of 33.7: that is, 21 percent.

The table for mortality in the ghetto can then be redesigned to look like Table 8.2.

What must be stressed again is that the data added on tuberculosis are strictly conjectural, based solely on Trunk's statement that 33.7 percent of ghetto dwellers died of that disease in 1941 (see Figure 8.2).

TYPHOID FEVER

This disease became a serious problem in the autumn of 1939, affecting Jews and Poles alike.[67] Nazi bombing of Warsaw caused the problem, because the destruction included the water-filtering stations. The populace was reduced to drinking water from the Vistula, unfiltered and frequently unboiled.[68] Typhoid fever was the predictable outcome. The first influx of refugees contributed to the problem by increasing the strain on the minimal water facilities available.[69]

At Czyste Hospital there were 2057 cases of typhoid between September and November 1939, or about 685 a month. By January 1940 the total had dropped to 104; in April it was only 10 cases, and the epidemic was over.[70] It had been a serious scare, and the massive number of patients in the fall, plus the shortage of food, made it difficult to treat the sick. An internist at Czyste commented that the available diet was exactly the opposite of what was required for typhoid patients. All the hospital had to give them were black bread and water. This man concluded that "it was obvious that the Germans tried to raise the mortality."[71]

Whether or not the Germans deliberately fomented the epidemic is uncertain. But thanks to ordinary public health measures, the disease was brought under con-

Table 8.2. Amended Causes of Death in the Warsaw Ghetto Based on the Speculations in Text and on Table 1 from Winick[66]

Year Months	Typhus	(%)	Hunger & Exhaustion	(%)	TB	(%)	Undetermined	(%)	Total
1939 Sept–Dec	5	(.07)	4	(.06)	544	(8.3)	2,056	(31.3)	6,560
1940 12	216	(2.3)	91	(1.01)	1,786	(21.0)	1,032	(11.5)	8,981
1941 12	1,991	(4.6)	10,971	(25.3)	14,572	(33.7)	10,653	(24.6)	43,239
1942 Jan–July	512	(1.3)	7,254	(18.4)	13,273	(33.7)	10,694	(27.2)	39,385
							22,511*		
Total	2,724	(2.8)	18,320	(18.7)	30,175	(30.7)	46,946	47.8	98,165

*Number unaccounted for when subtracting all subtotals from the overall total of 98,165; these are obviously also "undetermined."

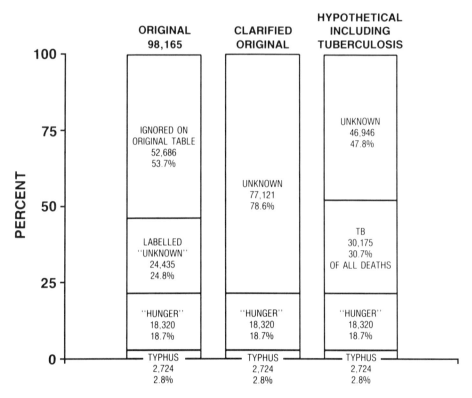

Figure 8.2. Graph of deaths within the Warsaw ghetto, 1940–42. The column of the left gives the proportional causes cited in Myron Winick (ed.), *Hunger Disease: Studies by the Jewish Physicians in the Warsaw Ghetto,* trans. Martha Osnos, New York, Chichester, Brisbane, and Toronto: John Wiley & Sons, 1979, Table 1). The central column shows the data readjusted to indicate total unknown causes of death; the column on the right shows the conjectural causes of death based on the author's speculations about the relative influence of tuberculosis on these data.

trol. One major factor was the eventual repair of the waterworks, so that reasonably clean water was again available.

In addition, immunization was carried out. Hagen states that the Polish state hygienic institute produced an antityphoid serum based on the strain of the organism then dominant in Warsaw.[72] Some type of vaccine was used widely and undoubtedly contributed to ending the epidemic. Between September 1939 and June 1940, the Vaccination Center of TOZ administered 24,663 antityphoid injections to 13,555 persons.[73]

After this, typhoid was not a problem in Warsaw. It was almost nonexistent in the ghetto, despite the poor water supply, because of regular repeated preventive immunizations of the whole population.[74] It was only in November 1942, after the ghetto was effectively dismembered and *Judenrat* services broke down, that typhoid returned,[75] and then it was not a major problem.

PSYCHOLOGICAL STRESS AND MENTAL DISORDER

In the 1940s, the concept of great physical and mental harm resulting from the pressure of unremitting tension had none of the force it has acquired since that time. But people react badly to stress whether they are aware of the concept or not. And the Warsaw ghetto provided every reason for a major epidemic of stress-related disorders.

One stress that had severe psychic results was the incessant bombing and shelling during the German attack on Warsaw in September 1939. "Crazy Elias" was one pitiful survivor of this period. He had been a scholar, a student of the Talmud, so shattered by the bombardment that he thought he was an air-raid siren. He howled all night, waking his entire building. "His sisters beat him, starved him and pushed him out of their room, so that he spent most of his time on the stairs."[76] Fortunately, such cases seem to have been rare.

The Nazi campaign of intimidation, humiliation, and brutality, leading to the ultimate and imminent likelihood of violent death, provided stresses in awful abundance. Many of their techniques have already been detailed, but one more should be examined because it fits so explicitly into this category. One of the main Polish prisons was the infamous Pawiak Prison, on Dzielna Street in the heart of what became the ghetto. But it was a general prison and throughout the ghetto's existence, all manner of political and criminal suspects and prisoners were brought into the ghetto to Pawiak, and some were taken out—often feet first, as the Western movies might have it. Christians and Jews, Poles and foreigners, prisoners of war and black marketeers, murderers and pickpockets.

Sometime in late 1941 or early 1942, the occupants of all flats in the buildings overlooking Pawia and Dzielna Streets—and thus the prison—had been ordered by the Germans to keep their windows blacked out totally, 24 hours a day. Presumably they didn't want to risk a public confrontation if it was known that they had introduced some popular figure into Pawiak. Or perhaps the edict represented simple cussedness. But the rule existed and was enforced. So, for hundreds of persons, one of the few consolations permitted to the Jews, the privilege of seeing the sky and enjoying a sunny day, was denied them. Few flats had electricity, the provision of which was intermittent at best anyway, so most of these people lived in perpetual darkness. A Jewish physician commented: "I need hardly describe what it means for the occupants' eyes and lungs, their state of mind, this continual dark existence without fresh air, even ghetto air."[77]

This same physician wrote in his diary about the general feeling of fear that by November 1942 was widespread, if not universal, among the few remaining Jews in Warsaw. He found it hard to describe the sensation of this incessant fear, suggesting that only a familiarity with the dark novels of Dostoyevsky could let anyone not there imagine how the ghetto dwellers lived with the sword of the *Umschlagplatz* hanging over their heads.[78] One clinician was surprised to find that the "perpetual nervous tension and fear" did not result in any increase in specific nervous diseases.[79] Perhaps one answer is that when everyone shares a situation there is consolation in that fact, in knowing that one's misery is widely shared rather than limited to oneself. But the strain affected at least some ghetto inhabitants. Janusz Korczak, a physician, observed in himself a strange weakness and physical instability. He found it difficult to step up onto a sidewalk; he staggered when a passerby brushed against him:

> And this is not weakness. Quite easily I lifted up a schoolboy, thirty kilograms of live, resistant weight. Not lack of strength, but of will. Like a drug addict. I even wondered if there wasn't something in tobacco, raw vegetables, in the air we breathe. For I am not alone in this.[80]

Fliederbaum and his colleagues, in their studies of hunger disease, noted what may be a related phenomenon: a striking increase in depression in the starving, even in young people. Many showed complete apathy, lack of interest in things around them, and sometimes incoherence.[81] Korczak sounds as if he may have been clinically depressed. He had every reason to be, as he struggled with such futility to keep his orphans dressed, fed, and cared for.

One expected consequence of this mental pressure would be suicide. Yet until the summer of 1942, when the massive deportations were carried out and irrefutable eyewitness accounts of Treblinka had been brought back into the ghetto, suicide was remarkably infrequent.[82] Chaim Kaplan, writing in his diary on 10 March 1940, credits the remarkably low suicide rate among Jews in Poland to some secret power. This power "keeps us alive and preserves us in spite of all the laws of nature." Moreover, Kaplan claims that this power did not inhere in German Jews, thus explaining their much higher suicide rate.[83] Dawidowicz suggested that the suicide rate in 1940 up to July 1942 was 65 percent of the prewar rate,[84] an estimate that is supported by a Joint report that in "the last so-called normal years"—that is, in the late 1930s—Warsaw had about 200 Jewish suicides annually, whereas in the immediately preceding four months of the war there had been "a couple of dozen, maximum 30 cases of Jewish suicides in Warsaw."[85]

Some of the suicides that did occur came at the time of the German occupation of Poland or shortly after. Berg relates how two of her teachers, both unequivocally Jewish-looking, took their own lives after suffering humiliations at Nazi hands.[86] The Opus factory was located in the same building as her parents' home in the fall of 1939, and Irena Bakowska recalls that the owner of the factory jumped several stories to his death when confronted by German demands in connection with the factory.[87]

The factors that suddenly cause people to kill themselves often are mysterious. Why today and not yesterday? Czerniakow mentioned an instance that shook him. A dental hygienist came to Czerniakow's home to work on his teeth; she was talking about the fate of their children, one of hers being missing, as was Czerniakow's son. The next morning she jumped to her death from a fourth-floor apartment.[88] Jumping from four- and five-story buildings was a method used relatively often in the ghetto. One case remains vivid in the memory of Janina David, a young girl who had twin girls living on the floor above. There had been an *Aktion* while the father was away:

> Mr. Roth, the father of the twins, flashed past and we heard him racing up the stairs calling to the girls. It was a hot sunny day and all the windows were open. We heard his steps, running from one room to another, then a short silence, then a large object

hurtled from above. It darkened our room for a moment and crashed like a thunderclap on the cement below. Father raced outside. Grandmother fainted. Mother and I busied ourselves with water and smelling salts. No one dared approach the window. Early next morning we moved out.[89]

Adam Czerniakow used poison to kill himself. Both as a chemical engineer and as head of the *Judenrat*, he would have easy access to such means. One of his associates recalled the day in the fall of 1939 when Czerniakow met with several new appointees to the *Judenrat* in his office. He made a point of showing them where he kept a key to a drawer in his desk in which he had placed a bottle containing 24 cyanide pills: The chairman was realistically prepared long before most of his constituents.[90] There were 24 councilors in the *Judenrat*.

At least one Jewish physician had been ready for two decades. In 1919 Janusz Korczak began a permanent practice of keeping poison at hand, tucked in the back of a drawer. According to a biographer, he kept both mercuric chloride and morphine pills.[91]

But efficient methods were not always available. Few Jews had guns. Poison was almost impossible to find. In the ghetto, one could not hang oneself in a room that was occupied by several other people. But this particular cultural inhibition later vanished in the nihilism of Treblinka. Gray remembers "the horrifying sound of a box overturning, the jerk as a body dangled, the death rattle. Then silence. Suicide was a kind of revolt, but it was the revolt of the defeated."[92] At Treblinka, Stiffel and other friends helped a Mr. Zmigrod to die. In the barracks where they lived temporarily until their value as laborers was gone, they gathered around him "while he swallowed a bottle of barbiturate pills, taking them, one by one, like a gourmet enjoying an hors d'oeuvre."[93]

There were some Jews who were willing to pay thousands of zloty for a revolver so that they could shoot their families and themselves. Fabulous sums were paid for small packages of veronal.[94]

When suicide did occur, it often was of a nature formed by the circumstances of ghetto existence. Millie Eisen, a nurse, remembers her horror at finding her own patients leaping to their death from the upper stories of the hospital.[95] But by the autumn of 1942 few illusions were left. Similarly, one knew what to expect when arrest loomed: In Warsaw, Wiszowski, the Jewish butcher, and his father were charged with secretly slaughtering cows. They were sentenced to death. Wiszowski's father committed suicide when the Nazis came to arrest him.[96]

The various major crises that further complicated the difficult and uncertain life of the Jews often produced their own flurry of suicides. Thus, when a sudden increase was reported in October 1940, the fact that the Jews were preparing to move into the ghetto probably explains the change.[97]

Nor is it difficult to find an explanation for the increase in the number of suicides during August and September 1942. Although there were 155 recorded suicides in August 1942,[98] even that number is small among a population shrinking by about 6000 daily but still numbering over 300,000. In September 1942, as the deportation ended (temporarily), only 60 suicides were recorded. However, ghetto mechanisms were breaking down by then, and the process of collecting statistics may not have been efficient. Almost certainly, a suicide taking place inside the

Umschlagplatz would not have been tallied. There, Nowogrodzki observed someone nearby reaching for poison. He washed it down with a little water. He took this
poison in front of crowds of people. "Nobody interferes. He is passing away. Now
he is delivered."[99]

This behavior contrasts with that accorded another friend while they were still
in the ghetto. This woman took sleeping pills, and two Warsaw physicians pumped
out her stomach. Surely she could have been left alone. Later that day, consumed
by terror, the woman left the shop, wandered into the ghetto "like a sleepwalker,"
and was never seen again.[100] This ethical issue came up often for the medical personnel in the ghetto's hospitals. Tosia Goliborska told Edelman that her mother
had taken poison and her brother-in-law had saved her. "Can you imagine such a
moron? To save her just so that a few days later she could be dragged to the
Umschlagplatz."[101] When a young couple were brought to the admitting office at
Czyste, having taken Garonal during the 1942 *Aktion*, Wigdorowicz treated them.
She did so more or less automatically, all the while wondering why.[102]

Without question, the most common suicide method was poison. When the
head nurse at Czyste received a life ticket and her daughter did not, Mrs. Tenenbaum handed the ticket to her daughter, assuring her that she would be right back.
She then went upstairs and took a large quantity of barbiturates.[103] And after the
entire hospital had been taken to the *Umschlagplatz*, a doctor named Irka took a
bottle of barbiturates, put on a pink nightgown, and went to bed.[104]

That, at least, is how Edelman remembered the event. Recently, Irka has published her own recollection. She is actually Dr. Adina Blady Szwajger, a Warsaw
pediatrician. Her nightgown *was* pink.

> There was only one phial of luminal in the first-aid cabinet. That wouldn't be
> enough. But there was a bottle of vodka on the table, actually only a few dregs at
> the bottom. Half a glass. I poured the vodka into a glass and thought that together
> with the luminal it should be enough.[105]

But it wasn't. She was saved for another half-century of service to her community. Nevertheless, she has spent those years trying to cope with her own feelings of
inadequacy because she had deliberately killed sick children rather than letting
them be sent to Treblinka: "I thought that I had no right to carry out my profession.
After all, one does not start one's work as a doctor by leading people not to life but
to death."[106]

The favorite poison probably was cyanide. References to it abound. Edelman
has described how the substance was procured in the ghetto. Henryk Grabowski, a
Pole, was assisting couriers from the Jewish fighting organizations to collect arms
and other needed materials. Once, he managed to obtain 200 grams of cyanide,
which the Jews wanted to have on their persons in case of arrest. The cyanide came
in small blue-gray cubes. Grabowski first tested it on a cat. He scratched off a little
powder and sprinkled it over some sausage, which the cat ate and immediately died.
So, "Henryk could give it to Wilner without any compunctions. Because Henryk,
as the owner of a bacon and meat stand, had his peddler's honor and couldn't sell
bad merchandise to a friend."[107]

Cyanide was expensive, and the demand for it was high. One ghetto inhabitant reported having a piece of potassium cyanide that was her family's only belonging except the clothes on their back. The cyanide had been obtained "at a fantastic price."[108] Months later, this woman, now in hiding on the Christian side of Warsaw, lamented the fact that "Our only remaining treasure, the potassium cyanide, has disintegrated. It is of no further use to us, and there is no chance of securing another supply. But never mind. What is fated will be."[109] Similarly, Dr. Szwajger discovered to her dismay that the cyanide she had been issued as a courier in the underground was stale. She had set great store on avoiding torture by using the cyanide if captured.[110]

Zofiowka

Caring for mental patients put severe strains on an already laboring, seriously flawed medical system. The seriously ill could not be kept at home, given the crowded living conditions. Families sometimes chased their mad relatives into the streets, hoping that the *Ordnungsdienst* would look after them. If there was space to do so, occasionally a patient would be locked into a room indefinitely, food being shoved in through a small opening, and often without any removal of body wastes; the results were predictably appalling.[111]

For some, the answer was Zofiowka. This was a prewar institution for the mentally ill, maintained by the Jewish community in the suburb of Otwock. Like all Jewish institutions, Zofiowka suffered from the chronic inability of the *Judenrat* to obtain sufficient funds to permit its operation. In the spring of 1940, when the community officials were still trying to organize their activities, the staff at Zofiowka were unpaid and threatening to discharge all their mentally ill patients if funds were not forthcoming.[112] Largely, though, their concerns were more medically oriented. The high mortality rate there was not sufficient to provide vacancies for the new cases arising in the ghetto. As a result of war experiences, Adler conjectured, the number of mental cases among the Jewish population in the ghetto was steadily rising.[113]

The traumas inflicted by the Nazis created madness on occasion, as was the case with Mietek Zucker. He defended his father from an attack by soldiers and was so severely beaten that he went mad.[114] There were as many as 400 patients at Zofiowka, all dying of hunger, many with stories similar to that of Zucker.[115] The director, a Dr. Miller, established a new service in an attempt to increase revenues. He set aside one small pavilion of 12 rooms "for people in need of a rest who could pay high rates, the income of which would help to maintain their indigent patients."[116] Thus it came about that an institution that was shunned before the war suddenly became highly desirable. Unfortunately, a rumor soon spread that Miller had laid on gourmet meals for potential clients, supposedly having obtained the money to pay for these by reducing the rations of the insane patients.[117] Whether there was any truth to this charge is unknown.

Adam Czerniakow, among others, escaped more than once to Zofiowka for a very brief "rest." On one of his official visits he learned that a long-time patient had died, an elderly Jew who nursed the delusion that he was the king of England. "Another who 'has black candles inside his body' tried to accost me but I managed to get away from him, claiming that I was not the Chairman."[118]

OTHER DISEASES

In addition to the above, there were innumerable other diseases and disorders affecting the Jews of Warsaw, just as there would be in any group of nearly half a million people. Some of these were common, though no less distressing for those who had them. Skin diseases were specially frequent—not surprising in a population cramped far too close together and without running water. Scabies was a common example—unpleasant and intensely itchy, though relatively easy to cure if sulfur is available. Scabies clinics were set up, both inside the ghetto and elsewhere in Warsaw,[119] and the disease was controlled.

Even less surprising was the incidence of venereal disease. Certainly at least some of the prostitutes on both sides of the wall would have had gonorrhea or syphilis or both, as would many of their clients. But some Jewish women acquired their disease in a more sinister way. Ringelblum records instances where Jewish women were taken off the streets, from cafes or stores, supposedly for compulsory labor. When the Germans returned them a few days later, some of them were infected, and obviously their labor, undoubtedly compulsory, was of a particular kind.[120]

Diseases affecting the gastrointestinal tract were so common as to be almost ubiquitous. Most often these disorders were of the common kinds, but some bizarre types defied diagnosis. For example, in the last months of 1939, while the ghetto was still only an amorphous plan in the minds of a few Nazis, an epidemic of diarrhea visited Warsaw. The diarrhea was severe and was accompanied by fever; there were many deaths, especially among the aged. It was not a colitis-type diarrhea, nor was it any form of dysentery. One medical observer speculated that at least some of the cases might have been tuberculosis of the gastrointestinal tract.[121] However, the disease ran its course and disappeared without any cause being discovered.

Two years later another disease arose, this time definitely affecting the lower bowel and thus identified as a colitis. But what type of colitis? It resembled the common variety of bacillary dysentery—caused by specific germs in the colon—but the resemblance was not total. The mucus and blood in the stools were expected, but the sudden collapse of the patients was not, nor was the astounding death rate of 60 percent.[122] The physicians caring for these unfortunates discovered that the systolic blood pressure, which normally should be about 110 or 120, fell suddenly in these patients to 60 or less; this occurred most often on the first or second day of the illness.

The reason for the spread of this epidemic was unknown. One theory, put forward by Dr. Abraham Milejkowski (brother of the head of the *Judenrat* health service), was that the cause was food contaminated when imported into the ghetto in carts otherwise used for hauling excrement.[123] This hypothesis was plausible since the disease was most severe during early 1942, when the ghetto was at its filthiest: The sewage system, never a strong point in that part of Warsaw, froze solid; refuse piled up in yards and streets because of a shortage of carts to haul it away and, presumably, a shortage of places to receive it. But the few carts that existed were being used to haul both human excrement and food.

Korczak, both a writer and a physician, recorded a pungent description of an outbreak of some sort of gastrointestinal complaint among the children in his orphanage. During it "the feces boiled in the chamber pots. On the surface of the thick, dark mass bubbles formed which, upon bursting, exuded a sweetish-putrid odor, which attacked not only the sense of smell but invaded as well the throat, eyes, ears, the brain."[124]

Dysentery, or *Durchfall*, was common on the wards of the Berson and Bauman Hospital. Tin buckets had to be put in the wards at night because afflicted children simply could not manage to get to the lavatories in time. By morning, the buckets were filled to overflowing, contributing to "a terrible stench of blood, pus and faeces."[125]

Another peculiar disease, never diagnosed scientifically, was known as "Volynian fever." The name identified the area in Poland from which it was thought the disease came, since its commencement seemed, in retrospect, to coincide with the arrival of Jewish refugees from Volynia. And perhaps that was the case.

Volynian fever differed completely from the bowel disorders just described. Characteristically, the victim developed fluctuating fever lasting for as long as several months. The fever waxed and waned but never disappeared totally. The disease affected particularly the lungs, which makes one wonder if it might not have been a variant of tuberculosis. It often ended fatally.[126] If it was tuberculosis, this would further expand the death toll from that disease.

In addition, Fliederbaum mentioned diphtheria, diffuse abscesses, and erysipelas as being extremely common, though few specific details seem to have survived. On the other hand, tonsillitis, scarlet fever, rheumatism, and meningitis were rare,[127] though there was a short-lived meningitis epidemic early in 1940.[128] Fliederbaum further noted that asthma and other allergic diseases were suddenly uncommon. Patients had spontaneous recoveries from such allergic disorders as urticaria, hay fever, asthma, and food allergy, as well as gastritis and enteritis.[129]

Scarlet fever may have been rare, but it did occur. Czerniakow recorded seeing cases during an inspection tour of Czyste.[130] And the same disease, simulated, once saved a family from harm. During an *Aktion* they painted a young boy with rouge, piled up medicine bottles and other medical paraphernalia around his bed, and stood about looking doleful. When the soldiers entered the room, the family gravely announced, "scarlet fever!" "There was scuffle and an oath. The Germans disappeared as if blown by a bomb."[131]

Chickenpox affected the children of the ghetto severely. Anna Braude-Heller, a pediatrician, recorded that the symptoms were much worse than customary, perhaps because starvation was vitiating the defense mechanisms of the body.[132]

Other conditions are referred to on occasion. Frostbite has been mentioned. One proposed preventive was to rub vodka on exposed parts,[133] though vodka was soon difficult to obtain. Appendicitis, of course, occurred as in any population. At least once, it was simulated in an attempt to keep a young man out of a labor camp. This particular case had a sad end. The man's fiancée was a nurse, who not only schooled him on the appropriate symptoms but also gave him a drug that caused a high fever. Apparently the drug also reactivated dormant tuberculosis, from which he died.[134]

Starkopf had the misfortune to suffer both infected tonsils and a hernia in the ghetto. The only treatment for his tonsils was surgical removal; this was done in his home, without anesthesia, seated in a chair and held firmly by his father. "I cannot possibly describe the pain."[135] He was perhaps relieved that no operation was carried out on his hernia. But there were still truss makers at work, and he acquired a rupture belt.[136]

Perhaps the strangest reference of all comes from Czerniakow's diary. On 11 February 1940 he noted that a serum had arrived in the ghetto from Belgium. Reputedly, it was beneficial against snakebite.[137] No explanation is suggested.

Czerniakow's own health was bad during the last three years of his life. Aside from being beaten badly, he recorded vomiting at his home[138] and suffering from both a headache and lumbago (*Hexenschuss*).[139] He was diagnosed as having enlargement of the heart and aorta[140] and inflammation of the trachea.[141] Given the strains under which he labored, such disorders are not surprising. He made a poignant entry in his journal on 26 December 1939: "At night I read a lot, constantly envying all the heroes of my novels because they lived in different times."[142]

9

The Children of the Ghetto

I would like to be a dog, because the Germans like dogs, and I would not have to be afraid that they would kill me.[1]

This was the response of a Jewish girl in the Warsaw ghetto when asked what she would like to be. Being a child in the ghetto was a lethal condition, nearly all of them dying before the war ended. In 1945, one Russian soldier who was a Jew broke down at seeing an eight-year-old Jewish girl in a Polish town; it was the first Jewish child he had seen in over a thousand miles.[2]

Although Jewish children shared all the experiences of their parents, there are enough unique aspects of their lives and deaths to justify a separate chapter. Numbers alone might dictate such an approach. Of the 400,000-plus inhabitants of the ghetto, about 100,000 were younger than 15 years old; of these, very few were babies. Many couples preferred not to have children, and of those who were born, the survival rate was low.[3] At least partly, this was because so little milk was available.[4]

Of the 100,000 children, at least three-quarters needed assistance and welfare.[5] And although the welfare system inevitably was flawed by uncontrollable exterior circumstances and by the sheer volume of destitution, many of these children did receive aid. A major source of assistance was CENTOS, (*Centrala Opieki nad Sierotami*, the National Society for the Care of Orphans), an organization that had a long tradition and that expanded its umbrella to include many needy children who were not orphans. But again, the volume of need made the task almost hopeless. Moreover, what facilities CENTOS had were significantly depleted from the first day of the war, when the CENTOS children's home in Otwock, 15 miles southeast of Warsaw, was severely damaged by German bombs, with many casualties.[6]

In Warsaw, CENTOS operated 20 centers to feed children and care for them during the day; 20 food kitchens for children; and thirty day centers for the children in refugee centers. Working through the house committees, CENTOS also organized "children's corners" in hundreds of apartment buildings.[7] At the height of its activities, CENTOS employed about 1000 Jews; many of them were also connected with underground resistance activities,[8] and their names appear on the rosters of those fighting the Nazis in January and April–May 1943.

TOZ (*Towarzystwo Ochrony Zdrowia Ludności Żydowskiej*, the Society to Protect the Health of the Jewish Population) was also prominently involved in trying to aid the children of the ghetto. Their special field was providing medical care, both curative and preventive. Before the ghetto was created, during 1940, TOZ physicians and nurses saw an average of 1800 children daily.[9] What they found was not encouraging, In August 1941, a staff of 11 TOZ physicians and 12 nurses examined 12,063 children from among a group of 30,816. They found that only 13 percent had an adequate diet; in 35 percent the diet was deemed passable, and 52 percent were unequivocally undernourished. "Of this number, 7,041 children were kept clean, 2,863 not clean and 2,260 covered with vermin. Free baths were given to 6,049 and thorough hair-cleaning administered to 2,485 children. 4,130 children were found in a state of absolute infirmity, requiring regular medical attention."[10] So, over one-third of the children examined were clinically ill and needed medical care. The situation deteriorated steadily. In January 1942, TOZ doctors examined 1861 children, finding only 3 percent in good health and 65 percent in bad health. More than half of the children examined were both dirty and lice-ridden.[11]

The chief concern of CENTOS was fighting to feed and house large numbers of abandoned or orphaned children. But despite their best efforts and the complementary work of TOZ, only a fraction of those in need received help. The problem was lack of funds, a lack so severe that for a time in 1940 the number of children fed by these organizations actually fell.[12]

Many of the children were described as apathetic, but this was the symptom of a late stage in the process of starvation. In fact, before the gradual but inexorable effects of starvation took hold, the ghetto children were extremely active. Many children became beggars, particularly refugee children struggling to cope in a strange city. Often they stood near the hospital buildings or near the telephone building, waiting and hoping.[13] By the spring of 1942, it was estimated that 4000 children were begging for their bread in the streets of gentile Warsaw, perhaps half of them Jewish children who had taken the potentially fatal risk of crossing the wall (see Figures 9.1 and 9.2).[14]

The involvement of children in smuggling has been mentioned in Chapter 6. Their size, their quickness, and the hope that the German, Polish, and Jewish guards would be lenient with children were reasons for this involvement. Hundreds of Jewish children, especially between the ages of 10 and 12, found ways to sneak over the walls or through the sewers to the Aryan side of Warsaw, where they stuffed potatoes into the lining of their coats and return with clothing so swollen that the children looked like balloons.[15] Usually they dug these potatoes out of the fields and sold then to Jews in the ghetto if they did not have a family to support.[16] Unfortunately, it was when stuffed with contraband that they were most likely to be discovered and beaten or, too often, killed.

Wigdorowicz cites the case of two children who came under her care after being shot while part of a smuggling gang. One was a 10-year-old girl, the other her 8-year-old brother. Both had gunshot wounds, but the girl was determined that they could not and would not stay in the hospital. Finally persuaded to trust the staff a little, she undressed herself, in the process unwinding yards and yards of bloodstained white wool from around her body. Her brother was also swaddled. The wool was their stock, which they were trying to smuggle out and sell in Aryan Warsaw.[17]

When children were not shot, they often were badly abused. The Polish police, the "Blues," were notoriously cruel, sometimes forcing children caught smuggling to crawl back and forth through barbed wire until they bled, or to crawl through narrow sewers filled with sewage.[18]

Figure 9.1. Poor teen-agers in the Warsaw ghetto (Bundesarchiv, Koblenz).

Figure 9.2. Child in the Warsaw ghetto (from Joe J. Heydecker, *Das Warschauer Getto,* 1983).

Not all German guards were cruel to children. The much touted German weakness for the young was often hidden, but sometimes it did shine through. Lewin records one instance he himself observed of kindness and compassion by some decent Germans, who let Jewish children get away with "crimes" that might have brought their deaths.[19] And there were other occasions when this occurred. But generally, the treatment was harsh and violent, though sometimes unusual. For example, Ringelblum recorded one strange occurrence when a group of children were taken from a synagogue on Powszechna Street and forced to give blood—presumably to be used in resuscitating wounded German soldiers.[20]

More typical, unfortunately, was the experience of an interviewee, Millie Eisen, who stepped outside the hospital where she was nursing, one rainy night, for some fresh air. Within a few seconds she saw several Germans grab a boy trying to sell cigarettes and kick him to death.[21]

Orphans roamed the streets, subject to the weather. In the first week of October 1941, when the first snows blanketed Warsaw, as many as 70 children froze to death on the steps and in the ruins of destroyed buildings.[22] There were not enough orphanages to house and feed them all.

They formed smuggling gangs and became "wild" children, refusing aid when it was proffered. In at least some cases their efforts at smuggling were successful, and they "were used to plenty of food, to vodka and cigarettes; they were sexually active."[23] Their smuggling skills and general knowledge of the tricks of surviving helped at least a few children last through the war on the Aryan side.[24]

Children seemed to have lost their fear of death, or at least lost any discomfort at its propinquity. In one courtyard in the ghetto, children were seen playing a game that involved tickling a corpse.[25] Janusz Korczak once saw a dead boy lying on the sidewalk. Nearby "three boys [fixed] something with some rope. At a certain moment they glanced at the body and moved away a few paces, not interrupting their game."[26]

But while they were learning firsthand about such grim matters, their education was grossly deficient in other ways. For example, these children of Warsaw could not see their own city, except for the few cramped blocks of the ghetto plus the immediately surrounding area, visible over the wall from the upper floors of ghetto buildings. Teachers were reduced to showing them pictures of the various sights of Warsaw, to try to instruct them in the geography of their native city.[27] Other teaching was carried out, including Hebrew lessons. This forbidden activity was initiated by CENTOS, using their children's kitchens and day centers as a cover. Here, lessons were given on a wide scale.[28] Many other organizations also conducted secret teaching, often slanted to the political viewpoint of the sponsors. Some groups emphasized teaching in Polish, some in Yiddish. English and Russian were favorite foreign languages.

Other efforts to promote the well-being of children occurred under the aegis of individuals and organizations. CENTOS, apparently making the largest contribution here, arranged for "summer camp" for many Jewish children—camp without leaving the ghetto. CENTOS workers and colleagues "exploited every patch of greenery to be found in the ghetto" to run these camps, providing the children at least a glimpse of normal life, a recollection of better times.[29]

Janina David remembers one playground, which was opened on a bombed-out site on her family's street. Her mother somehow found the money to enroll her for three afternoons a week, but her two closest friends had no money and were unable to join her. It was dangerous to be in the streets all day, courtyards were too small and too crowded, and the foul smell from the rubbish heap was often unbearable. "The playground was too crowded to allow any running about but there were a few trees and grass patches there, and even a few flowers managed to grow for a time."[30] There was just enough space for a game of net ball, but it generated long lines of children awaiting a turn. Though not ideal, the playground was better than the streets.

One of the last major public events held in the ghetto, under the collective responsibility of many organizations, was "Children's Month." This celebration and demonstration took place in the autumn of 1941; 1 million zloty was raised, specifically earmarked to help children.[31]

Attempting to maintain welfare institutions such as orphanages in the ghetto was heartbreaking work. The inevitable conclusion to their existence became more and more widely recognized, though some Jews clung to their hope of a better day until the very end. The need for institutional space grew rapidly as more and more children were orphaned or separated from their parents and guardians. The ability to maintain children—to feed, house, and clothe them and see that they had medical care—diminished steadily. Many institutions were reduced to becoming beggars themselves, not literally with a cup or an out-thrust hand in the street, but by visiting the *Judenrat*, the Joint, and all other institutional sources of possible income. When these were exhausted, the few rich Jews of the ghetto were sought out. Janusz Korczak spent a large proportion of his time, particularly during the last year in the ghetto, in such painful and often unproductive pursuits. One day:

> I returned utterly shattered from my "round." Seven calls, conversations, climbing of stairs, questions. The result: fifty zlotys and a promise of five zlotys a month. One is supposed to support two hundred people![32]

Dr. Korczak (born Henryk Goldszmidt) is a focal figure in any account of the children of the Warsaw ghetto, and of the preceding two decades as well (see Figure 9.3). He was a physician and, under the name of Korczak, a highly successful writer; he was also totally devoted to the care of orphaned children. In his latter capacity he was influential, not just in Poland but throughout Europe, because of his innovative approach. He introduced a democratic system of courts run by the children and penalties supervised by them.[33] His approach was pragmatic, nonauthoritarian, and wholly realistic; tasks and lessons were directed not to airy abstractions but, rather, to coping with the existing situation.

He took on many children who had been abandoned for long times, and who were tough and distrustful when they arrived. Korczak was too realistic not to know that he failed with some, but his score was extremely high.

Years afterward one woman remembered the enormous pride she felt at the orphanage when she received the first dress, undershirt, and underpants she had ever owned. On a Saturday afternoon she went to visit relatives. She lifted her skirt as she walked down the street so that everyone, "even the boys," could see her beautiful underpants.[34]

Figure 9.3. Dr. Janusz Korczak (Henryk Goldszmit, 1878–1942).

Perhaps the most revealing anecdote demonstrating Korczak's love and understanding of children is the story of his lecture to medical students about the heart of a child. The lecture took place in the radiology department at the Berson and Bauman children's hospital. After the students were in their places, he entered the room with a young boy holding his hand. Korczak removed the boy's shirt, placed him behind a fluoroscopic screen, and darkened the room. On the screen, the lad's heart could be seen beating rapidly. "Don't ever forget this sight," he said. "Before you raise a hand to a child, before you administer any kind of punishment, remember what his frightened heart looks like."[35] That was the end of the lecture.

In the ghetto, Korczak set up a system of toilet fees based entirely on the need to improve the hygiene in the orphanage: To urinate, each child had to catch 5 flies; bowel movement second class (bucket seat with hole), 10 flies; bowel movement first class (toilet seat), 15 flies—and every fly caught in isolation counted for two.[36]

Eliminating flies was prophylaxis against dysentery, a blight on the orphanage that Korczak commented on in his diary.[37] Of course, children suffered from all the disorders of the ghetto except those few associated with old age, a state beyond their hopes or expectations. Typhus, tuberculosis, and starvation all claimed their numbers. Of the so-called childhood diseases, diphtheria and scarlet fever seem to have been surprisingly rare, measles was more frequent, and whooping cough was a particular scourge of the very young[38] as was chickenpox.[39]

Korczak carried on, though his despair is evident in his diary.[40] Many doctors became emotionally blunted by the appalling conditions. Life had become cheap in the ghetto, and the sympathy of some medical men dissipated in the face of so much misery and death. "And yet, in the moments of greatest horror, there were doctors who went on believing that their duty was to strive and to save. One of this devoted band was Dr. Korman [a Warsaw pediatrician]." Michael Zylberberg remembers that he often furnished Korman with lists of people who were sick and too poor to pay a doctor, "and he went fearlessly from house to house trying to help and cure."[41]

Conditions in hospitals such as Berson and Bauman were horrendous. The details are spelled out in Chapter 5. Their cumulative impact on one observer, the scientist Ludwig Hirszfeld, is perhaps an adequate commentary:

> . . . I will say frankly that when I was visiting the two children's hospitals headed by Dr. Hellerowa . . . I had the impression that it would have been more humane not to prolong the life of these poor children.[42]

This painful ethical dilemma was faced remarkably often by ghetto physicians. Adina Szwajger was a physician at Berson and Bauman. When the hospital was to be emptied in 1942 and the fate of everyone entering the freight cars was well known, she gave morphine to a room full of sick babies to let them die in peace: "[J]ust as, during those two years of real work in the hospital, I had bent down over the little beds, so now I poured this last medicine into their tiny mouths."[43] She also describes the urgent need she and her colleagues felt for vodka to blot out the memories and the pangs of guilt.[44]

ORPHANAGES

One observer estimated that in November 1941 there were 10,000 orphans and deserted children in the ghetto, whereas the 14 CENTOS orphanages could house perhaps 2000 or so.[45] And even the orphanages were less than ideal havens. In May and June 1941, an estimated 25 percent of their inhabitants died.[46] The acceleration of disaster that marked the institution of the ghetto is indicated in the figures for the large municipal Jewish orphanage at Leszno 127. In a five-week period in the summer of 1940, 47 children died out of a population of 470. This figure was bad enough, but it became worse. When the ghetto opened, the orphanage had to move. Its new home was at Dzielna 39, where in May 1941 there were 178 deaths among the 600 children, and in June, another 155 deaths.[47]

The director of CENTOS during the war, Adolf Berman, reported figures for the summer of 1942, just before the deportations began, that are more positive. By July CENTOS had been able to set up more than 100 institutions providing aid to about 25,000 children—one-quarter of all the children in the ghetto.

These various efforts included partial or major support to 30 orphanages housing 4000 children. Among them were Janusz Korczak's orphanage, as well as Dobra Wola, at Dzielna 61 (400 children), and Beit Haydad on Wolność Street (1000 children). In addition to relief organizations, some other groups helped to provide and maintain orphanages.

Dobra Wola (Good Will) is a good example. On 1 November 1941 the workers of the brushmakers factory took over Dzielna 61, a building that had been almost totally ruined while it was a home for refugees. Using a fund of 70,000 zloty, the union renovated the building, which was modest but well equipped. In addition to over 400 beds there was a kitchen, classrooms, a hospital room, bath facilities, a playground, and central heating.[48] The brushmakers and CENTOS apparently joined forces in operating this institution. Purportedly, the Jewish bakers were to follow suit with an orphanage of their own, though whether or not it was actually opened is unknown.

Ludwig Hirszfeld was particularly impressed by Dobra Wola, though his account of its founding and history differs significantly from that provided by the Jewish informer cited above. Dobra Wola was directed by an educator, Mrs. Pinkiertowa. According to Hirszfeld, the institution was totally financed by a Mr. Weitz, a Krakow native who set up a brush factory producing various articles for the *Wehrmacht* and other German users. He became immensely rich and, according to Hirszfeld, wanted to use the money derived from the Nazis to help the Jews. Purportedly, Dobra Wola cost him 250,000 zloty a month.[49] Whether or not it earned him good will, other than Hirszfeld's, is unknown. In general, the men who ran shops and factories that earned large sums of German money were seen as avaricious and, usually, self-serving by the less affluent ghetto dwellers. Perhaps Dobra Wola benefited from the aid of both Weitz and his factory workers. Weitz may have donated the necessary money, the brushmakers their labor.

Of the several orphanages in the ghetto, the Korczak institution was best known and deservedly famous. It was forced into the newly created ghetto from its long-time location at Krochmalna 92.[50] It moved first to Chłodna 33[51] and then later, as the ghetto boundaries shrank, to Sienna 16.[52] There were also other orphanages, both private and public. The municipal orphanage also had to move. It had been on Płock Street and relocated at Dzielna 39 after the ghetto was opened. Here were gathered many of the street children; the mortality was very high.[53]

The largest orphanage was located at Wolność 14 and contained about 1000 children.[54] One of the smallest, opened as late as January 1942 and housing 50 street children, was located at Ogrodowa 29.[55]

THE DEPORTATIONS

When the relocations to the east began on 22 July 1942, the days of children in the ghetto were almost ended. Children were selectively deported out of proportion to their numbers in the population at that time. There were several reasons for this policy. First, those Jews permitted to remain in the ghetto were to be only productive workers. Moreover, both ideologically and pragmatically, the Nazis preferred to take the children. Nothing so destroys a people as the elimination of their children. Besides, no group was simpler for the police to remove than the children— there was little to fear from four- and eight-year-olds.

Among the earliest victims were the street children, who were rounded up and taken away by the *Ordnungsdienst* in the first day or two.[56] When 6000 or more Jews have to be taken to the *Umschlagplatz* and forced into the freight cars, groups of children are an easy target. Other dislocations occurred at the same time. When the Stawki Street division of Czyste was evacuated on Nazi orders the day before the deportations started, 40 or 50 convalescent children were sent to the Korczak orphanage,[57] and equal numbers to other institutions. On the second day of the *Aktion*, July 23, refugee shelters for children at Dzika 3 (250 orphans) and at Gęsia 6 (street children) were emptied.[58] This was the day that the chairman of the *Judenrat*, Adam Czerniakow, committed suicide.

When deportations began, none of the Jews knew certainly what was to be the fate of the deportees. Many believed, or made themselves believe, that in fact they were being relocated to some work area to the east. That is what the Nazis told them. One of the earliest clues indicating a probably lethal end for all was the fate of some of the first groups taken—children and old people. It quickly became known that the majority of these unfortunates had not been taken to the *Umschlagplatz* at all, but to the cemetery across Ogrodowa Street, where they were shot and buried in mass graves.[59] Yet, paradoxically, a few Jews, desperate to believe that some of them would survive, saw this action as confirming the likelihood of a good ending for the able-bodied: The destruction of the elderly and the very young might confirm the story of work colonies in the east, places where unproductive hands and mouths could not be tolerated.

On 30 July, the time came for the orphanages. The first to be struck was the Pnimia orphanage,[60] an institution with 50 refugee children at Ogrodowa 29.[61] Next, though the order of these events is uncertain, came the turn of orphanages at Wolność 12–14 (about 1200 children) and at Miła 18.[62] Early in August, Korczak's orphanage was emptied, as well as those at Twarda 7 (headed by Dombrowski and Sternfeld) and at Śliska 28 (Broniatowska).[63] The date was 5 August 1942.[64]

One of the lasting inspirational images of the Warsaw ghetto comes from these days. Shining over the years, it symbolizes both the destruction of the Jews and the courage of so many of them. When the Nazis came for the children at Korczak's orphanage, he was told that he was exempted. But Korczak knew how frightened his children were, and he would not abandon them. Many people saw the procession through the streets toward the *Umschlagplatz* that day—Janusz Korczak leading a column of children, carrying a tired youngster in his arms, the children each with a tiny bundle containing some fragment of food for the journey; only the youngest could have preserved many illusions at this stage, and certainly Korczak did not. "Halina Berg," who had a "little sister" among the children, watched them go by that day. Her memory is indelible,[65] as is that of Dr. Wisniewski.[66]

Janusz Korczak spurned an opportunity to escape and save himself, and he went to his death along with his charges.[67] There is no doubt on that point. What must be emphasized is that although it is Korczak's name that has been associated with this inspirational example of unreserved dedication, and although his exemplary reputation is deserved, it is a distinction that he shares with many others.[68] Dozens of nurses, physicians, and administrators chose not to attempt to escape, to save themselves, but remained with their young charges and died with them.[69]

Unhappily if inevitably, some were not capable of such altruism. Though mother love was prominently and frequently displayed in the ghetto, occasional exceptions occurred. Lewin noted in mid-August the report that a few mothers, presented with a cruel variation of "Sophie's choice," chose to try to live. People returning from the *Umschlagplatz* told how women, seized the day before, "were freed if they sacrificed their children. To our pain and sorrow many women saved themselves in this way."[70] Adina Szwajger collected children abandoned at the *Umschlagplatz*. Maybe they were left in the faint hope that they would be saved, or perhaps because they might have been detriments to their mothers' survival. Szwajger couldn't tell. "Fear of death is something that can't be described."[71]

The streets contained pitiful sights in those ghastly days of July, August, and September 1942. Just before the *Aktion* ended, five tiny children, two- and three-year-olds, had been sitting on a camp bed in the open for over 24 hours; presumably their mothers had already been taken to the *Umschlagplatz*. The children cried piteously, screaming for food—doomed.[72]

Eugenia Pernal is haunted by her memories from this time. She noticed four children, between about 4 and 12 years of age, on the street. She took charge of them as they were hustled along to the *Umschlagplatz*. Then, after finding a morsel of bread for them to eat and telling them she would be back, she found a way to save herself and did. But she never went back.[73]

After this first deportation ended, the ghetto was almost empty of children. Of perhaps 36,000 persons legally in the ghetto—as many as 20,000 more were hidden in various places—fewer than 1000 were under 10 years or over 60 combined.[74] Nevertheless, the work of the dedicated professionals went on, and CENTOS tried to set up a small orphanage.[75] All of this activity ended in January 1943 with the deportations that occurred then.

CHILDBIRTH

The attitude of the Jews of the ghetto to childbirth inevitably was strongly affected by what they saw going on around them. They knew how increasingly unlikely it was that children could survive. This conclusion naturally affected their feelings about having children in the ghetto. The birth rate fell drastically. In Warsaw at the beginning of 1942, the ratio of births to deaths was 1:45,[76] whereas normally it approximately 1:1.

Nevertheless, there were some births. Maternity hospitals were located at Elektoralna 11, Twarda 35, and Ceglana 17.[77] But babies also were born in Czyste Hospital, in the mother's home, and even in bunkers while hiding from the Nazis.

Dr. Wigdorowicz describes one childbirth that took place at the Leszno 1 division of Czyste. She remembered being horrified at first that anyone would dream of having a baby at such a time. Then her human sympathy took over, faced with a terrified mother whose husband had been in a labor camp for eight months; she had three children at home and had had no money to pay for an abortion. She had already sold her last pillow to put some food in her children's mouths.[78]

Not everyone was unsympathetic to the idea of creating new Jews despite the uncompromisingly bleak outlook. One unknown diarist commented, on seeing two pregnant Jewish women in the Warsaw ghetto: "If in today's dark and pitiless times a Jewish woman can gather enough courage to bring a new Jewish being into the world and rear him, this is great heroism and daring. . . . At least symbolically these nameless Jewish heroines do not allow the total extinction of the Jews and of Jewry."[79]

The Starkopf family couldn't afford an obstetrician, so their baby daughter was delivered at home with the help of a midwife. Pele, the mother, lay on the dining room table. Because anesthetics were impossible to find, she had the baby while she was fully conscious. The next day, the midwife returned and stitched up Pele's episiotomy, again without anesthesia.[80]

Far worse was the experience of an anonymous Jewish woman who gave birth, in January 1943, while hidden along with several others in an attic. The Nazis were searching for hidden Jews to be either shot on the spot or taken to the *Umschlagplatz* and hence to Treblinka. The young woman gave birth without uttering a sound: "[E]very sound, every murmur, even the slightest, caused antipathy and hostility among our companions of misfortune."[81] What of the baby's cries? It died later, it is said, from lack of nourishment.

Crying, noisy children were a serious problem in the bunkers. Discovery by the Germans meant certain death. In one of the Miła Street bunkers, in April 1943, some of the Jews tried to persuade mothers of crying children to give them Gardenal (a barbiturate preparation). At first the women were too frightened for their children to agree, but eventually they gave their approval.[82] The drug must have worked, since an observer lived to tell the story.

One young doctor in hiding with, among others, a pregnant woman remembers the joy the expectant woman radiated at feeling the baby move in her belly. But when it was born, she smothered the child because its crying would have betrayed the group. The doctor carried the body away in a cardboard box.[83]

The Starkopf baby survived its birth and later was also drugged, though under different circumstances. The parents devised a plan for escape. To succeed, the scheme required a "dead" baby for them to follow, weeping, to the Jewish cemetery. There, with suitable bribes, they could see an empty casket buried and then escape over the cemetery wall.[84] A doctor friend injected the little girl with something that put her to sleep, and the plan worked.[85]

But if some babies not only were born, but were welcomed, many were not. Edelman relates an experience during one of the late deportations in the ghetto. While the Nazis were clearing out patients on the first floor of the hospital, a baby was being born upstairs. A doctor and a nurse were with the mother:

> And when the baby was born, the doctor handed it to the nurse, and the nurse laid it on one pillow, and smothered it with another one. The baby whimpered for a while and then grew silent. This woman was nineteen years old. The doctor didn't say a thing to her. Not a word. And this woman knew herself what she was supposed to do.[86]

This nurse survived the war and became a prominent pediatrician.

In another situation, Edelman remembered, it was 8 September 1942. A hospital in a vocational school was being liquidated. As the Germans entered the ground floor, a doctor poisoned a number of children, giving them cyanide. "She saved those children from the gas chamber. People thought she was a hero."[87] The heroism was not only that she saved these sick children from a hideous final few hours, but also that the cyanide she used was her own. Having given it to shorten the sufferings of these children, she had none left for herself.

Children who survived the ghetto and the subsequent concentration camps usually did so at great cost, physically and mentally. When Dachau was liberated, the American commander forced the German inhabitants of the town to visit the camp and see with their own eyes what Nazism had achieved. An elderly woman, correctly dressed all in black, spoke to one inmate, expressing her compassion. "'It must have been very difficult for people your age to endure all this suffering.' 'How old do you think I am?' Livia asked her. 'Maybe sixty, maybe sixty- two,' replied the German woman. 'Fourteen,' replied Livia.'" The German woman crossed herself and fled in horror.[88]

10

Education in the Ghetto

Initially, teaching was forbidden at every level within the Jewish population, although some elementary schools eventually were permitted to open. Education ceased throughout Poland in the autumn of 1939; in small towns and in cities, the efforts to trick the Germans into permitting what was forbidden began immediately and were often successful, at least for a while. In the town of Ryki, between Warsaw and Lublin, the former high school teachers persuaded the German educational office that there was a need for trained salesmen and clerks to work in rural commune stores; under this guise, they began to provide high school education for the local teenagers.[1] Such efforts went on all over the country, including every Jewish community and ghetto. One student was able to complete high school with teachers from her private Jewish girl's school. Every day there was a change of venue from one student's home to the next.[2]

Zylberberg and several other teachers, abetted by the efforts of their former headmaster (himself not a Jew), set up a school first in the area of their prewar school and, later, inside the ghetto. The headmaster, Professor Marian Odrzywolski, collected and filed progress reports so that the students could receive credit after the war. Once they were forced into the ghetto, the teachers were able to locate a former convent on Nowolipki Street, vacated by the Poles, and established a school for fee-paying students, "but each class had free places for poor children of good ability. We continued to function in the heart of the ghetto till the summer of 1942."[3]

Eventually the Nazis became more permissive. They decreed that a few Polish primary schools might be opened. Characteristically, however, the Nazis still forbade schools in the Jewish quarter of Warsaw to open on the pretext that doing so would encourage an epidemic of typhus. In addition to allowing some primary school education—in the Warsaw ghetto, once teaching finally was permitted, perhaps 7000 of the 50,000 children of school age were able to receive some schooling[4]—the Nazis also made one other important exception to their no-education decree: As was the case outside the ghetto, a few technical or trade schools were opened under German authority. On 31 August 1940, Hans Frank, governor general of the Nazi *Generalgouvernement*, issued a decree authorizing the *Judenrat* to provide elementary and vocational schools for the Jewish population.[5]

Even before this date, word of the planned change in policy reached the ghetto. Adam Czerniakow noted in his diary for 18 August that permission had been granted "to conduct some vocational courses"; on 19 August he named the vocational education commission, and by 21 August he noted with evident pride that within three days they had started the vocational courses.[6] Although it did not begin operation for some months, the course of particular importance to this book was one designed to train personnel needed to fight epidemics.

By 30 June 1941, vocational education was active in the ghetto. There were 24 courses for boys (832 being enrolled), 24 for girls (818 enrolled), and 16 coeducational schools with 681 students. Thus a total of 2331 students were getting some sort of vocational training.[7]

AN UNDERGROUND MEDICAL SCHOOL

Czerniakow played a major role in obtaining permission to set up the medical vocational course.[8] He recorded some of the negotiations in his diary. On 23 April 1941 the concept had not yet been approved, as on that date at Gestapo headquarters he presented to SS Sergeant Gerhard Mende the project of Zweibaum's lectures.[9] Eighteen days later, Dr. Josef Stein gave the first lecture, on the topic, "Life and Death."[10] The site of the school was also found with the help of Czerniakow.

What the Germans approved was the creation of Sanitary Courses for Fighting Epidemics. The organizer was Docent Juliusz Zweibaum (see Figure 10.1), formerly of the Warsaw University medical school, although some authors have given Hirszfeld the credit.[11] The evidence of contemporary documentation and that of surviving faculty and students makes it clear that Zweibaum was indeed the originator. He planned a school to provide the early years of basic medical education; later, when Hirszfeld became active in the ghetto, he undertook to organize the superior course for fourth- and fifth-year studies.[12]

The course, as well as its true nature, was widely known within the ghetto. Halina Berg heard about the Zweibaum school by word of mouth, and she passed the information on to her friend Karolina Borman.[13] They both became students. After

Figure 10.1. Docent Juliusz Zweibaum, ca 1957 (courtesy of Dr. Marek Balin).

the war, both completed their education, one in medicine and the other in pharmacy. Not surprisingly, Ringelblum's archival network also knew of the school, for he recorded in October 1941 that the university professors Hirszfeld and Zwajbojm (Zweibaum) were giving university-level medical courses and that students were working in an anatomy lab.[14]

The creators of the clandestine medical school had one unanticipated advantage in dealing with the occupying Nazis. The Germans were terrified of epidemic diseases. Though their claim that the Jews were especially susceptible to typhus, used as an excuse for quarantining them within the ghetto, was false, it is probable that many Germans believed their own paranoid propaganda.[15] This fear may have been influential in obtaining approval for the courses to "combat epidemics" at a time when little other education was permitted except some basic teaching for very young children.

FINDING A BUILDING

At the western edge of the ghetto was a building that had been taken over as the *Arbeitsamt*, or Department of Labor, at the corner of Leszno and Żelazna streets, Leszno 84,[16] opposite one of the ghetto gates.[17] This structure was a former secondary school, or *Kolegium*, and it was the upper floors of the *Kolegium* that were taken over for medical teaching.[18] In the beginning, the students actually had to leave the ghetto to get to the school, passing the inspection of the guards at the *wacha*, or inspection point. These guards usually included two German soldiers, two Polish policemen (known as "Blues" because of their navy blue uniforms), and two members of the *Ordnungsdienst* or Jewish Order Service, the internal police created by the *Judenrat*.[19] Later, according to Makower, who taught there, a bridge was built over the street wall from Żelazna to a first-floor entrance (the second story in North American terms).[20]

The Germans visualized a program for a few weeks or months that would produce technicians capable of applying antiepidemic techniques. The medical teachers within the ghetto used the approved courses as a front to give clandestine medical education, and from May 1941 until July 1942 that is what they did.

The faculty of the ghetto school considered it a division of Warsaw University and, so long as this was possible, there was both consultative and administrative cooperation. Student records were communicated to the faculty offices outside the ghetto and, for a while, some exchange of lecturers was arranged.[21] Nevertheless, as the isolation of the ghetto became more absolute, these medical contacts could not be maintained. The situation within the ghetto became so appalling that, from the viewpoint of ordinary Poles outside the ghetto, the existence of anything as ambitious as a Jewish medical school seemed unlikely.[22]

The Primary Course

This term designated the first two years of the traditional Polish medical education, during which the students were taught the basic medical sciences. As has been mentioned, the formal teaching of the preclinical subjects in the underground school was carried out in the large building at the corner of Leszno and Żelazna streets that housed the *Arbeitsamt*.[23] Because it had been a secondary school before the war, there were blackboards on the walls[24] and it had laboratory facilities for teaching biology and chemistry,[25] though some students recall these facilities as being small and cramped, so that one had to peer over the shoulders of other students to see what was going on.[26]

The former secondary school served many functions in the war years, only one of which was the medical school. The students remember the rooms as being on the third or fourth floor, large rooms—huge, according to one student[27]—that were bright in the daylight hours.[28] Here, instruction was given largely by lectures; some laboratory space was available, though the facilities seem to have been primitive.[29] The students sat on benches, as in classrooms everywhere.[30] Vladka Meed was probably in one of these classrooms while trying to escape a Nazi roundup in 1942; she was in the *Arbeitsamt* and describes "a huge, deserted room, its furnishings consisting of two long benches, a desk, a chair, and two unlocked closets for storing medical supplies."[31]

Lectures in Polish,[32] which were described to the Germans as basic outlines of anatomy, hygiene, and public health, were in fact medical lectures designed for medical students.[33] The curriculum included physics, biology, histology, anatomy, and both organic and inorganic chemistry.[34] Books were in scant supply and had to be passed from one set of hands to the next on a strict rota,[35] though the shortage was somewhat alleviated when Ludwig Hirszfeld was able to influence Czerniakow to give 5000 zloty (ca. $1000) for purchasing texts.[36]

Anatomy

Ironically, despite the high mortality rate in the ghetto, anatomical specimens were scarce. Skulls had to be smuggled into the school, and histological and pathological slides were passed from student to student so that all would have the opportunity to examine them.[37] Bodies were readily available, but preservatives were not.[38] Thus much of the practical teaching of anatomy took place in prosectoria or hospital morgues;[39] Pernal remembers the room where she learned anatomy as having a tile floor and being properly equipped for that type of work.[40] In general, the principle was that dissections were done on fresh bodies: Died yesterday, dissected today.[41] One student remembers vividly how a cadaver's neck was kept stretched by placing a brick under it,[42] and another was struck by the emaciated appearance of the bodies and by the fact that the male sex organs were so much less conspicuous than she had imagined—not having had a previous opportunity to make such observations on a subject living or dead.[43]

Actually, the teaching of anatomy took place both in the classroom and in the prosectorium. Ludwig Stabholz and his assistant, Dr. Krugeberg, taught in the classroom, using books, charts, and prepared specimens; Henry Fenigstein taught anatomy to first-year students and pathology to third-year students in the prosectorium or autopsy room.[44] A few fortunate students had access to skulls and other teaching material because their parents were physicians or dentists.[45]

The faculty obtained some demonstration tables and histological preparations surreptitiously, through colleagues connected with Warsaw University,[46] particu-

larly Drs. Orlowski and Konopacki,[47] and Dr. Edward Loth. The last named—
though notoriously antisemitic before the war—carried pathological anatomy specimens preserved in formaldehyde into the ghetto for his former student, Ludwig
Stabholz, to use in demonstrating normal anatomy in the classroom.[48]

The clandestine nature of all teaching made subterfuge a routine and necessary
practice. One student finished high school by meeting with a teacher and three or
four fellow students, alternately in each student's home, ready to simulate an ordinary social gathering should Germans arrive unexpectedly.[49] Such extreme secrecy
was unnecessary in the medical school because of its quasi-legal status, but Tadeusz
Stabholz recalls that lectures would begin as simple descriptions of epidemic diseases—the sanitary courses cover—and then quickly shift to the actual subject
under consideration, physiology, or pathology, or biochemistry. A roll was kept of
those present, for the information of Dr. Zweibaum's office, but this potentially
incriminating document vanished quickly once the students had signed in.[50] Moreover, pamphlets and books relating to epidemics were left scattered on a table in
the lecture room and disinfectant was spread around, making the room redolent of
anti-epidemic measures.[51] But at least one writer believes that the precautions
against discovery were illusory; Zablotniak claims that the Germans were well
aware that the classes were going on, but were so much more concerned with other
matters (he suggests the possible threat of armed resistance by the Jews) that they
ignored the teaching.[52] This seems an unlikely hypothesis. When fighting finally did
break out in the ghetto in January 1943, the Nazis were stunned; nothing had prepared them for armed resistance. Had they been concerned about this possibility,
the medical school could have been eliminated in one raid on the assembled students, conveniently collected together daily in a room above one of the Germans'
own institutions, the *Arbeitsamt*. But this action never was taken.

In the evenings, particularly in the winter months, the darkened lecture rooms
were lit by carbide lamps, widely remembered as being helpful but unpleasantly
smelly.[53] The hallways and stairwells were especially cold and dark.[54] The rooms
were inadequately heated, though this was even more a problem when attempting
to study at home at night. There the entire experience was difficult and worrisome;
if you studied with another student, the visitor had to plan to stay overnight because
the curfew was enforced strictly.[55] Groups of three or four students commonly gathered to study and to teach each other.[56] Often, intellectual activity was disturbed by
hearing an automobile approaching through the dark streets. This was always
alarming because only the Nazis—usually the Gestapo—drove automobiles within
the ghetto at night.[57]

One major difficulty connected with the school was the danger involved in
reaching it. The school building was actually outside the ghetto walls, though only
a few meters. Consequently, until the bridge referred to earlier was constructed,
each student had to pass the scrutiny of German, Polish, and Jewish police guards.
In addition to the regular documents, required of all inhabitants of the ghetto, a
student card of some kind apparently also was used for identification.[58] With the
constant potential for violence, the students were apprehensive and fearful.[59] This
corner was a hazard for all inhabitants of the ghetto, not just the medical students.
One official noted dryly:

Another bit of amusement for the gendarmes was to stop people at the corner of Zelazna and Leszno. People had to pass through there even though it was close to an outpost of gendarmes. . . . there were frenzied beatings with any object at hand.[60]

One student found it increasingly difficult to force herself to attend the sessions.[61] Not surprisingly, perhaps, it is the female students who recall this more often than the male ones; hearing the cries of fellow students being raped in the guardhouse would have made the risk abundantly clear.[62] However, male students were also in danger, frequently being beaten on their way to classes.[63] Because the school building was outside the ghetto, some of the more Aryan-looking male students risked everything by removing their armbands and exploring Warsaw outside the ghetto. Not only was this action of great danger to them, but in addition, it might have compromised the school had they been caught.[64] The danger cannot be overestimated; Hirszfeld remembers hearing shouting from the streets during classes: The guard down on the street was killing a Jew.[65]

In addition to their formal courses in the evenings, the preclinical students had other learning opportunities. During the daytime, students were welcomed into the hospitals and clinics of the ghetto, where they could find both unlimited ways to be of service and teachers avid to teach.[66] Only those who did not need to work could take advantage of this opportunity, but there were many whose parents remained able to support them, at least for a time. Fenigstein, working as a pathologist in Czyste Hospital at Stawki 8, combined informal lectures with practical demonstrations, after which the students dissected the part of the body being studied; much of this was done during the regular hospital hours, in the daytime, and represented extra instruction for those students able to allot the time to it.[67] Fenigstein's anatomical teaching supplemented the more didactic lecturing of Ludwig Stabholz and his colleagues in the evening sessions. Lectures were followed by the study of *preparats* (formalin-preserved pathological specimens used, in this case, for teaching normal anatomy).

The Superior Course

The so-called superior course consisted of the final four clinical years of medical education in the Polish system at the time. Clinical teaching was carried out in the hospitals and clinics of the ghetto. Like everything else in that compressed, strangling world, the hospital system of the Warsaw ghetto was a complex, patched-together, inefficient, and overstrained entity. Before the war, Czyste Hospital had been a superior institution, well equipped and competently staffed.

During the ghetto period, the hospital occupied portions of several buildings, none of them designed as hospitals and none of them adequate. A children's hospital was located on Sienna and Sliska streets.[68] Additional small hospitals, clinics, and other health-related institutions also carried on medical work, but the Czyste Hospital was the main arena for this activity. Student work in anatomy, and in all laboratory and clinical subjects, was also carried out in numerous makeshift hospitals and clinics in the ghetto.

The faculty of the underground medical school attempted to teach clinical medicine in this environment. The students' activities were largely what one would expect in any medical school. They learned to give injections, to write prescriptions, and to examine patients. Occasional lectures were attended during the daytime, and the students did clerkships in rotation through the usual medical and surgical services.[69] Dr. Wisniewski was a cardiologist, and he taught students in the wards: skills such as percussion of the chest, listening to and understanding the heart sounds, all the material that would be taught about hearts and heart disease in any medical school.[70] Not surprisingly, given the conditions in the ghetto, students often were pressed into service as orderlies or nurses. One young man, previously a medical student outside Poland who arrived in Warsaw in March 1942, found himself working in the desperately busy pathology department with Dr. Fenigstein.[71]

The survivors relate a spectrum of experiences that clearly put this school quite outside customary bounds. Balin served in the hospital at the *Umschlagplatz*, where, briefly until he ran away, he was forced by the Nazis to select, from among the patients—*his* patients—those for "transportation" (the euphemism for extermination at Treblinka).[72] Pernal has described the wounds swarming with maggots in her pediatric patients.[73] Eisen saw a boy kicked to death on the street by several German soldiers,[74] and late in the existence of the ghetto, in the very last hospital, on Gęsia Street,[75] many of her patients threw themselves off the roof of the building to their deaths when the German trucks arrived to take them to the *Umschlagplatz*.[76] Borman found a dying woman in the street, who, just as she expired, gave birth to a living baby.[77]

The medical students had examinations regularly. The results were recorded and, it is believed, were communicated to the so-called Zaorski School outside the ghetto as long as this remained possible. One physician who was active in the school remembers that students' marks were to be submitted orally to Professor Hirszfeld, whose responsibility it was to convey them in turn to Prof. Franciszek Czubalski, who was in charge of clandestine medical education on the Aryan side in connection with the Zaorski school.[78] Dr. Stabholz gave only oral exams to his anatomy students,[79] and Balin recalls having only orals in surgery, several examiners taking part.[80] The survivors all remember undergoing numerous oral exams,[81] and there were usually written exams as well. At least one survivor has stressed how seriously these were taken, unsuccessful candidates often weeping over their failure.[82] Year-end examinations for the first-year class were held on 20 January 1942, and the senior-level exams were held two weeks later.[83]

No records exist of the names, or even of how many students there were in the underground school, although one estimate is that as many as 500 persons may have obtained some medical education during the 14 months the school existed.[84] Borman thinks there may have been 250 in the first year alone,[85] while Ludwig Stabholz remembers about 100 in a class.[86] If this last figure can be multiplied by two, for each year that he taught anatomy in the primary course, that would come close to Borman's figure. An anonymous contributor to "Oneg Shabbat," the ghetto archives, claimed that in 1941 there were three parallel groups of 60 students each in the primary course—the first two years of medicine.[87] With such a hidden enterprise, some uncertainty about details seems impossible to avoid. In the clinical classes, Tadeusz Stabholz recalls groups of 30 or more, though these figures would be more difficult to document, since the clinical students were located in a variety of hospitals and clinics.[88]

Few of these men and women survived the deportations to Treblinka that began on 22 July 1942. One estimate is that after the war, about 50 students received certificates confirming their participation in the underground medical school.[89] Fortunately both for himself and for his students, Dr. Zweibaum survived the war; because all records had been destroyed, he personally attested to the progress and accomplishments of several of the students, and they were able to begin their studies with credit for the work already done.[90] Borman believes that of the approximately 250 students in her own class, only about 8 both survived the war and resumed medical studies in Poland;[91] of course, some students completed their education elsewhere.[92] At least one of these, who finished her degree after the war at Wroclaw University, considers that she learned more in the underground school.[93] Some students continued their education in fields such as law, pharmacy, and dentistry.

THE MEDICAL FACULTY

We are able to identify many of those who taught in the ghetto medical college. For quite different reasons, three of the most important people in the underground medical school were Dr. Izrael Milejkowski, Docent Dr. Juliusz Zweibaum, and Prof. Dr. Ludwig Hirszfeld. The first was head of the department of health that was one of the necessary but involuntary creations of the *Judenrat* when responsibility for their city within a city was thrust upon the Jews. The second, before the war a teacher in the medical faculty of Warsaw University, was the titular head of the clandestine school. And the third, a world-famous scientist who had been forced into the ghetto despite being baptized (in accordance with Nazi doctrine that Jewishness was racial, not religious; one was a Jew by Nazi definition if one or more grandparents was Jewish), became a teacher whose charisma and reputation did much for the credibility of the school.

Izrael Milejkowski (1887–1943) became, on 18 September 1939, head of the Health Division of the KK, and then carried on this work with the newly appointed *Judenrat*.[94] Although Milejkowski played a significant role in encouraging the creation of the medical school, his chief contribution to the medical history of the ghetto was his promotion and support of the teams conducting research into starvation, described in Chapter 6. On 18 January 1943 he was captured in the ghetto, with the remnants of a TOZ team, and taken to Treblinka. En route, according to unverifiable reports, he committed suicide.[95]

Juliusz Zweibaum (1887–1959) was the person whose name is most closely associated with creating the school. It was Zweibaum who set up the technical courses that screened the medical school operation. His area of personal research interest was histology.[96] One of his students recalls his lectures on that topic, at which time his enthusiasm was evident.[97] Another categorized him as being quiet, self-possessed, and very nice.[98] Before the war, he had been docent in the Warsaw medical faculty after graduating from Bologna in 1913.[99] The rank of docent, roughly the same as that of associate professor, was the highest that a Jew could attain in prewar Polish universities.

Ludwig Hirszfeld (1884–1954) was by far the most scientifically prominent member of the faculty.[100] His presence in the ghetto during its short, traumatic existence was both scientifically relevant and curiously ironic. Not only was he an authority on several of the diseases that affected the Jews of Warsaw, but he also had done highly original studies on the blood groups and their inheritance, one among several fields that the Nazi authorities bastardized to create a "scientific" rationale for some of its ultimately lethal racial dogma. During World War I he served in Serbia, attempting to control epidemics of typhus and bacillary dysentery, and described the organism that came to be known as *Salmonella hirszfeldi*. In accordance with Nazi dogma, his baptism as a Catholic, performed many years before, was ignored and he was forced to enter the ghetto early in 1941. He escaped to the Aryan side in 1943 and survived the war.[101]

Hirszfeld is remembered by the students from the clandestine school as a gifted teacher; he is one of the few teachers in the school for whom we can discern some flavor of personality from the skimpy records extant. Wygodzka found him an exciting lecturer,[102] and Berg described him as "a poet of his science."[103] He told one class that they would be better off learning to be gravediggers than physicians.[104] Bakowska recalls clearly his statement, based on epidemiological principles, that everyone in the ghetto would be dead within five years, even if the Nazis did nothing more to them than keep them there.[105] Not all memories are favorable. Though Hirszfeld's stature as a scientist is unchallenged, it is obvious that several of the interviewees didn't like him as a person. Wisniewski considered him to be lacking in character.[106] Wygodzka emphasized that he was no saint; his autobiography, written after the war, she found unpleasant. "He loved himself, and it's written like that—with profound love for himself."[107] And Bakowska found that his family, converted Jews, behaved like aristocrats in the ghetto,[108] a characteristic they shared with many of their fellow converts to Christianity. Hirszfeld's wife, Prof. Hanna Hirszfeldowna, proved herself an able clinician when she took responsibility for a ward in the children's hospital.[109]

Henryk Makower (1904–64) taught in the primary course, in the lecture hall located on the top floor of the *Arbeitsamt*. "It was big and convenient and the work went at full speed. Being among these terrific, intelligent and bright young people, I found myself feeling more lively. . . . What a pleasure when you pose a question during a lecture and promptly receive a logical, smart answer that shows that the student is following the thoughts of the teacher and understands him."[110]

Other teachers included Josef Stein (1904–43), Wladyslaw Sterling (1876–1943), Henryk Lewenfisz-Wojnarowski (1894–1956),[111] Hilai Lachs,[112] M. Centnerszwer, Henryk Stabholz (1882–1941),[113] and the three interviewees, Ludwig Stabholz, Henry Fenigstein, and Bernard Waksman (Bronislaw Wisniewski). Fenigstein is fondly remembered by several of the students as a friendly, outgoing, encouraging young man.[114] Professor Centnerszwer was about 5 feet 7 inches tall and stout. He was a close friend of Professor Świętosławski, the minister of education just before the war, and of the Polish president, Prof. Ignacy Moscicki; according to a former student, Centnerszwer talked with these men regularly on the telephone and retained his professorship only through the personal intervention of the president. Centnerszwer was sympathetic to Zionism.[115]

It is a measure of the times that *The Martyrdom of Jewish Physicians in Poland* lists 14 men as those most heavily involved in the school. Of these, two survived the war.[116]

TUITION

Inevitably, both the teachers in the medical school and their students were affected by economic conditions. A senate "of sorts" had been set up, and it was decided that the students must pay for their education, just as everyone else paid for goods or services. The school had to be self-sufficient. The monthly fee was set at 60 zloty, though about a quarter paid only 40 zloty and a number paid nothing, receiving a "bursary" from the *Judenrat*.[117] Since the school functioned only in the evenings for the primary students,[118] this may have been less prejudicial economically than it seems, because students worked at other jobs in the daytime when there were other jobs. From this income, the teachers in the school received salaries of between 200 and 300 zloty per month.[119] In May 1942, a writer in the ghetto estimated that feeding a family required 1000 zloty per month.[120] The medical school had a yearly budget of about 67,000 zloty, and of that, the income from student fees was 64,000; the *Judenrat* paid 3687 zloty toward the cost of printing lecture notes—none seem to have survived—and they permitted the school to operate without paying rent.[121]

The payment of fees by these students remains a topic of debate today. One of the students thought the fees might have been as much as 500 zloty a month, though she was vague on the topic since, as she pointed out, her parents were well off and her father paid the fees for her.[122] She may be remembering an annual figure. She also recognized that the fees would be extremely high for anyone who was significantly less well off, and remembered students dropping out when they or their parents could no longer afford to continue the payments.[123] But another student believes that while those who could do so were expected to pay, those who could not pay were permitted to continue.[124] One woman now living in the United States, whose name has not been revealed to me, reportedly remains bitter to this day, believing that she was prevented from attending the school because she lacked the necessary tuition.[125]

MOTIVATION AND DEDICATION

Perhaps the fundamental question to be asked about the clandestine school, aside from the specific details of its existence, is why? Why did faculty and students undertake this hazardous and apparently futile enterprise?

It may be useful to see motivation at two levels. There may be general motivations, driving all or most of the participants, and, in addition, individual, personal, sometimes idiosyncratic motives. For example, we can recognize in the efforts of Dr. Zweibaum and his colleagues to create a school, and in the aspirations of the students who enrolled, a motivation at one level no different from that of those associated with any other medical school. There existed an abundance of medical talent, a mass of patients for teaching purposes, a prospective student body lacking other intellectual activity, and a perceived need to replenish the ranks of the profession because of attrition both ordinary and extraordinary. Ergo, start a medical school. Or, if one was a student, attend a medical school.

A majority of those involved centered their rationale (no matter how self-delusively) on an attempt to lead a normal life. In the words of one student, "I felt that I must play normal. Everything is normal, otherwise I couldn't exist."[126] Another referred to study as "the miraculous way of getting away from reality, of forgetting the bleak lot, the today and tomorrow, the bestiality and barbarity."[127] These students expressed one common attitude: They were bored in the ghetto. Some were from families sufficiently well off that they had no need to work. Others worked at routine jobs during the day, but they were young, bright, and ambitious. They needed more. Their anatomy teacher observed that "They wanted to learn. They had nothing to do, only to learn. It was not possible to go anywhere."[128]

The students who had already completed some years of study had also, of course, the pressure of an unfinished task driving them to complete their education. As one of them put it, "some of us were very anxious to learn. We had a lot of experience, a lot of exposure, and we wanted to know."[129]

But these were by no means the sole motives. No ordinary medical school, this was a clandestine activity. Its forbidden nature constituted a factor in motivation, as well as, more obviously, in the day-to-day operations of the school. Most survivors believe that the underground medical school should be seen as a form of rebellion, of refusal to accept full control of their lives by the Germans. This feeling was expressed in various ways: a "beautiful case of passive resistance,"[130] "sort of a resistance, not with machine guns or anything, but a different way,"[131] "one was fighting the war in a special way,"[132] and the idea that the Germans can have my body, "but they will not have my soul."[133] The students worked "as if we wouldn't care what will happen tomorrow."[134] "It was not an escape from the dreadful reality but an expression of opposition to the iniquity and the desecration of cherished values."[135] Dawidowicz quotes Chaim Kaplan, who defended even the frivolity of dancing within the ghetto because it could be interpreted as a protest against the oppressors;[136] if dancing was a protest, how much stronger was the protest of clandestine higher education?

All of these motivations must be seen within the context of the ghetto and the realities of life there. Borman noted: "We had the choice of total desperation, total demoralization, suicide (some did commit suicide), escapism (whiskey [more likely, vodka] or whatever they could find), but instead we started to study."[137]

True, these statements about motivation were made 40 years after the short life of the school had ended. But the opinions, and the manner in which they were stated, have a ring of authenticity. Also, none of those interviewed gave this last, defiant motive alone, and most expressed more prosaic reasons before mentioning their perception of the school as a form of resistance.

And there were other reasons, or motivations, that varied widely. Fenigstein taught simply because he enjoyed teaching. When he heard that he might be able to be involved in the underground school, "I grabbed this opportunity because it was not just a plain job, but it was something which was, for me, challenging, interesting, which I enjoyed."[138] At the other extreme were students who used the classes as an escape from confinement in the home and from the dangers of being found walking the streets, where one was subject to indiscriminate abuse. Jewish women were known to have been rounded up and used for sexual purposes by the Nazis.[139] According to one of the students, some women attended the school at least partly because it offered a way of hiding for part of the day in an environment that was dangerous but safer than the streets.[140] Prosaically enough, some students attended simply because their parents wanted them to become physicians.[141] At least one student enrolled because her mother pushed her, telling her that she needed to plan to be educated and to survive.[142] Another woman decided to become a physician at the age of 10, under the influence of her parents, both of whom were dentists, and an uncle, a doctor.[143]

Gutman has suggested that the members of the various youth movements within the ghetto became "a kind of existential enclave,"[144] permitting the members to function differently—in this case, much more positively and forcefully—than the general population there. Perhaps a similar devotion to a common and positive purpose enveloped the medical students from the underground school, enabling them also to pursue a future goal when the future looked so desperate. For the few who survived, that impossible future came to pass.

The underground medical school in the Warsaw ghetto was created for two not mutually exclusive reasons: to carry on normal life and to flout German regulations. Similarly, students studied in the school for two not mutually exclusive reasons: to further their education and to defy the Germans.

Thus both faculty and students had double goals that, although they could be held simultaneously, nevertheless were antithetical: to lead life normally and to combat the obvious abnormality in their lives. For the few survivors who continued their education after the war and who have had useful professional careers, it must be a source of some satisfaction, despite the attendant tragedies that distorted all their lives, to realize that they did succeed in fending off the awful pressures of their times.[145] They lived on what was forbidden, and against all odds they put their clandestine education to use. Milejkowski was right: *Non omnis moriar.*[146]

OTHER FACULTIES

Medicine was not the only professional course offered in the ghetto. Nursing education went on without a break and apparently with the approval of the Germans, a notable exception to their general policy of minimal education for the Jews.[147] This experience is outlined in Chapter 4.

In addition, some teaching was conducted in dentistry, chemistry, and pharmacy. Little seems to have been recorded about the first two groups. Hirszfeld relates that he was given permission by Dr. Hagen to give a lecture course to dentists on general pathology.[148] Whether this was a true course or merely a series of lectures is uncertain. The reference to teaching of chemistry is even more cryptic; Czerniakow mentions in his diary that he visited the school of chemistry, which looked like a garbage dump.[149] Nothing else has been uncovered about this school, which could have been connected with the medical school or the school of pharmacy.

There was a school of pharmacy in the Warsaw ghetto. One anonymous memoir states that there were 50 students and suggests that the course was offered by Professor Hirszfeld,[150] though this seems unlikely, both because pharmacy was not his field and because he was meticulous in his autobiography in setting out his various activities and yet does not mention a school of pharmacy. The students entered a nine-month course, for which they were expected to pay 50 zloty a month.[151] Czerniakow spoke at the inauguration of the course in December 1941,[152] and at least one of the medical student interviewees had friends in the course.[153] This activity awaits its historian.

11

Surviving the Catastrophe

... we have learned that even the faintest glimmer of hope for personal survival was more powerful than any fear of selection.[1]

Millions of persons died in Europe during World War II. For Jews the figure generally used is 6 million, though accurate accounting will never be possible. The number of Jews in Poland shrank from 3 million to a few thousand. Given the circumstances, it is perhaps remarkable that any survived.

Yet some did, and the purpose of this chapter is to examine how and why that was the case. It will emphasize the specific group of men and women who have been the source of so much firsthand information for this book—those interviewees who were survivors of the Warsaw ghetto.

LEAVING THE GHETTO

There were three ways for the Jews of Warsaw to leave the ghetto. About 140,000 "left" by dying there. About 400,000 were relocated to various camps, particularly Treblinka (of all these Jews, only a dozen or two survived to 1945). And about 20,000 escaped from the ghetto into Warsaw and other cities and towns, to attempt to survive as pretended Christians, or into the forests to hide or to fight with the partisans or the official resistance. Although full details on the experiences of the last two groups do not fit properly into a history of the ghetto, a fairly full description of the three deportations will be given, up to the departure of the trains for extermination or concentration camps. After that point, only a brief mention of events will be made to round out the picture. Similarly, the fate of escapees, while having its own fascination and a few hundred happy endings, can only be alluded to for the period after the Jews physically departed from the ghetto.

Escaping Over the Walls or Through the Gates

Escapers used many routes. Some simply walked out the gates, usually after bribing the necessary Jewish, Polish, and German guards or others. Some left through the gates disguised as workers, perhaps as part of a column of Jews going to some work site. The sewers were also used as escape routes, in particular at the time of the uprising of the Jews in April–May 1943. The cemetery was a common route, since there were sympathetic employees there plus a quiet, little-patrolled environment. The going rate, in autumn 1942, was 75 zloty to be helped up a ladder and over the cemetery wall.[2]

Innumerable escape methods were used, some successfully, many not. One "medical" approach was that of faking the death of a family member, who would be taken to the cemetery, followed by the rest of the family, from where they would all attempt to escape. In one instance, a Dr. Levy pronounced a six-year-old girl dead from illness, and the family escaped after following the undertaker from the home on Walicow 6 to the Jewish cemetery.[3] As described in Chapter 9, at least one baby was the "deceased," having been appropriately drugged.

Faked illness was also a promising approach. In October 1941, two ex-army officers, though under arrest, were in Czyste Hospital on Stawki Street. They had been admitted because of suspected typhus, a contrived condition. They subsequently escaped, apparently with the connivance of some of the medical staff.[4]

Once one succeeded in escaping physically, the truly difficult part began. Survival in Warsaw or other Polish cities, towns, and villages required many assets, particularly a generous dose of luck. Of this latter asset there were many examples. When Sabina Gurfinkiel-Glocerowa was attempting to escape early in 1943, she used the method of mingling with a group of workers leaving via one of the gates. But she was interrogated and searched at a police post and was saved only by incredible good fortune. A Jewish policewoman in the *Ordnungsdienst* came into the post while Gurfinkiel-Glocerowa was being examined. This woman had once been her patient, and she managed to get her through.[5]

To survive outside, either authentic papers or passable forgeries were required. These were difficult to obtain, especially authentic documents; all kinds were expensive. One family eventually purchased Argentinian papers, though they have since decided that the papers were fraudulent; at any rate they were unable to attempt to use them, perhaps fortunately, since they survived without them.[6] Many who sought freedom via passports and visas from sympathetic countries, particularly several South American nations, found the papers a snare pulled tight by the Nazis just as escape seemed imminent.[7]

Halina Berg tried to buy a birth certificate in the autumn of 1942 but failed.[8] She fled into Aryan Warsaw without papers but ultimately was able to get a genuine *Kennkarte*, or identification card, and survived.[9] Marek Balin, a medical student, received help from a Polish physician, a Dr. Slominski, who visited the ghetto regularly on official public health duties. He was also in the *Armja Krajowa*, the underground army, and he obtained false papers for Balin.[10]

Of course, one needed a "good face." A Jew who was immediately identifiable as such on the basis of facial appearance was unlikely to survive. Meed, who did survive, noted that "[m]y salient features were, indeed, 'Aryan'—a rather small nose, grey-green eyes, straight light brown hair."[11] But appearance alone wasn't enough; one needed to control one's eyes, prevent them from darting about suspiciously, and ideally, one needed to look happy. This rarely was an easy task for a Jew struggling for life in a hostile environment, usually having already lost relatives and friends to the death camps.[12] Moreover, the effect of appearance was inconsistent. In many cases, Jews with typically Semitic appearances came through the war without any attempt at exploitation, whereas those with typically Slavic faces were caught. "'Good appearance' involved the entire style of existence, behavior, clothing, speech, etc."[13] It was not easy to maintain the pretense of being a gentile.[14] Kubar discovered one hazard that shows some of the hidden dimensions of the problem. After she left the ghetto, she found a home with an elderly Polish spinster. They became fond of one another, but one area of uneasiness concerned bathing. Kubar was in the habit of bathing her entire body every day. To the Polish lady this was at least bizarre, possibly suspicious. Why would anyone behave in this remarkable way? Surely her guest's morals ought to be examined, for no one of sound virtue would feel the need to bathe daily.[15] In the end, Kubar survived, but she had never thought that her bathing habits might have brought her undue attention.

Edelman, a leader in the 1943 uprising, escaped through the sewers. He found it difficult to adjust to the relative normality of gentile Warsaw. When he was riding a streetcar for the first time in many months,

> a horrible thing happened to him. He was seized by the wish not to have a face. Not because he was afraid that someone would notice him and denounce him; no, he suddenly felt that he had a repugnant, sinister face. The face from the poster "JEWS-LICE-TYPHUS." Whereas everybody else around him had fair faces. They were handsome, relaxed. They could be relaxed because they were aware of their fairness and beauty.[16]

For those whose appearance was dangerously Jewish, there was also the option of plastic surgery. But this branch of medicine was relatively undeveloped then. One needed money, or a physician friend who was both sympathetic and skillful, or both. With these, the attempt could be made. Dr. Wisniewski, himself a physician, was able to have the shape of his nose altered. His good friend Dr. Andrzej Trojanowski performed the operation in the early autumn of 1942.[17] He survived, perhaps at least partly due to his altered facial appearance. Dr. Felix Kanabus, a Polish surgeon, performed many operations during the war. Some were done to alter the shape of a nose; others—more than 70—were intended to disguise the existence of a circumcision. All this surgery had to be done in Kanabus' office or in patients' homes because they could not be admitted to any hospital in Warsaw. Kanabus worked in cooperation with Dr. Trojanowski and Dr. Jan Grocholski, who was executed by the Nazis in 1942.[18]

A few Poles made a gruesome living by blackmailing Jews, threatening to report them to the Gestapo; often these *szmalcownicy*,[19] or blackmailers, would bleed their victim dry and then turn them in. Only one-quarter to one-third of those who escaped from the ghetto survived until 1945.[20] A tragic case in point was that of Halina Berg; a boy accused her of being a Jew and stole everything she had.[21] Later, Berg and her mother, who had escaped together, had to be separated because of the difficulty in finding safe housing. Soon afterward, the mother was betrayed. Halina never saw her again.[22]

The *Armja Krajowa*, operating underground in Aryan Warsaw, made some attempts to discourage the activities of the *szmalcownicy*. One method involved scrutinizing their mail. Thanks to members of the *Armja Krajowa* who worked in the post office, it was possible to monitor mail sent to the Gestapo. Some of this mail contained denunciations of Jews. At least a few of the senders of such letters were tried by the underground and executed.[23]

Some experiences with gentile Poles were happier. Several books have documented the self-sacrifice made by many Poles, and the immense risks run in order to try to save the lives of Jews, some of them prewar friends or colleagues but more often strangers.[24] Death was the penalty decreed for any Pole found aiding or sheltering a Jew.[25] Balin was one who was aided. Peasants hid him and fed him after he escaped from the train going to Treblinka. He paid them with gold coins sewn into his clothing. He then returned to Warsaw, where a Christian woman who had formerly worked for Balin's aunt hid him in her home on Ogrodowa Street for a while.[26]

Some escapes became lengthy, complicated hegiras. When Irena Bakowska and her family left the ghetto, using false papers, they traveled to the village of Zakrzowek, near Lublin, where the local Jews had not yet been deported. They lived there in hiding for some time. There was a Gestapo detachment in the area, which was bribed generously to permit the Jews to live. They did so for some time, but ultimately all the Jews had to flee. The family returned to Warsaw, from where Bakowska and her sister, in the guise of Catholic Polish girls, were sent to Germany to do manual labor.[27] By some miracle, all four members of the family survived, almost a unique event for that time and place. Eugenia Pernal, who escaped into Warsaw in August 1942,[28] was sheltered in a girlfriend's home. Ultimately she also was sent to Germany on forced labor as a Polish girl and survived.[29]

Housing was a particularly difficult problem. A worker in an underground group dedicated to aiding Jews in hiding noted that the reports of her fellow workers constantly referred to the unceasing hunt for a room or a corner in a room, for someplace to hide.[30] Most Poles lived in apartment buildings that had concierges. It was difficult to conceal one stranger under these circumstances, and two or more increased the likelihood of discovery significantly. Even Jews who had been on the Aryan side for some time were faced with frequent moves. These were sometimes necessary because of suspicion cast upon them by others in a building; sometimes by greed on the part of the host or hostess, who might demand ever higher sums for risking their lives; and for innumerable other reasons as well.

The conclusion of the first massive deportations produced one supportive action. During the deportations, the Jews sent messages to the outside world, informing people about the horrendous mass murder taking place and appealing for help. In general, the response was pitifully limited. But one extremely helpful group came into being. On 27 September, a Provisional Committee was set up in Warsaw, largely by gentiles. Its aims were to help Jews escape from the ghetto and to then provide them with shelter, papers, and money. On 4 December 1942, that committee was disbanded and a Council for Aid to Jews (*Roda Pomocy Żydom*) replaced it. Some funding came from the Polish government in exile in London.[31]

They coined a cryptonym, Żegota, since using any title with the word "Jew" (*Żydom*) in it was potentially lethal. The Council included representatives of the democratic political parties in Poland plus two Jews from the Warsaw ghetto.[32] In Warsaw alone, where about 20,000 Jews were hidden among the gentile population, 4000 received assistance from Żegota.[33] In addition, an effort was mounted to rescue specific individuals from concentration camps and settle them in hiding in

Warsaw. Some successes were recorded, though often the end result continued to be tragedy. For example, Ringelblum was removed from a camp and established in Warsaw in the Aryan area. Unfortunately, the historian and his family later were betrayed and killed.[34] These rescue efforts were extremely expensive. Rescue from a camp cost about 50,000 zloty ($10,000) for bribes and other expenses, and installing someone in reasonably safe hiding required another 5000 to 10,000 zloty.[35]

A special problem arose when an illegal person needed medical care. It was dangerous to assume that an unknown nurse or doctor was sympathetic. Fortunately for some who were in this predicament, *Żegota* provided invaluable assistance.

Żegota set up an office to provide medical aid to Jews, aid punishable by death if discovered by the Nazis.[36] This operation was headed by Dr. Ludwig Rostkowski, an ophthalmologist, who created a secret medical support network with a group of his colleagues. "The physicians working in this program visited and treated patients living in hiding free of charge and, if necessary, found a space for them in a hospital."[37] A system of secret mailboxes was established where addresses of sick Jews could be left along with a description of symptoms. A liaison worker for *Żegota* collected these notes and conveyed them to Rostkowski, who assessed the problems, selected appropriate doctors to visit the patients, and sent instructions to these doctors via his son, a medical student.[38] In this way, the hidden Jews were relieved of the fear that they might become seriously ill and be unable to get assistance.

Some Jews in hiding, however, lacked access to this clandestine medical service. In at least one instance this led to tragedy. A woman named Clara Hechtman became insane while in hiding. Becoming manic and uncontrollable, she created a moral crisis among the group of Jews with whom she shared a hiding place. Finally, to save the rest of the group, who would certainly be discovered if she was not silenced, they felt obliged to poison her. She died and was secretly buried.[39]

Sometimes assistance in escaping came from unexpected directions. For example, a Roman Catholic priest in what became the ghetto was Marcelli Godlewski. This man had been a notorious antisemite before the war, using the pulpit to attack Jews viciously. After the ghetto was established his church remained within the walls, a source of consolation to the baptized Jews forced into the ghetto. There were 1540 such Jews (Jews by Hitlerian decree) in the ghetto at the beginning of 1941, with churches on Grzybow Square and on Leszno Street.[40] Godlewski also remained in the ghetto. But, apparently intensely moved by the desperate plight of the Jews in the ghetto, he began to help them actively. A tall man with long gray hair, Godlewski assisted those hoping to flee into the city by providing papers and by putting them in contact with Catholic families who might help the escapers in various ways.[41] Moreover, a tunnel purportedly was excavated from a building near the church on Leszno Street, used both as an escape route and as a way of bringing supplies into the ghetto.[42]

The Deportation of July–September 1942

On 18 July 1942, rumors of an upcoming *Aktion* began to circulate in the ghetto. Tension rose rapidly, despite the assurances of German officials that they knew of no such impending event. By the 19th, Chairman Czerniakow was in a sorry state: "Today I took 2 headache powders, another pain reliever, and a sedative, but my head is still splitting. I am trying not to let the smile leave my face."[43] Keeping up the morale of his people was essentially the only positive action left to Czerniakow.

The first move made by the Germans was to require of the *Judenrat*, on 21 July, that the branch of Czyste Hospital at Stawki 6–8 be cleared of all patients immediately. Czerniakow protested this order. Czyste contained hundreds of patients with infectious diseases and had the only reasonably well-equipped pharmacy in the ghetto. Auerswald replied that he held the manager of the hospital as a hostage. The building was evacuated.[44]

When the deportations began, Heinz Auerswald, the *Kommissar*, ceased to be in charge. The Gestapo and the *Umsiedlung*, or Deportation Division, had full responsibility.[45] The *Judenrat* was essentially powerless. Only the *Ordnungsdienst* had a role to play, one that earned them the loathing of their fellow Jews. The German staff planning of this *Aktion* was undertaken by Franz Novak, who was convicted of war crimes after the war and served six years' imprisonment. Herman Höfle, another key figure in the deportation proceedings, hung himself in his cell on 20 August 1962 rather than face trial.[46]

On 22 July the deportation began under the direct supervision of Herman Höfle, Globocnik's chief of staff at Krakow,[47] and the following day Czerniakow conveyed the strongest possible final message to the Jews in the ghetto. Finally using the cyanide that he had kept hidden in his desk since 1939, he committed suicide.

The deportation had four stages:[48]

1. 22–30 July: the main responsibility for fulfilling the daily quota of deportees (6000–9000 daily) lay with the members of the *Ordnungsdienst*.
2. 31 July to 14 August: SS forces (with their helpers—young Ukrainians, Lithuanians, and Latvians who served as auxiliaries) took complete responsibility for supplying Treblinka with its victims.
3. 15 August to 6 September: all documentation began to be ignored, and the reign of terror intensified.
4. 6–12 September: this was the period known as the "Kettle" or the "Cauldron," when every Jew remaining in the ghetto was required to be on the streets within a prescribed area of a few blocks, near the *Umschlagplatz*, at which time those who had approved jobs received special passes, the so-called life tickets. The rest were sent to Treblinka.

During this eight-week-long *Aktion*, about 75 percent of the Jews in the ghetto were either sent to Treblinka, and death, or were killed in the ghetto. Approximately 60,000 survived, just over 35,000 "legally" and the rest in hiding.[49]

Of this massive *Aktion*, which resulted in the deaths of a third of a million of Warsaw's Jews, a vast amount has been written. Perhaps one of the most moving depictions was written by Vladka Meed, a young woman who turned 20 the same year. She recorded in her diary the expulsion of the Jews living in the Small Ghetto; they were trudging toward the *Umschlagplatz* and Treblinka:

A tremendous churning black tide. . . . There were *rickshas* carrying invalids; men, women, and children, the young and the old, trudging along. Face after face passed below us, faces apathetic, agitated, terrified, some tense, others bereft of hope. We watched intently, searching for a familiar face among the thousands shuffling past. The sight made my head reel. All the faces blended in confusion; only bowed heads and bundles and bent backs, a single wave of humanity. The marchers were silent,

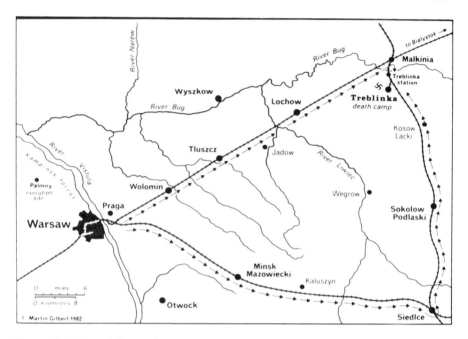

Figure 11.1. Map of deportations of Polish Jews out of the Warsaw ghetto beginning 22 July 1942 (from Martin Gilbert, *The Macmillan Atlas of the Holocaust,* Da Capo, New York 1984, p. 109).

the atmosphere stifling, only the sound of footsteps, all sorts of footsteps—the slow and nimble, adults and children. . . .[50]

The deportations were a massive tragedy, a tapestry of human misery and German brutality. About 350,000 Jews from the Warsaw ghetto were deported, most of them making their final journey to Treblinka, only 70 miles north east of the city (see Figure 11.1). Except for the smallest handful who managed to escape in one way or another, all died there. Thousands more perished at Auschwitz, Majdanek, Bergen-Belsen, Dora, or other camps.

Those who went to Treblinka usually died within a few hours. Tadeusz Stabholz was sent to Auschwitz—and survived. He heard the orchestra made up of Jewish musicians, playing near the entrance,[51] and described the infamous gateway to death.[52] As was the rule at such places, the men were separated from the women; Stabholz's fiancée went with the women to her death. He is haunted still by his failure either to help her or to die with her.[53]

The first place emptied in the ghetto, the first sacrifice to the gas chambers at Treblinka, was Dzika 3, where there was a large refugee "point" or station housing about 1200, including 200 children, as well as a youth home containing 60 adolescents.[54] Dzika 3 was adjacent to the *Umschlagplatz*, and refugees, especially children, were an easy target. But taking refugees first also contributed to the psychological state that the Germans were seeking. The native Varsovian Jews in the ghetto, still a large majority, could delude themselves a little longer. They assured each other that the deportation was only to rid the ghetto of Jews who couldn't contribute economically, by moving them to an area further east where there might be

Figure 11.2. Corner of Stawki and Djika Streets, and the *Umschlagplatz,* Warsaw ghetto, presumably post-war. Translation of Yiddish writing on reverse of original: "This is the terrible building where our brothers and sisters were confined after the tragic Aktion in the Warsaw ghetto, and from which they were loaded on the freight cars for transport to Treblinka and Majdanek. For this to the glory of God." (Translation by Mrs. Mali Fenigstein.) (courtesy of Dr. L. Stabholz, Tel Aviv).

Figure 11.3. The main building at the *Umschlagplatz,* Warsaw (Le Centre de Documentation Juive Contemporaine, Paris).

Figure 11.4. Loading Jews onto a train at the *Umschlagplatz*, destined for Treblinka (Le Centre de Documentation Juive Contemporaine, Paris).

Figure 11.5. Jews at the *Umschlagplatz* waiting deportation to Treblinka (Le Centre de Documentation Juive Contemporaine, Paris).

work for them to do. As Gutman puts it, "At each stage of the operation, they landed a blow to one section of the population while reinforcing the illusions of the rest that they were among the privileged and immune from harm"[55] (see Figures 11.2 to 11.5).

Others taken early on were the inmates of the prisons,[56] another group outside the boundaries of society to most people. But not all deportation was forced. Lewin mentions talking with the wife of a lawyer from Łódź who had gone to the *Umschlagplatz* with her two daughters twice by 26 July 1942. They had gone to give themselves up for relocation on the promise of food, having eaten nothing for two days; but they were sent away because there were huge crowds of people giving themselves up.[57] Among these was the Zionist historian Dr. Tulo Nussenblat. He was last seen trying to escape from the ghetto, carrying a heavy valise loaded with the documents he needed to complete his biography of Theodore Herzl. He refused to discard them, his one familiar point in the midst of a catastrophic event.[58] Ultimately, he went to the *Umschlagplatz*.

The roundups in the street created an atmosphere of paralyzing fear among the ghetto residents. Once it was learned that papers might not save one, the experience of being in such an *Aktion* was terrifying. Here is the account of one survivor:

> How did it look, the catching of people on the street? I had an occasion to "satisfy" my curiosity about it walking one day on Leszno Street. . . . All of a sudden, a truck approached with Germans, Ukrainians, and SP [Jewish police]. They blocked the exits on Karmelicka, Solna, and Żelazna Streets in order to direct the traffic towards Karmelicka Street. They did it at a very fast pace. In front of each house there was a Ukrainian standing with a gun ready to shoot. We wanted to reach a house nearby that had a passageway through to Ogrodowa Street. The police were chasing and directing us toward the crowds, marching us forward quickly. There was an old friend of ours from Lodz that joined us on the street. . . . All of a sudden, one of us had the idea of hiding in the Department of Health at Leszno 68. There were no Ukrainians in front of that building, only SP were standing there. Finally, after lengthy persuasion, they let us in; once there we could breathe easier.[59]

The Umschlagplatz

What became the dreaded *Umschlagplatz*, the gateway to Treblinka, had until 22 July 1942 been simply a railroad freight yard and was the site of entry into the ghetto for many of the meager goods received. But the *Umschlagplatz* became a place of terror, chaos, cruelty, and death. For those weeks in July, August, and September 1942, and again in 1943, the freight hauled was people—the Jews of Warsaw. The *Umschlagplatz* was a large square into which ran railway tracks. It lay immediately north of Stawki Street, from which it was separated by the large buildings at Stawki 6–8.[60] These buildings, still standing in 1990, are four stories high, well constructed, with tan-colored stone facings. It was these buildings that were the main nonsurgical division of Czyste Hospital until its forced abandonment on 21 July 1942 to provide space for deportees who could not be taken away by train on the same day they were rounded up.

The anguish of the times is evident in the recollections of a young girl, torn from her grandfather in the *Umschlagplatz* because she had a life ticket and he did not:

Behind me Grandfather was no longer visible, but he still held my hand and suddenly I felt his lips in my palm. In the next moment his hand was free. I craned my neck and called him but the swirling crowd had swallowed him already. I held my left hand clenched throughout the day, treasuring his kiss. . . .[61]

The former hospital at Stawki 6–8 thus became an overnight holding place for Jews awaiting deportation to Treblinka. Sometimes the trains were full and a group would be held overnight, to be removed the next day. Hundreds, sometimes thousands, of Jews were crammed into this building, which became a cesspool. Toilets were not working, there was no running water, and the victims were crowded together without respect to age or sex. One man who had worked in the hospital for months before the summer *Aktion* found it unrecognizable when he was forced to return. It was jammed with desperate Jews and it was filthy, the floors covered with feces and vomit, the smell indescribable.[62]

Most of the survivors who have been interviewed had personal experience with the *Umschlagplatz*, that "hell on earth."[63] Their memories often give them pain. Eugenia Pernal found four children in the street nearby when she was being taken there; they either had no parents or had been separated from them. She managed to find them a little food, but given the opportunity to escape alone she did so— and still feels guilty.[64] Typifying the chaos of the time, she had been taken there despite wearing her nurse's uniform and having correct papers that should have brought about her immediate release. She spent a terrified night before she was rescued the following day by a friend of her brother.[65]

Although she might have been sent to Treblinka despite her uniform, at least in the early days of the deportation, having a medical or related profession often was lifesaving. Indeed, Ringelblum identified nurses as being "the only ones who saved people from deportation without [asking for] money."[66] This is too narrow a statement, but many nurses certainly labored heroically to save their fellow Jews.

Sabina Gurfinkiel-Glocerowa described ambulances from Czyste that smuggled medical people, and presumably some made to look medical, away from the *Umschlagplatz*.[67] Wdowinski identified the *Judenrat* secretary, Nahum Remba, and his wife, as having heroically commandeered an ambulance, which they used to rescue children from the *Umschlagplatz*.[68]

Remba, a Zionist who had been in the *kehilla* before the war and then became personnel secretary in the *Judenrat*,[69] operated out of a two-room first aid station set up at the *Umschlagplatz*. He was assisted by Ala Gołąb-Grynberg[70] and several nurses or nursing students from the Czyste school. They identified important people from the ghetto world in the milling crowds forced into the great square of the *Umschlagplatz*. Remba or one of the nurses took these individuals to the first aid station as if they were ill. To get them out of the *Umschlagplatz*, these people had to be seen by the Germans to be unwell, so many subterfuges were used to simulate illness or injury. According to Edelman, the most drastic was not to simulate but to create injury: "So these girls from the emergency rooms, those nurses, would break the legs of those people who had to be saved. They would wedge a leg up against a wooden block and then smash it with another block. All this in their shiny white robes of model students."[71] These now genuine patients could then be transported out of the *Umschlagplatz* in the makeshift ambulance that was kept there for that use.[72]

Marek Edelman was a part of this rescue apparatus. He stood by the gate with lists of people who should be saved and picked them out as "sick."[73] Technically he was working for Czyste Hospital, but they knew of his clandestine assignment, so he was given only nominal tasks by the hospital staff. For six weeks, he spent most of the daylight hours at the entrance to the *Umschlagplatz*. At the end of that time, he had watched almost 400,000 Jews shuffle past on their way to death.[74]

Gurfinkiel-Glocerowa and her daughter had a remarkable escape. They were taken to the *Umschlagplatz* because she had failed to get a life ticket, the pass stating one's employment in a protected field (the Germans gave only certain numbers, even to the hospitals).[75] But there was still a clinic operating in the Stawki building that had been a branch of Czyste. Gurfinkiel-Glocerowa and her daughter jumped over a fence into the hospital yard, she breaking a leg in the process.[76] She had to bribe a German soldier not to force them back across the fence again. Then a hospital employee who recognized her unlocked a door and let them in.[77] From the hospital windows she saw people with nurses' uniforms being saved,[78] as were people pretending, convincingly, to be doctors.[79]

Dr. Ludwig Stabholz, the anatomist, was able to rescue his mother from the dreaded *Umschlagplatz* by telling a guard she was his nurse.[80] They left in an ambulance. And Marek Balin was saved because of his white coat; though only a medical student, he claimed to be a staff member of Czyste; he was young enough to be salvageable, since at that time the Nazis were deporting only old or crippled doctors and nurses.[81] However, he then found himself among those at Czyste told that they must do the selecting themselves; a small percentage of the patients could stay in the hospital, but most were to be sent directly to the *Umschlagplatz*. Balin did this painful work for two hours but, sickened, ran away at the first opportunity.[82]

This selection took place on 15 August 1942, at the Trauma Division of Czyste, then located at Leszno 1. There were 600 patients there that day, though the usual number was about 200. The Nazis ordered a selection by the next morning. No more than 150 patients were to remain; the rest would be deported via the *Umschlagplatz*.[83] By mid-August 1942, most Jews knew the meaning of deportation: death at Treblinka. The medical staff was horrified at the order that would make them select fellow Jews to die. Nor were these healthy men and women. The patients were ill, crippled, unable to walk, and often in severe pain. The doctors were ordered to select their own patients, people they had dedicated their lives to comforting and treating, and whose lives they should be attempting to prolong.[84]

Ultimately, the selection was made. The gruesome choice had to be made during regular evening rounds, customarily carried out by house surgeons and volunteers. But on 15 August 1942 the heads of the surgical services were there: Drs. Rothaub, Borkowski, and Szenicer. Dr. Amsterdamski, the chief surgeon, had been held as a hostage. Patients' charts were to be marked with either a plus sign or a minus sign.

> They stopped at each bed for a longer time than usual. They whispered quietly, with anguished voices. They debated in Latin so the patients could not guess anything or comprehend the horror of this unusual consultation.[85]

But of course, the patients did guess what was happening. Dr. Szenicer held a handkerchief to his face to hide his emotion. Others were in tears. During the selection, Balin's chief of service disappeared, and he never saw him again.[86]

Balin's special personal trial during this agonizing selection for death was connected with a favorite patient, Chana Rosenfeld. She was a 16-year-old "criminal" who had been incarcerated in Gęsiówka for the crime of begging. While imprisoned, her feet froze and both had to be amputated. Balin was a senior medical student and had been assigned the task of trying to heal her, both in body and in mind. She was deeply depressed by the loss of both feet. By August, after several months, she had begun to improve rapidly. Now Balin knew she could not fail to be selected for the *Umschlagplatz*. And he was right. She went to Treblinka.[87]

Halina Berg had the bad luck to be taken to the *Umschlagplatz* twice, both times while in uniform; she had the astonishing good fortune to have been saved both times.[88] During this same terrible summer of 1942, Karolina Borman, her parents, and her sister also were caught up in an *Aktion* and found themselves in the mob of frightened humanity. They weren't put directly on a train and deported, but had to spend the night in the building at Stawki 6–8. This gave them enough time to bribe their way out.[89]

The pressures on individuals often assumed tragic dimensions. Morality was strained to the breaking point. Lewin describes agonized discussions with his relatives about his infirm, elderly mother. Finally, late in August 1942, the family agreed to spare her the trial of Treblinka. But the person chosen to carry out this decision couldn't do it. "I have given my permission to put her to sleep, eternal rest, rather than give her over to the executioners. But J. refuses to carry it out."[90] "J" was Jakub Tombeck, Lewin's brother-in-law, a physician.

Other physicians also hated the lonely responsibility but carried out the wishes of patients to be allowed to die quietly, spared the cruelty and humiliation of Treblinka and the gas chambers. Szwajger finally gave in to the pleas of a nurse, unable to do the deed herself, and prepared a lethal injection: "[T]hat gray-haired lady smiled at me and stretched out her arm. . . . I injected the morphine into her vein."[91]

The reaction of Germans to this wholesale evacuation, under conditions of great cruelty and to a fate that could less and less easily be hidden, was mixed. Some seemed to find it edifying. As has been mentioned, not all Jews were shipped to Treblinka; quite a large number, some hundreds, were shot in the Jewish cemetery. On 26 July a car drove up to the cemetery, and a German woman got out with her two young children. She took them into the cemetery, to a place where elderly Jews were being murdered. "She wanted to show the children how the Jews were dying."[92] Some German reactions seemed more humane. Dr. Hagen was on leave when the deportations began and he learned about them only on his return to Warsaw, 13 August. He claims that he immediately stopped any further work in the ghetto and determined to leave the *Generalgouvernement*.[93] Six months later he was transferred to the Russian front. This attitude helped no Jew, but at least it indicated some element of remorse or conscience.

The deportations were carried out with great brutality. The Jews were rounded up from streets, homes, and workplaces, beaten into columns, and shot if they resisted or attempted to escape. The victims of these shootings were men and women, old and young, babies and grandparents. The *Judenrat* reported 2305 deaths from bullet wounds in August 1942, 3158 in September.[94]

One physician has written about her experiences during the deportations while working in the Czyste operating rooms in the building at Leszno 1:

> It was situated in the former building of the Alcohol Monopoly belonging to the government, at Leszno 1. Next to the *Umschlagplatz* it was a true reflection of happenings in the ghetto. I did not leave the hospital even once during the whole action and we were swamped with work. We were literally bathing in blood during 24 hours non-stop. There were no interruptions from outside at that time. They left the hospital in peace practically to the end of action.
>
> They were supplying us with loads of work. . . . They brought wounded to the hospital constantly. The most common wounds were in the head and abdomen, and in second place were arms and legs. Shots, mostly from close range with dum-dum bullets, created atrocious wounds. I remember a young woman around 20 years old, whom I had seen already in bed on the hospital floor, covers drawn over her head in deep shock. She seemed to be sleeping quietly. When it came her turn to be operated on I removed her cover. In the middle of her abdomen was a wound the size of a dessert plate with the edges torn in shreds, and with the stomach, liver, and part of the intestine hanging out. The wound described above was the entry of the bullet. The exit was in the vicinity of the left lumbar loin, about the size of a human head. How could we operate there? The older doctors agreed with my opinion. When she regained consciousness she had horrible pain. All we could do was to give her morphine, with no limit. Within 24 hours came death, the deliverer. We were getting 60 or 70 of this kind of patient daily. . . . The operating room was busy non stop. Instruments were sterilized constantly. and on the table were long lines of victims. . . . In the air was a strong smell of fresh blood. Carts with new victims replaced those already operated on. Sweat ran down our faces and underwear stuck to the hot, wet torsos of operating surgeons. . . . The action was still in progress. A person turns into a robot. Cuts, sews, and—most important—tries not to think about it all.[95]

On 6 September, Czyste Hospital was ordered to return to its Stawki Street site, bringing together all remaining patients and staff from all locations in the ghetto. This action coincided with the beginning of the Cauldron. At this time, the first life tickets were issued. Henry Fenigstein received tickets for himself and his wife, the first of several times they were saved.[96] But many failed to get the lifesaving forms; some physicians had brought their aged parents to the hospital, hoping to find a way to save them, sometimes registering them as patients.[97] When it was obvious that most could not be saved, a wave of euthanasia occurred, tearful physicians giving lethal injections of morphine to mothers and fathers.[98] Others gave cyanide dissolved in water to desperately sick children, discarding ethical precepts so that the young ones would have a quiet and quick death, saved from the freight cars. Cyanide had become "the most precious, irreplaceable treasure."[99]

The psychological impact of these events was profound. Few are ever exposed to such pressures, and inevitably some coped better than others. Eugenia Pernal's father couldn't bring himself to flee. Although he had spent time in Siberia for political activities 20 years before, and had escaped from there, he wouldn't even contemplate trying to get illegal papers.[100] He died at Treblinka. Halina Berg's father was crushed by the impact of events. He had been a well-built man, a big man, but now to his daughter he appeared small and bent and afraid. A day or two after she noticed this, he was seized and sent to Treblinka.[101]

The general reaction probably paralleled Fenigstein's. He blocked fear. He was numb, simply doing whatever he had to do. He cared for others, but he didn't cry when they died.[102] Lewin went through the agonies of losing a beloved wife. He was distraught at what had happened but equally distressed at his own reaction: "I have no words to describe my desolation. I ought to go after her, to die. But I have no strength to take such a step."[103] He continued to deplore his own weakness often in the ensuing days. The gnawing torments of guilt at their own survival still trouble many Jews, though some have found peace from these thoughts. Stiffel, in his memoirs, speaks of the fact that his father went to the *Umschlagplatz* and to his death:

> Long after that day, I told myself that had I known my Father was going to his death, I would have joined him. Today, I am no longer ashamed to admit the obvious truth: I knew where he was going. I must have known by intuition that we were drowning in a sea of death, and I wanted to steer away from it, toward some shore of salvation.[104]

Meanwhile, those not deported had to go on as best they could. The *Judenrat* had a new chairman, Marc Lichtenbaum, replacing Czerniakow. The *Judenrat* previously had been located at Grzybowska 26 in the Small Ghetto.[105] After this portion of the ghetto was eliminated, the offices were moved to Zamenhof 19, a former military prison.[106]

The *Aktion* ended more or less officially on 21 September—the Day of Atonement—its last act being a major blow to the *Ordnungsdienst*, which despite promises of immunity was decimated by deportations. After this date activities continued at the *Umschlagplatz*, though in a more desultory way. Small parties of Jews continued to be sent to Treblinka or other camps until November. Then, on 22 November, the *Umschlagplatz* was closed. All still held there were released, as well as all Jews held in Warsaw prisons—Motokowska, Pawiak, Gęsiówka.[107] As if to suggest that everything was back to "normal," the Germans permitted the Jews to set up both a primary and a secondary school, though by this time there were few children left in the ghetto.[108]

For the months intervening until the events of 18–21 January 1943, the ghetto sank into its new shape and role. Essentially, the Warsaw ghetto had become nothing more than a massive labor camp. There were four separate and separated sections: (1) a central ghetto, containing the *Judenrat*, the remnants of the *Ordnungsdienst*, some small manufacturing shops, and the *Werterfassung*, an office charged with collecting abandoned Jewish possessions for the Nazis (this area contained about 35,000 Jews, both legal and illegal); (2) an area containing several large shops: Többens, on Leszno Street; K. G. Schultz, also on Leszno; Fritz Schultz, on Nowolipie; and some smaller ones (ca. 20,000 Jews); (3) the "Brushmakers' Shop," bound by Swietojerska, Bonifraterska, Wolowa, and Franciszkańska streets (ca 4000 Jews); and (4) the so-called Little Többens in the former Small Ghetto (ca. 2000 Jews).[109] All movement among these shops was strictly forbidden to the Jews, and many were shot on sight if seen outside the four circumscribed areas. Deaths in the ghetto in November 1942 totaled 414, of whom 124 were shot by the Nazis; only 3 were suicides, the remaining 287 dying natural deaths.[110]

Walls were being built around the shop areas, so that each workplace became a small separate prison. Many Jews—Lewin says most, but that must be an exaggeration—worked for the *Werterfassung*, collecting and delivering furniture, clothing, and other belongings of their former friends and neighbors, so that these items could be sold to Poles or shipped to Germany.[111]

The *Judenrat* continued to exist, though its hold over the Jews and its effectiveness were permanently eroded. Members of the *Judenrat* continued to have some personal security from deportation, as did their families. However, the latter were protected only when they were physically with the father or husband. Consequently, the *Judenrat* offices were overcrowded in their new location at Zamenhof 19.[112] Officials sat working at their desks, wives and children seated around them in fearful closeness.[113]

In addition to the 35,000 Jews remaining who had life tickets, there were perhaps 20,000 in hiding. These people were in a desperate situation. Because they lacked life tickets, they were shot by the Nazis whenever they were discovered. If a group was uncovered, it might be sent to Treblinka. These illegals were starving because, being illegal, they had no ration cards.[114]

The Germans used psychology to attack this group. They spread the word that they had established an *ehrlich*, or honesty block. Any illegal who reported there would receive amnesty, and would be fed, clothed, and put to work. Their isolation drove many Jews to risk themselves by choosing this route. They were fed and clothed for a few weeks, until the experiment failed to bring in any more Jews to surrender. They were all then killed.[115] The block was located in the area surrounded by Karmelicka, Nowolipki, Zamenhof, and Dzielna streets.

The Deportations of January 1943

The dreaded and inevitable next *Aktion* by the Nazis began on 19 January 1943. Few of the Jews remaining in the ghetto had any illusions; they knew that further deportations would take place. The ghetto, which actually was now a series of small, unconnected ghettos occupying only a fraction of the space of the original enclosure, had been relatively quiet since September. But random shootings continued, particularly of Jews found in the forbidden areas outside the small ghettos. The Jews, nevertheless, continued to attempt to find a way of living and coping. But the January raids essentially spelled the beginning of the end.

This short episode also gave the Jews their first experience at fighting the Germans militarily. Since the summer deportations, which had wrenched the bulk of the Jews to a ghastly death, the attitude toward open warfare had changed. The situation was vastly different. Before 22 July 1942, one of the chief arguments against fighting was the fact that this would place aged parents and young children at great risk of retaliation by the Nazis. But these groups, the old and the young, were now dead. Moreover, the deportations to Treblinka had included among their victims many of the community's political leaders, the older ones who had been opposed to open warfare. The previous preoccupation with the struggle to find food, shelter, and clothing[116] was washing away under the realization that they were certainly going to die and that they should not submit supinely; it was no longer possible to harbor real illusions about the ultimate fate of Poland's Jews.

There is no space here for detailed descriptions of the fighting organizations or the political battles that underlay their existence and activities. The two groups most prominently involved were the Jewish Fighting Organization, known by the acronym ŻOB (*Żydowska Organizacja Bojowa*),[117] of which Dr. Marek Edelman was a leader and one of the few survivors, and the Betarist group, the *Irgun Zvai Leumi*, or Jewish Military Organization, ŻZW (*Żydowski Zwiazek Wojskowy*), one of whose leaders was Dr. David Wdowinski.[118] Within these major subdivisions, the actual fighting units, the "battle groups," 22 in number, represented nine different political parties.[119]

They received some help from the Polish underground and, indirectly, from the Polish government in exile in London. Mostly they were on their own, however, forced to pursue a dangerous course of purchasing weapons of questionable effectiveness at enormous prices outside the ghetto and then smuggling them in. Money was scarce, and they instituted a system of taxation among their fellow Jews, many of whom gave voluntarily. Others, according to Wdowinski, were assessed at gunpoint, chiefly the immensely rich black marketeers.[120]

The remaining staff of what had been Czyste Hospital had regrouped in a building on Gęsia Street, bringing together those physicians and nurses who had been spared during the long summer *Aktion*. Like most of the others Jews, they worked to construct underground bunkers with hidden entrances under the buildings and the streets. Some of these bunkers were simple, others very elaborate and well equipped.

As soon as the German intention to conduct yet another *Aktion* was certain, as many people as possible went underground in the hope of saving themselves. In the case of the hospital, many doctors and nurses went into the Gęsia Street bunkers, as well as some ambulatory patients. Still hopeful of German decency to the bedridden, they left them with the on-duty staff; they had little choice. Unfortunately, their hopes were ill-founded. The Nazis killed many patients in their beds. Some patients, a few babies, nurses, and about 150 physicians were marched to the *Umschlagplatz*, herded into freight cars, and shipped to Treblinka.[121] Some of the physicians were prepared for this eventuality and there were many suicides in the cattle cars, often brought about by the kindly injection of an overdose of morphine.[122]

Morphine was used in the bunkers too. Life was very difficult there. Those hiding had to remain quiet, sometimes for days, and one nurse has vivid memories of injecting children with minimal doses of morphine to keep them from crying while the German soldiers were searching for them.[123] In one bunker, a mother smothered her crying baby to save the group from discovery.[124] In Wdowinski's bunker they hid successfully for three days, using opium to stop bowel action, codeine to suppress coughing, and caffeine to keep alert.[125]

Marek Balin was in a bunker at Miła 4, down the street from the bunker made famous by its defenders and by Leon Uris's novel, *Miła 18*.[126] He had moved there with his brother, sister, and mother, and remained at Miła 4, and intermittently in the bunker, almost until the final deportations of April–May 1943.[127]

To the everlasting credit of those medical professionals who survived this further disaster in January 1943, once the Germans had withdrawn and left them in relative peace, some of them decided that they must open Czyste yet again. There were still a few patients who needed medical help.[128] But for many, reviewing the events of the past months, it was obvious that the time to attempt to escape had come.

Opportunities came less and less frequently. Sabina Gurfinkiel-Glocerowa, a nurse who had been most devoted to her patients, had a young daughter named Lilka. In February 1943 Sabina made the difficult choice; she would leave her patients—fewer and fewer in number—and try to save her daughter. She overcame the anguish of leaving her colleagues and friends,[129] and on 14 February they set out.[130] An SS soldier stole her coffee and soap, and all of her syringes except one; these were all goods she had hoarded carefully, hoping to be able to sell or trade them in Warsaw.[131] As has been mentioned, the fortuitous intervention of an ex-patient saved her at the ghetto gate, and she and her daughter left. Soon they had to separate because of problems with living arrangements,[132] and although they met briefly once more,[133] Sabina Gurfinkiel-Glocerowa failed in her ultimate purpose. Though she survived, Lilka did not.

The Final Deportations and the Uprising of April–May 1943

> . . . to die in a gas chamber is by no means worse than to die in battle . . . the only undignified death is when one attempts to survive at the expense of somebody else.[134]

When the Nazis returned to complete the job they had begun in January 1943, they returned in force. *SS-und Polizeiführer* (General) Juergen Stroop directed a full-scale military operation against the Jews.[135] They brought a substantial force of troops[136] to deal with perhaps 750 Jewish men and women in the organized but poorly trained and inadequately armed fighting organizations—about 500 in the ŻOB, 250 in the ŻZW.[137] This force had a single field hospital. It included a doctor, nurses, and the equipment and medications appropriate to a military dressing station. One survivor noted proudly that there were even facilities for heating water.[138]

Several of the survivors remained in the ghetto until this last act in the massive tragedy: Millie Eisen, Henry Fenigstein, Tadeusz Stabholz, and Marek Balin. Their adventures were quite different.

Millie Eisen had continued to nurse as long as there was nursing to be done. But she had a "good face" and spoke Polish well. She had the good fortune and good timing to escape from the ghetto on 16 April 1943, three days before the massive German attacks began that convulsed the ghetto area for the next three weeks. She was helped by Dr. Josef Stein, the director of Czyste. Picking her way through cellars and attics until she reached the Jewish cemetery, she was then smuggled over the wall.[139]

For Henry Fenigstein and his wife Ala, there seemed a possibility of salvation. They had already been spared in September, during the Cauldron, when he received a life ticket because of his work in the pathology department (and, one can guess, because of the important role both Fenigsteins were playing in preparing the data on the hunger disease research). In the January deportations they had been in hiding and had the good luck to remain undetected.[140]

Over the previous months, Henry had made the acquaintance of a German of high rank through a mutual interest in stamp collecting.[141] This man had promised to assure that they would be sent to a work camp rather than an extermination camp. On the basis of this assurance, they went voluntarily though nervously to the *Umschlagplatz* in April, 1943.[142] Fenigstein, a physician, had a supply of powdered barbiturate with him so that they could take their own lives, should it become apparent that the German's promise had not been honored and they were headed toward Treblinka.[143] They were forced into a cattle car, but blessedly, as it must have seemed, went in a different direction.[144] They ended up in Lublin, where Henry and Ala were separated; she died in Majdanek, shot by the Nazis on 3 November 1943.

Tadeusz Stabholz fought against the Germans briefly in April 1943, and had the satisfaction of throwing three grenades and blowing up a car.[145] Later, he was betrayed in a bunker by a traitor, and was taken to the *Umschlagplatz*.[146] After two days there, he was shipped to Auschwitz on 6 May 1943.[147] His experiences there he has described in his book, *Seven Hells*.[148]

Marek Balin became separated from his family at Miła 4 when the uprising began and had to take shelter with friends living on Nowolipie Street. Finally, when the house began to burn down over their heads, they were forced to surrender. He was put up against a wall, then somehow was *not* shot; he wonders if the Nazis did not want to have too many bodies in the ghetto area because of the danger of epidemics.[149] Taken to the *Umschlagplatz*, he was crammed into a cattle car for several hours, a car so full that people were dying of suffocation. The train finally left for Treblinka. Once its destination was certain, Balin found an opening and escaped from the train. He was shot in the back by a guard before the train disappeared.[150] His subsequent adventures have already been mentioned briefly.

Figure 11.6. Razed Warsaw ghetto, probably 1944; X marks the ruins of Evangelic Hospital, Karmelicka Street (courtesy of Dr. Marek Balin).

Despite the chaos of these final weeks in the Warsaw ghetto, some attempts at normality were noted. Borzykowski visited the home of a rabbi on the first day of Passover. The home had been severely damaged, but the rabbi and his family were celebrating the *seder*. "Amidst this destruction, the table in the center of the room looked incongruous with glasses filled with wine, with the family seated around, the rabbi reading the Haggadah. His text was punctuated by explosions and the rattling of machine-guns; the faces of the family around the table were lit by the red light from the burning buildings nearby."[151]

When the fighting ended about 10 May 1943, the Germans had captured 56,065 Jews. Of these they killed about 7000 on the spot and sent the rest to the concentration camps or to Treblinka. About 6000 Jews were killed in the fighting.[152] Six months later, the Jewish National Committee reported that there had been massacres in the camps in the Lublin District (at which time Ala Fenigstein was killed). This spelled essentially the end of Warsaw's Jewry, for most of the survivors of the ghetto had been sent to these camps.[153]

After the courageous but doomed Jewish uprising ended, the Nazis began a systematic destruction of what remained of the ghetto, a process already far advanced by their policy of eliminating Jewish fighting men and women by burning down building after building. Ultimately, almost every structure in the previous ghetto vanished in huge piles of rubble, including the Great Synagogue on Tømackie Place (see Figures 11.6 and 11.7).

There was, however, a concentration camp in Warsaw in 1944, at a location on Gęsia Street in what had once been the ghetto.[154] So it continued to be a place for incarceration and death.

Figure 11.7. The Warsaw ghetto, razed, probably 1944 (courtesy of Dr. Marek Balin).

12

Statistics of Morbidity and Mortality in the Warsaw Ghetto

Throughout this book, reference has been made to the impact of various diseases and disorders on the inhabitants of the Warsaw ghetto. Often these statements have been bolstered by numerical data. These data have been cited from a wide variety of sources, many of them more or less contemporary to the events described. The purpose of this chapter is to examine the available data and their sources to try to conclude how reliable they are and to identify some spectrum of reliability if that is possible.

Two important caveats must be borne in mind when examining this material. The first is that essentially all data on morbidity and mortality from the ghetto come from the inhabitants of the ghetto—from the Jews. The second is that most postwar computations derive from only one or two data sources.

Germans have a reputation for precision and reliability with regard to numerical data. Whether or not there is any general truth in this stereotype, it is irrelevant when considering disease figures about the Warsaw ghetto. The figures are Jewish, not German. I do not mean to suggest that therefore the data are less reliable—not at all—simply that no Nazi statistical team collected data in the ghetto. The *Judenrat* collected data and supplied it, in regular reports and for special ad hoc purposes, as required by the Nazis.

The statistics are unreliable for several reasons, none of them connected with any intrinsic inability to deal with data scientifically in ordinary circumstances. The most important is relevant particularly to data for typhus. As has been emphasized in Chapter 7, much typhus was hidden, not only from the Germans but, more directly, from fellow Jews. The reasons need not be restated. Figures given for typhus in Czyste Hospital may well be accurate for that institution but cannot be seen as anything more than a rough guide to overall figures. People sickened, suffered, and often died at home and in the streets. No data are available for these cases except the roughest of estimates.

There are, of course, medical and social reasons why even the hospital statistics may be incorrect: Inadequate time to make an exact diagnosis because patients often died at or immediately after admission is one of them. But such reasons are unlikely to have a major impact. There also exists the possibility that figures were falsified. It was in the self-interest of the Jews, often in terms literally of survival, not to let the Nazis know precisely how many were ill or had died.

Second, the original sources of statistics are few in number. Chief among these is the "Oneg Shabbat" material, the Ringelblum Archive. More than half of this information was retrieved from its hiding place after the war. Among the archives were detailed *Judenrat* reports on many subjects, some of which contained statistics. These were the data that the Germans used in their own compilations. The flow of information is made explicit by Czerniakow in diary entries such as the following for 10 May 1941: "I delivered to Mende and Kra[a]tz a graphic compilation of the mortality rate among the Jews" for 1939, 1940, and the first few months of 1941.[1] The extant "Oneg Shabbat" archive is available to scholars at the Yad Vashem institution in Jerusalem. Some substantial portions have been translated into English, particularly in the volume *To Live with Honor and Die with Honor*, published by Yad Vashem in 1986.[2]

The other chief source for medical statistics is the hunger disease research conducted in the ghetto. This has appeared in French, Polish, and English.[3] Again, the extant material is only a portion of what was planned; the deportations of the summer of 1942 not only stopped the research but also prevented the completion of several of the chapters because their authors were killed at Treblinka.

Equally useful are the materials now located in archives such as that of the American Jewish Joint Distribution Committee in New York.[4] Invaluable detail came out of Warsaw in the form of documents about various Joint-sponsored and -supported activities. In particular, the reports on TOZ and CENTOS provide illuminating specifics on day-to-day activities inside the ghetto.

In addition to these three major repositories of statistical information, a few of the contemporary diaries should be mentioned. These rarely give detailed statistics but are invaluable for dating events, as well as for providing information about the names of persons involved in various activities, addresses, and some idea of emotions and morale. Chief among these sources are diaries kept by Czerniakow,[5] Ringelblum,[6] Lewin,[7] and Korczak.[8]

Memoirs compiled immediately after the war also have great value. The description of Czyste Hospital by Fenigstein was written soon after the war and gives us much detail not otherwise available from a physician who was there throughout the ghetto period.[9] Depositions made immediately after the war have been invaluable sources documenting other parts of this book but seldom contribute much of a statistical nature.

After these various materials, most accounts depend on one or more of the basic sources already cited. For example, the article by Lenski, who was himself a physician in the ghetto, refers frequently to Oneg Shabbat material.[10] It is nevertheless invested heavily with the personal observations of the author; these are invaluable but not statistical. The same is true of the other important article published by an author who cites the Ringelblum archive and the numbers collected by Jewish physicians who were in the ghetto: Isaiah Trunk.[11] But he warns readers that the numbers are flawed, though "fair approximations."[12] Wilhelm Hagen, the author of a paper giving the viewpoint of a member of the German medical staff in Warsaw,[13] cites what he terms superior data from his own office in 1941–43. But he ignores the fact that in referring to the ghetto, he also was dependent on Jewish data.

A final generalization needs to be made. As will be quickly apparent, the numerical data are incomplete. In some cases they are contradictory, and in a few instances obviously wrong. No criticism of the collectors and recorders of these statistics is intended. We are fortunate to have what does exist, collected under extremes of stress and danger that we can scarcely imagine. Nevertheless, in places the data are flawed, and these flaws prevent us from ever having absolutely reliable answers to the many questions that arise.

What do the data reveal?

TYPHUS

Despite the appalling conditions in the ghetto, the mortality from typhus seems to have been surprisingly low, although the morbidity was very high. One physician has estimated mortality as about 15 percent.[14] Reliable figures are impossible to obtain because so much disease was hidden. Thus almost all numerical data about typhus depend on extrapolations and estimates.

The more or less official statistics, recorded in the course of medical investigations carried out on starvation in the ghetto by Jewish physicians, have survived, and they are instructive though incomplete.[15] According to these data, 20,399 cases of typhus were reported between September 1939 and November 1942, when data collection ceased. Total deaths in this period were 98,165, of which 2724 were due to typhus, 18,320 to hunger, and 24,435 to undetermined causes. Thus the physicians in the ghetto could conclusively identify typhus as the cause of death in only 2.8 percent of total deaths, and they believed that the death rate from typhus among those reported to have the disease was 13.4 percent. There are enormous discrepancies between the gross number of dead and the three categories of deaths mentioned. For this fact there is no scientific explanation; one can only assume an inability to maintain statistics or to correct errors for obvious reasons.

Other writers have attempted to estimate the total number of cases of typhus and the total number of deaths. Hagen cites the following number of deaths (from all causes) for the first half of 1941: January 898, February 1023, March 1608, April 2068, May 3821, and June 4096.[16] But these gross figures are of little help, particularly given Hagen's estimate that only two-thirds of all deaths are reported.[17] He also states that on 4 July 1941 there were 578 cases of typhus in Czyste Hospital, with 50 new cases being added every day. He assumes that there must have been 3000 cases in the ghetto on that 4th of July, indicating his belief that only about 20 percent of patients reported to the hospital.[18] Again, this is Hagen's guess.

Czerniakow reported a somewhat different approach to indicating what impact typhus was having on mortality in the ghetto. The comparison was between data on the number of funerals recorded vis-à-vis the number of new cases of typhus reported. Table 12.1 summarizes the numbers:

Table 12.1. Funerals and Typhus Cases, Warsaw Ghetto[19]

Month	Funerals			Typhus (New Cases)	
	1938	1940	1941	1940	1941
October	379	457	4716	16	3438
November	413	445	4801	23	2156
December	437	581	NA	17	NA

The table documents a direct and unremarkable parallel between the incidence of new cases of typhus and the number of funerals. These figures do not *prove* that large numbers of Jews were dying of typhus, but they certainly corroborate other data to that effect.

Trunk presents the most specific and directly applicable statistics. In Table 12.2 he shows the relative prevalence of typhus in the ghetto and in Aryan Warsaw for the time of the second epidemic. Table 12.2 shows that the epidemic outside the ghetto became increasingly serious, but it was not nearly as severe as that occurring inside the ghetto. Nor are we given any information about the reliability of the numbers with respect to typhus outside the ghetto.

Trunk also published monthly figures on reported cases (Table 12.3). As can be seen, 1941 was the disastrous year, with 15,449 registered cases vs. 1758 in 1940. Trunk further reported that the mortality rate among this group was 167 out of 1266 patients admitted between February and June 1940 (13 percent); for 1941, mortality was 11.3 percent, and for 1942, 16.3 percent.[22] Lenski agreed with these mortality rates, citing an overall figure of about 15 percent in all age groups; the worst complication, he found, was encephalitis, which was almost invariably fatal.[23]

Hagen's final contribution to the statistics of typhus in the Warsaw ghetto was the statement that one approach had been to delouse an entire section of the ghetto in one day; this was carried out and 60 unreported cases of typhus were found in the course of this action, but since he does not indicate how large a whole section was, we do not gain much insight.[24] Presumably his reference is to the Krochmalna Street incident (see Chapter 7). Some of Hagen's data are subject to reinterpretation. Two graphs in his article on war and pestilence show the incidence of sickness from typhus among Jews and among non-Jewish Poles. The graphs do indeed show enormously higher morbidity for Jews in 1940–43. But the graphs also contain figures for 1916–21, and these reveal that there was essentially the same morbidity for Jews and for Poles in these years, when there was no ghetto and when conditions were thus more or less equal. Hagen does not seem to have noticed this aspect of his own data.[25]

Lenski discusses the unreliability of statistics from the ghetto. He cites one writer who estimated the number of cases of typhus at 150,000; Lenski, however, believes this is much too high. He states his own estimate as 100,000, basing this on the observation that the larger number was predicated on every family's having at

Table 12.2. Typhus in the Ghetto and in Aryan Warsaw[20]

Date	Cases in the Ghetto	Cases on the Aryan Side	Ratio of Aryan to Ghetto Cases	Ratio of Aryan Population to Jews
1940	1758	189	9.7	70
1941 Jan	57	5	8.6	70
Feb	134	78	36.8	70
Aug	1805	434	24.0	67
Sept	2492	450	18.0	67

Table No. 12.3. Reported Cases of Typhus Among the Jews of Warsaw[21]

Year	Month											
	Jan	Feb	Mar	Apr	May	Jun	Jul	Aug	Sep	Oct	Nov	Dec
1939												88
1940	191	214	398	407	335	123	68	18	—	—	—	—
1941	57	129	201	241	367	841	1742	1805	2492	3438	2156	1980
1942	1220	787	478	319	208	67						

least one case, but Lenski knew families that in fact had no cases.[26] On such slender grounds are some of these estimates based. Lenski cites an article from 1954 by Penson, head of the typhus ward at Czyste Hospital, also giving the number 100,000.[27] Finally, he states that mortality was 15 percent.[28]

TUBERCULOSIS

The discussion of tuberculosis data was so intimately involved in the general discussion of the disease that the detailed comments remain in Chapter 8. The revised mortality table used in the next section is based upon conjectures with regard to tuberculosis mortality. See Table 12.7, "Amended Causes of Death."

GENERAL MORTALITY

Before examining the few attempts to compile overall figures for mortality in the ghetto, it may be useful to point out the kinds of fragmentary information that exist, from which one can infer certain conclusions about death among the Jews. These inferences do not all give us the same degree of confidence in their accuracy.

Some observations are comparative and vague. Arad, for example, states that the death rate in Vilna rose from a prewar figure of 1.9 percent to 2.9 percent and adds that the change was far worse in Warsaw.[29] That is not helpful. According to Ringelblum, in January 1940, just five months after the war began, deaths among the Jews in Warsaw were averaging 50 to 70 a day compared with 10 a day before the war.[30] By April 1941 the death rate was said to be seven times higher than in November 1940 (though we don't know the rate then). Ringelblum goes on to point out that Jewish mortality in Warsaw had always been artificially high because so many sick Jews from all over Poland came to Czyste Hospital to be treated and, often, to die there.[31] He also identifies the ghetto hospitals as "places of execution" and says that the death rate was about 8 percent.[32] On Thursday, 8 May 1941, 210 Jews died, a record to that date,[33] though of course, the Nazis later found a way to break that record many times.

Lewin cites an estimate by Hurwicz, the *Judenrat* member responsible for the cemetery, that 12,000 Jews had been murdered by the Nazis and buried at the cemetery in a period of 23 months.[34] By comparison, another source says that between the end of the fighting in Poland in 1939 and July 1943, 35,000 to 40,000 non-

Jewish Varsovians were killed in or near Warsaw by the Germans.[35] This vague figure, with an admitted margin of error of at least 5000, suggests that data collection
was not easy outside the ghetto either. The chief reason for inaccuracy is that such
deaths often were executions, sometimes mass executions, carried out secretly by
the Nazis. The victims usually were buried unceremoniously in common graves,
uncounted and often unknown.

Street deaths in the ghetto numbered 846 for all of 1941,[36] and in March 1942,
290 bodies were found in the street.[37] Shoskes claims that there was a mortality rate
in the first six months of 1939 of 10/1000, which rose to 86/1000 in the first six
months of 1941.[38] Gutman's figures differ somewhat from these. He states that in
August 1939, 360 Jews died out of a population of 360,000, or 1/1000/month. But
for August 1941, out of a population of about 450,000 Jews, 5560 died, giving a
ratio of 81/1000.[39] Some authors contradict themselves, such as Trunk, who claims
in 1953 that 88,568 Jews died in Warsaw between September 1939 and August
1942,[40] whereas in 1972 he lists a mortality figure for the same period of 84,896.[41]
There is no explanation for what happened to the missing 3672 Jews. But using a
mortality index of 10.7, he concludes that at the 1939 rate, only 12,600 Jews should
have died in the three-year period. Thus the excess mortality blameable on hunger,
disease, and execution would be either 76,000 (88,568 − 12,600) or 72,296 (84,896
− 12,600). Lenski rounds off these numbers, stating that 80,000 died of disease and
other causes, 18,000 of these from starvation.[42]

Some figures cannot be reconciled, lacking knowledge of how the numbers were
constructed. Trunk cites a mortality rate in the ghetto for July 1941 of 153.8/
10,000. With a population of about 450,000, that means that 6985 Jews would have
died in the ghetto that month.[43] But *Unser Tsait* published figures stating that 5600
Jews died in July 1941.[44]

Trunk, who has compiled much of the statistical data that we have to use, prepared two tables of general mortality, one for several selected months between 1939
and 1942 (Table 12.4), the other a cumulative mortality table (Table 12.5).

Most confusing and least helpful are the extant data on causes of death. Table
12.6 was prepared by the hunger disease researchers.[47] What is important is how
little the table tells us. Only two diseases or disorders are listed as categories, typhus
and hunger/exhaustion. Adding these two figures gives a total of 21,044. The heading "Undetermined" tells us nothing. Indeed, it is misleading. Only 21,044 deaths
are due to "determined" causes, and all the rest are actually undetermined: 98,165
− 21,044 = 77,121. That is to say, when we attempt to discover the various causes
for the deaths of Jews in the ghetto, in numbers, the best that can be said is that
2724 (2.8 percent) died of typhus, 18,320 (18.7 percent) died of hunger and exhaustion, and 77,121 (78.6 percent) died of something else. The numbers may be accurate—they are the best we have—but they are not very useful.

If we add some totally speculative data about tuberculosis, the amended table
can be presented as in Table 12.7. If the tuberculosis data are reasonably correct,
we see that there remains a very large mass of deaths from "undetermined" causes:
38,149, or 45 percent. Barring the discovery of additional original documentation
from the ghetto years, the numbers cannot be refined further. We must accept the
vagueness that exists as, presumably, a permanent feature of the story of health and
disease in the Warsaw ghetto.

Table 12.4. Mortality Among Warsaw Jewry: Selected Months[45]

Year	Month	Population	No. of Deaths	Deaths/1000 Pop.
1939	August	380,500	360	0.9
1939	October	360,000	1850	5.1
1940	December	392,900	581	1.5
1941	December	416,700	4366	10.7
1942	April	400,000	4432	11.1

Table 12.5. Aggregate Mortality, Warsaw Jewry, 1939–42[46]

Year	Period	No. of Deaths	Average/Month	Increase Over 1940
1939	Sep–Dec	6,560	1,312	175.4
1940	Jan–Dec	8,981	748	100
1941	Jan–Dec	43,239	3,603	494.9
1942	Jan–Aug	29,788	4,255	571.2

Table 12.6. Causes of Death in the Warsaw Ghetto

Year Months	Typhus	(%)	Hunger & Exhaustion	(%)	Undetermined	(%)	Total
1939 Sep–Dec	5	(.07)	4	(.06)	2,056	(31.3)	6,560
1940 12	216	(2.3)	91	(1.01)	1,032	(11.5)	8,981
1941 12	1,991	(4.6)	10,971	(25.3)	10,635	(24.6)	43,239
1942 incomplete	512	(1.3)	7,254	(18.4)	10,694	(27.2)	39,385
Total	2,724		18,320		24,435		98,165

Table 12.7. Amended Causes of Death in the Warsaw Ghetto

Year Months	Typhus	(%)	Hunger & Exhaustion	(%)	TB	(%)	Undetermined	(%)	Total
1939 Sep–Dec	5	(.07)	4	(.06)	544	(8.3)	2,056	(31.3)	6,560
1940 12	216	(2.3)	91	(1.01)	1,786	(21.0)	1,032	(11.5)	8,981
1941 12	1,991	(4.6)	10,971	(25.3)	14,572	(33.7)	10,653	(24.6)	43,239
1942 Jan–Jly	512	(1.3)	7,254	(18.4)	13,273	(33.7)	10,694	(27.2)	39,385
							22,511*		
Total	2,724	2.8	18,320	18.7	30,175	30.7	46,946	47.8	98,165

*Number unaccounted for when subtracting all subtotals from the overall total of 98,165; these are obviously also "undetermined."

13

Conclusions

When the Warsaw ghetto vanished, the Jews of Poland had been under Nazi domination for 44 months. The ghetto itself ceased to exist in May 1943. It had been a living—and dying—entity for exactly 30 months. This book has attempted to show how the Jews tried to live, and succeeded in dying, during this time. The account being done, what can be concluded?

Perhaps most broadly, the great cliché of humanity is displayed yet again: We are tough and resilient and enormously adaptable under pressure. Not all of us, but enough so that it matters. Thus large numbers of Jews did survive many months of hunger, exposure, and disease. The fact they they could not withstand the ultimate murder process at Treblinka and similar camps does not alter the remarkable fact of their having survived until that point.

Conversely, we can see clearly how intimidation, coercion, and hunger can unite to suborn a population, or at least a substantial part of a population.

Fortunately, despite the appalling ferocity of the Nazi occupiers and the final destruction of millions of Jews, there is a positive side. Encouragingly often, the human spirit, the humane instinct, revealed itself as still existent. The Warsaw ghetto story is replete with instances, large and small, of self-sacrifice and of dedication to others in the face of bleakness and terror.

A good example of this ability to achieve despite adversity is the clandestine medical school. This school was a vigorously functioning enterprise for 15 months. The courses were well organized, popular, and highly respected in the ghetto. Nevertheless, in retrospect, it is easy to see how futile was the attempt to operate a medical school in the Warsaw ghetto. But the enterprise was no empty gesture. It was never that. Until the summer of 1942, perhaps the majority of the inhabitants of the ghetto believed that many of them would survive the war, though it was all too obvious that many would not. They had no precedent for believing otherwise; despite the centuries of anti-Jewish sentiment in Central Europe, its most violent expression was in pogroms, which, however frequent and grim, were isolated and sometimes spontaneous events that never rivaled the Holocaust in aims or results. Thus, even as conditions worsened rapidly for the Jews of Warsaw, they assumed that this large-scale "pogrom" would, like the others, end, and life would return more or less to normal.

There is nothing particularly Jewish in this optimistic attitude or in its continuation in the face of contrary evidence of the most dramatic kind. Soldiers in battle rely on the "foxhole syndrome," in which no matter how hard the fighting and how serious the casualties, each soldier is convinced that he will survive in his foxhole, though he recognizes all too clearly that his compatriots nearby may not. Similar instances abound in civil life and could be said to identify a basic psychological defense of humankind.

The medical school—and the innovative hunger research studies—are among the few genuinely positive achievements to be associated with the Warsaw ghetto. In addition to their general contribution to morale within the ghetto, and to our appreciation of the school and the research studies as victories of the human spirit, they achieved concrete goals.

For the medical school, a number of men and women who began their education there finished it after the war and practiced medicine for many decades. But without belittling this accomplishment in any way, one might respond that these Jews would have become doctors even if there had been no invasion of Poland, so the contribution of their practice is more apparent than real.

In the case of the hunger disease research, the case is otherwise. By taking advantage of the unparalleled opportunity of having so much hunger all about them, the medical researchers created a body of knowledge that was unique. These men and women would not have carried out this particular research had there been no ghetto. Although perhaps half of the work done has vanished into the gas chambers, what remains has been a significant contribution to our knowledge of the human body and the way it behaves in conditions of extreme hunger and starvation. This is a lasting achievement most aptly epitomized by Izrael Milejkowski's quotation from Horace: *Non omnis moriar*—"I shall not die completely."

The rest of the medical history of the ghetto is on a more mundane level. Although flawed, the attempt of the *Judenrat* and the numerous other organizations to respond to extremes of hunger, filth, and disease was heroic. The flaws were not of their own making, except for some cases where efficiency was sacrificed to pique or to vain dreams of personal power. The result of these efforts was largely predetermined by the Nazis through their failure to supply the necessary food, medicines, coal, and other supplies. But the vast majority of the Germans were, at best, indifferent to the fate of the Jews.

That fate was determined, prior to the 1942 deportations, largely by starvation and its attendant diseases. Of these, typhus was an awesome problem. So, it has been suggested, was tuberculosis.

All these disorders were part of the daily life of the Warsaw ghetto. The vast majority of ghetto inhabitants never entered the *Transferstelle*, knew of The Thirteen only by reputation, and had direct contact with the *Judenrat* only occasionally, aside from frequent dealings with members of the *Ordnungsdienst*. But they knew every nuance of hunger in its soul- and body-destroying, ceaseless gnawing. They watched relatives eaten alive by tuberculosis. They knew firsthand the panicky feeling when typhus was rumored to exist in the next block.

This was life in the Warsaw ghetto. For almost one quarter of the Jews there, it was also death. The only consolation to those left behind was that the dead were spared Treblinka.

Notes

Introduction

1. CENTOS is the acronym for *Centrala Opieki nad Sierotami*, the National (Jewish) Society for the Care of Orphans.

2. Adolf Berman, "The Fate of the Children in the Warsaw Ghetto," in Yisrael Gutman and Livia Rothkirchen (eds.), *The Catastrophe of European Jewry: Antecedents, History, Reflections* (Jerusalem: Yad Vashem, 1976), pp. 400–21; p. 400.

3. Suicide among German Jews has been analyzed by Konrad Kwiet in "The Ultimate Refuge: Suicide in the Jewish Community Under the Nazis," *Leo Baeck Institute Year Book*, Vol. 29: 1984, pp. 135–67.

4. Yisrael Gutman, *The Jews of Warsaw, 1939–1943: Ghetto, Underground, Revolt* trans. Ina Friedman (Bloomington and Indianapolis: Indiana University Press, 1989), pp. xxi + 487; p. xvii.

5. Gutman, *Jews of Warsaw*, p. 120.

6. Gutman, *Jews of Warsaw*, p. 167.

7. Isaiah Trunk, *Judenrat: The Jewish Councils in Eastern Europe Under Nazi Occupation* (New York: The Macmillan Co., 1972), pp. xxxv + 664, illust.

8. Gutman, *Jews of Warsaw*, p. 178.

9. Gutman, *Jews of Warsaw*, p. 479.

10. Betty Jean Lifton, *The King of Children: A Biography of Janusz Korczak* (New York: Farrar, Straus and Giroux, 1988), p. 404; see p. 180 regarding Korczak educating his Jewish orphans in the Polish language in the hope of fostering better relations with gentile Poles.

11. Isaac Bashevis Singer, *Shosha* (London: Penguin Books, 1979), p. 251; Isaac Bashevis Singer, *The Family Moskat*, trans. A. H. Gross (New York: Farrar, Straus & Giroux, 1988), p. 611.

12. Cited in Abraham Lewin, *A Cup of Tears: A Diary of the Warsaw Ghetto* (London: Fontana/Collins, 1990), pp. xii + 308, illust.; p. 21.

13. See Shmuel Almog, "What's in a Hyphen?" *SICSA Report* (newsletter of the Vidal Sassoon International Center for the Study of Antisemitism, Hebrew University of Jerusalem), No. 2, Summer 1989, pp. 1–2.

Chapter 1

1. Henry Fenigstein, interview, HCM 3–82, Toronto, Ontario, 21 January 1982, pp. 5–6.

2. Irena Bakowska, interview, HCM 3–83, Kingston, Ontario, 1 February 1983, p. 8; Eugenia Pernal, interview, HCM 4–87, Toronto, Ontario, 19 May 1987, p. 24.

3. Bakowska, interview, HCM 3–83, p. 9.

4. Fenigstein, interview, HCM 3–82, pp. 5–6.

5. New York, Archives of the American Jewish Joint Distribution Committee (hereafter, AAJJDC), AR3344, file 842, Persecutions (Pre-War), from a report on "The Situation of the Jewish Students in Poland," p. 6.

6. Yisrael Gutman, *The Jews of Warsaw, 1939–1943: Ghetto, Underground, Revolt*, trans. Ina Friedman (Bloomington and Indianapolis: Indiana University Press, 1989), pp. xxi + 487; p. xvii.

7. AAJJDC, AR3344, file 842, Persecutions (Pre-War); "The Situation of the Jewish Students in Poland," p. 3.

8. Janina Zaborowska (a gentile medical student before the war), interview, HCM 76–85, Oakville, Ontario, 12 September 1985, pp. 15–16.

9. Richard M. Watt, *Bitter Glory: Poland and Its Fate, 1918–1939* (New York: Simon and Schuster, 1979), p. 363; AAJJDC, AR3344, file 842, Persecutions (Pre-War); "The Situation of the Jewish Students in Poland."

10. Ludwig Stabholz, interview, HCM 5–87, Tel Aviv, Israel, 11 June 1987, pp. 1–2.

11. Henry Fenigstein, as Told to Saundra Collis, *The Holocaust and I: Memoirs of a Survivor* (Toronto: Unpublished MS, 1990), pp. 521 + xlii; pp. 501–02.

12. Ryszard Zablotniak, "Das geheime Medizin- und Pharmazie-studium in Polen in den Jahren 1939 bis 1945," *Zeitschrift für Arztliche Fortbildung* 83: 363–66, 1989; p. 363.

13. Egon Tramer, interview, HCM 24–85, Winnipeg, Manitoba, 9 March 1985, p. 1.

14. Marek Balin, interview, HCM 7–83, Timberlake, Ohio, 16 May 1983, pp. 6–7.

15. AAJJDC AR3344, file 842, Persecutions (Pre-War); letter L. Neustadt, AJDC Warsaw, to Bernhard Kohn, AJDC New York, 26 October 1938.

16. Lucy S. Dawidowicz, *From That Place and Time: A Memoir, 1938–1947* (New York and London: W. W. Norton & Co., 1989), pp. xiv + 333; p. 172.

17. Hanna Hirszfeldowna (ed.), *The Story of One Life, from "Historia Jednego Zycia" by Ludwig Hirszfeld*, trans. F. R. Camp and F. R. Ellis (Fort Knox, KY: Blood Transfusion Division, United States Army Medical Research Laboratory, n.d.), p. 368; pp. 212–13.

18. This paragraph is derived from Rose Klepfisz and Emil Lang, *Annotated Catalogue of the Archives of the American Jewish Joint Distribution Committee, 1933–1944* (New York: AJJDC, n.d.), p. 57.

19. AAJJDC AR3344, file 840, Medical Care: TOZ, Warsaw, 1933–1942; L. Neustadt, "Organization to Safeguard the Health of the Jewish Population in Poland: TOZ," January 1936, p. 1. For a summary of TOZ activities in its first 20 years, see the report by the general secretary, Leo Wulman, "Between Two Wars: A Review of Social Medical Work for Jews in Poland, 1919–1939," *Jewish Social Service Quarterly* 16:267–73, 1940.

20. AAJJDC AR3344, file 822, Child Care Association CENTOS, 1935–1941; unattributed report, "Organization for Child Protection and Aid for Orphans in Poland: CENTOS," January 1936, p. 4.

21. AAJJDC AR3344, file 821, Child Care: General, 1932–1940; unsigned copy of a letter from the secretary of the AJDC to Mr. A. Ray Katz, Baltimore, 3 March 1932.

22. All street addresses used in this book are given in the European style: street name followed by building number.

23. AAJJDC AR3344, file 840, Medical Care: TOZ, Warsaw, 1933–1942; from "Pictures of Jewish Misery in Warsaw," hand-dated June 1935; p. 4.

24. Janina David, *A Square of Sky: Recollections of My Childhood* (New York: W. W. Norton & Co., 1964), p. 222; p. 106.

25. AAJJDC AR3344, file 843, Poland: Reconstructions, General; "Activities and Plans of the JDC in Poland."

26. AAJJDC AR3344, file 821, Child Care: General, 1932–1940; from an untitled, unattributed report on JDC-sponsored programs in Poland, 1937; p. 9.

27. AAJJDC AR3344, file 821, Child Care: General, 1932–1940; from an untitled, unattributed report on JDC-sponsored programs in Poland, 1937.

28. AAJJDC AR3344, file 822, Child Care Association CENTOS, 1935–1941; from a

report on "CENTOS: The Plight of the Jewish Children in Ostrog, N/H," October 1937, p. 4.

29. AAJJDC AR3344, file 841, Medical Care: Other Organizations; letter, B. C. Vladek and others, Medem Sanitarium near Warsaw, to Joseph Hyman, AJDC, New York, 22 February 1938.

Chapter 2

1. Cited in Yisrael Gutman, *The Jews of Warsaw, 1939–1943: Ghetto, Underground, Revolt*, trans. Ina Friedman (Bloomington and Indianapolis: Indiana University Press, 1989), pp. xxi + 487; p. 15.

2. This paragraph is derived chiefly from Wheeler-Bennett's study of the Brest-Litovsk Treaty; see John W. Wheeler-Bennett, *Brest-Litovsk: The Forgotten Peace, March 1918* (New York: W. W. Norton & Co., 1971), pp. xvi + 478; pp. 104ff.

3. Wheeler-Bennett, *Brest-Litovsk*, p. 109.

4. R. F. Leslie, Antony Polonsky, Jan M. Ciechanowski, and Z. A. Pelczynski, *The History of Poland since 1863* (Cambridge: Cambridge University Press, 1983), pp. xii + 499; p. 138.

5. Lucy S. Dawidowicz, *From That Place and Time: A Memoir, 1938–1947* (New York and London: W. W. Norton & Co., 1989), pp. xiv + 333; p. 148.

6. Dawidowicz, *From That Place*, p. 144.

7. These reports are cited in Harry Kenneth Rosenthal, *German and Pole* (Gainesville: University Presses of Florida, 1978), p. 97.

8. Cited in Dawidowicz, *From That Place*, pp. 176–77.

9. See Harry K. Rosenthal, *German and Pole*, (Gainesville: University Presses of Florida, 1978), p. 115.

10. Robert M. Kennedy, *The German Campaign in Poland (1939)* (Washington, DC: Department of the Army, 1956), p. 113.

11. Gutman, *Jews of Warsaw*, p. 12.

12. Gutman, *Jews of Warsaw*, p. 13.

13. The education of Poles, Christian as well as Jewish, was carried on with concealed vigor in many centers during the years of Nazi occupation. Medical studies on many levels of complexity and sophistication were pursued in Edinburgh, by escaped Polish students, and in many cities within Poland. This work has been summarized by Witold Rudowski and Ryszard Zablotniak, "Clandestine Medical Studies in Poland, 1939–1945," *Journal of the Royal College of Surgeons of Edinburgh* 23: 239–52, 1978. According to these authors, there were at least seven different medical schools or courses in Warsaw at different times, many of which were incorporated into the Jan Zaorski School in Aryan Warsaw, which began in March 1941 and had about 1900 students; the Zweibaum School in the ghetto, with about 500 students, was the next largest (for a recent description, see Charles G. Roland, "An Underground Medical School in the Warsaw Ghetto," *Medical History* 33: 399–419, 1989). Of course, the ghetto school operated for only 14 months, whereas the non-Jewish schools lasted for several years. See also Leonard J. Bruce-Chwatt and Zbigniew Bankowski, "An Unknown Page in the History of Medicine," *Journal of the American Medical Association* 201: 946–48, 1967, regarding the Zaorski School. Some of those students who were fortunate enough to escape from the Nazi orbit continued their medical education in Scotland; see J. Rostowski, *History of the Polish School of Medicine, University of Edinburgh* (Edinburgh: University of Edinburgh, 1955).

14. For example, in the Polish schools that were permitted to function outside the ghetto,

"teachers and pupils had to pretend they were engaged upon a simple grammar lesson, or the like, when German inspectors entered the classroom." Z. Stypulkowski, *Invitation to Moscow* (London: Thames and Hudson, 1951), p. 51.

15. Heinrich Himmler memorandum, May 1940, in Helmut Krausnick, "Denkschrift Himmlers," *Vierteljahreshefte für Zeitgeschichte*, V, 197; cited in Joachim Remak (ed.), *The Nazi Years: A Documentary History* (New York: Simon & Schuster, 1986), p. 127.

16. Leon Wulman and Joseph Tenenbaum, *The Martyrdom of Jewish Physicians in Poland*, ed. Louis Falstein (New York, Exposition Press, 1963), pp. xii + 500; p. 177.

17. Gutman, *Jews of Warsaw*, pp. 14–15.

18. David Wdowinski, *And We Are Not Saved* (New York: Philosophical Library, 1985), pp. xxi + 222, illust.; p. 27.

19. Wdowinski, *And We Are Not Saved*, p. 24.

20. Wdowinski, *And We Are Not Saved*, p. 26.

21. Alain Stanke, *So Much to Forget: A Child's Vision of Hell* (N.p.: Gage Publishing, 1977), pp. iii + 164; pp. 87–89.

22. Gutman, *Jews of Warsaw*, p. 198.

23. Apolinary Hartglas, "How Did Cherniakow [*sic*] Become Head of the Warsaw Judenrat?" *Yad Vashem Bulletin* 15: 4–7, 1964; p. 7; New York, Archives of the AJJDC AR3344, file 796, Reports, 1939 (Oct.– Dec.); report of Mr. Henryk Szoszkies on his experiences in Poland, Paris, 5 December 1939.

24. Jacob Apenszlak (ed.), *The Black Book of Polish Jewry: An Account of the Martyrdom of Polish Jewry Under the Nazi Occupation* (New York: Howard Fertig, 1982), pp. 222ff.

25. Dawidowicz has emphasized the vastly enhanced area of responsibility of the *Judenrat* over the *Kehilla*, the latter being a *Gemeinschaft* institution, whereas the former was forced to become a *Gesellschaft* institution, i.e., one devoted to providing crucial services, yet without the necessary funding. Lucy S. Dawidowicz, *The War Against the Jews, 1939–1945* (Toronto: Bantam Books, 1986), p. 229. The *Judenrat* has been explored extensively in Isaiah Trunk, *Judenrat: The Jewish Councils in Eastern Europe Under Nazi Occupation* (New York: The Macmillan Co., 1972).

26. Gutman, *Jews of Warsaw*, pp. 48–50.

27. Anonymous, *The German New Order in Poland* (London: Hutchinson & Co., 1942), pp. 560–61.

28. Officially, German citizens were forbidden to have sexual relations with Jews because of the supposed danger of "race defilement." See Helen Fein, *Accounting for Genocide: National Responses and Jewish Victimization during the Holocaust* (Chicago and London: University of Chicago Press, 1984), p. 21. In fact, opportunity often overrode edict, especially during the early days of the war, before the Jews were effectively isolated from the rest of Warsaw within the walled ghetto. Jewish girls and women apparently were demanded by the Nazis for service in brothels intended for German soldiers stationed in Warsaw; see affidavit of Dr. Henryk Szoszkies, 14 January 1940, published in Apenszlak, *Black Book*, pp. 26–28.

29. Gutman, *Jews of Warsaw*, p. 252.

30. Schon, in Arad, *Documents*, pp. 221–22.

31. Gutman, *Jews of Warsaw*, p. 53.

32. Fein, *Accounting for Genocide*, p. 221. The planning and implementation of the Warsaw ghetto has been described extensively. Useful sources include Joseph Kermish (ed.), *To Live with Honor and Die with Honor! . . . Selected Documents from the Warsaw Ghetto Underground Archives, "O.S."* [*"Oneg Shabbath"*] (Jerusalem: Yad Vashem, 1986); and Gutman, *Jews of Warsaw*.

Chapter 3

1. "Extracts from the Warsaw ghetto diary of Chaim A. Kaplan, 1940," in Yitzhak Arad, Yisrael Gutman, and Abraham Margoliot (eds.), *Documents on the Holocaust: Selected Sources on the Destruction of the Jews of Germany and Austria, Poland, and the Soviet Union* (New York: Ktav Publishing House, 1981), p. 202.

2. This categorization is adapted from the five-stage schema devised by Hilberg. See Raul Hilberg, Stanislaw Staron, and Josek Kermisz (eds.), *The Warsaw Diary of Adam Czerniakow: Prelude to Doom*, trans. S. Staron and the staff of Yad Vashem (New York: Stein & Day, 1982), pp. viii + 420; p. 28.

3. New York, Archives of the American Jewish Joint Distribution Committee (hereafter, AAJJDC), AR3344, file 796, Reports, 1939 (Oct.–Dec.); from "Report on the Bombings of Warsaw," by Sara Goldstein, age 19; undated but apparently contemporary.

4. Joanna K. M. Hanson, *The Civilian Population and the Warsaw Uprising of 1944* (Cambridge: Cambridge University Press, 1982), pp. xiii + 345; p. 5.

5. Isaiah Trunk, *Judenrat: The Jewish Councils in Eastern Europe Under Nazi Occupation* (New York: The Macmillan Co., 1972), pp. xxxv + 664; p. 115.

6. AAJJDC AR3344, file 796, Reports, 1939 (Oct.–Dec.); report of JDC from 1 September 1939, forwarded to Amsterdam 27 December 1939, p. 2.

7. Hanson, *The Civilian Population*, p. 11.

8. Izak Arbus, *The Number on My Forehead: A Survivor's Story* (MS, 1990), p. 224; p. 38.

9. Arbus, *The Number on My Forehead*, p. 37.

10. Irena Bakowska, interview, HCM 3–83, Kingston, Ontario, 1 February 1983, p. 15–16.

11. David Wdowinski, *And We Are Not Saved* (New York: Philosophical Library, 1985), pp. xxi + 222; p. 28.

12. Hilberg et al., *The Warsaw Diary of Adam Czerniakow*, p. 115, entry of 6 February 1940.

13. Hilberg et al., *The Warsaw Diary of Adam Czerniakow*, p. 114.

14. Jacob Sloan (ed.), *Notes from the Warsaw Ghetto: The Journal of Emmanuel Ringelblum* (New York: Schocken Books, 1974), pp. xxvii + 369; p. 20, entry of 14 February 1940.

15. Henry Fenigstein, as Told to Saundra Collis, *The Holocaust and I: Memoirs of a Survivor* (Toronto: Unpublished MS, 1990), pp. 521 + xlii; p. xiv.

16. E. P. Kulawiec (ed. and trans.), *The Warsaw Ghetto Memoirs of Janusz Korczak* (Washington, DC: University Press of America, 1979), pp. xvii + 127; p. 70.

17. AAJJDC AR3344, file 796, Reports, 1939 (Oct.– Dec.); from a report prepared by Szoszkies in Paris, 5 December 1939, p. 4.

18. Yisrael Gutman, *The Jews of Warsaw, 1939–1943: Ghetto, Underground, Revolt*, trans. Ina Friedman (Bloomington and Indianapolis: Indiana University Press, 1989), pp. 48–50.

19. Lucy S. Dawidowicz, *The War Against the Jews, 1933–1945* (Toronto and New York: Bantam Books, 1986), pp. xxxx + 466; p. 205.

20. Hanna Hirszfeldowna (ed.), *The Story of One Life, from "Historia Jednego Zycia" by Ludwig Hirszfeld* trans. F. R. Camp and F. R. Ellis (Fort Knox, KY: Blood Transfusion Division, United States Army Medical Research Laboratory, n.d.), p. 368; p. 192.

21. Hilberg et al., *The Warsaw Diary of Adam Czerniakow*, p. 90, entry of 18 November 1939.

22. Arbus, *The Number on My Forehead*, p. 43.

23. Hilberg et al., *The Warsaw Diary of Adam Czerniakow*, p. 157, entry of 4 June 1940.

24. AAJJDC AR3344, file 796, Reports, 1939 (Oct.–Dec.); from report by Henryk Szosz-kies, Paris, 5 December 1939, p. 3.

25. Christopher R. Browning, "Nazi Ghettoization Policy in Poland: 1939–41," *Central European History* 19: 343–68, 1986; Gutman, *Jews of Warsaw*, p. 50.

26. Waldemar Schon, cited in Arad et al., *Documents on the Holocaust*, p. 223.

27. Hilberg et al., *The Warsaw Diary of Adam Czerniakow*, p. 135.

28. Sloan, *The Journal of Emmanuel Ringelblum*, p. 133.

29. Hilberg et al., *The Warsaw Diary of Adam Czerniakow*, p. 405. The zloty was, and is, the unit of currency in Poland. In 1939, 5 zlotys were the equivalent of approximately $1 (U.S.); by 1943, 800 zlotys were equal to $1. See Sybil Milton (ed. and trans.), *The Stroop Report: The Jewish Quarter of Warsaw Is No More!* (London: Secker & Warburg, 1980), n. 32.

30. Raul Hilberg, *The Destruction of the European Jews* (New York and London: Holmes and Meier, 1985), pp. xii + 1274; p. 247.

31. Christopher R. Browning, "Nazi Resettlement Policy and the Search for a Solution to the Jewish Question, 1939–1941," *German Studies Review* 9: 497–519, 1986; Browning, "Nazi Ghettoization Policy in Poland."

32. Browning, "Nazi Resettlement Policy," p. 511.

33. Hilberg et al., *The Warsaw Diary of Adam Czerniakow*, p. 169.

34. Hilberg et al., *The Warsaw Diary of Adam Czerniakow*, p. 39; this passage is based on German documents published in *Faschismus-Gett-Massenmord* (Berlin: Rütten and Loening, 1961), pp. 108–13.

35. For a full discussion of the Madagascar plan, see Leni Yahil, "Madagascar: Phantom of a Solution for the Jewish Question," in Bela Vago and George L. Mosse, (eds.) *Jews and Non-Jews in Eastern Europe, 1918–1945* (New York and Toronto: John Wiley & Sons; Jerusalem: Israel Universities Press, 1974), pp. 315–34.

36. Browning, "Nazi Resettlement Policy," p. 512.

37. Wilhelm Hagen, "Krieg, Hunger und Pestilenz in Warschau, 1939–1943," *Gesundheitswesen und Desinfektion* 8: 115–28; 9: 129–43, 1973; p. 130.

38. Gutman, *Jews of Warsaw*, p. 53. In Vilna a year later, the first *Aktion* was also carried out on Yom Kippur, 1 October 1941; see Yitzhak Arad, *Ghetto in Flames: The Struggle and Destruction of the Jews in Vilna in the Holocaust* (New York: Holocaust Library, 1982), p. 500; p. 136.

39. Schon, in Arad et al., *Documents*, pp. 221–22.

40. Helen Fein, *Accounting for Genocide* (New York: The Free Press, 1979), p. 221. The planning and implementation of the Warsaw ghetto has been described extensively. Useful sources include Joseph Kermish (ed.), *To Live with Honor and Die with Honor! . . . Selected Documents from the Warsaw Ghetto Underground Archives, "O.S."* [*"Oneg Shabbath"*] (Jerusalem: Yad Vashem, 1986), and Gutman, *Jews of Warsaw.*

41. Gutman, *Jews of Warsaw*, p. 61.

42. AAJJDC AR3344, file 817, Reports: Commission for Polish Relief (CPR), 1939–1941; Report of an Inspection Trip Made by Messrs. John Hartigan and Columba P. Murray, Jr., Representatives of the Commission for Polish Relief, undated but by context early November 1940; p. 1.

43. Karolina Borman, interview, HCM 23-82, Kingston, Ontario, 26 September 1982, p. 4.

44. "Grace Dover" [pseudonym], interview, HCM 36-85, Port Dover, Ontario, 4 April 1985, p. 40.

45. Eugenia Pernal, interview, HCM 4–87, Toronto, Ontario, 19 May 1987, p. 3.

46. Wdowinski, *And We Are Not Saved*, p. 5.

47. For a discussion of the ZWW, see Chaim Lazar, *Muranowska 7: The Warsaw Ghetto Uprising*, trans. Yosef Shachter (Tel Aviv: Massada-P.E.C. Press Ltd., 1966), p. 341, illust.

48. Abraham Lewin, *A Cup of Tears: A Diary of the Warsaw Ghetto* (London: Fontana/Collins, 1990), pp. xii + 308; p. 274.

49. Stanislaw Adler, *In the Warsaw Ghetto, 1940–1943: An Account of a Witness* (Jerusalem: Yad Vashem, 1982), pp. xviii + 334; p. 94.

50. Adler, *In the Warsaw Ghetto*, p. 93.

51. Noemi Makowerowa (ed.), *Henryk Makower: Pamietnik z getta warszawskiego, pazdziernik 1940-styczen 1943* (Wrocław, Warszawa, Kraków, Gdansk, Łodż: Zakład Narodowy im. Ossolinskich Wydawnictwo, 1987), p. 213; p. 11.

52. Lewin, *A Cup of Tears*, p. 254.

53. Jean Amery, "In the Waiting Room of Death: Reflections on the Warsaw Ghetto," in Sidney Rosenfeld and Stella P. Rosenfeld (ed. and trans.), *Radical Humanism: Selected Essays* (Bloomington: Indiana University Press, 1984), pp. 21–36; p. 29.

54. Gutman, *Jews of Warsaw*, p. 60.

55. Isaiah Trunk, "Epidemics and Mortality in the Warsaw Ghetto, 1939–1942," *YIVO Annual of Jewish Social Science* 8: 82–122, 1953; p. 87.

56. Trunk, "Epidemics and Mortality," p. 87. Trunk's figures are based on the number of ration cards issued. The precise figures are: October 1939, 359,827; December 1940, 392,911; March 1941, 445,000; April 1941, 450,000; June 1941, 435,700; October 1941, 394,348; and June 1942, 400,000 (see pp. 87, 89, 90, and 91, respectively). It can be assumed that additional small numbers of Jews lived in the ghetto. The rich probably did not bother to register for ration cards, particularly the nouveau riches, who had access to unlimited food via smuggling operations.

57. Hanson, *The Civilian Population*, pp. 8–9.

58. Gutman, *Jews of Warsaw*, p. 63.

59. Lewin, *A Cup of Tears*, p. 261, n. 85.

60. Jan Karski [Jan Kozielewski], *Story of a Secret State* (Boston: Houghton Mifflin Co., 1944), pp. vi + 391; p. 334.

61. Arbus, *The Number on My Forehead*, p. 67.

62. Makowerowa, *Henryk Makower*, p. 196.

63. Hilberg et al., *The Warsaw Diary of Adam Czerniakow*, p. 286, entry of 7 October 1941.

64. Gutman, *Jews of Warsaw*, p. 108.

65. Hilberg et al., *The Warsaw Diary of Adam Czerniakow*, p. 208, entry for 19 October 1940.

66. Trunk, "Epidemics and Mortality," p. 89. By comparison, in 1990 the population density in Tokyo was 24,463, that of Toronto was 20,001, that of New York City was 11,473, and that of London was 10,551. But Bombay packed in Indians to a total of 120,299 per square mile and Hong Kong to an astonishing 247,004. Figures from *The World Almanac and Book of Facts, 1991* (New York: World Almanac, 1990), p. 960; p. 771.

67. Hilberg et al., *The Warsaw Diary of Adam Czerniakow*, p. 314, entry of 11 January 1942.

68. Anonymous, *The Warsaw Ghetto: The 45th Anniversary of the Uprising* (Warsaw: Interpress Publishers, 1988), pp. 92 + unnumbered illustrations; Anonymous, *Scenes of Martyrdom and Fighting of Jews on the Polish Land, 1939–1945* (Warsaw, 1978), pp. [60], text in English, Polish, Hebrew, French, Russian, and German; Milton, *The Stroop Report*.

69. Joseph Marcus, *Social and Political History of the Jews in Poland, 1919–1939* (Berlin, New York, Amsterdam: Mouton Publishers, 1983), p. 78.

70. Betty Jean Lifton, *The King of Children: A Biography of Janusz Korczak* (New York: Farrar, Straus and Giroux, 1988), p. 404, illust.

71. Gutman, *Jews of Warsaw*, p. 38.

72. Apolinary Hartglas, "How Did Cherniakow [*sic*] Become Head of the Warsaw Judenrat?" *Yad Vashem Bulletin* 15: 4–7, 1964; p. 5.

73. Makowerowa, *Henryk Makower*, p. 108.

74. See, for example, Hirszfeld's description of their precipitate expulsion from their home; Hirszfeldowna, *The Story of One Life*, p. 191.

75. Gutman, *Jews of Warsaw*, p. 59.

76. Sloan, *The Journal of Emmanuel Ringelblum*, p. 138.

77. Adler, *In the Warsaw Ghetto*, p. 171.

78. Sloan, *The Journal of Emmanuel Ringelblum*, pp. 214–15.

79. Lewin, *A Cup of Tears*, p. 84, entry for 21 May 1942.

80. Hilberg et al., *The Warsaw Diary of Adam Czerniakow*, p. 159.

81. Trunk, *Judenrat*, p. 218.

82. From the report of a Gestapo informer, cited in Christopher R. Browning and Israel Gutman, "The Reports of a Jewish 'Informer' in the Warsaw Ghetto—Selected Documents," *Yad Vashem Studies* 17: 247–93, 1986; p. 263.

83. Jerusalem, Yad Vashem Archives, YVA 03/2358, Testimony of Dr. Stanislaw Waller, n.d., p. 4.

84. Michael Zylberberg, *A Warsaw Diary, 1939–1945* (London: Vallentine, Mitchell, 1969), p. 220; p. 49.

85. Hilberg et al., *The Warsaw Diary of Adam Czerniakow*, p. 347, entry of 25 April 1942.

86. Hilberg et al., *The Warsaw Diary of Adam Czerniakow*, p. 347, entry of 27 April 1942.

87. Hilberg et al., *The Warsaw Diary of Adam Czerniakow*, p. 367, entry of 16 June 1942.

88. Lewin, *A Cup of Tears*, p. 261, n. 92.

89. Adler, *In the Warsaw Ghetto*, p. 237.

90. Gutman, *Jews of Warsaw*, p. 31.

91. Janina David, *A Square of Sky: Recollections of My Childhood* (New York: W. W. Norton & Co., 1964), p. 222; p. 135.

92. Lewin, *A Cup of Tears*, p. 257, n. 52.

93. Adam Starkopf, *There Is Always Time to Die*, ed. Gertrude Hirschler (New York: Holocaust Library, 1981), p. 242; pp. 87–88.

94. David Graber, "Some Impressions and Memories," cited in Kermish (ed.), *To Live with Honor*, p. 60.

95. Hilberg et al., *The Warsaw Diary of Adam Czerniakow*, p. 352, entry of 12 May 1942.

96. Lewin, *A Cup of Tears*, pp. 71–72, entry of 13 May 1942.

97. Tolla Kelson, a former nurse at Czyste and Berson and Bauman Hospital, and her husband were in hiding in 1943. They "had spotless Aryan documents. One day the Gestapo raided the villa. Tolla and her husband were discovered; their appearance and their documents were of no avail. The beasts examined her husband physically, discovered he was a Jew, and immediately shot them." Bernard Goldstein, *The Stars Bear Witness*, trans. Leonard Shatzkin, (New York: Viking Press, 1949), p. 295; p. 228.

98. Hilberg et al., *The Warsaw Diary of Adam Czerniakow*, p. 353.

99. Hilberg et al., *The Warsaw Diary of Adam Czerniakow*, p. 225, entry of 23 April 1941.

100. Alexander Donat, *The Holocaust Kingdom: A Memoir* (New York: Holocaust Library, 1978), p. 7.

101. Hilberg et al., *The Warsaw Diary of Adam Czerniakow*, p. 201, entry of 24 September 1940.

102. Hilberg, *The Destruction of the European Jews*, p. 241.

103. Jan Kapczan, "Account of the Ways of Financial Management in the Jewish Communities in the Occupied Territory during the War," in Kermish, *To Live with Honor*, p. 296.

104. Frank Stiffel, *The Tale of the Ring: A Kaddish* (Toronto, New York, London, Sydney, and Auckland: Bantam Books, 1985), p. 348; p. 51.

105. Trunk, *Judenrat*, p. 247.

106. Gutman, *Jews of Warsaw*, pp. 22–23.

107. Adler, *In the Warsaw Ghetto*, p. 207.

108. Gutman, *Jews of Warsaw*, p. 24.

109. Browning, "Nazi Ghettoization Policy," p. 363.

110. Lewin, *A Cup of Tears*, p. 254, n. 31.

111. Helena Szereszewski, "In the Financial Department of the Judenrat (Memories of the Warsaw Ghetto)," in *Extermination and Resistance: Historical Records and Source Material* (Kibbutz Lohamei Haghettaot: Ghetto Fighter's House in Memory of Yitzhak Katznelson, 1958), pp. 65–78; p. 65.

112. Gutman, *Jews of Warsaw*, p. 112. For a general outline of how the postal service functioned, see the chapter by Peretz Opoczynski in Kermish, *To Live with Honor*, pp. 157–63.

113. New York, Archives of the AJJDC AR3344, file 811, Publicity: General, (May) 1937–1942, 1944; from *Unser Tsait*, August 1942.

114. Janina Zaborowska, interview, HCM 76–85, Oakville, Ontario, 12 September 1985, p. 15.

115. Lewin, *A Cup of Tears*, p. 269.

116. AAJJDC AR3344, file 811, Publicity: General, (May) 1937–1942, 1944; from *Unser Tsait*, June 1942.

117. Halina Berg [pseudonym], interview, HCM 6–84, Milpitas, California, 14 September 1984, pp. 33–34.

118. Sloan, *The Journal of Emmanuel Ringelblum*, p. 182.

119. Before the end of 1941, eight Jews caught outside the ghetto without permission were executed by the Nazis. According to Dr. Izrael Milejkowski, "his superior, Dr. Wilhelm Hagen, was directly responsible for the execution. It was the only way, Hagen claimed, to stop Jews from spreading typhus outside the Ghetto." (See Donat, *Holocaust Kingdom*, p. 47.) Hagen does not deny this, though he qualifies it; leaving should be punished by flogging, with additional and heavy fines for wealthy Jews. Only vagrant Jews should be shot for their "crime." See Hagen, "Krieg, Hunger und Pestilenz," p. 125.

120. N. Rosen, "The Problem of Work in the Jewish Quarter—July 1942," in Kermish, *To Live with Honor*, pp. 251–52.

121. Borman, interview, HCM 23–82, 26 September 1982, p. 37.

122. See, for example, the scathing letter from A. M. Rogowy, 5 September 1941, in Kermish *To Live with Honor*, pp. 317ff; also Anonymous, "Economic Life in the Ghetto as of Its Establishment in November 1940," in Kermish, *To Live with Honor*, p. 537.

123. Rabbi Itzhak Katz, "Things I Intended to Say," in Kermish, *To Live with Honor*, p. 356.

124. Adler, *In the Warsaw Ghetto*, p. 124.

125. Natan Koninski, "The Profile of the Jewish Child," in Kermish, *To Live with Honor*, p. 390.

126. Gutman, *Jews of Warsaw*, pp. 40–41.

127. Kulawiec, *The Warsaw Ghetto Memoirs*, p. 27.

128. Gutman, *Jews of Warsaw*, p. 106.

129. Adler, *In the Warsaw Ghetto*, pp. 232–33.

130. Gutman, *Jews of Warsaw*, p. 44.

131. Adolf Berman, "The Fate of the Children in the Warsaw Ghetto," in Yisrael Gutman and Livia Rothkirchen (eds.), *The Catastrophe of European Jewry: Antecedents, History, Reflections* (Jerusalem: Yad Vashem, 1976), pp. 400–21; p. 403.

132. Gutman, *Jews of Warsaw*, p. 106.

133. Figures from Trunk, "Epidemics and Mortality," p. 91.

134. Haim Baram, cited in Shalom Cholavsky, "The German Jews in the Minsk Ghetto," *Yad Vashem Studies* 17: 219–45, 1986; p. 223.

135. Vladka Meed, *On Both Sides of the Wall: Memoirs from the Warsaw Ghetto*, trans. Steven Meed (New York: Holocaust Library, 1979), pp. 276, illust., p. 22.

136. Gutman, *Jews of Warsaw*, p. 45.

137. Bakowska, interview, HCM 3–83, p. 29.

138. Berg, interview, HCM 6–84, pp. 19ff.

139. Dr. Egon Tramer, interview, HCM 24–85, Winnipeg, Manitoba, 9 March 1985, p. 5.

140. Stiffel, *The Tale of the Ring*, p. 63.

141. Adler, *In the Warsaw Ghetto*, p. 256.

142. Hanna Krall, *Shielding the Flame: An Intimate Conversation with Dr. Marek Edelman, the Last Surviving Leader of the Warsaw Ghetto Uprising*, trans. Joanna Stasinska and Lawrence Weschler, (New York: Henry Holt and Co., 1986), pp. xiii + 124; p. 48.

143. Hilberg et al., *The Warsaw Diary of Adam Czerniakow*, p. 326, entry of 15 February 1942. Mrs. Judt was the former mistress of a German officer and claimed special privileges in the ghetto on the strength of that relationship. Her final "privilege" was to be shot by the Germans rather than being shipped to Treblinka (p. 178, n.5).

144. Hilberg et al., *The Warsaw Diary of Adam Czerniakow*, p. 323, entry of 6 February 1942.

145. Adler, *In the Warsaw Ghetto*, p. 40.

146. Trunk, "Epidemics and Mortality," p. 115.

147. Gutman, *Jews of Warsaw*, p. 18.

148. Trunk, "Epidemics and Mortality," p. 88.

149. Trunk, "Epidemics and Mortality," pp. 115–16.

150. Anonymous, "Report for January of the 'Refugees' Township,' Dzika-Stawki," in Kermish, *To Live with Honor*, p. 327.

151. Sloan, *The Journal of Emmanuel Ringelblum*, p. 252.

152. Hirszfeldowna, *The Story of One Life*, p. 230.

153. *Biuletyn Informacyjny*, 30 April 1942, cited in Władyslaw Bartoszewski, *The Warsaw Ghetto: A Christian's Testimony*, trans. Stephen G. Cappellari (Boston: Beacon Press, 1987), pp. x + 117; p. 13.

154. *Biuletyn Informacyjny*, 30 April 1942.

155. Trunk, "Epidemics and Mortality," p. 115.

156. Sloan, *The Journal of Emmanuel Ringelblum*, p. 205.

157. Hilberg et al., *The Warsaw Diary of Adam Czerniakow*, p. 338, entry of 25 March 1942.

158. Hilberg et al., *The Warsaw Diary of Adam Czerniakow*, p. 339, entry of 1 April 1942.

159. Hilberg et al., *The Warsaw Diary of Adam Czerniakow*, p. 340, entry of 5 April 1942.

160. Hagen, "Krieg, Hunger und Pestilenz," p. 128.

161. Gutman, *Jews of Warsaw*, p. 113.

162. Hilberg et al., *The Warsaw Diary of Adam Czerniakow*, p. 332, entry of 4 March 1942, in which Czerniakow notes that "For several days we are again without electricity."

163. Tadeusz Stabholz, interview, HCM 26–82, Cleveland, Ohio, 4 December 1982, p. 21.

164. Henryk Rubinlicht, in Howard Roiter, *Voices from the Holocaust* (New York: William-Frederick Press, 1975), p. 221; p. 110–11.

165. Wdowinski, *And We Are Not Saved*, p. 40.

166. Anonymous, "Children's Playroom at 28 Sliska Street: A Report," in Kermish, *To Live with Honor*, p. 480.

167. Fliederbaum, in Myron Winick (ed.), *Hunger Disease: Studies by the Jewish Physicians in the Warsaw Ghetto*, trans. Martha Osnos (New York, Chichester, Brisbane, and Toronto: John Wiley & Sons, 1979), pp. xiv + 261; p. 16.

168. Stiffel, *The Tale of the Ring*, pp. 53–54.

169. Zylberberg, *A Warsaw Diary*, p. 43.

170. Zylberberg, *A Warsaw Diary*, p. 45.

171. Hilberg et al., *The Warsaw Diary of Adam Czerniakow*, entry for 19 December 1939, p. 101.

172. Trunk, *Judenrat*, p. 189. In May 1943 the Great Synagogue was totally destroyed by the Nazis as retribution against the Jews for their bloody revolt in April and May.

173. Trunk, *Judenrat*, p. 193.

174. Yaffa Eliach, *Hasidic Tales of the Holocaust* (New York: Avon Books, 1982), pp. xxxii + 312; p. 198–99.

175. David, *A Square of Sky*, p. 136.

176. Sloan, *The Journal of Emmanuel Ringelblum*, p. 184.

177. Hilberg et al., *The Warsaw Diary of Adam Czerniakow*, p. 300.

178. Hilberg et al., *The Warsaw Diary of Adam Czerniakow*, p. 279, entry for 11 September 1941.

179. Trunk, "Epidemics and Mortality," p. 117.

180. Zylberberg, *A Warsaw Diary*, p. 31.

181. Sloan, *The Journal of Emmanuel Ringelblum*, p. 138.

182. Bakowska, interview, HCM 3–83, 1 February 1983, p. 13.

183. Zylberberg, *A Warsaw Diary*, p. 31.

184. Sloan, *The Journal of Emmanuel Ringelblum*, p. 211.

185. Adler, *In the Warsaw Ghetto*, p. 167.

186. Hilberg et al., *The Warsaw Diary of Adam Czerniakow*, p. 297.

187. Fenigstein, interview, HCM 11–82, pp. 8–9.

188. Fenigstein, interview, HCM 11–82, p. 11.

189. Wdowinski, *And We Are Not Saved*, p. 41.

190. This problem is a frequent topic in World War II prisoner of war accounts, especially those relating experiences in the Far East. Only a sample is cited here: Norman Q. Brill, "Neuropsychiatric Examination of Military Personnel Recovered from Japanese Prison Camps," *Bulletin U.S. Army Medical Department* 5: 429–38, 1946; Kenneth Harrison, *The Brave Japanese* (Adelaide: Rigby Ltd., 1966), pp. 280; Gerald Klatskin, William T. Salter, and Frances D. Humm, "Gynecomastia due to Malnutrition: I. Clinical Studies," *American Journal of the Medical Sciences* 213: 19–30, 1947.

191. Anonymous, "[Youth and Their Education in the Ghetto]," in Kermish, *To Live with Honor*, p. 496.

192. Gutman, *Jews of Warsaw*, p. 115.

193. Stiffel, *The Tale of the Ring*, p. 57.

194. Henry Orenstein, *I Shall Live: Surviving Against All Odds, 1939–1945* (New York, London, Toronto, Sydney, Tokyo: Touchstone Book, Simon & Schuster, 1989), pp. xiv + 272; p. 124.

195. Adler, *In the Warsaw Ghetto*, p. 256.

196. Hilberg, et al., *The Warsaw Diary of Adam Czerniakow*, p. 330.

197. Alan Adelson and Robert Lapides (eds.), *Łódź Ghetto: Inside a Community Under Siege* (New York: Viking Press, 1989), pp. xxi + 526; p. 44.

198. Millie Eisen, interview, HCM 58–85, Greyslake, Illinois, 20 June 1985, p. 3, 9.

199. Hilberg et al., *The Warsaw Diary of Adam Czerniakow*, p. 132, entry for 27 March 1940.

200. Sloan, *The Journal of Emmanuel Ringelblum*, p. 120.

201. Lewin, *A Cup of Tears*, p. 87, entry of 22 May 1942.

202. Krall, *Shielding the Flame*, p. 40.

203. Sloan, *The Journal of Emmanuel Ringelblum*, p. 249, entry of January 1942.

204. Adler, *In the Warsaw Ghetto*, p. 68. He was also an owner of the saloon To Tu on Leszno Street. On 18 May 1942, perhaps to Czerniakow's secret relief, Czerwinski died of a heart attack.

205. Adler, *In the Warsaw Ghetto*, p. 48; see Hilberg et al., *The Warsaw Diary of Adam Czerniakow*, p. 355, entry for that date.

206. Martin Gray, with Max Gallo, *For Those I Loved*, 2nd ed., trans. Anthony White (London: W. H. Allen, 1984), pp. xvi + 349; p. 47.

207. "Answers to a Questionnaire by H. Rosen," in Kermish, *To Live with Honor*, p. 749.

208. Adler, *In the Warsaw Ghetto*, p. 257.

209. Ringelblum records an instance where three Jewish women were raped by Germans at Tłomackie 2, their screams resounding through the house (Sloan, *The Journal of Emmanuel Ringelblum*, p. 24). Such crimes were common.

210. Kubar had a Jewish friend in hiding on the gentile side of Warsaw who was raped in an abandoned building by a Polish blackmailer; Zofia S. Kubar, *Double Identity: A Memoir* (New York: Hill and Wang, 1989), p. 42. Among some bands of partisans ostensibly fighting the Germans, Jewish women who were members of the band seemed nevertheless to be considered fair game; Brysk's father, a surgeon in one such band, was kept busy doing abortions on these unfortunate girls and women. See Miriam Brysk, interview, HCM 5–84, Galveston, Texas, 31 May 1984, p. 17.

211. Cited in Roiter, *Voices from the Holocaust*, pp. 221; p. 94.

212. Krall, *Shielding the Flame*, p. 44.

213. Hilberg et al., *The Warsaw Diary of Adam Czerniakow*, p. 153, entry for 24 May 1940.

214. Gutman, *Jews of Warsaw*, p. 90.

215. Hirszfeldowna, *The Story of One Life*, p. 244.

216. Lewin, *A Cup of Tears*, pp. 93–94.

217. Gutman, *Jews of Warsaw*, p. 90.

218. Gutman, *Jews of Warsaw*, p. 110.

219. Gutman, *Jews of Warsaw*, p. 275.

220. Lewin, *A Cup of Tears*, pp. 130–31.

221. Gutman, *Jews of Warsaw*, p. 39.

222. Gutman, *Jews of Warsaw*, p. 97.

223. Browning, "Nazi Ghettoization Policy."

224. Browning, "Nazi Ghettoization Policy," p. 355.

225. Adler, *In the Warsaw Ghetto*, pp. 82–83.

226. Gutman, *Jews of Warsaw*, p. 24.

Chapter 4

1. David Wdowinski, *And We Are Not Saved* (New York: Philosophical Library, 1985), pp. xxi+222; p. 45.

2. Wilhelm Hagen, "Krieg, Hunger und Pestilenz in Warschau, 1939–1943," *Gesundheitswesen und Desinfektion* 8: 115–28; 9: 129–43, 1973; p. 118.

3. Raul Hilberg, Stanislaw Staron, and Josef Kermisz (eds.), *The Warsaw Diary of Adam Czerniakow: Prelude to Doom*, trans. S. Staron and the staff of Yad Vashem (New York: Stein & Day, 1982), pp. viii+420; p. 139, entry of 10 April 1940.

4. Isaiah Trunk, *Judenrat: The Jewish Councils in Eastern Europe Under Nazi Occupation* (New York: The Macmillan Co., 1972), pp. xxxv+664; pp. 159–60.

5. New York, Archives of the American Jewish Joint Distribution Committee (hereafter, AAJJDC), AR3344, file 840, Medical Care: TOZ, Warsaw, 1933–1942; from "TOZ: Report of Activities for May 1941," p. 2.

6. Noemi Makowerowa (ed.), *Henryk Makower: Pamietnik z getta warszawskiego, pazdziernik 1940–styczen 1943* (Wroclaw, Warsaw, Krakow, Gdansk, and Lodz: Zaklad Narodowy im. Ossolinskich Wydawnictwo, 1987), pp. 213; p. 184.

7. Hanna Hirszfeldowna (ed.), *The Story of One Life, from "Historia Jednego Zycia" by Ludwig Hirszfeld*, trans. F. R. Camp and F. R. Ellis (Fort Knox, KY: Blood Transfusion Division, United States Army Medical Research Laboratory, n.d.), p. 368; p. 210.

8. Stanislaw Adler, *In the Warsaw Ghetto, 1940–1943: An Account of a Witness* (Jerusalem, Yad Vashem, 1982), pp. xviii+334; pp. 196–97.

9. Adler, *In the Warsaw Ghetto*, pp. 197–98.

10. Hirszfeldowna, *The Story of One Life*, p. 212.

11. Charles G. Roland, "An Underground Medical School in the Warsaw Ghetto, 1941–2," *Medical History* 33: 399–419, 1989.

12. Myron Winick (ed.), *Hunger Disease: Studies by the Jewish Physicians in the Warsaw Ghetto*, trans. Martha Osnos, (New York, Chichester, Brisbane, and Toronto: John Wiley & Sons, 1979), pp. xiv+261, illust.

13. Leon Wulman and Joseph Tenenbaum, *The Martyrdom of Jewish Physicians in Poland*, ed. Louis Falstein, (New York: Exposition Press, 1963), p. 118.

14. AAJJDC AR3344, file 840, Medical Care: TOZ, Warsaw, 1933–1942; "TOZ: Report on Activities for May 1941," p. 2.

15. AAJJDC AR3344, file 840, Medical Care: TOZ, Warsaw, 1933–1942; "TOZ: Report on Activities for May 1941," p. 4.

16. AAJJDC AR3344/840, Medical Care: TOZ, Warsaw, 1933–1942; from "Some Facts About the Activities of TOZ in Poland," Dr. L. Wulman, 27 March 1940, P. 3.

17. AAJJDC AR3344, file 798, Report, 1940 (Apr.–Aug.); from Minutes, meeting of Committee on Poland and Eastern Europe, AJDC, 11 April 1940, p. 1.

18. Yisrael Gutman, *Jews of Warsaw, 1939–1943: Ghetto, Underground, Revolt*, trans. Ina Friedman (Bloomington and Indianapolis: Indiana University Press, 1989), pp. xxi+487; p. 40.

19. AAJJDC AR3344, file 798, Report, 1940 (Apr.–Aug.); Troper, AJDC, reporting his meetings with David Guzik and L. Neustadt, from minutes of a meeting of the Committee on Poland and Eastern Europe, AJDC, 11 April 1940.

20. AAJJDC AR3344, file 799, Report 1940 (Sept.–Dec.); from "Explanations to the Report Lists About the Activities of the American Joint Distribution Committee, Warsaw-Cracow," 1 January to 30 September 1940, p. 3.

21. AAJJDC AR3344, file 799, Report 1940 (Sept.–Dec.); from year-end report for 1940.

22. As an example, see the reply of Henrietta Buchman to an agonized and impassioned letter from Dr. Leon Wulman demanding that more be done for Polish Jews: AAJJDC

AR3344, file 840, Medical Care: TOZ, Warsaw, 1933–1942, letter dated 17 September 1940.

23. This appeal from TOZ Warsaw was forwarded to Mrs. Buchman by the indefatigable Dr. Wulman, 6 November 1941; AAJJDC AR3344/840, Medical Care: TOZ, Warsaw, 1933–1942.

24. AAJJDC AR3344, file 840, Medical Care: TOZ, Warsaw, 1933–1942; report from Dr. L. Wulman, 27 May 1940, p. 1.

25. AAJJDC AR3344, file 840, Medical Care: TOZ, Warsaw, 1933–1942; letter, Dr. M. Koenigstein, president, and Dr. J. Rozenblum, secretary, TOZ Warsaw, to The Administrators of the AJDC, 4 December 1940.

26. AAJJDC AR3344, file 840, Medical Care: TOZ, Warsaw, 1933–1942; memorandum from AJDC Budapest to AJDC Lisbon, 14 May 1941.

27. See Adolf Berman, "The Fate of the Children in the Warsaw Ghetto," in Yisrael Gutman and Livia Rothkirchen (eds.), *The Catastrophe of European Jewry: Antecedents, History, Reflections* (Jerusalem: Yad Vashem, 1976), pp. 400–21.

28. Berman, "The Fate of the Children," p. 409.

29. Gutman, *Jews of Warsaw*, p. 43.

30. Gutman, *Jews of Warsaw*, p. 42.

31. SKSS performed its self-help tasks throughout the war. When needed, and within the limits of what was possible, it helped non-Jewish Poles with food, clothing, medicine, money, child care, orphan and refugee care, care for the families of prisoners of war, and care for prisoners; they provided patients with coupons so that they could have access to physicians, dentists, and midwives for services they could not afford: Hanson, *The Civilian Population*, pp. 33–35.

32. Gutman, *Jews of Warsaw*, p. 41.

33. Gutman, *Jews of Warsaw*, p. 42; Lucy S. Dawidowicz, *The War Against the Jews, 1933–1945* (Toronto and New York: Bantam Books, 1986), pp. xxxx+466; pp. 242–43.

34. Gutman, *Jews of Warsaw*, pp. 40–43; Dawidowicz, *The War Against the Jews*, p. 246.

35. Wdowinski, *And We Are Not Saved*, p. 37.

36. Wdowinski, *And We Are Not Saved*, p. 38.

37. AAJJDC AR 3344, file 800, Report 1941–1942 (Aug.); from "Budget Estimate of the Jewish Welfare Institution for the I Semester of 1942," p. 10 (TOZ) and 8 (CENTOS).

38. Dawidowicz, *The War Against the Jews*, p. 244.

39. Dawidowicz, *The War Against the Jews*, p. 244.

40. Abraham I. Katsh (ed. and trans.), *The Warsaw Diary of Chaim A. Kaplan* (New York: Collier Books, 1973), p. 410; entry for 8 March 1942, p. 302.

41. Joseph Kermish (ed.), *To Live with Honor and Die with Honor! . . . Selected Documents from the Warsaw Ghetto Underground Archives "O.S."* [*"Oneg Shabbath"*] (Jerusalem: Yad Vashem, 1986), pp. xliv+790; p. 336.

42. Dawidowicz, *The War Against the Jews*, p. 246.

43. Dawidowicz, *The War Against the Jews*, p. 247.

44. Betty Jean Lifton, *The King of Children: A Biography of Janusz Korczak* (New York: Farrar, Straus and Giroux, 1988), p. 404; pp. 275–76.

45. Dawidowicz, *The War Against the Jews*, p. 246.

46. Gutman, *Jews of Warsaw*, p. 293.

47. Wdowinski, *And We Are Not Saved*, p. 142.

48. Jacob Sloan (ed.), *Notes from the Warsaw Ghetto: The Journal of Emmanuel Ringelblum* (New York: Schocken Books, 1974), pp. xxvii+369; p. 131.

49. Gutman, *Jews of Warsaw*, p. 110.

50. Cited in "Answers to a Questionnaire by Dr. Milejkowski," in Kermish, *To Live with Honor*, p. 741.

51. Ryszard Zablotniak, "Wydzial Lekarski w Getcie Warszaw-skim," *Biuletyn Żydowskiego Instytutu Historycznego* 74: 81–86, 1970; p. 84.

52. Makowerowa, *Henryk Makower*, p. 106.

53. Henryk Rosen, "The Problem of Work in the Jewish Quarter—July 1942," in Kermish, *To Live with Honor*, p. 254.

54. Balin commented on the disappearance, from day to day and without explanation, both of fellow students and of teachers. Balin, HCM 7–83, p. 26 and 34.

55. Yitzhak Katznelson, *Vittel Diary*, trans. Myer Cohen (Israel: Beit Lohamei Hagettaot and Hakibbutz Hameuchad, 1972), p. 98.

56. Ryszard Zablotniak, "Das geheime Medizin- und Pharmazie-studium in Polen in den Jahren 1939 bis 1945," *Zeitschrift für Arztliche Fortbildung* 83: 363–66, 1989; p. 365.

57. Sloan, *Notes From the Warsaw Ghetto*, pp. xxvii + 369; p. 108.

58. AAJJDC, AR3344, file 840, Medical Care: TOZ, Warsaw, 1933–1942; from a report from Dr. L. Wulman, 27 May 1940.

59. Michael Temchin, *The Witch Doctor: Memoirs of a Partisan* (New York: Holocaust Library, 1983), p. 185, illust.; p. 24.

60. AAJJDC AR3344, file 796, Reports, 1939 (Oct.–Dec.); from anonymous "Notes on the Activity of American Joint Distribution Committee from Sept. 1, 1939," forwarded by U.S. consul, Warsaw, to Amsterdam, 27 December 1939, p. 3.

61. AAJJDC AR3344, file 798, Report, 1940 (Apr.–Aug.); from an unattributed document, "The Situation," hand-dated "May 1940 (?)," p. 10.

62. Hirszfeldowna, pp. 205–06.

63. Hilberg et al., *The Warsaw Diary of Adam Czerniakow*, pp. viii + 420; p. 110, entry of 22 January 1940.

64. Hilberg et al., *The Warsaw Diary of Adam Czerniakow*, p. 116, entry of 10 February 1940.

65. Hilberg et al., *The Warsaw Diary of Adam Czerniakow*, p. 170, entry of 4 July 1940.

66. Mordecai Lenski, "Problems of Disease in the Warsaw Ghetto," *Yad Vashem Studies* 3: 283–93, 1975; p. 285.

67. Hilberg et al., *The Warsaw Diary of Adam Czerniakow*, p. 121, entry of 23 February 1940.

68. Adler, *In the Warsaw Ghetto*, pp. xviii + 334, port., map., p. 165.

69. Ludwig Stabholz, interview, HCM 5–87, 11 June 1987, p. 5; "Dr. Ludwik Marceli Sztabholz—lekarz-chirurg," undated copy of an affidavit made shortly after World War II ended, gift of Dr. Stabholz, 11 June 1987; also Yad Vashem Archives, YVA Y63/36-l.

70. Hilberg et al., *The Warsaw Diary of Adam Czerniakow*, p. 185, entry of 16 August 1940.

71. Hilberg et al., *The Warsaw Diary of Adam Czerniakow*, p. 190, entries of 25 and 27 August 1940.

72. Hilberg et al., *The Warsaw Diary of Adam Czerniakow*, p. 193, entry of 3 September 1940.

73. Hilberg et al., *The Warsaw Diary of Adam Czerniakow*, p. 196, entry of 9 September 1940.

74. Hilberg et al., *The Warsaw Diary of Adam Czerniakow*, p. 195, footnote by the editors.

75. Henry Shoskes [Henryk Szoszkies], *No Traveler Returns* (Garden City, NY: Doubleday, Doran & Co., 1945), p. 55.

76. Sloan, *The Journal of Emmanuel Ringelblum*, p. 19.

77. Makowerowa, *Henryk Makower*, pp. 213, port.; p. 16.

78. Sloan, *The Journal of Emmanuel Ringelblum*, p. 88, entry for 19 November 1940.

79. Shoskes, *No Traveler Returns*, p. 34.

80. Hilberg et al., *The Warsaw Diary of Adam Czerniakow*, p. 213, entries for 4 and 5 November 1940.

81. Hilberg et al., *The Warsaw Diary of Adam Czerniakow*, p. 198, entry for 18 September 1940.

82. Hilberg et al., *The Warsaw Diary of Adam Czerniakow*, p. 148, entry for 10 May 1940.

83. Hilberg et al., *The Warsaw Diary of Adam Czerniakow*, p. 309.

84. Abraham Lewin, *A Cup of Tears: A Diary of the Warsaw Ghetto* (London: Fontana/Collins, 1990), pp. xii + 308; p. 101, entry of 27 May 1942.

85. Sloan, *The Journal of Emmanuel Ringelblum*, p. 10.

86. Hilberg et al., *The Warsaw Diary of Adam Czerniakow*, p. 364, entry of 8 June 1942.

87. AAJJDC AR3344, file 840, Medical Care: TOZ, Warsaw, 1933–1942; from letter, Dr. Leon Wulman, secretary, American Committee of OSE, to Mrs. Henrietta Buchman, AJDC, New York, 5 December 1941.

88. Adler, *In the Warsaw Ghetto*, p. 41.

89. Adler, *In the Warsaw Ghetto*, pp. 196–98.

90. Zofia S. Kubar, *Double Identity: A Memoir* (New York: Hill and Wang, 1989), p. 209; p. 31.

91. Michael Zylberberg, *A Warsaw Diary, 1939–1945* (London: Vallentine, Mitchell, 1969), p. 220; pp. 50ff.

92. Makowerowa, *Henryk Makower*, p. 99.

93. Sloan, *The Journal of Emmanuel Ringelblum*, p. 159.

94. Sloan, *The Journal of Emmanuel Ringelblum*, p. 160.

95. Howard Roiter, *Voices from the Holocaust* (New York: William-Frederick Press, 1975), p. 221; p. 115.

96. Roiter, *Voices from the Holocaust*, p. 117.

97. Wdowinski, *And We Are Not Saved*, pp. 76–77.

98. Ludwig Stabholz, interview, HCM 5–87, 11 June 1987, p. 24.

99. Sloan, *The Journal of Emmanuel Ringelblum*, p. 148.

100. Sloan, *The Journal of Emmanuel Ringelblum*, p. 166.

101. Trunk, *Judenrat*, p. 195.

102. Temchin, *The Witch Doctor*, p. 36.

103. The best source for information about the fate of individual Jewish physicians is the one painstakingly gathered and published in 1963, *The Martyrdom of Jewish Physicians in Poland*. The editors have made a prodigious effort to obtain information about these men and women, and the book is invaluable. Having said that, it must also be noted that the book is flawed—hardly surprising, given the massive anonymity that attended the fate of so many millions of Jews during the war. Dr. Henry Fenigstein, for example, whose name appears often in this book as one of the important interviewees, is listed in this source as having died during the Holocaust. Noting this caveat, the book is essential: Leon Wulman and Joseph Tenenbaum, *The Martydrom of Jewish Physicians in Poland*, ed. Louis Falstein (New York: Exposition Press, 1963), pp. xii + 500, illust.

104. Lewin, *A Cup of Tears*, p. 267.

105. Ludmilla Zeldowicz, "Personal Notes on Stanislaw Adler," in Adler, *In the Warsaw Ghetto*, p. xiii.

106. Adler, *In the Warsaw Ghetto*.

107. Lewin, *A Cup of Tears*, p. 168.

108. Lewin, *A Cup of Tears*, p. 171.

109. Adler, *In the Warsaw Ghetto*, p. 293.

110. Adler, *In the Warsaw Ghetto*, p. 233.

111. Sloan, *The Journal of Emmanuel Ringelblum*, p. 114.

112. Adler, *In the Warsaw Ghetto*, p. 232.

113. Adler, *In the Warsaw Ghetto*, p. 108.

114. Adler, *In the Warsaw Ghetto*, p. 232.

115. Hagen, "Krieg, Hunger und Pestilenz," p. 123.

116. Hagen, "Krieg, Hunger und Pestilenz," p. 124.

117. Eisen, interview, HCM 58–85, Greyslake, Illinois, 20 June 1985, p. 9.

118. Hilberg et al., *The Warsaw Diary of Adam Czerniakow*, p. 247.

119. Hilberg et al., *The Warsaw Diary of Adam Czerniakow*, p. 20.

120. Adler, *In the Warsaw Ghetto*, p. 130.

121. Sloan, *The Journal of Emmanuel Ringelblum*, p. 251.

122. Sloan, *The Journal of Emmanuel Ringelblum*, p. 189.

123. Adler, *In the Warsaw Ghetto*, p. 233.

124. Christopher R. Browning and Israel Gutman, "The Reports of a Jewish 'Informer' in the Warsaw Ghetto—Selected Documents," *Yad Vashem Studies* 17: 247–93, 1986; p. 263.

125. Adler, *In the Warsaw Ghetto*, pp. 233–34.

126. Gutman, *Jews of Warsaw*, p. 92.

127. Adler, *In the Warsaw Ghetto*, p. 133.

128. Hilberg et al., *The Warsaw Diary of Adam Czerniakow*, p. 247, entry for 6 June 1941.

129. Sloan, *The Journal of Emmanuel Ringelblum*, p. 185.

130. Korczak mentions his struggles to abstract donations at several places in his diary; see E. P. Kulawiec (ed. and trans.), *The Warsaw Ghetto Memoirs of Janusz Korczak* (Washington, DC: University Press of America, 1979), pp. 44, 50, and 60–61.

131. Makowerowa, *Henryk Makower*, p. 105.

132. Hirszfeldowna, *The Story of One Life*, pp. 226–27.

133. Makowerowa, *Henryk Makower*, p. 105.

134. Makowerowa, *Henryk Makower*, pp. 107-08.

135. Hilberg et al., *The Warsaw Diary of Adam Czerniakow*, p. 277, n. 10, entry for 9 September 1941.

136. Hirszfeldowna, *The Story of One Life*, p. 226.

137. Hirszfeldowna, *The Story of One Life*, pp. 226–27.

138. Hirszfeldowna, *The Story of One Life*, p. 227.

139. Henry Fenigstein, as Told to Saundra Collis, *The Holocaust and I: Memoirs of a Survivor* (Toronto: Unpublished MS, 1990), pp. 521 + xlii; pp. xx-xxi.

140. Hirszfeldowna, *The Story of One Life*, p. 230.

141. Hirszfeldowna, *The Story of One Life*, pp. 208-09.

142. Hirszfeldowna, *The Story of One Life*, p. 213.

143. Hirszfeldowna, *The Story of One Life*, p. 210.

144. Hirszfeldowna, *The Story of One Life*, p. 210.

145. Hilberg et al., *The Warsaw Diary of Adam Czerniakow*, p. 324, entry of 11 February 1942.

146. Balin, interview, HCM 7–83, 16 May 1983, p. 12.

147. Makowerowa, *Henryk Makower*, p. 195.

148. Hilberg et al., *The Warsaw Diary of Adam Czerniakow*, p. 98.

149. Sloan, *The Journal of Emmanuel Ringelblum*, p. 141.

150. Trunk, *Judenrat*, p. 158.

151. Gutman, *Jews of Warsaw*, p. 92.

152. Wdowinski, *And We Are Not Saved*, p. 64.

153. Trunk, *Judenrat*, p. 158.

154. *Der Wecker*, an underground periodical published by the Bund in the ghetto, No. 5/29, 15 February 1942. Cited in Trunk, *Judenrat*, p. 158.

155. Trunk, *Judenrat*, pp. 159–60.

156. AAJJDC AR 3344, file 800, Report 1941–1942 (Aug.); letter from Dr. B. Tschlenoff to Joseph J. Schwartz, AJDC, Geneva, 8 January 1942.

157. AAJJDC AR3344, file 801, Report (Sept.) 1942–1943; letter from Dr. Weichert, Krakow, to the Committee for the Assistance of the War-Stricken Jewish Population, Geneva, 15 July 1943.

158. Hilberg et al., *The Warsaw Diary of Adam Czerniakow*, p. 176.

159. Hilberg et al., *The Warsaw Diary of Adam Czerniakow*, p. 156.

160. Lewin, *A Cup of Tears*, pp. [xii] + 308; p. 282.

161. Dr. Hagen arrived in Warsaw 6 February 1941, and Schrempf departed 10 February; Wilhelm Hagen, *Auftrag und Wirklichkeit: Sozialarzt im 20.Jahrhundert* (Munchen-Grafelfing: Werk-Verlag Dr. Edmund Banaschewski, 1978), p. 255, p. TR-1.

162. Hagen, "Krieg, Hunger und Pestilenz," p. 116.

163. AAJJDC AR3344, file 841, Medical Care: Other Organizations; from "Summary of Application dated February 24, 1939, from the Nurses' Training School of Warsaw."

164. AAJJDC AR3344, file 841, Medical Care: Other Organizations; from "Summary of Application dated February 24, 1939, from the Nurses' Training School of Warsaw."

165. AAJJDC AR3344, file 841, Medical Care: Other Organizations; from "Report of Nurses' Training School, Warsaw, 1937–38," by Sabina Schindler, Directress."

166. AAJJDC AR3344, file 841, Medical Care: Other Organizations; from "Summary of Application dated February 24, 1939, from the Nurses' Training School of Warsaw."

167. AAJJDC AR3344, file 841, Medical Care: Other Organizations; Report of the Activities of the School of Nursing in Warsaw, from April 1st, 1938 to March 31st, 1939," p. 1.

168. AAJJDC AR3344, file 841, Medical Care: Other Organizations; Report of the Activities of the School of Nursing in Warsaw, from April 1st, 1938 to March 31st, 1939," p. 3.

169. AAJJDC AR3344, file 841, Medical Care: Other Organizations; Report of the Activities of the School of Nursing in Warsaw, from April 1st, 1938 to March 31st, 1939," p. 2.

170. AAJJDC AR3344, file 841, Medical Care: Other Organizations; Report of the Activities of the School of Nursing in Warsaw, from April 1st, 1938 to March 31st, 1939," p. 4.

171. AAJJDC AR3344, file 841, Medical Care: Other Organizations; Report of the Activities of the School of Nursing in Warsaw, from April 1st, 1938 to March 31st, 1939," p. 5.

172. AAJJDC AR3344, file 841, Medical Care: Other Organizations; from memorandum, Henrietta KI. Buchman to Moses A. Leavitt, AJDC, 18 June 1940.

173. Adina Blady Szwajger, *I Remember Nothing More: The Warsaw Children's Hospital and the Jewish Resistance*, trans. Tasja Darowska and Danusia Stok (New York: Pantheon Books, 1990), pp. xx + 184, illust., maps; p. 62.

174. Vladka Meed, *On Both Sides of the Wall: Memoirs from the Warsaw Ghetto*, trans. Steven Meed (New York: Holocaust Library, 1979), p. 276; p. 106.

175. Meed, *On Both Sides of the Wall*, p. 103.

176. Bronislawa J. Wygodzka, interview, HCM 1–88, New York City, 8 January 1988, p. 24.

177. Bernard Goldstein, *The Stars Bear Witness*, trans. Leonard Shatzkin (New York: Viking Press, 1949), p. 295; p. 133.

178. Hilberg et al., *The Warsaw Diary of Adam Czerniakow*, p. 178, entry for 29 July 1940. The dancing school was run by Mrs. Regina Judt (see Chapter 3).

179. Goldstein, *The Stars Bear Witness*, p. 65.

180. Wygodzka, interview, HCM 1–88, 8 January 1988, p. 24.

181. Eugenia Pernal, interview, HCM 4–87, Toronto Ontario, 19 May 1987, p. 5.

182. [Stanislaw Rozycki?], "The School System," in Kermish, *To Live with Honor*, p. 512.

183. Goldstein, *The Stars Bear Witness*, p. 133.

184. Anonymous, "B: Clandestine Schooling, Secondary Schools, and Universities, Jewish Youth," in Kermish, *To Live with Honor*, p. 460.

185. Helena Szereszewski, "In the Financial Department of the Judenrat (Memories of the Warsaw Ghetto)," in *Extermination and Resistance: Historical Records and Source Material* (Kibbutz Lohamei Haghettaot: Ghetto Fighter's House in Memory of Yitzhak Katznelson, 1958), pp. 65–78; p. 77.

186. Szereszewski, "Financial Department of the Judenrat," p. 68.

187. Hanna Krall, *Shielding the Flame: An Intimate Conversation with Dr. Marek Edelman, the Last Surviving Leader of the Warsaw Ghetto Uprising*, trans. Joanna Stasinska and Lawrence Weschler (New York: Henry Holt and Co., 1986), pp. xiii + 124; pp. 77–78.

188. Szereszewski, "Financial Department of the Judenrat," p. 75.

189. Sabina Gurfinkiel-Glocerowa, "Szpital na Czystem," Yad Vashem Archives 03/398 0–3/2–2 undated, ca. 1945, p. 51; p. 9.

190. HCMU/OHA, interview of Eugenia Pernal, HCM 4–87, pp. 16–18.

191. Eisen, interview, HCM 58–85, 20 June 1985, 58 pp; p. 2.

192. Michael Zylberberg, "The Trial of Alfred Nossig," *Wiener Library Bulletin* 22: 41–45, 1969.

193. Eisen, interview, HCM 58–85, 20 June 1985, p. 28.

194. Eisen, interview, HCM 58–85, 20 June 1985, p. 5.

195. Balin, interview, HCM 7–83, 16 May 1983, p. 32.

196. Gurfinkiel-Glocerowa, "Szpital na Czystem," p. 46.

197. Gurfinkiel-Glocerowa, "Szpital na Czystem," p. 51.

198. Berman, "The Fate of the Children," p. 417.

Chapter 5

1. Jacob Apenszlak (ed.), *The Black Book of Polish Jewry: An Account of the Martyrdom of Polish Jewry Under the Nazi Occupation* (New York: Howard Fertig, 1982), p. 38.

2. Marek Balin, interview, HCM 7–83, 16 May 1983, p. 21.

3. New York, Archives of the American Jewish Joint Distribution Committee (hereafter AAJJDC), AR3344, file 841, Medical Care: Other Organizations; article in *L'Univers Israelite*, France, 28 July 1939.

4. Polish names present certain difficulties with regard to spelling. In general, I have adopted spellings that were in use in 1939–43. The exception, of which Dr. Stabholz's name is an example, is that in cases where I have interviewed a survivor, I have used the spelling of the name as given to me; usually such names have been anglicized, since many of these men and women live in the English-speaking world. Thus the name appears as "Sztabholc" in contemporary documents, but because both Dr. Taddeusz Stabholz and Dr. Ludwig Stab-

holz use the latter spelling, I have also done so wherever the name occurs, except in direct quotations from wartime documents, where all original spellings have been preserved.

5. Joanna K. M. Hanson, *The Civilian Population and the Warsaw Uprising of 1944* (Cambridge, London, New York, New Rochelle, Melbourne, and Sydney: Cambridge University Press, 1982), pp. xiii + 345; p. 6.

6. Jerusalem, YVA 03/398 0–3/2-2, "Szpital na Czystem," testimony of Sabina Gurfinkiel-Glocerowa, undated, ca. 1945, p. 3.

7. Gurfinkiel-Glocerowa, "Szpital na Czystem," p. 2.

8. Gurfinkiel-Glocerowa, "Szpital na Czystem," p. 4.

9. Henry Fenigstein, as Told to Saundra Collis, *The Holocaust and I: Memoirs of a Survivor* (Toronto: Unpublished MS, 1990), pp. 521 + xlii; pp. v-vi.

10. Gurfinkiel-Glocerowa, "Szpital na Czystem," p. 4.

11. Gurfinkiel-Glocerowa, "Szpital na Czystem," p. 4.

12. Gurfinkiel-Glocerowa, "Szpital na Czystem," p. 6.

13. Schrempf was at one time the city health officer for Frankfurt-on-Main, but was relieved of his duties in 1933 as being politically unreliable; see Wilhelm Hagen, "Krieg, Hunger und Pestilenz in Warschau, 1939–1943," *Gesundheitswesen und Desinfektion* 8: 115–28; 9: 129–43, 1973; p. 118.

14. Fenigstein, *The Holocaust and I*, p. xi.

15. Jerusalem, Yad Vashem Archives 033/1558 E 104-4-7. Dr. Emil Apfelbaum describes events at Czyste Hospital in 1939–43, Conversation between Apfelbaum and Stefania Beylin, Warsaw, 1945, trans. Martha and Robert Osnos, 9 pp., p. 3. Dr. Apfelbaum, who was head of internal medicine at Czyste, considered that Schrempf was able and energetic but totally devoid of compassion; "He believed in typical rigid German methods of punishment and applied them with an iron fist." He remained in medical control over the ghetto until replaced by Dr. Wilhelm Hagen early in 1941.

16. Anonymous, "Assimilationists and Neophytes at the Time of War-Operations and in the Closed Jewish Quarter," in Joseph Kermish (ed.), *To Live with Honor and Die with Honor! . . . Selected Documents from the Warsaw Ghetto Underground Archives "O.S."* [*"Oneg Shabbath"*] (Jerusalem: Yad Vashem, 1986), pp. xliv + 790; pp. 629–30.

17. Anonymous, "Assimilationists and Neophytes at the Time of War-Operations and in the Closed Jewish Quarter," in Kermish, *To Live with Honor*, pp. 629–30.

18. Dr. Malowist, in Kermish, *To Live with Honor*, pp. 629–30.

19. Bronislawa J. Wygodzka, interview, HCM 1–88, 8 January 1988, p. 21.

20. Jerusalem, YVA 03/2358, testimony of Dr. Stanislaw Waller, n.d., pp. 4–6.

21. Gurfinkiel-Glocerowa, "Szpital na Czystem," pp. 6–7.

22. Millie Eisen, interview, HCM 58–85, 20 June 1985, p. 3.

23. Raul Hilberg, Stanislaw Staron, and Josef Kermisz, (eds.), *The Warsaw Diary of Adam Czerniakow: Prelude to Doom*, trans. S. Staron and the staff of Yad Vashem (New York, Stein & Day, 1982), pp. viii + 420; p. 103, entry of 30 December 1939.

24. Hilberg et al., *The Warsaw Diary of Adam Czerniakow*, pp. 96–7.

25. Hilberg et al., *The Warsaw Diary of Adam Czerniakow*, p. 100, entry of 17 December 1939.

26. Hilberg et al., *The Warsaw Diary of Adam Czerniakow*, p. 119, entry of 20 February 1940.

27. Hilberg et al., *The Warsaw Diary of Adam Czerniakow*, p. 101, entry of 19 December 1939.

28. Balin, interview, HCM 7–83, pp. 10–11.

29. Gurfinkiel-Glocerowa, "Szpital na Czystem," pp. 10–11.

30. Isaiah Trunk, "Epidemics and Mortality in the Warsaw Ghetto, 1939–1942," *YIVO Annual of Jewish Social Science* 8: 82–122, 1953; p. 101.

31. Hilberg et al., *The Warsaw Diary of Adam Czerniakow*, p. 146, entry of 6 May 1940.

32. Fenigstein, *The Holocaust and I*, p. iv.

33. Balin, interview, HCM 7–83, 16 May 1983, p. 8.

34. Balin, interview, HCM 7–83, 16 May 1983, p. 31.

35. Anonymous, "[Special Schools]," in Kermish, *To Live with Honor*, p. 516.

36. Tadeusz Stabholz, interview, HCM 26–82, 4 December 1982, 46 pp., p. 12.

37. Fenigstein, interview, HCM 3–82, 21 January 1982, p. 7.

38. Frank Stiffel, *The Tale of the Ring: A Kaddish* (Toronto, New York, London, Sydney, and Auckland: Bantam Books, 1985), p. 348; p. 56.

39. Hilberg et al., *The Warsaw Diary of Adam Czerniakow*, p. 146, entry of 6 May 1940.

40. Jacob Sloan (ed.), *Notes From the Warsaw Ghetto: The Journal of Emmanuel Ringelblum* (New York: Schocken Books, 1974), pp. xxvii + 369; p. 107.

41. Sloan, *The Journal of Emmanuel Ringelblum*, pp. 86–87.

42. Sloan, *The Journal of Emmanuel Ringelblum*, p. 107.

43. Hilberg et al., *The Warsaw Diary of Adam Czerniakow*, p. 203, entry of 30 September 1940.

44. Hilberg et al., *The Warsaw Diary of Adam Czerniakow*, p. 204, entry of 3 October 1940.

45. Hilberg et al., *The Warsaw Diary of Adam Czerniakow*, p. 207, entry of 15 October 1940.

46. Hilberg et al., *The Warsaw Diary of Adam Czerniakow*, p. 207, entry of 14 October 1940.

47. Hilberg et al., *The Warsaw Diary of Adam Czerniakow*, p. 222n.

48. Tadeusz Stabholz, interview, HCM 26–82, 4 December 1982, p. 13.

49. Gurfinkiel-Glocerowa, "Szpital na Czystem," pp. 14–15.

50. Marek Balin, interview, HCM 7–83, p. 8; Tadeusz Stabholz, interview, HCM 26–82, p. 11.

51. Bernard Goldstein, *The Stars Bear Witness*, trans. Leonard Shatzkin (New York: Viking Press, 1949), p. 295; p. 65.

52. The main hospital at Leszno 1, which could contain about 200 patients under reasonable conditions, held 600 in 1942: Jerusalem, YVA 03/441, testimony of Marek Balin, "Selekcja w szpitalu."

53. Fenigstein, *The Holocaust and I*, p. xvi.

54. David Wdowinski, *And We Are Not Saved* (New York: Philosophical Library, 1985), p. 63.

55. The *Umschlagplatz* was a railway freight loading area just at the edge of the ghetto; from here, trains left regularly from 22 July 1942, for many weeks, taking the ghetto inhabitants to their deaths at Treblinka and other camps.

56. Fenigstein, interview, HCM 11–82, 31 March 1982, p. 3.

57. Fenigstein, *The Holocaust and I*, p. xvi.

58. Noemi Makowerowa (ed.), *Henryk Makower: Pamietnik z getta warszawskiego, pazdziernik 1940–styczen 1943* (Wrocław, Warszawa, Kraków, Gdansk, and Lodż: Zakład Narodowy im. Ossolinskich Wydawnictwo, 1987), p. 213; p. 112.

59. Hilberg et al., *The Warsaw Diary of Adam Czerniakow*, p. 102, entry for 24 December 1939.

60. Gurfinkiel-Glocerowa, "Szpital na Czystem," p. 18.

61. These street addresses are derived from several sources, particularly Louis Falstein (ed.), *The Martyrdom of Jewish Physicians in Poland* (New York: Exposition Press, 1963), especially pp. 113–17, 197–99, and 227–30. See also Henry Fenigstein, *The Warsaw Jewish Hospital during the Nazi Regime* (Frankfurt: Buchdruckerei Joh. Wagner & Sohne, 1948), 20 pp. Exactly what portion of the hospital activities was carried out at each location changed

from time to time and is difficult to determine with certainty; moreover, some sections changed locations. Undoubtedly some have not been mentioned here because the archival material is incomplete; this general problem characterizes all studies of this time and place.

62. Jerzy Winkler, "The Ghetto Combatting Economic Servitude," in Kermish, *To Live with Honor*, p. 581.

63. Anonymous, "Jewish Social Self-Help, Municipal Care-Taking Committee Warsaw: Report on the Activities of TOPOROL, first semi-period, 1st December 1940–31st May 1941," in Kermish, *To Live with Honor*, p. 525.

64. Tadeusz Stabholz, interview, HCM 26–82, p. 13.

65. Trunk, "Epidemics and Mortality," p. 101.

66. Sloan, *Journal of Emmanuel Ringelblum*, p. 194.

67. Hilberg et al., *The Warsaw Diary of Adam Czerniakow*, p. 288, entry for 14 October 1941.

68. Stabholz, interview, HCM 26–82, p. 20.

69. Jerusalem, YVA 033/1558 E 104-4-7, testimony of Dr. Emil Apfelbaum, head of the Department of Medicine, Czyste Hospital, during the war years, trans. Martha Osnos and Robert Osnos.

70. Trunk, "Epidemics and Mortality," p. 102.

71. Sloan, *Journal of Emmanuel Ringelblum*, p. 128.

72. Piszczek, interview, HCM 2–88, p. 9.

73. Balin, interview, HCM 7–83, p. 32.

74. Borman, interview, HCM 23–82, p. 12.

75. Sloan, *Journal of Emmanuel Ringelblum*, p. 142.

76. Isaiah Trunk, *Judenrat: The Jewish Councils in Eastern Europe Under Nazi Occupation* (New York: Macmillan Co., 1972), pp. xxxv+664; p. 161. Trunk is citing the Ringelblum Archive.

77. Trunk, "Epidemics and Mortality," p. 103.

78. Fenigstein, interview, HCM 11–82, p. 2.

79. Fenigstein, *The Holocaust and I*, p. xvii.

80. Hilberg et al., *The Warsaw Diary of Adam Czerniakow*, p. 330, entry of 25 February 1942.

81. Hilberg et al., *The Warsaw Diary of Adam Czerniakow*, p. 106, entry of 9 January 1940.

82. Hilberg et al., *The Warsaw Diary of Adam Czerniakow*, p. 123, entry of 2 March 1940.

83. Hilberg et al., *The Warsaw Diary of Adam Czerniakow*, pp. 130, 259.

84. Hilberg et al., *The Warsaw Diary of Adam Czerniakow*, p. 116, entry of 8 February 1940.

85. Hilberg et al., *The Warsaw Diary of Adam Czerniakow*, p. 164, entry of 21 June 1940.

86. Hilberg et al., *The Warsaw Diary of Adam Czerniakow*, p. 165, entry of 24 June 1940.

87. Hilberg et al., *The Warsaw Diary of Adam Czerniakow*, p. 169, entry of 1 July 1940.

88. Hilberg et al., *The Warsaw Diary of Adam Czerniakow*, p. 171, entry of 7 July 1940.

89. Hilberg et al., *The Warsaw Diary of Adam Czerniakow*, p. 258, entry of 18 July 1941.

90. Hilberg et al., *The Warsaw Diary of Adam Czerniakow*, p. 300, entry of 18 November 1941.

91. Trunk, "Epidemics and Mortality," pp. 103–04.

92. Ludwig Stabholz, interview, HCM 5–87, pp. 25–26.

93. Fenigstein, *The Holocaust and I*, p. xvii.

94. Trunk, "Epidemics and Mortality," p. 103.

95. Stanislaw Adler, *In the Warsaw Ghetto, 1940–1943: An Account of a Witness* (Jerusalem: Yad Vashem, 1982), pp. xviii + 334; p. 139.

96. Trunk, *Judenrat*, p. 160.

97. Vladka Meed, trans. Steven Meed, *On Both Sides of the Wall: Memoirs from the Warsaw Ghetto* (New York: Holocaust Library, 1979), p. 276; p. 58.

98. Fenigstein, *The Holocaust and I*, p. 143.

99. Fenigstein, *The Holocaust and I*, p. xxvii.

100. Gurfinkiel-Glocerowa, "Szpital na Czystem," pp. 16–17.

101. Fenigstein, *The Holocaust and I*, pp. xl–xlii.

102. Wdowinski, *And We Are Not Saved*, pp. xxi + 222, illust.; Henryk Fenigstein, *Warshewer Yidisher Shpitol heisn Nazi Rezhim* (Frankfurt-am-Main: Buchdruckerei Joh. Wagner & Sohne, 1948), p. 20; Fenigstein, *The Holocaust and I*, pp. 521 + xlii; and Gurfinkiel-Glocerowa, "Szpital na Czystem."

103. Hanna Hirszfeldowna (ed.), *The Story of One Life*, from *Historia Jednego Zycia by Ludwig Hirszfeld*, trans. F. R. Camp and F. R. Ellis (Fort Knox, KY: Blood Transfusion Division, United States Army Medical Research Laboratory, n.d.), p. 368.

104. Kermish, *To Live with Honor*.

105. In particular, all the Fenigstein interviews (Henry Fenigstein, interview, HCM 3–82, Toronto Ontario, 21 January 1982, 29 pp.; Fenigstein, interview, HCM 11–82, 31 March 1982, 16 pp.; and Fenigstein, interview, HCM 17–82, 28 June 1982, 19 pp.). Also Marek Balin, interview, HCM 7–83, 16 May 1983, 46 pp.; Tadeusz Stabholz, interview, HCM 26–82, Cleveland, Ohio, 4 December 1982, 46 pp.; Ludwig Stabholz, interview, HCM 5–87, Tel Aviv, Israel, 11 June 1987, 33 pp.; Irena Piszczek, interview, HCM 2–88, Montreal, PQ, 23 June 1986, 18 pp.; Bronislaw Wisniewski, interview, HCM 2–89, New York City, 3 May 1989, 36 pp.; Kazimierz Zakrzewski, HCM 9-90, Warsaw, Poland, 2 November 1990, 27 pp.; and Karolina Karolowicz, HCM 10-90, Warsaw, Poland, 3 November 1990, 25 pp.

106. Abraham Lewin, *A Cup of Tears: A Diary of the Warsaw Ghetto* (London: Fontana/Collins, 1990), pp. xii + 308; p. 264, n. 117.

107. Lewin, *A Cup of Tears*, p. 289, n. 347.

108. Hilberg et al., *The Warsaw Diary of Adam Czerniakow*, p. 100n.

109. Fenigstein, *The Holocaust and I*, p. xxviii.

110. Gurfinkiel-Glocerowa, "Szpital na Czystem," p. 25.

111. Gurfinkiel-Glocerowa, "Szpital na Czystem," p. 26.

112. Gurfinkiel-Glocerowa, "Szpital na Czystem," p. 26.

113. Balin, interview, HCM 7–83, 16 May 1983, p. 16.

114. Re. Treblinka, see especially Alexander Donat (ed.), *The Death Camp Treblinka: A Documentary* (New York: Holocaust Library, 1979), p. 320; Raul Hilberg, *The Destruction of the European Jews* (New York and London: Holmes & Meier, 1985), pp. xii + 1274; Gitta Sereny, *Into that Darkness: An Examination of Conscience* (New York: Vintage Books, 1983), pp. 380 (based on extensive interviews with Frank Stangl, commandant at Treblinka, and others who were there as SS staff, Jewish prisoners, and others); and Aharon Weiss, "Categories of Camps—Their Character and Role in the Execution of the 'Final Solution of the Jewish Question'," in *The Nazi Concentration Camps: Structure and Aims: The Image of the Prisoner: The Jews in the Camps: Proceedings of The Fourth Yad Vashem International Historical Conference* (Jerusalem: Yad Vashem, 1984), pp. 115–33. The book by Steiner is useful though fictionalized in the sense that explicit details of conversation are offered as if fact: Jean-François Steiner, *Treblinka*, trans. Helen Weaver (New York: Simon and Schuster, 1967), pp. 415.

115. Balin, interview by Roland, HCM 7–83, p. 15.

116. Gurfinkiel-Glocerowa, "Szpital na Czystem," p. 39. Mrs. Gurfinkiel-Glocerowa identifies the administrator as Dr. [Henryk] Stabholc, but this must be a slip of memory, as Stabholc had not been in this position since the autumn of 1939 and had died of a surgical infection months before the deportations began.

117. Jerusalem, YVA 03/2358, testimony of Dr. Stanislaw Waller, n.d., p. 6.

118. Fenigstein, *The Holocaust and I*, p. xxx.

119. Wdowinski, *And We Are Not Saved*, p. 74.

120. Lewin, *A Cup of Tears*, p. 229: "On the first day of the Christmas holidays a few Jews were killed on Leszno and Smocza Streets because they were 'wandering around' on their own in the streets."

121. Lewin, *A Cup of Tears*, entry for 5 October 1942, p. 187.

122. Fenigstein, *The Holocaust and I*, p. xxxi.

123. *Likwidacja żydowskiej Warszawy*, trans. and cited in Lewin, *A Cup of Tears*, p. 289.

124. Trunk, *Judenrat*, p. 156.

125. Adina Blady Szwajger, *I Remember Nothing More: The Warsaw Children's Hospital and the Jewish Resistance*, trans. Tasja Darowska and Danusia Stok (New York: Pantheon Books, 1990), pp. xx + 184, illust., maps; p. 59.

126. Fenigstein, *The Holocaust and I*, p. xxxi.

127. Goldstein, *The Stars Bear Witness*, p. 156.

128. Fenigstein, *The Holocaust and I*, p. 158.

129. Gurfinkiel-Glocerowa, "Szpital na Czystem," p. 36.

130. Fenigstein, *The Holocaust and I*, p. 158.

131. Stabholz, interview, HCM 26–82, 4 December 1982, p. 28.

132. Fenigstein, *The Holocaust and I*, pp. 162–63.

133. Gurfinkiel-Glocerowa, "Szpital na Czystem," p. 37.

134. Lewin, *A Cup of Tears*, p. 192, entry for 20 October 1942.

135. Anonymous, "Social Data for November, 1942," in Kermish, *To Live with Honor*, p. 165.

136. Hirszfeldowna, *The Story of One Life*, pp. 278–79.

137. Gurfinkiel-Glocerowa, "Szpital na Czystem," pp. 40–41.

138. Wdowinski, *And We Are Not Saved*, p. 89.

139. Yisrael Gutman, *Jews of Warsaw, 1939–1943: Ghetto, Underground, Revolt,* trans. Ina Friedman (Bloomington and Indianapolis: Indiana University Press, 1989), p. 309.

140. Martin Gray, with Max Gallo, *For Those I Loved*, 2nd ed., trans. Anthony White (London: W. H. Allen, 1984), pp. xvi + 349; p. 199.

141. Toby Knobel Fluek, *Memories of My Life in a Polish Village, 1930–1949* (New York: Alfred A. Knopf, 1990), p. 110, illust.; p. 86.

142. Tadeusz Pankiewicz, *The Cracow Ghetto Pharmacy*, trans. Henry Tilles (New York: Holocaust Library, 1987), pp. xi + 155, illust.; pp. 74, 115–16.

143. Jack Eisner, *The Survivor*, ed. Irving A. Leitner (New York: Bantam Books, 1982), p. 263; pp. 130–31.

144. Fenigstein, *The Holocaust and I*, pp. 164–65.

145. Gurfinkiel-Glocerowa, "Szpital na Czystem," p. 45.

146. Jerusalem, Yad Vashem Archives 03/2360, Testimony of Judyta Braude, Tel Aviv, 4 July 1962, 14 pp., p. 3.

147. Jerusalem, Yad Vashem Archives 03/2360, Braude, p. 3.

148. Hilberg et al., *The Warsaw Diary of Adam Czerniakow*, p. 177, entry of 24 July 1940.

149. AAJJDC AR3344, file 840, Medical Care: TOZ, Warsaw, 1933–42, unattributed "Report of the Work of the TOZ from September 1, 1939 to June 1940, p. 4.

150. Myron Winick (ed.), *Hunger Disease: Studies by the Jewish Physicians in the Warsaw Ghetto*, trans. Martha Osnos (New York, Chichester, Brisbane, and Toronto: John Wiley & Sons, 1979), pp. xiv + 261; p. 60.

151. Hirszfeldowna, *The Story of One Life*, p. 248.

152. Szwajger, *I Remember Nothing More*, p. 19.

153. Goldstein, *The Stars Bear Witness*, p. 156.

154. This paragraph is derived chiefly from Goldstein, *The Stars Bear Witness*, p. 156.

155. Adler, *In the Warsaw Ghetto*, p. 63.

156. Hilberg et al., *The Warsaw Diary of Adam Czerniakow*, p. 234, entry of 12 May 1941.

157. Makowerowa, *Henryk Makower*, p. [3].

158. Meed, *On Both Sides of the Wall*, p. 110.

159. Pernal, interview, HCM 4–87, 19 May 1987, p. 5.

160. Trunk, "Epidemics and Mortality," p. 104.

161. Pernal, interview, HCM 4–87, p. 29.

162. Trunk, "Epidemics and Mortality," p. 104.

163. A. Favel, *Faithful Unto Death: The Story of Arthur Zygielbaum* (Montreal: Zygielbaum Branch Workmen's Circle, 1980), p. 68. According to L. Stabholz, anesthetics were available at Czyste; see L. Stabholz, interview, HCM 5–87, Tel Aviv, Israel, 11 June 1987, p. 24. Thus the physicians were preserved from having to use the rough and ready techniques necessarily followed in some guerrilla hospitals, where there were no anesthetics of any kind. One interviewee recalls her father, a surgeon, literally punching surgical patients to knock them unconscious so that surgery could be performed: see Miriam Brysk, interview, HCM 5–84, 31 May 1984, p. 15.

164. Anonymous, "A Visit to the Most Unfortunate of Children," in Kermish, *To Live with Honor*, p. 401.

165. Pernal, interview, HCM 4–87, p. 29.

166. Pernal, interview, HCM 4–87, p. 16; Anna Braude-Heller et al., in Winick, *Hunger Disease*.

167. Pernal, interview, HCM 4–87, p. 30.

168. Braude-Heller et al., in Winick, *Hunger Disease*, p. 52.

169. Pernal, interview, HCM 4–87, p. 31.

170. Pernal, interview, HCM 4–87, pp. 27–29.

171. Eisen, interview, HCM 58–85, 20 June 1985, pp. 21–22.

172. AAJJDC, AR3344, file 811, Publicity: General, (May) 1937–1942, 1944; from the American labor newspaper published in Yiddish, *Unser Tsait*, April 1942.

173. Chaim Lazar, *Muranowska 7: The Warsaw Ghetto Uprising*, trans. Yosef Shachter (Tel Aviv: Massada-P.E.C. Press Ltd., 1966), p. 341; p. 75.

174. Lazar, *Muranowska 7*, p. 85.

175. Lazar, *Muranowska 7*, p. 79.

Chapter 6

1. Dr. Emil Apfelbaum-Kowalski, in Myron Winick (ed.), *Hunger Disease: Studies by the Jewish Physicians in the Warsaw Ghetto*, trans. Martha Osnos (New York, Chichester, Brisbane, and Toronto: John Wiley & Sons, 1979), pp. xiv + 261; p. 127.

2. Mordecai Lenski, "Problems of Disease in the Warsaw Ghetto," *Yad Vashem Studies* 3: 283–93, 1975; p. 284.

3. Wilhelm Hagen, "Krieg, Hunger und Pestilenz in Warschau, 1939–1943," *Gesundheitswesen und Desinfektion* 8: 115–28; 9: 129–43, 1973; p. 136.

4. Winick, *Hunger Disease*, p. 35.

5. Eugenia Pernal, interview, HCM 4–87, 19 May 1987, p. 36.

6. Abraham Lewin, *A Cup of Tears: A Diary of the Warsaw Ghetto* (London: Fontana/Collins, 1990), pp. xii + 308; p. 276, n. 218.

7. Frank Stiffel, *The Tale of the Ring: A Kaddish* (Toronto, New York, London, Sydney, and Auckland: Bantam Books, 1985), p. 348; p. 52.

8. Translated by David Chazen; cited in Philip Friedman (ed.), *Martyrs and Fighters: The Epic of the Warsaw Ghetto* (New York: Frederick A. Praeger, 1954), p. 324; p. 73.

9. Lucy S. Dawidowicz, *The War Against the Jews, 1933–1945* (Toronto and New York: Bantam Books, 1986), pp. xxxx + 466; p. 214.

10. Karolina Borman, interview, HCM 3–84, 28 March 1984, pp. 36–37.

11. Halina Birenbaum, *Hope Is the Last to Die: A Personal Documentation of Nazi Terror*, trans. David Welsh (New York, Twayne Publishers, 1971), pp. iv + 246; p. 8.

12. Adam Starkopf, *There Is Always Time to Die*, ed. Gertrude Hirschler (New York: Holocaust Library, 1981), p. 73.

13. David Wdowinski, *And We Are Not Saved* (New York: Philosophical Library, 1985), pp. xxi + 222; p. 42.

14. Bronislaw Wisniewski, interview, HCM 2–89, 3 May 1989, p. 14.

15. Raul Hilberg, Stanislaw Staron, and Josef Kermisz (eds.), *The Warsaw Diary of Adam Czerniakow: Prelude to Doom*, trans. S. Staron and the staff of Yad Vashem (New York: Stein and Day, 1982), pp. viii + 420; p. 243.

16. Jacob Sloan, *Notes from the Warsaw Ghetto: The Journal of Emmanuel Ringelblum* (New York: Schocken Books, 1974), p. 130.

17. Ludwig Stabholz, interview, HCM 5–87, Tel Aviv, Israel, 11 June 1987, p. 30.

18. Sloan, *The Journal of Emmanuel Ringelblum*, pp. 204-05.

19. Starkopf, *Always Time to Die*, p. 74.

20. Sloan, *The Journal of Emmanuel Ringelblum*, p. 138.

21. Anonymous, "Snapshots from the Warsaw Ghetto," 21 April 1941, in Joseph Kermish (ed.), *To Live with Honor and Die with Honor! . . . Selected Documents from the Warsaw Ghetto Underground Archives "O.S."* [*"Oneg Shabbath"*] (Jerusalem: Yad Vashem, 1986), pp. xliv + 790; p. 78.

22. Stiffel, *The Tale of the Ring*, p. 54.

23. Jerusalem, Yad Vashem Archives (hereafter, YVA), 033/1558 E 104-4-7, testimony of Dr. Emil Apfelbaum, former head of the department of medicine, Czyste Hospital, p. 5. (Statement made in 1945; translated by Martha Osnos and Robert Osnos.)

24. Howard Roiter, *Voices from the Holocaust* (New York: William-Frederick Press, 1975), p. 221; p. 96.

25. Roiter, *Voices from the Holocaust*, p. 99.

26. Stanislaw Adler, *In the Warsaw Ghetto, 1940–1943: An Account of a Witness* (Jerusalem: Yad Vashem, 1982), p. 123.

27. Wdowinski, *And We Are Not Saved*, pp. 39–40.

28. Adler, *In the Warsaw Ghetto*, p. 42.

29. Henry Shoskes [Henryk Szoszkies], *No Traveler Returns* (Garden City, NY: Doubleday, Doran & Co., 1945), pp. xiii + 267; p. 55.

30. Hilberg et al., *The Warsaw Diary of Adam Czerniakow*, p. 300, entry for 19 November 1941.

31. Hilberg et al., *The Warsaw Diary of Adam Czerniakow*, pp. 261–62, entry for 25 July 1941.

32. Adler, *In the Warsaw Ghetto*, p. 122.

33. Lewin, *A Cup of Tears*, pp. 93–94, entry for 23 May 1942.

34. New York, Archives of the American Jewish Joint Distribution Committee (here-

after, AAJJDC), AR3344, file 840, Medical Care: TOZ, Warsaw, 1933–1942; letter, Dr. L. Wulman to Mrs. Henrietta Buchman, AJDC, New York, 6 November 1941, p. 2.

35. Adler, *In the Warsaw Ghetto*, pp. 64–65.

36. Adler, *In the Warsaw Ghetto*, p. 130.

37. Isaiah Trunk, "Epidemics and Mortality in the Warsaw Ghetto, 1939–1942," *YIVO Annual of Jewish Social Science* 8: 82–122, 1953; p. 91.

38. Joanna K. M. Hanson, *The Civilian Population and the Warsaw Uprising of 1944* (Cambridge, London, New York, New Rochelle, Melbourne, and Sydney: Cambridge University Press, 1982), pp. xiii + 345; p. 27.

39. AAJJDC AR3344, file 798, Report, 1940 (Apr.–Aug.); from Minutes of a Meeting of the AJDC Committee on Poland and Eastern Europe, 11 April 1940, p. 1.

40. AAJJDC AR3344, file 796, Reports, 1939 (Oct.–Dec.); record of a telephone conversation with Morris Troper, Geneva, 6 November 1939.

41. Hanson, *The Civilian Population*, p. 27.

42. Sloan, *The Journal of Emmanuel Ringelblum*, p. 41.

43. Hanson, *The Civilian Population*, p. 27.

44. Zofia S. Kubar, *Double Identity: A Memoir* (New York: Hill and Wang, 1989), p. 209; p. 171.

45. Hagen, "Krieg, Hunger und Pestilenz," p. 142.

46. Hanson, *The Civilian Population*, p. 35.

47. Figures from *Okupacja i ruch oporu w dzienniku Hansa Franka, 1939–1945*, Vol. 1 (Warsaw, 1972), cited in Yisrael Gutman, *Jews of Warsaw, 1939–1943: Ghetto, Underground, Revolt*, trans. Ina Friedman (Bloomington and Indianapolis: Indiana University Press, 1989), pp. xxi + 487; p. 66; Dr. Wilhelm Hagen states that the official ration for Jews was 200 calories; see his "Krieg, Hunger und Pestilenz," p. 119.

48. Gutman, *Jews of Warsaw*, p. 66.

49. Gutman, *Jews of Warsaw*, p. 109.

50. Gutman, *Jews of Warsaw*, pp. 94–95. The exact figures are 36 kilograms of bread (at 18.15 zloty/kilogram), for 653.40 zloty; 2 kilograms groats (25 zloty/kilogram), 50.00 zloty; 48 kilograms of potatoes (6.75 zloty/kilogram), 324.00 zloty; and 1.2 kilograms of fats (72.30 zloty/kilogram), 86.76 zloty.

51. Hanson, *The Civilian Population*, pp. 21–22; she shows that the cost of feeding a family of four rose from 61.27 zloty in 1938 to 1568 zloty in 1941 in gentile Warsaw; in the same period, salaries doubled from 150 to 300 zloty.

52. Gutman, *Jews of Warsaw*, p. 72. Food prices were higher in the ghetto because the profits of the black marketeers took an even larger bite than they did outside the ghetto.

53. J. H. Bolton, "Personal Experiences as a Prisoner of War, with Special Reference to Dietetics," in H. L. Tidy (ed.), *Inter-Allied Conferences on War Medicine, 1942–1945* (New York: Staples Press Ltd., 1947), p. 370.

54. A. Allen Goldbloom, Abraham Lieberson, and Charles D. Rosen, "Malnutrition and Vitamin Deficiency in Recently Released Prisoners of War," *American Journal of Digestive Diseases* 15: 115–18, 1948; p. 115.

55. Deborah Darlene Buffton, "The Ritual of Surrender: Northern France Under Two Occupations, 1914–1918/1940–1944" (Ph.D. thesis, University of Wisconsin at Madison, 1987), p. 85.

56. Hanson, *The Civilian Population*, p. 27. Hagen, "Krieg, Hunger und Pestilenz," p. 125. Hagen wrote this article 30 years after the events, so it must be seen as possibly self-serving; nevertheless, in the ghetto he was considered to be one of the better Germans.

57. Hilberg et al., *The Warsaw Diary of Adam Czerniakow*, p. 269.

58. Christopher R. Browning, "Nazi Ghettoization Policy in Poland: 1939–41," *Central European History* 19: 343–68, 1986; p. 365.

59. Marie "Missie" Vassiltchikov, *The Berlin Diaries, 1940–1945* (London: Chatto & Windus, 1985), pp. xii + 320; p. 23.

60. Lewin, *A Cup of Tears*, p. 127.

61. [Yehoshua Perle], "4580," in Kermish, *To Live with Honor*, p. 666.

62. Trunk, "Epidemics and Mortality," p. 93.

63. Trunk, "Epidemics and Mortality," p. 93; Lenski provides similar if slightly less explicit estimates, suggesting a figure of 800 calories for refugees and perhaps 1500 for the middle class (Lenski, "Problems of Disease," p. 287).

64. Julian Fliederbaum, cited in Winick, *Hunger Disease*, p. 13.

65. Trunk, "Epidemics and Mortality," p. 121.

66. Trunk, "Epidemics and Mortality," p. 120.

67. AAJJDC AR3344, file 840, Medical Care: TOZ, Warsaw, 1933–1942; from "Report of the Work of the TOZ, Sept. 1, 1939 to June 1940," p. 9.

68. Hanna Krall, *Shielding the Flame: An Intimate Conversation with Dr. Marek Edelman, the Last Surviving Leader of the Warsaw Ghetto Uprising*, trans. Joanna Stasinska and Lawrence Weschler (New York: Henry Holt and Co., 1986), pp. xiii + 124; pp. 16–17.

69. Gutman, *Jews of Warsaw*, pp. 85–86.

70. Gutman, *Jews of Warsaw*, p. 101.

71. Trunk, "Epidemics and Mortality," p. 93.

72. AAJJDC AR3344, file 811, Publicity: General, (May) 1937–1942, 1944; *Unser Tsait*, April 1942.

73. Wisniewski, interview, HCM 2–89, 3 May 1989, p. 14.

74. Dawidowicz, *The War Against the Jews*, p. 250.

75. Rabbi Gelertner, Central Refugee Committee, 1941, in Kermish, *To Live with Honor*, p. 415.

76. Rabbi Gelertner, in Kermish, *To Live with Honor*, p. 416.

77. Rabbi Gelertner, in Kermish, *To Live with Honor*, p. 417.

78. AAJJDC AR3344, file 796, Reports, 1939 (Oct.–Dec.); memorandum, Mr. Borenstein, Warsaw, to AJDC, New York, 22 October 1939.

79. AAJJDC AR3344, file 796, Reports, 1939 (Oct.–Dec.); letter David Guzik and L. Neustadt, AJDC, Warsaw, to AJDC Angers, 12 November 1939.

80. AAJJDC AR3344, file 796, Reports, 1939 (Oct.–Dec.); draft of monthly budget, December 1939.

81. AAJJDC AR3344, file 840, Medical Care: TOZ, Warsaw, 1933–1942; from "Report of Work of the TOZ, Sept. 1, 1939 to June 1940," p. 10.

82. AAJJDC AR3344, file 799, Report 1940 (Sept.–Dec.); from "Explanations to the Report Lists about the Activities of the American Joint Distribution Committee, Warsaw-Cracow," 1 January to 30 September 1940.

83. AAJJDC AR3344, file 797, Reports, 1940 (Jan.–Mar.); from memorandum "Activities of the JDC After the Outbreak of the War," Warsaw, 8 February 1940, unsigned, p. 1.

84. AAJJDC AR3344, file 799, Report 1940 (Sept.–Dec.); from "Explanations to the Report Lists About the Activities of the American Joint Distribution Committee, Warsaw-Cracow," 1 January to 30 September 1940, unsigned, p. 1.

85. Anonymous, "The Jewish Quarter in Warsaw," in Kermish, *To Live with Honor*, p. 146.

86. Hanson, *The Civilian Population*, p. 34.

87. Hilberg et al., *The Warsaw Diary of Adam Czerniakow*, pp. 250 and 255, entries for 20 June and 4 July 1941.

88. Hilberg et al., *The Warsaw Diary of Adam Czerniakow*, p. 271, entry for 23 August 1941.

89. Isaiah Trunk, *Judenrat: The Jewish Councils in Eastern Europe Under Nazi Occupation* (New York: The Macmillan Co., 1972), pp. xxxv + 664; p. 146.

90. [Peretz Opoczynski], "Warsaw Ghetto Chronicle—September 1942," entry for 14 September, in Kermish, *To Live with Honor*, p. 107.

91. YVA 033/1558 E 104-4-7, Apfelbaum, p. 7.

92. Anonymous, "Scenes from a Children's Hospital," Document ARI/PH/3-2-3, 20.3.1941, in Kermish, *To Live with Honor*, p. 404.

93. Anonymous, "Scenes from a Children's Hospital," in Kermish, *To Live with Honor*, p. 405.

94. Anonymous, "Jewish Welfare Society," Document ARI/LXV, in Kermish, *To Live with Honor*, p. 345.

95. Hilberg et al., *The Warsaw Diary of Adam Czerniakow*, p. 293, entry of 27 October 1941.

96. Lewin, *A Cup of Tears*, p. 91.

97. For a synoptic account of many of these efforts, see "The Profile of the Jewish child," in Kermish, *To Live with Honor*, pp. 371–91.

98. Gutman, *Jews of Warsaw*, p. 125.

99. AAJJDC AR3344, file 799, Report 1940 (Sept.–Dec.); letter from O. I. Hirsch and P. I. Meyerheim, *Reichsvereinigung der Juden in Deutschland*, to AJDC, 11 October 1940. They report that the expenses of the AJDC in Warsaw for September 1940 were $20,000, and the cost of passages was $27,000.

100. AAJJDC AR3344, file 797, Reports, 1940 (Jan.–Mar.); memorandum of discussions between Morris C. Troper, chairman of AJDC, Europe, and Dr. Ludwick Rajchman, representative of the Polish government for Medical Aid and Health, Paris, 26 January 1940.

101. AAJJDC AR3344, file 887, Relief Supplies: 1937, 1940–1944; "Draft Memorandum to be Presented at Administration Committee Meeting, 12/16/40," Alfred Jaretzki, Jr., 13 December 1940.

102. AAJJDC AR3344, file 817, Reports: Commission for Polish Relief (CPR), 1939–1941; quote from CPR News Bulletin No. 1, 20 October 1939; the president of CPR was Henry Noble MacCracken, president, Vassar College; see letter, MacCracken to William J. Donavan, 1 November 1939.

103. AAJJDC AR3344, file 817, Reports: Commission for Polish Relief (CPR), 1939–1941; News Release, Commission for Polish Relief, New York, 15 June 1940, p. 3.

104. AAJJDC AR3344, file 817, Reports: Commission for Polish Relief (CPR), 1939–1941; letter, Maurice Pate, CPR, to Paul Baerwald, chairman, AJDC, 17 September 1940.

105. AAJJDC AR3344, file 817, Reports: Commission for Polish Relief (CPR), 1939–1941; extract of letter from C. P. Murray, Berlin, to Maurice Pate, CPR, New York, 2 August 1940. This was verified by an American Red Cross official who also witnessed personally the arrival of Red Cross supplies at Cracow and their subsequent distribution "without regard to race, creed or politics"; see AAJJDC AR3344, file 798, Report, 1940 (Apr.–Aug.); letter, James T. Nicholson to Ernest J. Swift, 26 April 1940.

106. AAJJDC AR3344, file 817, Reports: Commission for Polish Relief (CPR), 1939–1941; letter from Maurice Pate and Chauncey McCormick, CPR, to the directors of the *Rada Polonii*, 19 December 1940.

107. Hilberg et al., *The Warsaw Diary of Adam Czerniakow*, pp. 237–38, entry of 19 May 1941. There are 100 groszy in one zloty.

108. Hilberg et al., *The Warsaw Diary of Adam Czerniakow*, p. 321, entry of 2 February 1942.

109. Browning, "Nazi Ghettoization Policy," p. 358.

110. Cited in Gutman, *Jews of Warsaw*, p. 67.

111. In his Introduction to Winick, *Hunger Disease*, p. 4.

112. Hilberg et al., *The Warsaw Diary of Adam Czerniakow*, p. 248.

113. Sloan, *The Journal of Emmanuel Ringelblum*, p. 149.

114. Hagen, "Krieg, Hunger und Pestilenz," p. 136.

115. Hagen, "Krieg, Hunger und Pestilenz," p. 121.

116. AAJJDC AR3344, file 887, Relief Supplies: 1937, 1940–1944; memorandum, Moses A. Leavitt to Louis Rosner, 16 July 1941.

117. Sloan, *The Journal of Emmanuel Ringelblum*, p. 137.

118. Sloan, *The Journal of Emmanuel Ringelblum*, p. 172.

119. Hilberg et al., *The Warsaw Diary of Adam Czerniakow*, p. 330, entry for 26 February 1942.

120. Sloan, *The Journal of Emmanuel Ringelblum*, p. 137.

121. Wdowinski, *We are not Saved*, p. 40.

122. Sloan, *The Journal of Emmanuel Ringelblum*, p. 216.

123. Roiter, *Voices from the Holocaust*, p. 90.

124. Sloan, *The Journal of Emmanuel Ringelblum*, p. 187.

125. Dawidowicz, *The War Against the Jews*, p. 210.

126. Gutman, *Jews of Warsaw*, pp. 140–41.

127. Gutman, *Jews of Warsaw*, p. 233.

128. Gutman, *Jews of Warsaw*, p. 286; although the text reads December 1943, it is obvious from the context that 1942 was intended.

129. See Harrison E. Salisbury, *The 900 Days: The Siege of Leningrad* (New York and Evanston, IL: Harper & Row, Publishers, 1969), pp. ix + 635, illust.; pp. 452–53, 474–81.

130. Egon Tramer, MD, interview, HCM 24–85, Winnipeg Manitoba, 9 March 1985, p. 8.

131. Trunk, "Epidemics and Mortality," p. 96.

132. Hilberg et al., *The Warsaw Diary of Adam Czerniakow*, p. 328, entry for 20 February 1942.

133. Pernal, interview, HCM 4–87, 19 May 1987, p. 33.

134. Hanna Hirszfeldowna (ed.), *The Story of One Life, from "Historia Jednego Zycia" by Ludwig Hirszfeld*, trans. F. R. Camp and F. R. Ellis (Fort Knox, KY: Blood Transfusion Division, United States Army Medical Research Laboratory, n.d.), p. 368; p. 238.

135. Adler, *In the Warsaw Ghetto*, pp. 257–58.

136. Trunk, *Judenrat*, p. 146.

137. Reay Tannahill, *Flesh and Blood: A History of the Cannibal Complex* (London: Hamish Hamilton, 1975), pp. ix + 209; p. 173.

138. Jonas Turkow, *Azoy iz es Geven* (Buenos Aires: CFPJ, 1948), p. 129.

139. Turkow, *Azoy iz es Geven*, pp. 190–91; cited in Philip Friedman (ed.), *Martyrs and Fighters: The Epic of the Warsaw Ghetto* (New York: Frederick A. Praeger, 1954), p. 324; p. 63.

140. E. P. Kulawiec (ed. and trans.), *The Warsaw Ghetto Memoirs of Janusz Korczak* (Washington, DC: University Press of America, 1979), pp. xvii + 127; p. 39.

141. Lewin, *A Cup of Tears:*, pp. 214–15.

142. "Because of the unique population that was available for study, observations could be made which had never been made before and some of which have never been made since." Myron Winick, "Preface," in Winick, *Hunger Disease*, p. ix; an earlier book summarized the project, its findings, and the researchers: Leonard Tushnet, *The Uses of Adversity* (New York: Thomas Yoseloff, 1966), pp. 108.

143. Emil Apfelbaum (ed.), *Maladie de Famine: Recherches Cliniques sur la Famine Exécutées dans la Ghetto de Varsovie en 1942* (Warsaw: American Joint Distribution Committee, 1946), p. 264.

144. Emil Apfelbaum (ed.), *Choroba Glodowa: Badania Kliniczne Nad Glodem Wykonane w Getcie Warszawskim z Roku 1942* (Warsaw: American Joint Distribution Committee, 1946), p. 265.

145. Winick, *Hunger Disease*, 1979.

146. Henry Fenigstein, as Told to Saundra Collis, *The Holocaust and I: Memoirs of a Survivor* (Toronto: Unpublished MS, 1990), pp. 521+xlii; p. 134.

147. Izrael Milejkowski, in Introduction, Winick, *Hunger Disease*, p. 4.

148. YVA 033/1558 E 104-4-7, Apfelbaum, p. 6.

149. Ancel Keys, Josef Brozek, Austin Henschel, Olaf Mickelsen, and Henry Longstreet Taylor, *The Biology of Human Starvation* (Minneapolis: University of Minnesota Press, 1950), Vol. 1, pp. 1-766, illust.; vol. 2, pp. 767-1385.

150. These paragraphs are derived from Chapter One of *Hunger Disease*, by Dr. Julian Fliederbaum, Dr. Ari Heller, Dr. Kazimierz Zweibaum, and Jeanne Karchi, entitled "Clinical Aspects of Hunger Disease in Adults," pp. 13-36. This research has also been summarized by Lenski, "Problems of Disease," pp. 292-93.

151. Fliederbaum et al., in Winick, *Hunger Disease*, p. 14.

152. Michael Zylberberg, *A Warsaw Diary, 1939-1945* (London: Vallentine, Mitchell, 1969), p. 220; p. 72.

153. From Chapter Two of *Hunger Disease*, "Clinical Aspects of Hunger Disease in Children," by Drs. Anna Braude-Heller, Israel Rotbalsam, and Regina Elbinger, pp. 47-57.

154. This paragraph is based on a modern assessment of the ghetto research written by Michael Katz, in Winick, *Hunger Disease*, p. 67.

155. From Chapter Three of *Hunger Disease*, by Julian Fliederbaum, with the collaboration of Dr. Ari Heller, Dr. Kazimierz Zweibaum, Suzanne Szejnfinkel, Dr. Regina Elbinger, and Fajga Ferszt, "Metabolic Changes in Hunger Disease," pp. 71-114.

156. Robert Bernstein and Myron Winick in Winick, *Hunger Disease*, p. 116.

157. Fliederbaum et al., in *Hunger Disease*, p. 101.

158. Derived from Chapter Four of *Hunger Disease*, by Dr. Emil Apfelbaum-Kowalski with the collaboration of Dr. Ryszard Pakszwer, Jeanne Zarchi (medical student), Dr. Ari Heller, and Dr. Zdzisław Askanas, "Pathophysiology of the Circulatory System in Hunger Disease," p. 127-52.

159. Apfelbaum-Kowalski et al., *Hunger Disease*, p. 147.

160. Apfelbaum-Kowalski et al., *Hunger Disease*, p. 134.

161. See Chapter Six of *Hunger Disease*, by Dr. Szymon Fajgenblat, "Ocular Disturbances in Hunger Disease," pp. 199-202.

162. From Chapter Seven of Winick, *Hunger Disease*, by Dr. Joseph Stein with the collaboration of Dr. Henryk Fenigstein, "Pathological Anatomy of Hunger Disease," pp. 209-54.

163. Stein and Fenigstein, *Hunger Disease*, pp. 216-17.

164. Henry Fenigstein, interview, HCM 11-82, 31 March 1982, p. 2.

165. Stein and Fenigstein, *Hunger Disease*, pp. 209-10.

166. For example, Borman remembered being assigned to assist with autopsies on victims of starvation who were part of the research: see Borman, interview, HCM 23-82, p. 13.

167. Six cases are presented with full microscopic data; they are discussed in the French edition of Apfelbaum, *Maladie de Famine*, 1946, pp. 43-72, and in the Polish edition, *Choroba Glodowa*, 1946, pp. 42-67. For some reason, the editors of the English translation omitted this information.

168. Dr. Fenigstein was responsible for the macroscopic studies—descriptions, weights, etc.—of the body organs. Fenigstein, *The Holocaust and I*, p. xxvi.

169. Personal communication, H. Fenigstein to C. G. Roland, ALS, 8 February 1991.

170. Stein and Fenigstein, *Hunger Disease*, p. 218.

171. Stein and Fenigstein, *Hunger Disease*, p. 220.

172. Fenigstein, interview, HCM 3–82, 21 January 1982, p. 8.

173. Stein and Fenigstein, *Hunger Disease*, p. 222.

174. Stein and Fenigstein, *Hunger Disease*, p. 219.

175. Hilberg et al., *The Warsaw Diary of Adam Czerniakow*, p. 375, entry for 6 July 1942.

176. Izrael Milejkowski, in Introduction, *Hunger Disease*, p. 3.

177. Fenigstein, *The Holocaust and I*, p. 161. The chapter in *Hunger Disease* is Chapter Seven, "Pathological Anatomy of Hunger Disease," by Dr. Joseph Stein with the collaboration of Dr. Henryk Fenigstein. Mrs. Ala Fenigstein was killed in Majdanek on 3 November 1943.

178. Winick (ed.), *Hunger Disease*, p. 43.

179. AAJJDC AR3344, file 801, Report (Sept.) 1942–1943; letter from Herbert Katzki, secretary, AJDC Lisbon, to A. G. Brotman, London, 2 July 1943.

Chapter 7

1. J. Stanisławski, *McKay's English-Polish Polish-English Dictionary* (New York: Random House, 1988), pp. 463+416.

2. Trunk, for example, in his otherwise accurate and useful article, refers to "all typhus cases, including abdominal typhus, spotted typhus and others" (p. 119). But "abdominal typhus" is typhoid fever and "spotted typhus" is typhus. Isaiah Trunk, "Epidemics and Mortality in the Warsaw Ghetto, 1939–1942," *YIVO Annual of Jewish Social Science* 8: 82–122, 1953.

3. This confusion is made explicit in one memoir in which the author writes that his wife "pasted on our apartment door a crudely-lettered sign reading 'Fleckfieber'—the German term for typhoid fever." Adam Starkopf, *There Is Always Time to Die*, ed. Gertrude Hirschler (New York: Holocaust Library, 1981), p. 242; p. 71.

4. One of the survivors interviewed in connection with the research reported here, a nurse, referred regularly to typhoid fever in her interview, though it was evident from the context that she meant typhus. See Millie Eisen, interview, HCM 58–85, 20 June 1985, p. 11.

5. See, for example, the article by Dr. Wilhelm Hagen, "Krieg, Hunger und Pestilenz in Warschau, 1939–1943," *Gesundheitswesen und Desinfektion* 8: 115–28, 9: 129–43, 1973. One translator, reading Hagen's phrase "Typhus, Pocken, und Fleckfieber" (p. 115), rendered it as "typhus, smallpox, and spotted fever" when it should have been "typhoid fever, smallpox, and typhus."

6. Hans Zinsser, *Rats, Lice and History: Being a Study in Biography, which, after Twelve Preliminary Chapters Indispensable for the Preparation of the Lay Reader, Deals With the Life History of Typhus Fever. . . .* (Boston: Little, Brown, and Co., 1935), pp. xii+301; see p. 241.

7. See the Loeb Library volume *Hippocrates*, Vol. VI, translated by Paul Potter (Cambridge, MA: Harvard University Press, and London: William Heinemann Ltd., 1988), pp. 201–19; note that the index entry under "Typhus" reads "not the modern disease: E39, E40, E41, E42, E43," p. 339.

8. Ralph H. Major, *Classic Descriptions of Disease, With Biographical Sketches of the Authors* (Springfield, IL: Charles C. Thomas, 1959), pp. xxxii+679; p. 163.

9. Hieronymi Fracastorii, *De Contagione et Contagiosis Morbis et Eorum Curatione*, Libri III, trans. Wilmer Cave Wright (New York and London: G. P. Putnam's Sons, 1930), p. 103.

10. "Few women died of this disease, very few old men, almost no Jews, but many young people and children, and they were of the best families." Fracastorii, *De Contagione*, p. 103.

11. Major, *Classic Descriptions*, p. 165.

12. Major, *Classic Descriptions*, p. 169.

13. Major, *Classic Descriptions*, pp. 169–70.

14. James Lind, *An Essay on the Most Effectual Means of Preserving the Health of Seamen in the Royal Navy, and a Dissertation on Fevers and Infection* (1779), in Christopher Lloyd (ed.), *The Health of Seamen: Selections from the Works of Dr. James Lind, Sir Gilbert Blane, and Dr. Thomas Trotter* (London: Navy Records Society, 1965), p. 94.

15. Charles Nicolle, "Investigations on Typhus: Nobel Lecture," in *Nobel Lectures: Physiology or Medicine, 1922–1941* (Amsterdam: Elsevier Publishing Co., 1965), p. 181.

16. Wesley W. Spink, *Infectious Diseases: Prevention and Treatment in the Nineteenth and Twentieth Centuries* (Minneapolis: University of Minnesota Press, 1978), pp. 326–27.

17. Zinsser, *Rats, Lice and History*, p. 168.

18. E. P. Kulawiec (ed. and trans.), *The Warsaw Ghetto Memoirs of Janusz Korczak* (Washington, DC: University Press of America, 1979), p. 9.

19. The following description is derived chiefly from Zinsser, *Rats, Lice and History*, pp. 216ff.

20. John D. C. Bennett and Lydia Tyszczuk, "Deception by Immunisation, Revisited," *British Medical Journal* 2: 1471–72, 1990.

21. Philippe Aziz, *Doctors of Death*, Vol. 3: *When Man Became a Guinea Pig for Death*, trans. E. Bizub and P. Haentzler (Geneva: Ferni Publishers, 1976), pp. 107–08.

22. Alexander Mitscherlich and Fred Mielke, *Doctors of Infamy: The Story of the Nazi War Crimes*, trans. Heinz Norden (New York: Henry Schuman, 1949), pp. xxxix + 172; pp. 42–51.

23. Mitscherlich, *Doctors of Infamy*, p. 45.

24. It is not possible to tell precisely who Ding's subjects were, or how many there were, since he uses only percentages to describe his results, not absolute numbers. He identifies his subjects as physicians, health-care workers, soldiers, and civilians (*Ärzte, Pflege-personal, Soldaten und Zililangehörige*). Erwin Ding, "Über die Schutzwirkung verschiedener Fleck-fieberimpfstoffe beim Menschen und den Fleckfieberverlauf nach Schutzimpfung," *Zeitschrift für Hygiene und Infektionskrankheiten* 124: 670–682, 1943.

25. Robert Jay Lifton, *The Nazi Doctors: Medical Killing and the Psychology of Genocide* (New York: Basic Books, 1986), p. 269.

26. Lifton, *The Nazi Doctors*, p. 291.

27. Cited in Trunk, "Epidemics and Mortality," p. 83.

28. Trunk, "Epidemics and Mortality," p. 83.

29. Robert Proctor, *Racial Hygiene: Medicine Under the Nazis* (Cambridge, MA, and London: Harvard University Press, 1988), p. 205.

30. Hanna Hirszfeldowna (ed.), *The Story of One Life, from "Historia Jednego Zycia" by Ludwig Hirszfeld*, trans. F. R. Camp and F. R. Ellis (Fort Knox, KY: Blood Transfusion Division, United States Army Medical Research Laboratory, n.d.), p. 368; p. 186.

31. Yisrael Gutman, *Jews of Warsaw, 1939–1943: Ghetto, Underground, Revolt*, trans. Ina Friedman (Bloomington and Indianapolis: Indiana University Press, 1989), pp. xxi + 487; p. 26.

32. Philip Friedman (ed.), *Martyrs and Fighters: The Epic of the Warsaw Ghetto* (New York: Frederick A. Praeger, 1954), p. 324; p. 42.

33. Christopher Browning, "Genocide and Public Health: German Doctors and Polish Jews, 1939–41" *Holocaust and Genocide Studies* 3: 21–36, 1988; see p. 23.

34. Browning, "Genocide," p. 23.

35. Hagen, "Krieg, Hunger und Pestilenz," p. 117.

36. Browning, "Genocide," p. 22.

37. Joanna K. M. Hanson, *The Civilian Population and the Warsaw Uprising of 1944* (Cambridge, London, New York, New Rochelle, Melbourne, and Sydney: Cambridge University Press, 1982), pp. xiii+345; p. 31.

38. Browning, "Genocide," p. 23.

39. Hagen, "Krieg, Hunger und Pestilenz," p. 125.

40. Browning, "Genocide," p. 27.

41. Cited in Raul Hilberg, *The Destruction of the European Jews* (New York and London: Holmes & Meier, 1985), pp. xii+1274; p. 262.

42. Hagen, "Krieg, Hunger und Pestilenz," p. 122.

43. Browning, "Genocide," p. 24.

44. Browning, "Genocide," p. 24.

45. Cited in Wilhelm Hagen, *Auftrag und Wirklichkeit: Sozialarzt im 20.Jahrhundert* (Munich-Grafelfing: Werk-Verlag Dr. Edmund Banaschewski, 1978), p. 255; p. 188. Hagen has been held up by many as one of the arch foes of the Jews of Warsaw. Waller, a surviving physician from the ghetto, expressed his opinion in unequivocal terms: "It was [Hagen's] job to increase the speed of epidemics in the ghetto and later to prevent their spread to the Aryan side of Warsaw. More specifically, the task was to create every possible condition for increasing the size of the epidemics." Jerusalem, Yad Vashem Archives, YVA 03/2358, Testimony of Dr. Stanislaw Waller, n.d., p. 9. On the other hand, Hilberg cites a document in which Hagen protested to Leist in September 1941 that a plan to sever the Small Ghetto was "insanity" (*Wahnsinn*): Hagen to Leist, 22 September 1941. Zentrale Stelle der Landesjustizverwaltungen, Ludwigsburg, Polen 365c, p. 58; cited in Hilberg, *The Destruction of the European Jews*, pp. xii+1274; p. 226.

46. Hagen, *Auftrag und Wirklichkeit*, p. 181.

47. Jerusalem, Yad Vashem Archives 0–53/145/57–265, *Arbeitstagung der Abteilung Gesundheitswesen im der Regierung in Bad Krynica vom 13–16.10.1941*. During their occupation of Poland in World War I, the Germans also created a dichotomy between disease prevention and soap availability. The authorities guaranteed a small supply of soap by placing severe restrictions on its manufacture. The relevant edict expressly forbade the making of soap with fat. Proper soap was not to be used for personal hygiene. "Such limitations . . . reduced the opportunities for the occupied to improve their own hygienic conditions, flying in the face of German claims that they were the agents of improved hygiene." (See Pam Maclean, "Control and Cleanliness: German–Jewish Relations in Occupied Eastern Europe during the First World War," *War and Society* 6: 47–69, 1988; p. 56.) A similar charge could be made for World War II.

48. Hagen, "Krieg, Hunger und Pestilenz," p. 121.

49. Christopher R. Browning, "Nazi Ghettoization Policy in Poland, 1939–41," *Central European History* 19:343–68, 1986, p. 351.

50. Hilberg, *The Destruction of the European Jews*, p. 266.

51. Browning, "Genocide," p. 28.

52. Henry Fenigstein, interview, HCM 11–82, 31 March 1982, p. 4. This explanation was also put forward by another of the survivors of Czyste Hospital; Marek Balin observed that "because of the typhus they have to start autopsies" in the Czyste Hospital inside the ghetto. (Balin, interview, HCM 7–83, 16 May 1983, p. 10.)

53. For a description of the subversion of medical education by Nazism, see Michael

Kater, *Doctors Under Hitler* (Chapel Hill, NC, and London: University of North Carolina Press, 1989), pp. xii + 426; pp. 111–16.

54. Proctor, *Racial Hygiene*, p. 195.

55. Benno Müller-Hill, *Murderous Science: Elimination by Scientific Selection of Jews, Gypsies, and Others, Germany, 1933–1945*, trans. George R. Fraser (Oxford, New York, and Tokyo: Oxford University Press, 1988); p. 41, for example, describes the murder of 6400 mental patients by the SS as part of this program.

56. M. Dworjetski, "Jewish Medical Resistance during the Catastrophe," in *Extermination and Resistance: Historical Records and Source Materials*, Vol. 1 (Kibbutz Lohamei Hagettaot, Israel: Ghetto Fighters' House, 1958), pp. 118–19.

57. Isaiah Trunk, *Judenrat: The Jewish Councils in Eastern Europe Under Nazi Occupation* (New York: The Macmillan Co., 1972), pp. xxxv + 664; p. 191. The edict was issued 26 January 1940.

58. Jacob Sloan, *Notes from the Warsaw Ghetto: The Journal of Emmanuel Ringelblum* (New York: Schocken Books, 1974), p. 7, entry of 8 February 1940.

59. New York, Archives of the American Jewish Joint Distribution Committee (hereafter AAJJDC), AR 3344, file 800, Report 1941–1942 (Aug.); from a report by S. A. Desick, AJDC, "General Situation of the Jews in Poland," 13 February 1942, p. 5.

60. Koblenz, *Bundesarchiv*, German Federal Archives, R 70 (Poland), Folder 1, 27 June 1941.

61. Balin, interview, HCM 7–83, p. 16.

62. Sloan, *The Journal of Emmanuel Ringelblum*, p. 85.

63. Ludvik Stabholz, interview, HCM 5–87, p. 26.

64. B. Markowski, "Some Experiences of a Medical Prisoner of War," *British Medical Journal* 2: 361–63, 1945; see p. 361.

65. Lifton, *The Nazi Doctors*, pp. 180ff.

66. Sloan, *The Journal of Emmanuel Ringelblum*, p. 197.

67. Stanislaw Adler, *In the Warsaw Ghetto, 1940–1943: An Account of a Witness* (Jerusalem: Yad Vashem, 1982), pp. xviii + 334; p. 304.

68. *Jüdisches Volksblatt* no. 50 (1902); cited by Proctor, *Racial Hygiene*, p. 196.

69. Izak Arbus, *The Number on My Forehead: A Survivor's Story* (MS, 1990), p. 224; p. 64.

70. See, for example, A. W. Crosby, "Virgin Soil Epidemics as a Factor in the Aboriginal Depopulation in America," *William and Mary Quarterly* 33: 289–99, 1976.

71. Hirszfeld discusses and disposes of this argument in his unsigned memorandum, "Denkschrift über die Epidemieverbreitung in Warschau," YVA AZIH Ring II/85, [1940].

72. Schon, in Yitzhak Arad, Yisrael Gutman, and Abraham Margoliot (eds.), *Documents on the Holocaust: Selected Sources on the Destruction of the Jews of Germany and Austria, Poland, and the Soviet Union*, (New York: Ktav Publishing House, Inc., 1981). p 227; Donat gives the figures as 37 percent of the population in an area equalling 4.6 percent of greater Warsaw: Alexander Donat, *The Holocaust Kingdom: A Memoir* (New York: Holocaust Library, 1978), p. 35.

73. According to Schon, who was head of the Department of Resettlement in the Warsaw District, "The German Army and population must in any case be protected against the Jews, the immune carriers of the bacteria of epidemics." *Documents*, p. 225.

74. Mordecai Lenski, "Problems of Disease in the Warsaw Ghetto," *Yad Vashem Studies* 3: 283–93, 1975; p. 285.

75. Karolina Borman, interview, HCM 23–82, 26 September 1982, p. 10.

76. Chaim Lazar, *Muranowska 7: The Warsaw Ghetto Uprising*, trans. Yosef Shachter (Tel Aviv: Massada-P.E.C. Press Ltd., 1966), p. 29.

77. Henry Fenigstein, as Told to Saundra Collis, *The Holocaust and I: Memoirs of a Survivor* (Toronto: Unpublished MS, 1990), pp. 521 + xlii; p. xviii.

78. Lenski, "Problems of Disease," p. 290.

79. Pernal, interview, HCM 4–87, Toronto, Ontario, 19 May 1987, p. 7.

80. Pernal, interview, HCM 4–87, 19 May 1987, pp. 7–8.

81. Arbus, *The Number on My Forehead*, pp. 75–76.

82. Fliederbaum, in Myron Winick (ed.), *Hunger Disease: Studies by the Jewish Physicians in the Warsaw Ghetto*, trans. Martha Osnos (New York, Chichester, Brisbane, and Toronto: John Wiley & Sons, 1979), p. 18.

83. Lenski, "Problems of Disease," pp. 290–91.

84. Bronislaw Wisniewski, interview, HCM 2–89, New York, New York, 3 May 1989, 36 pp., p. 12.

85. Hagen, *Auftrag und Wirklichkeit*, p. 181.

86. Trunk, "Epidemics and Mortality," p. 107.

87. Hirszfeldowna, *The Story of One Life*, p. 187.

88. 2 November 1939: "We were burying the victims of typhus": Raul Hilberg, Stanislaw Staron, and Josek Kermisz (eds.), *The Warsaw Diary of Adam Czerniakow: Prelude to Doom*, trans. S. Staron and the Staff of Yad Vashem (New York: Stein & Day, 1982), p. 87.

89. Lenski, "Problems of Disease," p. 285. But note that Czerniakow recorded very substantial numbers of deaths from typhus, mostly among refugees: 944 in December 1939 and 1004 in January 1940 (Hilberg et al., *The Warsaw Diary of Adam Czerniakow*, p. 129, entry of 16 March 1940).

90. AAJJDC AR3344/840, Medical Care: TOZ, Warsaw, 1933–1942; from a report by Dr. L. Wulman, "Some Facts about the Activities of the TOZ in Poland," 27 March 1940, p. 1.

91. David Wdowinski, *And We Are Not Saved* (New York: Philosophical Library, 1985), pp. xxi + 222; pp. 43–44; Eisen, interview, HCM 58–85, 20 June 1985, pp. 3–4.

92. Fenigstein, *The Holocaust and I*, pp. ix-x.

93. Gutman, *Jews of Warsaw*, p. 55.

94. AAJJDC AR3344, file 797, Reports, 1940 (Jan.–Mar.); from the memorandum, "Activities of the JDC After the Outbreak of the War," unsigned, Warsaw, 8 February 1940, p. 1.

95. Hilberg et al., *The Warsaw Diary of Adam Czerniakow*, p. 116, entry of 9 February 1940.

96. Gutman, *Jews of Warsaw*, p. 50.

97. Hilberg et al., *The Warsaw Diary of Adam Czerniakow*, p. 151, entry of 17 May 1940.

98. AAJJDC AR3344, file 840, Medical Care: TOZ, Warsaw, 1933–1942; from "Report of the Work of the TOZ, Sept. 1, 1939 to June 1940," p. 8.

99. Sloan, *The Journal of Emmanuel Ringelblum*, p. 42, entry of 27 May 1940.

100. Hilberg et al., *The Warsaw Diary of Adam Czerniakow*, p. 158, entry of 5 June 1940.

101. Trunk, "Epidemics and Mortality," pp. 95–97.

102. Sloan, *The Journal of Emmanuel Ringelblum*, p. 105, entry of 7 December 1940.

103. Hagen, *Auftrag und Wirklichkeit*, p. 166.

104. A. Favel, *Faithful Onto Death: The Story of Arthur Zygielbaum* (Montreal: Zygielbaum Branch Workmen's Circle, 1980), p. 67.

105. Hagen, "Krieg, Hunger und Pestilenz," p. 121.

106. Hagen, "Krieg, Hunger und Pestilenz," p. 121.

107. Trunk, *Judenrat*, p. 343.

108. Sloan, *The Journal of Emmanuel Ringelblum*, p. 177.

109. Sloan, *The Journal of Emmanuel Ringelblum*, p. 191.

110. Hilberg et al., *The Warsaw Diary of Adam Czerniakow*, p. 248, entry of 13 June 1941.

111. Hilberg et al., *The Warsaw Diary of Adam Czerniakow*, p. 263, entry of 29 July 1941.

112. Sloan, *The Journal of Emmanuel Ringelblum*, p. 189, June 1941.

113. Anonymous, "Scenes from a Children's Hospital," in Joseph Kermish (ed): *To Live with Honor and Die with Honor! . . . Selected Documents from the Warsaw Ghetto Underground Archives*, "O. S." ["Oneg Shabbat"] (Jerusalem: Yad Vashem, 1986), p. 406.

114. Noemi Makowerowa (ed.), *Henryk Makower: Pamietnik z getta warszawskiego, pazdziernik 1940-styczen 1943* (Wrocław, Warsaw, Kraków, Gdansk, and Łodż: Zakład Narodowy im. Ossolinskich Wydawnictwo, 1987), p. 213; p. 184.

115. Sloan, *The Journal of Emmanuel Ringelblum*, p. 194.

116. *Documents on the Holocaust*, p 245.

117. Eugenia Pernal, interview, HCM 4–87, 19 May 1987, pp. 8 and 13; see also Helen Fein, *Accounting, for Genocide: National Responses and Jewish Victimization during the Holocaust*, (Chicago and London: University of Chicago Press, 1979), p. 228.

118. Lenski, "Problems of Disease," p. 288.

119. Adler, *In the Warsaw Ghetto*, p. 202.

120. Hagen, "Krieg, Hunger und Pestilenz," p. 123.

121. Hilberg et al., *The Warsaw Diary of Adam Czerniakow*, p. 252, entry of 26 June 1941.

122. Hilberg et al., *The Warsaw Diary of Adam Czerniakow*, p. 277, entry of 9 September 1941.

123. Sloan, *The Journal of Emmanuel Ringelblum*, p. 246.

124. Adler, *In the Warsaw Ghetto*, pp. 136–37.

125. Trunk, "Epidemics and Mortality," pp. 101–02.

126. Jerusalem, Yad Vashem Archives 033/1558 E 104-4-7, Dr. Emil Apfelbaum describes events at Czyste Hospital, 1939–1943: Conversation between Apfelbaum and Stefania Beylin, Warsaw, 1945, trans. Martha Osnos and Robert Osnos, p. 7.

127. Sloan, *The Journal of Emmanuel Ringelblum*, p. 194.

128. Fenigstein, *The Holocaust and I*, p. xviii.

129. Sloan, *The Journal of Emmanuel Ringelblum*, p. 230.

130. Hilberg et al., *The Warsaw Diary of Adam Czerniakow*, p. 301, entry of 23 November 1941.

131. Fenigstein, *The Holocaust and I*, p. xxxii.

132. AAJJDC AR3344, file 811, Publicity: General, (May) 1937–1942, 1944; from *Unser Tsait*, April 1942.

133. Fliederbaum et al., in Winick, *Hunger Disease*, p. 35.

134. Trunk, "Epidemics and Mortality," p. 96.

135. Isaac Bashevis Singer, *Shosha* (London: Penguin Books, 1979), p. 68.

136. Joseph Hyams, *A Field of Buttercups* (Englewood Cliffs, NJ: Prentice-Hall, 1968), p. 273, map., p. 5.

137. Sloan, *The Journal of Emmanuel Ringelblum*, p. 28.

138. Hilberg et al., *The Warsaw Diary of Adam Czerniakow*, p. 147, entry of 7 May 1940.

139. Trunk, "Epidemics and Mortality," pp. 111–12.

140. Hagen, "Krieg, Hunger und Pestilenz," p. 126.

141. Hilberg et al., *The Warsaw Diary of Adam Czerniakow*, p. 272, entry of 29 August 1941.

142. Leon Poliakov, *Harvest of Hate: The Nazi Program for the Destruction of the Jews of Europe* (New York: Holocaust Library, 1986), pp. 87–88.

143. Trunk, "Epidemics and Mortality," pp. 111–12.

144. The following description derives from the report of 31 August 1941, prepared for the *Judenrat* by an unidentified officer in that organization. It is published in its entirety in Hilberg et al., *The Warsaw Diary of Adam Czerniakow*, pp. 275–76.

145. Hilberg et al., *The Warsaw Diary of Adam Czerniakow*, pp. 275–76.

146. Balin, interview, HCM 7-83, pp. 40–42.

147. Lenski, "Problems of Disease," p. 289.

148. [Ludvik Hirszfeld], "Denkschrift über die prophylaktischen Massnahmen im jüdischen Viertel" and "Denkschrift über die Ursachen des Flecktyphus in Warschau und Vorschlüge zu seiner Bekämpfung," YVA AZIH Ring I/85, 15 May 1940.

149. Hirszfeldowna, *The Story of One Life*, p. 200.

150. Makowerowa, *Henryk Makower*, p. 107.

151. Sloan, *The Journal of Emmanuel Ringelblum*, p. 196.

152. When Eugenia Pernal's brother had typhus, the whole family went into quarantine in the Leszno 109 site. See Pernal, interview, HCM 4-87, 19 May 1987, p. 14.

153. Trunk, "Epidemics and Mortality," p. 106.

154. Fenigstein, *The Holocaust and I*, p. xix.

155. Hilberg et al., *The Warsaw Diary of Adam Czerniakow*, pp. 327–28, entry of 20 February 1942.

156. Sloan, *The Journal of Emmanuel Ringelblum*, p. 196.

157. Hagen, "Krieg, Hunger und Pestilenz," p. 124.

158. Sloan, *The Journal of Emmanuel Ringelblum*, p. 135.

159. Hagen, "Krieg, Hunger und Pestilenz," p. 121.

160. Sloan, *The Journal of Emmanuel Ringelblum*, p. 135.

161. Hagen, "Krieg, Hunger und Pestilenz," p. 121.

162. Lenski, "Problems of Disease," p. 289.

163. Lenski, "Problems of Disease," p. 289.

164. Cited in Michael R. Marrus, *The Holocaust in History* (Toronto: Lester and Orpen Dennys, 1987), pp. xv + 267; pp. 136–37.

165. Hirszfeldowna, *The Story of One Life*, p. 257.

166. Lenski, "Problems of Disease," p. 289.

167. Hilberg et al., *The Warsaw Diary of Adam Czerniakow*, p. 140.

168. Hilberg et al., *The Warsaw Diary of Adam Czerniakow*, p. 114, entry of 3 February 1940.

169. Sloan, *The Journal of Emmanuel Ringelblum*, p. 16.

170. Sloan, *The Journal of Emmanuel Ringelblum*, p. 16.

171. Trunk, "Epidemics and Mortality," p. 109.

172. Trunk, "Epidemics and Mortality," p. 108.

173. Sloan, *The Journal of Emmanuel Ringelblum*, p. 294.

174. AAJJDC AR3344, file 840, Medical Care: TOZ, Warsaw, 1933–1942; from "Report of the Work of the TOZ, from Sept. 1, 1939 to June 1940," p. 6.

175. Sloan, *The Journal of Emmanuel Ringelblum*, p. 169.

176. Sloan, *The Journal of Emmanuel Ringelblum*, p. 19, entry for 12 February 1940.

177. Sloan, *The Journal of Emmanuel Ringelblum*, p. 169.

178. Trunk, "Epidemics and Mortality," p. 113.

179. Hirszfeldowna, *The Story of One Life*, p. 219.

180. Sloan, *The Journal of Emmanuel Ringelblum*, p. 196.

181. Ringelblum reported that the original ghetto contained 1500 buildings in 100 city blocks; see Sloan, *The Journal of Emmanuel Ringelblum*, p. 59.

182. Hagen, "Krieg, Hunger und Pestilenz," p. 121.

183. Anonymous, "Street Traffic," in Kermish, *To Live with Honor*, p. 154.

184. Janina Zaborowska, interview, HCM 76–85, 12 September 1985, pp. 4–5.

185. Sloan, *The Journal of Emmanuel Ringelblum*, p. 195.

186. Janina David, *A Square of Sky: Recollections of My Childhood* (New York: W. W. Norton & Co., 1964), p. 222; p. 150.

187. Hirszfeldowna, *The Story of One Life*, p. 238.

188. Hirszfeldowna, *The Story of One Life*, pp. 218–21.

189. Hirszfeldowna, *The Story of One Life*, p. 221.

190. Hilberg et al., *The Warsaw Diary of Adam Czerniakow*, p. 104, entry of 3 January 1940.

191. Hilberg et al., *The Warsaw Diary of Adam Czerniakow*, p. 115, entry of 5 February 1940.

192. Hilberg et al., *The Warsaw Diary of Adam Czerniakow*, p. 104, entry of 7 January 1940.

193. Trunk, "Epidemics and Mortality," p. 108.

194. Trunk, "Epidemics and Mortality," pp. 110–11.

195. Trunk, "Epidemics and Mortality," pp. 110–11.

196. Hilberg et al., *The Warsaw Diary of Adam Czerniakow*, p. 165, entry of 24 June 1940.

197. Trunk, "Epidemics and Mortality," p. 111.

198. Sloan, *The Journal of Emmanuel Ringelblum*, p. 130.

199. Sloan, *The Journal of Emmanuel Ringelblum*, p. 35, entry for April 1940.

200. Anonymous, "Contents of a conversation with a Member of the Order Police," in Kermish, *To Live with Honor*, p. 316.

201. Hirszfeldowna, *The Story of One Life*, pp. 219–20.

202. Hirszfeldowna, *The Story of One Life*, pp. 216–17.

203. Hagen, "Krieg, Hunger und Pestilenz," p. 122.

204. Hagen, *Auftrag und Wirklichkeit*, p. TR 6.

205. Hagen, "Krieg, Hunger und Pestilenz," p. 117.

206. Hagen, "Krieg, Hunger und Pestilenz," p. 126.

207. Trunk, "Epidemics and Mortality," p. 109.

208. Fenigstein, *The Holocaust and I*, pp. 282–83.

209. Henry Fenigstein, interview, HCM 3–82, 21 January 1982, p. 21.

210. John D. C. Bennett, and Lydia Tyszczuk, "Deception by Immunisation, Revisited," *British Medical Journal* 2: 1471–72, 1990, p. 1471.

211. Sloan, *The Journal of Emmanuel Ringelblum*, p. 219.

212. Frank Stiffel, *The Tale of the Ring: A Kaddish* (Toronto, New York, London, Sydney, and Auckland: Bantam Books, 1985), p. 348; p. 43.

213. Eisen, interview, HCM 58–85, Greyslake, Illinois, 20 June 1985, 58 pp., p. 25.

214. Hilberg et al., *The Warsaw Diary of Adam Czerniakow*, p. 96, entry for 2 December 1939, where he records being feverish at night after having his second typhus vaccination.

215. Hilberg et al., *The Warsaw Diary of Adam Czerniakow*, p. 274, entry of 2 September 1941.

216. Hilberg et al., *The Warsaw Diary of Adam Czerniakow*, p. 324, entry of 12 February 1942.

217. Hirszfeldowna, *The Story of One Life*, p. 213. Hirszfeld also produced antidysentery

vaccine in his own lab, which was sold and the proceeds used at least partly to raise the salaries of his lab workers, who were starving.

218. Hagen, "Krieg, Hunger und Pestilenz," p. 127.

219. Hagen, "Krieg, Hunger und Pestilenz," p. 127.

220. Henry Shoskes, *No Traveler Returns* (Garden City, NY: Doubleday, Doran & Co., 1945), pp. xiii + 267; p. 56.

221. Sloan, *The Journal of Emmanuel Ringelblum*, p. 219.

222. Hanson, *The Civilian Population*, p. 32.

223. Borman, interview, HCM 23–82, p. 12.

224. AAJJDC AR3344, file 800, Report 1941–1942 (Aug.); letter to Joseph Schwartz from Dr. B. Tschlenoff, Geneva, 8 January 1942.

225. AAJJDC AR3344, file 840, Medical Care: TOZ, Warsaw, 1933–1942; letter from Elias Sternbuch, St. Gall, to Mr. Rosenheim, president, Agudas Israel World Organization, New York, 7 November 1941.

226. AAJJDC AR3344, file 801, Report (Sept.) 1942–1943; letter, Moses A. Leavitt, AJDC, to Samuel A. Goldsmith, Jewish Charities of Chicago, 6 November 1942.

227. AAJJDC AR3344/801, letter, Leavitt to Goldsmith, 6 November 1942.

228. Hagen, *Auftrag und Wirklichkeit*, p. 182.

229. Henry Fenigstein, interview, HCM 3–82, 21 January 1982, p. 21.

230. Bennett and Tyszczuk, "Deception by Immunisation," p. 1471.

231. Wdowinski, *And We Are Not Saved*, p. 39.

232. Trunk, "Epidemics and Mortality," p. 97.

233. Hilberg et al., *The Warsaw Diary of Adam Czerniakow*, p. 305, entry of 4 December 1941.

234. Hilberg et al., *The Warsaw Diary of Adam Czerniakow*, p. 290, entries of 16 and 18 October 1941.

235. Hilberg et al., *The Warsaw Diary of Adam Czerniakow*, p. 367, entry of 16 June 1942.

236. Adolf Berman, "The Fate of the Children in the Warsaw Ghetto," in Yisrael Gutman and Livia Rothkirchen (eds.), *The Catastrophe of European Jewry: Antecedents, History, Reflections* (Jerusalem: Yad Vashem, 1976), pp. 400–21; p. 405.

237. Sloan, *The Journal of Emmanuel Ringelblum*, p. 195.

238. Fenigstein, *The Holocaust and I*, p. xx.

239. Hilberg et al., *The Warsaw Diary of Adam Czerniakow*, p. 246, entry of 4 June 1941.

240. Hagen, "Krieg, Hunger und Pestilenz," p. 122.

241. Hilberg et al., *The Warsaw Diary of Adam Czerniakow*, p. 294, entry of 29 October 1941.

242. Hirszfeldowna, *The Story of One Life*, p. 233.

243. Makowerowa, *Henryk Makower*, p. 106.

244. Makowerowa, *Henryk Makower*, citing a biographical account by Dr. Edward Stocki.

245. Bennett and Tyszczuk, "Deception by Immunisation," p. 1471.

246. Sloan, *The Journal of Emmanuel Ringelblum*, p. 219.

247. Adler, *In the Warsaw Ghetto*, p. 42.

248. Adler, *In the Warsaw Ghetto*, p. 126.

249. Sloan, *The Journal of Emmanuel Ringelblum*, p. 211, entry for September 1941.

250. Hirszfeldowna, *The Story of One Life*, p. 217.

251. Ludwig Stabholz, interview, HCM 5–87, Tel Aviv, Israel, 11 June 1987, p. 6.

252. Fenigstein, *The Holocaust and I*, p. xix.

253. Sloan, *The Journal of Emmanuel Ringelblum*, p. 255, entry for January 1942.

254. Hilberg et al., *The Warsaw Diary of Adam Czerniakow*, p. 322, entry of 5 February 1942.

255. Hilberg et al., *The Warsaw Diary of Adam Czerniakow*, p. 102, entry of 24 December 1939.

256. Hilberg et al., *The Warsaw Diary of Adam Czerniakow*, p. 257, entry of 10 July 1941.

257. Hilberg et al., *The Warsaw Diary of Adam Czerniakow*, pp. 248–49, entry of 14 June 1941.

258. Hilberg et al., *The Warsaw Diary of Adam Czerniakow*, p. 293, entry of 22 October 1941.

259. Winick, *Hunger Disease*.

260. Eisen, interview, HCM 58–85, 20 June 1985, 58 pp., p. 8.

261. Hirszfeldowna, *The Story of One Life*, p. 281.

262. Hirszfeldowna, *The Story of One Life*, p. 214.

263. Hirszfeldowna, *The Story of One Life*, p. 211.

264. Hirszfeldowna, *The Story of One Life*, p. 212.

265. Hagen, "Krieg, Hunger und Pestilenz," p. 121.

266. Hirszfeldowna, *The Story of One Life*, p. 214.

Chapter 8

1. New York, Archives of the American Jewish Joint Distribution Committee (hereafter, AAJJDC), AR3344, file 841, Medical Care: Other Organizations; letter, B. C. Vladeck and others, Medem Sanitarium, to Joseph Hyman, AJDC New York, 22 February 1938.

2. Isaiah Trunk, "Epidemics and Mortality in the Warsaw Ghetto, 1939–1942," *YIVO Annual of Jewish Social Science* 8: 82–122, 1953; p. 121.

3. Wilhelm Hagen, "Krieg, Hunger und Pestilenz in Warschau, 1939–1943," *Gesundheitswesen und Desinfektion* 8: 115–28, 9: 129–43, 1973; p. 118.

4. Hagen, "Krieg, Hunger und Pestilenz," p. 118.

5. Hagen, "Krieg, Hunger und Pestilenz," p. 120.

6. Hagen, "Krieg, Hunger und Pestilenz," p. 129.

7. Wilhelm Hagen, *Auftrag und Wirklichkeit: Sozialarzt im 20.Jahrhundert* (Munich-Grafelfing: Werk-Verlag Dr. Edmund Banaschewski, 1978), p. 255; p. 170.

8. Hagen, *Auftrag und Wirklichkeit*, p. 161.

9. Hagen, *Auftrag und Wirklichkeit*, p. 171.

10. Henry Fenigstein, as told to Saundra Collis, *The Holocaust and I: Memoirs of a Survivor* (Toronto: Unpublished MS, 1990), p. xiv.

11. Jacob Sloan: *Notes from the Warsaw Ghetto: The Journal of Emmanuel Ringelblum* (New York: Schocken Books, 1974), p. 131..

12. AAJJDC AR3344, file 800, Report 1941–1942 (Aug.); from "General Situation of the Jews in Poland," S. A. Desick, AJDC NY, 13 February 1942, p. 8.

13. Mordecai Lenski, "Problems of Disease in the Warsaw Ghetto," *Yad Vashem Studies* 3: 283–93, 1975; p. 291.

14. Raul Hilberg, Stanislaw Staron, and Josef Kermisz (eds.), *The Warsaw Diary of Adam Czerniakow: Prelude to Doom*, trans. S. Staron and the staff of Yad Vashem (New York: Stein & Day, 1982), pp. viii + 420; p. 329, entry for 23 February 1942.

15. AAJJDC AR3344, file 841, Medical Care: Other Organizations; letter, Henrietta K. Buchman, AJDC New York, to M. J. Kellner, Springfield, Illinois, 9 November 1939.

16. AAJJDC AR3344, file 841, Medical Care: Other Organizations; letter, Adolph Held,

chairman, Jewish Labor Committee, New York, to M. M. Feld, Jewish Community Council, Houston Texas, 12 August 1940.

17. Adina Blady Szwajger, *I Remember Nothing More: The Warsaw Children's Hospital and the Jewish Resistance*, trans. Tasja Darowska and Danusia Stok (New York: Pantheon Books, 1990), pp. xx + 184, illust., maps, p. 28.

18. Szwajger, *I Remember Nothing More*, p. 43.

19. Personal communication, Wladyslaw Lewin to C. G. Roland, ALS, 15 February 1991.

20. Hagen, "Krieg, Hunger und Pestilenz," p. 141.

21. Clarissa Henry and Marc Hillel, *Of Pure Blood*, trans. Eric Mossbacher, (New York, St. Louis, and San Fransisco: McGraw-Hill Book Co., 1976), p. 256, illust.

22. Trunk, "Epidemics and Mortality," p. 121.

23. Fliederbaum, in Myron Winick (ed.): *Hunger Disease: Studies by the Jewish Physicians in the Warsaw Ghetto*, trans. Martha Osnos (New York, Chichester, Brisbane, and Toronto: John Wiley & Sons, 1979), p. 35.

24. F. M. Lipscomb, "Medical Aspects of Belsen Concentration Camp," *Lancet* 2: 313–15, 1945; p. 314.

25. J. W. D. Megaw, "Davis, W.A. [U.S. Typhus Commission], *Typhus at Belsen*, 29 mimeographed pages, four tables and one map [Field Headquarters A.P.O. 887, U.S. Army, dated July 26, 1945]," *Bulletin of War Medicine* 6: 398–99, 1946; p. 398.

26. Charles Richet, "Notes medicales sur le camp de Buchenwald en 1944–1945," *Bulletin de l'Academie de Medecine* 129: 377–88, 1945; p. 382.

27. Esmond R. Long, "Tuberculosis in German Prison Camps," *Military Surgeon* 97: 449–50, 1945; p. 450.

28. Michael Kater, *Doctors Under Hitler* (Chapel Hill, NC, and London: University of North Carolina Press, 1989), pp. xii + 426; pp. 124–25.

29. Sierakowiak, in Alan Adelson and Robert Lapides (eds.), *Lodz Ghetto: Inside a Community Under Siege* (New York: Viking Press, 1989), pp. xxi + 526; p. 151.

30. Sierakowiak, in Adelson, *Lodz Ghetto*, pp. 159 + 161.

31. Josef Stein and Henryk Fenigstein, Chapter Seven in Winick, *Hunger Disease*, p. 216.

32. Winick, *Hunger Disease*.

33. Trunk, "Epidemics and Mortality."

34. Lenski, "Problems of Disease."

35. Michal Szejnman, Chapter Five in Winick, *Hunger Disease*, p. 164.

36. Trunk, "Epidemics and Mortality," p. 103.

37. Szejnman, in Winick, *Hunger Disease*, p. 164.

38. Lenski, "Problems of Disease," p. 291.

39. Emil Apfelbaum-Kowalsi, Chapter Four in Winick, *Hunger Disease*, p. 133.

40. Szwajger, *I Remember Nothing More*, p. 44.

41. Anna Braude-Heller, Israel Rotbalsam, and Regina Elbinger, Chapter Two in Winick, *Hunger Disease*, p. 49.

42. Julian Fliederbaum, Chapter One in Winick, *Hunger Disease*, p. 21.

43. Braude-Heller, in Winick, *Hunger Disease*, p. 48.

44. Braude-Heller, in Winick, *Hunger Disease*, p. 52.

45. Braude-Heller, in Winick, *Hunger Disease*, p. 55.

46. Apfelbaum-Kowalski, in Winick, *Hunger Disease*, p. 18.

47. Braude-Heller, in Winick, *Hunger Disease*, p. 49.

48. Braude-Heller, in Winick, *Hunger Disease*, p. 54.

49. Apfelbaum-Kowalski, in Winick, *Hunger Disease*, p. 18.

50. Apfelbaum-Kowalski, in Winick, *Hunger Disease*, p. 36.

51. Braude-Heller, in Winick, *Hunger Disease*, p. 52.

52. Braude-Heller, in Winick, *Hunger Disease*, p. 55.

53. Apfelbaum-Kowalski, in Winick, *Hunger Disease*, p. 21.

54. Hagen, "Krieg, Hunger und Pestilenz"; Hagen, *Auftrag und Wirklichkeit*.

55. Trunk, "Epidemics and Mortality."

56. Hagen, "Krieg, Hunger und Pestilenz," p. 120.

57. Hagen, "Krieg, Hunger und Pestilenz," p. 135.

58. Pakebusch to Krüger, December 1942, reproduced in Hagen, "Krieg, Hunger und Pestilenz," p. 141.

59. Letter, R. Brandt (Himmler's deputy) to Dr. Conti, 29 March 1943. Reproduced in Hagen, "Krieg, Hunger und Pestilenz," p. 143.

60. Trunk, "Epidemics and Mortality," p. 121.

61. In Winick, *Hunger Disease*, p. 35.

62. Trunk, "Epidemics and Mortality," p. 97.

63. Trunk, "Epidemics and Mortality," p. 120.

64. Trunk, "Epidemics and Mortality," p. 97.

65. Apfelbaum-Kowalski, in Winick, *Hunger Disease*, p. 35.

66. Winick, *Hunger Disease*.

67. Lenski, "Problems of Disease," pp. 284–85.

68. Lenski, "Problems of Disease," p. 285; Hagen, "Krieg, Hunger und Pestilenz," p. 117.

69. Fenigstein, *The Holocaust and I*, p. xiv.

70. Trunk, "Epidemics and Mortality," p. 85.

71. Jerusalem, YVA 033/1558 E 104-4-7, Dr. Emil Apfelbaum describes events at Czyste Hospital in 1939–1943 in Conversation between Apfelbaum and Stefania Beylin, Warsaw, 1945, trans. Martha Osnos and Robert Osnos, p. 4.

72. Hagen, "Krieg, Hunger und Pestilenz," p. 117.

73. AAJJDC AR3344, file 840, Medical Care: TOZ, Warsaw, 1933–1942; from "Report of the Work of the TOZ from Sept. 1, 1939 to June 1940."

74. Noemi Makowerowa (ed.), *Henryk Makower: Pamietnik z getta warszawskiego, pazdziernik 1940–styczen 1943* (Wrocław, Warsaw, Kraków, Gdansk, and Łodż: Zakład Narodowy im. Ossolinskich Wydawnictwo, 1987), p. 213; p. 125.

75. Abraham Lewin, *A Cup of Tears: A Diary of the Warsaw Ghetto* (London: Fontana/Collins, 1990), pp. [xii]+308; p. 198.

76. Janina David, *A Square of Sky: Recollections of My Childhood* (New York: W. W. Norton & Co., 1964), p. 222, illust., p. 117.

77. Lewin, *A Cup of Tears*, p. 97, entry for 25 May 1942.

78. Lewin, *A Cup of Tears*, p. 205, entry for 11 November 1942.

79. Lenski, "Problems of Disease," p. 287.

80. E. P. Kulawiec (ed. and trans.), *The Warsaw Ghetto Memoirs of Janusz Korczak* (Washington, DC: University Press of America, 1979), pp. xvii+127; p. 45.

81. Fliederbaum et al., in Winick, *Hunger Disease*, p. 36.

82. Lewin, *A Cup of Tears*, p. 119, entry of 5 June 1942.

83. Abraham I. Katsch (ed. and trans.), *The Warsaw Diary of Chaim Kaplan* (New York: Collier Books, 1973), entry for 10 March 1940, p. 131.

84. Lucy S. Dawidowicz, *The War Against the Jews, 1933–1945* (Toronto and New York: Bantam Books, 1986), pp. xxxx+466; p. 217.

85. AAJJDC AR3344, file 798, Report, 1940 (Apr.–Aug.); from "The Situation," an unsigned 13-page report hand-dated "May 1940 (?)," p. 5.

86. Halina Berg [pseudonym], interview, HCM 6–84, 14 September 1984, p. 5.

87. Irena Bakowska, interview, HCM 3–83, 1 February 1983, p. 16.

88. Hilberg et al., *The Warsaw Diary of Adam Czerniakow*, p. 279, entry for 15 September 1941.

89. David, *A Square of Sky*, p. 187.

90. Apolinary Hartglas, "How Did Cherniakow [*sic*] Become Head of the Warsaw Judenrat?" *Yad Vashem Bulletin* 15: 4–7, 1964; p. 7.

91. Betty Jean Lifton, *The King of Children: A Biography of Janusz Korczak* (New York: Farrar, Straus and Giroux, 1988), p. 404; p. 103.

92. Martin Gray with Max Gallo, *For Those I Loved*, 2nd ed., trans. Anthony White (London: W. H. Allen, 1984), pp. xvi + 349; p. 126.

93. Frank Stiffel, *The Tale of the Ring: A Kaddish* (Toronto, New York, Sydney, and Auckland: Bantam Books, 1985), p. 79.

94. Henry Shoskes, *No Traveler Returns* (Garden City, NY: Doubleday, Doran & Co., 1945), p. 164.

95. Eisen, interview, HCM 58–85, 20 June 1985, p. 20.

96. AAJJDC AR3344, file 811, Publicity: General, (May) 1937–1942, 1944; item translated from the Yiddish newspaper *Unser Tsait*, April 1942.

97. Hilberg et al., *The Warsaw Diary of Adam Czerniakow*, p. 205, entry for 10 October 1940.

98. Lewin, *A Cup of Tears*, p. 282, citing a German report dated 12 October 1942.

99. H. Nowogrodzki, cited in Philip Friedman (ed.), *Martyrs and Fighters: The Epic of the Warsaw Ghetto* (New York: Frederick A. Praeger, 1954), p. 324; p. 159.

100. Stiffel, *The Tale of the Ring*, p. 64.

101. Hanna Krall, *Shielding the Flame: An Intimate Conversation with Dr. Marek Edelman, the Last Surviving Leader of the Warsaw Ghetto Uprising*, trans. Joanna Stasinska and Lawrence Weschler, (New York: Henry Holt and Co., 1986), pp. xiii + 124; pp. 46–47.

102. Makowerowa, *Henryk Makower*, pp. 115–16.

103. Krall, *Shielding the Flame*, pp. 46–47.

104. Krall, *Shielding the Flame*, p. 108.

105. Szwajger, *I Remember Nothing More*, pp. 50–51.

106. Szwajger, *I Remember Nothing More*. p. 166.

107. Krall, *Shielding the Flame*, p. 101.

108. Friedman, *Martyrs and Fighters*, p. 102.

109. Letter of Franciska Rubinlicht, 9 November 1943. Cited in Howard Roiter, *Voices from the Holocaust* (New York: William-Frederick Press, 1975), p. 119.

110. Szwajger, *I Remember Nothing More*, p. 83.

111. Adler, *In the Warsaw Ghetto*, p. 109.

112. Hilberg et al., *The Warsaw Diary of Adam Czerniakow*, p. 156, entry for 31 May 1940.

113. Stanislaw Adler, *In the Warsaw Ghetto 1940–1943: An Account of a Witness* (Jerusalem: Yad Vashem, 1982), p. 109.

114. Sloan, *The Journal of Emmanuel Ringelblum*, p. 35.

115. Sloan, *The Journal of Emmanuel Ringelblum*, p. 158.

116. Adler, *In the Warsaw Ghetto*, p. 108.

117. Adler, *In the Warsaw Ghetto*, p. 109.

118. Hilberg et al., *The Warsaw Diary of Adam Czerniakow*, p. 185, entry for 17 August 1940.

119. Janina Zaborowska, interview, HCM 76–85, 12 September 1985, pp. 11–12.

120. Sloan, *The Journal of Emmanuel Ringelblum*, p. 20.

121. Lenski, "Problems of Disease," p. 284.

122. Lenski, "Problems of Disease," p. 291.

123. Lenski, "Problems of Disease," p. 292.

124. Kulawiec, *The Warsaw Ghetto Memoirs of Janusz Korczak*, p. 90.

125. Szwajger, *I Remember Nothing More*, p. 42.

126. Lewin, *A Cup of Tears*, p. 126, entry for 9 June 1942.

127. Fliederbaum, in his chapter in Winick, *Hunger Disease*, p. 36. In contrast, Hanson cites figures to show that scarlet fever was increased in Aryan Warsaw, as was diphtheria, measles, whooping cough and, she claims, malaria: see Joanna K. M. Hanson, *The Civilian Population and the Warsaw Uprising of 1944* (Cambridge, London, New York, New Rochelle, Melbourne, and Sydney: Cambridge University Press, 1982), pp. xiii + 345; p. 32.

128. Szwajger, *I Remember Nothing More*, p. 23.

129. In Winick, *Hunger Disease*, p. 22.

130. Hilberg et al., *The Warsaw Diary of Adam Czerniakow*, p. 288, entry for 14 October 1941.

131. David, *A Square of Sky*, p. 101.

132. Braude-Heller et al., in Winick, *Hunger Disease*, p. 56.

133. Adam Starkopf, *There Is Always Time to Die*, ed. Gertrude Hirschler (New York: Holocaust Library, 1981), p. 242; p. 56.

134. Makowerowa, *Henryk Makower*, pp. 116–17.

135. Starkopf, *There Is Always Time to Die*, p. 68.

136. Starkopf, *There Is Always Time to Die*, p. 105.

137. Hilberg et al., *The Warsaw Diary of Adam Czerniakow*, p. 117.

138. Hilberg et al., *The Warsaw Diary of Adam Czerniakow*, p. 85, entry for 21 October 1939.

139. Hilberg et al., *The Warsaw Diary of Adam Czerniakow*, p. 182, entry for 9 August 1940.

140. Hilberg et al., *The Warsaw Diary of Adam Czerniakow*, p. 333, entry for 9 March 1942.

141. Hilberg et al., *The Warsaw Diary of Adam Czerniakow*, p. 336, entry for 21 March 1942.

142. Hilberg et al., *The Warsaw Diary of Adam Czerniakow*, p. 102.

Chapter 9

1. Hanna Hirszfeldowna (ed.), *The Story of One Life, from "Historia Jednego Zycia" by Ludwig Hirszfeld*, trans. F. R. Camp and F. R. Ellis (Fort Knox, KY: Blood Transfusion Division, United States Army Medical Research Laboratory, n.d.), p. 368; p. 198.

2. Miriam Brysk, interview, HCM 5–84, 31 May 1984, p. 21.

3. Myron Winick (ed.), *Hunger Disease: Studies by the Jewish Physicians in the Warsaw Ghetto*, trans. Martha Osnos (New York, Chichester, Brisbane, and Toronto: John Wiley & Sons, 1979), pp. xiv + 261; p. 109.

4. Jacob Sloan (ed.), *Notes from the Warsaw Ghetto: The Journal of Emmanuel Ringelblum* (New York: Schocken Books, 1974), pp. xxvii + 369; p. 206.

5. Adolf Berman, "The Fate of the Children in the Warsaw Ghetto," in Yisrael Gutman and Livia Rothkirchen (eds.), *The Catastrophe of European Jewry: Antecedents, History, Reflections* (Jerusalem: Yad Vashem, 1976), p. 403.

6. New York, Archives of the American Jewish Joint Distribution Committee (hereafter, AAJJDC), AR3344, file 796, Reports, 1939 (Oct.–Dec.); see "Notes on Activities of American Joint Distribution Committee from Sept. 1, 1939," forwarded by the U.S. consul in Warsaw to Amsterdam, 27 December 1939; p. 2.

7. Berman, "The Fate of the Children," pp. 403-04.

8. Berman, "The Fate of the Children," p. 406.

9. AAJJDC AR3344, file 798, Report, 1940 (Apr.–Aug.); from an unattributed report, "The Situation," hand-dated "May 1940 (?)," p. 9.

10. AAJJDC AR3344, file 799, Report 1940 (Sept.–Dec.); from "Explanations to the Report Lists about the Activities of the American Joint Distribution Committee, Warsaw-Cracow," 1 January to 30 September 1940, p. 2.

11. AAJJDC AR3344, file 840, Medical Care: TOZ, Warsaw, 1933–1942; from letter, Dr. Leon Wulman, secretary, the American Committee of OSE, to Mrs. Henrietta Buchman, AJDC, New York, 6 November 1941.

12. AAJJDC AR3344, file 811, Publicity: General, (May) 1937–1942, 1944; from the American Yiddish paper *Unser Tsait*, June 1942.

13. Sloan, *The Journal of Emmanuel Ringelblum*, p. 204.

14. Teresa Prekerowa, "The Relief Council for Jews in Poland, 1942–1945," in Chimen Abramsky, Maciej Jachimczyk, and Antony Polonsky (eds.), *The Jews in Poland* (Oxford: Basil Blackwell, 1986), pp. xi + 264; p. 169.

15. Abraham Lewin, *A Cup of Tears: A Diary of the Warsaw Ghetto* (London: Fontana/Collins, 1990), pp. [xii] + 308.

16. Elwood McQuaid, *Zvi* (West Collingswood, NJ: Friends of Israel Gospel Ministry, Inc., 1978), p. 202; p. 30.

17. Noemi Makowerowa (ed.), *Henryk Makower: Pamietnik z getta warszawskiego, pazdziernik 1940-styczen 1943* (Wrocław, Warsaw, Kraków, Gdansk, and Lodż: Zakład Narodowy im. Ossolinskich Wydawnictwo, 1987), p. 213; pp. 113–14.

18. Stanislaw Adler, *In the Warsaw Ghetto, 1940–1943: An Account of a Witness* (Jerusalem: Yad Vashem, 1982), p. 94.

19. Lewin, *A Cup of Tears*, p. 64.

20. Sloan, *The Journal of Emmanuel Ringelblum*, p. 39.

21. Millie Eisen, interview, HCM 58–85, 20 June 1985, p. 6.

22. Sloan, *The Journal of Emmanuel Ringelblum*, p. 233.

23. Adler, *In the Warsaw Ghetto*, p. 260.

24. One such group of youthful survivors, living on their wits, is described in Joseph Ziemian, *The Cigarette Sellers of Three Crosses Square*, trans. Janina David (Minneapolis: Lerner Publications Co., 1975).

25. Sloan, *The Journal of Emmanuel Ringelblum*, p. 174.

26. E. P. Kulawiec (ed. and trans.), *The Warsaw Ghetto Memoirs of Janusz Korczak* (Washington, DC: University Press of America, 1979), pp. xvii + 127; p. 43.

27. Sloan, *The Journal of Emmanuel Ringelblum*, p. 190.

28. Berman, "The Fate of the Children," p. 405.

29. Berman, "The Fate of the Children," p. 404.

30. Janina David, *A Square of Sky: Recollections of My Childhood* (New York: W. W. Norton & Co., 1964), p. 222; p. 151.

31. Berman, "The Fate of the Children," p. 406.

32. Kulawiec, *The Warsaw Ghetto Memoirs*, p. 44.

33. There have been several biographies of Korczak, of which the following representative works have been consulted here; of these, the most comprehensive is the book by Lifton. See Mark Bernheim, *Father of the Orphans: The Story of Janusz Korczak* (New York: Lodestar Books, E. P. Dutton, 1989), pp. xv + 160, illust., a book for children; Betty Jean Lifton, *The King of Children: A Biography of Janusz Korczak* (New York: Farrar, Straus and Giroux, 1988), p. 404, illust.; and Alicja Szlązakowa, *Janusz Korczak* (Warszawa: Wydawnicto Szkolne i Pedagogiczne, 1978), p. 146, illust.

34. Quoted in Lifton, *The King of Children*, p. 119.

35. Lifton, *The King of Children*, p. 144.

36. Kulawiec, *The Warsaw Ghetto Memoirs*, pp. 81–2.

37. Kulawiec, *The Warsaw Ghetto Memoirs*, p. 90.

38. Hirszfeldowna, *The Story of One Life*, p. 233.

39. Braude-Heller, in Myron Winick (ed.), *Hunger Disease*, p. 56.

40. Kulawiec, *The Warsaw Ghetto Memoirs*.

41. Michael Zylberberg, *A Warsaw Diary, 1939–1945* (London: Vallentine, Mitchell, 1969), pp. 220; p. 50.

42. Hirszfeldowna, *The Story of One Life*, p. 248.

43. Adina Blady Szwajger, *I Remember Nothing More: The Warsaw Children's Hospital and the Jewish Resistance*, trans. Tasja Darowska and Danusia Stok (New York: Pantheon Books, 1990), pp. xx + 184, illust., maps, p. 57.

44. Szwajger, *I Remember Nothing More*; see pp. 27, 108, and 166, for example.

45. Anonymous, "The Life and Fate of Children," in Joseph Kermish (ed.), *To Live with Honor and Die with Honor! . . . Selected Documents from the Warsaw Ghetto Underground Archives "O.S." ["Oneg Shabbath"]* (Jerusalem: Yad Vashem, 1986), pp. xliv + 790; pp. 386–87.

46. Adler, *In the Warsaw Ghetto*, pp. xviii + 334; p. 79.

47. Anonymous, "A Visit to the Most Unfortunate of Children," in Kermish, *To Live with Honor*, p. 397.

48. Christopher R. Browning and Israel Gutman, "The Reports of a Jewish 'Informer' in the Warsaw Ghetto—Selected Documents," *Yad Vashem Studies* 17: 247–93, 1986; p. 264.

49. Hirszfeldowna, *The Story of One Life*, pp. 247–48.

50. Some of the streets of Warsaw have been renamed since World War II. The building that housed the Korczak orphanage, at Krochmalna 92, is still a children's institution, now identified as Jaklorawska 8. Korczak's name and a handsome bust are displayed prominently.

51. Lifton, *The King of Children*, p. 261.

52. Lifton, *The King of Children*, p. 286.

53. Kulawiec, *The Warsaw Ghetto Memoirs*, p. 119.

54. Lewin, *A Cup of Tears*, p. 279, n. 252.

55. Raul Hilberg, Stanislaw Staron, and Josef Kermisz (eds.), *The Warsaw Diary of Adam Czerniakow: Prelude to Doom*, trans. S. Staron and the staff of Yad Vashem (New York: Stein & Day, 1982), p. 320, entry for 31 January 1942.

56. Berman, "The Fate of the Children," p. 408.

57. Kulawiec, *The Warsaw Ghetto Memoirs*, p. 99.

58. Berman, "The Fate of the Children," pp. 408-09.

59. Berman, "The Fate of the Children," p. 413.

60. Lewin, *A Cup of Tears*, p. 276, n. 210.

61. Berman, "The Fate of the Children," p. 413.

62. Lewin, *A Cup of Tears*, p. 149.

63. Berman, "The Fate of the Children," p. 414.

64. Wladyslaw Bartoszewski, *The Warsaw Ghetto: A Christian's Testimony*, trans. Stephen G. Cappellari (Boston: Beacon Press, 1987), pp. x + 117; p. 33.

65. Halina Berg [pseudonym], interview, HCM 6–84, 14 September 1984, pp. 17–18.

66. Wisniewski, interview, HCM 2–89, p. 18.

67. According to one writer, Korczak and his children were not deported to Treblinka, but rather were among those taken to the cemetery and shot: see Henry Shoskes, *No Traveler Returns* (Garden City, NY: Doubleday, Doran & Co., 1945), pp. 128–29. But this is certainly an instance of confusion; Shoskes left Warsaw in the autumn of 1939, so he was certainly not

an eyewitness. Although some children were dealt with in this way, the progress of Korczak and the children was observed all along their march through the ghetto to the *Umschlagplatz* and onto the freight cars.

68. Berman, "The Fate of the Children," pp. 414–15.

69. Kulawiec, *The Warsaw Ghetto Memoirs*, p. 122.

70. Lewin, *A Cup of Tears*, p. 157, entry for 16 August 1942.

71. Szwajger, *I Remember Nothing More*, p. 52.

72. Lewin, *A Cup of Tears*, p. 177, entry for 11 September 1942.

73. Eugenia Pernal, interview, HCM 4–87, 19 May 1987, p. 19.

74. Yisrael Gutman, *Jews of Warsaw, 1939–1943: Ghetto, Underground, Revolt*, trans. Ina Friedman (Bloomington and Indianapolis: Indiana University Press, 1989), pp. xxi + 487; p. 270.

75. Berman, "The Fate of the Children," p. 420.

76. Raul Hilberg, *The Destruction of the European Jews* (New York and London: Holmes & Meier, 1985), pp. xii + 1274; p. 269.

77. AAJJDC AR3344, file 840, Medical Care: TOZ, Warsaw, 1933–1942; from TOZ report on activities for May, 1941, p. 2.

78. Makowerowa, *Henryk Makower*, p. 117.

79. Cited in Lucy S. Dawidowicz, *The War Against the Jews, 1933–1945* (Toronto and New York: Bantam Books, 1986), pp. xxx + 466; p. 221.

80. Adam Starkopf, *There Is Always Time to Die*, ed. Gertrude Hirschler (New York: Holocaust Library, 1981), p. 242; p. 66.

81. Halina Birenbaum, *Hope Is the Last to Die: A Personal Documentation of Nazi Terror*, trans. David Welsh (New York: Twayne Publishers, 1971), pp. iv + 246; p. 57.

82. Adler, *In the Warsaw Ghetto*, p. 306.

83. Szwajger, *I Remember Nothing More*, pp. 136–37.

84. Starkopf, *There is Always Time to Die*, p. 110.

85. Starkopf, *There is Always Time to Die*, p. 112.

86. Hanna Krall, *Shielding the Flame: An Intimate Conversation with Dr. Marek Edelman, the Last Surviving Leader of the Warsaw Ghetto Uprising*, trans. Joanna Stasinska and Lawrence Weschler, (New York: Henry Holt and Company, 1986), pp. xiii + 124; p. 47.

87. Krall, *Shielding the Flame*, p. 9.

88. Yaffa Eliach, *Hasidic Tales of the Holocaust* (New York: Avon Books, 1982), pp. xxxii + 312; pp. 98–99.

Chapter 10

1. Zofia S. Kubar, *Double Identity: A Memoir* (New York: Hill and Wang, 1989), p. 209; 153–54.

2. Halina Berg [pseudonym], interview, HCM 6–84, 14 September 1984, p. 8.

3. Michael Zylberberg, *A Warsaw Diary, 1939–1945* (London: Vallentine, Mitchell, 1969), p. 220; p. 40.

4. Yisrael Gutman, *Jews of Warsaw, 1939–1943: Ghetto, Underground, Revolt*, trans. Ina Friedman (Bloomington and Indianapolis: Indiana University Press, 1989), pp. xxi + 487; p. 84.

5. Lucy S. Dawidowicz, *The War Against the Jews, 1933–1945* (Toronto and New York: Bantam Books, 1986), p. 253.

6. Raul Hilberg, Stanislaw Staron, and Josef Kermisz (eds.), *The Warsaw Diary of Adam Czerniakow: Prelude to Doom*, trans. S. Staron and the staff of Yad Vashem (New York: Stein & Day, 1982), pp. viii + 420; pp. 186, 188.

7. Isaiah Trunk, *Judenrat: The Jewish Councils in Eastern Europe Under Nazi Occupation* (New York: The Macmillan Co., 1972), pp. xxxv+664; p. 200.

8. Henry Fenigstein, interview, HCM 17–82, 28 June 1982, p. 2.

9. Hilberg et al., *The Warsaw Diary of Adam Czerniakow*, p. 225, entry of 23 April 1941.

10. Hilberg et al., *The Warsaw Diary of Adam Czerniakow*, p. 233, entry of 11 May 1941. One of the last lectures—perhaps the very last—was given on 3 July 1942 by David Wdowinski on the topic of mental disturbances during and after typhoid fever: David Wdowinski, *And We Are Not Saved* (New York: Philosophical Library, 1985), pp. xxi+222; p. 57.

11. Gutman, for example, speaks of "a course in medicine by Professor Hirszfeld geared to the level of a professional school of medicine." *Jews of Warsaw*, p. 105. This error probably reflects the remarkable prestige of Hirszfeld, who most certainly was an important figure in the school. Similarly, in Bernard Goldstein, *Die Sterne sind Zeugen: Der Untergang der polnischen Juden* (Munich: Deutscher Taschenbuch Verlag GmbH & Co., 1965), p. 79, the only name cited in connection with the school (*Die Sanitaterkurse*) was that of Hirszfeld. Hirszfeld himself gives credit to Zweibaum: "Docent Zweibaum obtained a permit to organize a course for the sanitary personnel. The fact was that this was a clandestine first year in medical study": Hanna Hirszfeldowna, *The Story of One Life, from "Historia Jednego Zycia" by Ludwig Hirszfeld*, trans. F. R. Camp and F. R. Ellis (Fort Knox, KY: Blood Transfusion Division, United States Army Medical Research Laboratory, n.d.), p. 209.

12. Marek Balin, interview, HCM 7–83, 16 May 1983, p. 11; Hirszfeldowna, *The Story of One Life*, p. 209.

13. Karolina Borman, interview, HCM 23–82, 26 September 1982, p. 6; Berg, interview, HCM 6–84, Milpitas, California, 14 September 1984, 49 pp., p. 41.

14. Jacob Sloan (ed.), *Notes from the Warsaw Ghetto: The Journal of Emmanuel Ringelblum* (New York: Schocken Books, 1974), pp. xxvii+369; p. 225.

15. Browning, "Nazi Ghettoization," pp. 347–48.

16. Noemi Makowerowa (ed.), *Henryk Makower: Pamietnik z getta warszawskiego, pazdziernik 1940–styczen 1943* (Wrocław, Warsaw, Kraków, Gdansk, Łodź: Zakład Narodowy im. Ossolinskich Wydawnictwo, 1987), p. 213; p. 183.

17. Hirszfeldowna, *The Story of One Life*, p. 207.

18. Hirszfeldowna, *The Story of One Life*, p. 207.

19. Abraham Lewin, *A Cup of Tears: A Diary of the Warsaw Ghetto* (London: Fontana/Collins, 1990), pp. xii+308; p. 263. On the *Ordnungsdienst* see Gutman, *Jews of Warsaw*, pp. 85–90. Several of the ex-students interviewed have commented on how worrisome it was to have to leave the ghetto each day and travel the few feet from the ghetto gate on Leszno to the school. Although the guards knew of the school, of course, they could be arbitrary in allowing students through. On at least one instance, a woman student was forced into the guards' quarters and raped. Sadly, but realistically, the teacher urged the students to ignore her cries and try to work. (See Borman, HCM 23–82, p 16; also Irena Bakowska, interview, HCM 3–83, 1 February 1983, p. 31.)

20. Makowerowa, *Henryk Makower*, p. 184.

21. Borman, interview, HCM 23–82, p. 10; Tadeusz Stabholz, interview, HCM 26–82, p. 24.

22. One Christian Polish interviewee, herself a medical student in Warsaw during the war, expressed doubts in 1985 that such a school could have existed in the ghetto, because conditions were known to be so hopeless there; Janina Zaborowska, interview, HCM 76–85, 12 September 1985, p. 13.

23. Ludwig Stabholz, interview, HCM 5–87, 11 June 1987, p. 12; Halina Berg, interview, HCM 6–84, 14 September 1984, p. 12.

24. Eugenia Pernal, interview, HCM 4–87, 19 May 1987, p. 13.

25. Bronislawa J. Wygodzka, interview, HCM 1–88, 8 January 1988, p. 14.

26. Borman, interview, HCM 23–82, 26 September 1982, p. 18.

27. Berg, interview, HCM 6–84, 14 September 1984, p. 12.

28. Pernal, interview, HCM 4–87, p. 12; L. Stabholz, interview, HCM 5–87, p. 29; Bakowska, HCM 3–83, p. 29.

29. Borman, interview, HCM 23–82, p. 15; Berg, interview, HCM 6–84, p. 43–44; L. Stabholz, interview, HCM 5–87, p. 14.

30. Balin, interview, HCM 7–83, p. 16.

31. Vladka Meed, *On Both Sides of the Wall: Memoirs from the Warsaw Ghetto*, trans. Steven Meed (New York: Holocaust Library, 1979), p. 276; pp. 60–61.

32. Anonymous, "The School System," in Joseph Kermish (ed.), *To Live with Honor and Die with Honor! . . .* Selected Documents from the Warsaw Ghetto Underground Archives "O.S." ["Oneg Shabbath"] (Jerusalem: Yad Vashem, 1986), p. 503.

33. The Jews had had experience with clandestine education and had proven their capacity for fooling the Germans. As early as 1935 in Germany, when Jews were banned from attending universities, a *Hochschule fur die Wissenschaft des Judentums* was transformed secretly into a Jewish university; the Nazis had been told that it was a religious school (which at that time they were prepared to tolerate) and they accepted this as fact; see Dawidowicz, *War Against the Jews*, p. 186.

34. Bakowska, interview, HCM 3–83, 1 February 1983, 55 pp., p. 38.

35. Several of the students remember this system of passing books from one to the next (see Pernal, HCM 4–87, p. 23; Borman, HCM 23–82, p. 14). However, others recall no shortage of books (see Berg, HCM 6–84, p. 43); Balin had the good fortune to study with students from a very well-to-do family who had apparently unlimited books and equipment, a situation that certainly was atypical (Balin, HCM 7–83, p. 14).

Only three texts used in the ghetto are identifiable with certainty. Dr. Ludwik Stabholz owns two anatomical texts that were given him by his professor at Warsaw University, Dr. Edward Loth, and that he used in teaching students in the underground school. They are Adam Bochenek, *Anatomja Człowieka: Podręcznik dla Słuchaczów Szkól Wyższych i lekarzy* [*Human Anatomy: A Textbook for Students of Higher Schools and Physicians*], Vol. 2 (Kraków: Nakładem Polskiej Academji Umiejętnosci, 1921), and Vol. 3, 1928; and Zygmunt Messing, *Krótki Zarys: Anatomji I Fizjologji Ośrodkowego Układu Nerwowego* [*Synopsis of Anatomy and Physiology of the Central Nervous System*] (Warszawa: University of Warsaw, 1922–23), p. 263. Balin, Borman, and Tadeusz Stabholz remember using the Sobotta atlas (see Borman, HCM 23–82, p. 14; T. Stabholz, HCM 26–82, p. 18): Joh. Sobotta, *Atlas der deskriptiven Anatomie des Menschen*, 3 vols. (Munich and Berlin: J. F. Lehmanns Verlag, 1941); Dr. Borman's copy is in the author's possession.

36. Hirszfeldowna, *The Story of One Life*, p. 211.

37. Borman, HCM 23–82, p. 18.

38. Henry Fenigstein, interview, HCM 17–82, 28 June 1982, p. 5.

39. Berg, interview, HCM 6–84, p. 13; Henry Fenigstein, interview, HCM 3–82, p. 9; L. Stabholz, interview, HCM 5–87, p. 9.

40. Pernal, interview, HCM 4–87, Toronto Ontario, 19 May 1987, 36 pp., p. 13.

41. Wygodzka, interview, HCM 1–88, New York City, 8 January 1988, 28 pp., p. 13.

42. Bakowska, interview, HCM 3–83, p. 29.

43. Borman, interview, HCM 23–82, p. 13; Bakowska, interview, HCM 3–83, p. 27.

44. Henry Fenigstein, as Told to Saundra Collis, *The Holocaust and I: Memoirs of a Survivor* (Toronto: Unpublished MS, 1990), pp. 521 + xlii; p. xxiv.

45. Bakowska, interview, HCM 3–83, p. 28; Berg, interview, HCM 6–84, pp. 43–44.

46. Juliusz Zweibaum, Kurs przysposobienia sanitarnego do walki z epidemiami w getcie Warszawskim w latach, 1940–1942." [Courses of Sanitary Training], *Archiwum Historji Meydcyny* 21:355, 1958.

47. Edwarda Mark, "Konspiracyjne wyzsze szkoly medyczne," *Sluzba Zdrowia* p. 3, 1962.

48. L. Stabholz, interview, HCM 5–87, pp. 13–14.

49. Bakowska, interview, HCM 3–83, p. 20.

50. T. Stabholz, interview, HCM 26–82, pp. 12, 14.

51. T. Stabholz, interview, HCM 26–82, pp. 16–17.

52. Ryszard Zablotniak, "Das geheime Medizin- und Pharmazie-studium in Polen in den Jahren 1939 bis 1945," *Zeitschrift für Arztliche Fortbildung* 83: 365, 1989.

53. T. Stabholz, HCM 26–82, pp. 18, 21; Bakowska, in Borman, HCM 23–82, p. 29; Fenigstein, HCM 17–82, p. 4.

54. Borman, HCM 23–82, p. 14; Bakowska, HCM 3–83, p. 22.

55. Wygodzka, interview, 8 January 1988, HCM 1–88, p. 16.

56. Balin, interview, HCM 7–83, Timberlake, Ohio, 16 May 1983, 46 pp., p. 19.

57. Bakowska, HCM 3–83, p. 32; Borman, HCM 23–82, p. 9; Borman, HCM 3–84, p. 18, 44. An anonymous historian in the ghetto has described the significance of hearing the approach of an automobile at that time: "Every night people were killed. The procedure was established. A car would stop in front of the house. Steps would reverberate. Someone would leave the flat under escort. A shot would then be fired in the gateway or on the nearest street-corner. At night, the ears were kept cocked in fear lest the car passing in the street should stop. Knocking on the front door of a building made the hearts of all its inhabitants thump in the instinctive, mortal fear of all living creatures": from "The Last Stage of Resettlement is Death," in Kermish, *To Live with Honor*, p. 706.

58. Berg, interview, HCM 6–84, p. 10.

59. Bakowska, interview, HCM 3–83, pp. 25–26; Borman, interview, HCM 23–82, p. 17.

60. Stanislaw Adler, *In the Warsaw Ghetto, 1940–1943: An Account of a Witness* (Jerusalem: Yad Vashem, 1982), p. 115.

61. Borman, interview, HCM 23–82, p. 14.

62. Borman, interview, HCM 23–82, 13, 31; Bakowska, HCM 3–83, pp. 23, 25–26.

63. "Often the German soldiers beat the male students if they thought they looked too semitic, so that on later days we would see our colleagues attending with bandaged heads"; see Alicja Zawadzka-Wetz, *Refleksje Pewnego Życia* (Paris: Instytut Literacki, 1967), p. 23. Zawadzka-Wetz was herself a student in the underground medical school.

64. Borman was quite worried that this would happen; HCM 23–82, p. 17.

65. Hirszfeld, *The Story of One Life*, p. 14.

66. Marek Balin, interview, HCM 7–83, 16 May 1983, p. 14.

67. Pernal, interview, HCM 4–87, pp. 27–29.

68. Balin, interview, HCM 7–83, pp. 9, 12, 26.

69. Stabholz, interview, HCM 26–82, p. 15.

70. Bronislaw Wisniewski, interview, HCM 2–89, New York, 3 May 1989, 36 pp., pp. 24–25.

71. Frank Stiffel, *The Tale of the Ring: A Kaddish* (Toronto and New York: Bantam Books, 1985), p. 56.

72. Balin, HCM 7–83, p. 13.

73. Pernal, HCM 4–87, pp. 28–29.

74. HCMU/OHA, interview of Millie Eisen, 20 June 1985, HCM 58–85, p. 6.

75. A moving and detailed eyewitness account of Czyste Hospital during its last months in the ghetto, particularly the period on Gesia Street, is contained in YVA 03/398 0–3/2–2, Sabina Gurfinkiel-Glocerowa, "Szpital na Czystem," 51 pp.

76. Eisen, interview, HCM 58–85, p. 19.

77. Borman, interview, HCM 3–84, p. 39.

78. Dr. Bronislaw Wisniewski, personal communication, TLS 13 May 1898 to C. G. Roland.

79. L. Stabholz, interview, HCM 5–87, p. 15.

80. Balin, interview, HCM 7–83, 16 May 1983, 46 pp., p. 14.

81. See, e.g., T. Stabholz, interview, HCM 26–82, p. 18, and Balin, interview, HCM 7–83, p. 12.

82. Berg, interview, HCM 6–84, pp. 42–43.

83. Anonymous, "[Special Schools]," cited in Kermish, *To Live with Honor*, p. 516.

84. This is the figure given in Zweibaum, pp. 355–56; also cited in Mark, "Konspiracyjne."

85. Borman, interview, HCM 23–82, p. 19.

86. L. Stabholz, interview, HCM 5–87, p. 11.

87. Anonymous, "The school system," cited in Kermish, *To Live with Honor*, p. 514.

88. T. Stabholz, interview, HCM 26–82, p. 20.

89. Zweibaum, "Kurs przysposobienia," pp. 355–56. Since Zweibaum was the originator of the school, his evidence in this regard should have weight.

90. Wygodzka, interview, HCM 1–88, p. 13; Borman, interview, HCM 23–82, pp. 32–33; Balin, interview, HCM 7–83, p. 25; Bakowska, interview, HCM 3–83, p. 23–24.

91. Borman, interview, HCM 23–82, p. 17.

92. Not surprisingly, in universities outside Poland, no credit was given for the clandestine studies; see T. Stabholz, interview, HCM 26–82, pp. 40–41.

93. Irena Piszczek, interview, HCM 2–88, 23 June 1986, p. 11.

94. Hilberg et al., *The Warsaw Diary of Adam Czerniakow*, pp. 33, 75.

95. See Joseph Tenenbaum, "Nazi Rule in Poland and the Jewish Medical Profession," in Leon Wulman and Joseph Tenenbaum, *The Martyrdom of Jewish Physicians in Poland*, ed. Louis Falstein (New York: Exposition Press, 1963), p. 205.

96. See, for example, two articles on epithelial histology: J. Zweibaum, "Sur la survie de l'épithélium vibratile *in vitro*," *Comptes Rendus Hebdomadaires des Seances et Memoires de la Societe de Biologie et de ses Filiales* 93: 782–84, 1925, and J. Zweibaum, "Analyse histophysiologique de l'épithélium vibratile en état de survie *in vitro*," ibid., 93: 785–87, 1925.

97. Zawadzka-Wetz, *Refleksje*, p. 23.

98. Wygodzka, interview, HCM 1–88, New York City, 8 January 1988, 28 pp., p. 17.

99. See *Martyrdom of Jewish Physicians*, pp. 55–56.

100. Biographical sketch based on the following: H. Schadewaldt, "Ludwik Hirszfeld," *Dictionary of Scientific Biography* 6: 432–34, 1972; Falstein, *Martyrdom*, pp. 61–62; his biography, *Historia Jednego Zycia* (Warszawa: Instytut Wydawniczy Pax, 1967), in translation, Hirszfeldowna, *The Story of One Life*; and from interviews. Note his article on racial serological differences: Ludwik Hirschfeld [*sic*] and Hanna Hirschfeld, "Serological Differences Between the Blood of Different Races," *Lancet* 2: 675–79, 1919. See also L. Hirschfeld, "A New Germ of Paratyphoid," *Lancet* 1: 296–97, 1919.

101. Falstein, *Martyrdom*, pp. 61–62, and Schadewaldt, "Ludwig Hirszfeld." See also William H. Schneider, "Chance and Social Setting in the Application of the Discovery of the Blood Groups," *Bulletin of the History of Medicine* 57: 545–62, 1983, especially pp.

555ff regarding Hirszfeld, his discoveries, and their application to racial theories by the Nazis.

102. Wygodzka, interview, HCM 1–88, p. 16.

103. Berg, interview, HCM 6–84, p. 10.

104. Berg, interview, HCM 6–84, p. 15.

105. Bakowska, interview, HCM 3–83, p. 22; in his memoirs, Hirszfeld gives a statistical computation and concludes that the ghetto might have lasted eight years before it disappeared (Hirszfeldowna, *The Story of One Life*, p. 230). With regard to his speaking ability, Hirszfeld has recorded how impressed he was, as a student, by the theatrical lecturing style of his professor of philosophy in Berlin, Simml: "later I endeavored to give my lectures the same plasticity of expression I found in Simml." Hirszfeldowna, *The Story of One Life*, p. 5. And in describing the ghetto period specifically, he wrote, "Never before did I speak with such lucidity and fire," p. 207.

106. Wisniewski, interview, HCM 2–89, 3 May 1989, pp. 19–20.

107. Wygodzka, interview, HCM 1–88, 8 January 1988, pp. 16–17.

108. Bakowska, interview, HCM 3–83, 1 February 1983, p. 25.

109. Adina Blady Szwajger, *I Remember Nothing More: The Warsaw Children's Hospital and the Jewish Resistance*, trans. Tasja Darowska and Danusia Stok (New York: Pantheon Books, 1990), pp. xx + 184, illust., maps, p. 40.

110. Makowerowa, *Henryk Makower*, pp. 184–85.

111. He also taught Wygodzka after the war, and she remembers his annoying but unconscious habit, when speaking on the telephone, of nodding or shaking his head, without speaking, in answer to questions; Wygodzka, HCM 1–88, p. 21.

112. Wygodzka recalls him as "a fine old man with white hair," who spoke in an unusual high-pitched voice; Wygodzka, HCM 1–88, p. 20.

113. According to Tadeusz Stabholz, his father developed an infection after operating with inadequately sterilized instruments and died in the ghetto about April, 1941; T. Stabholz, HCM 26–82, p. 17.

114. For example, Borman, interview, HCM 23–82, p. 10; Eisen, interview, HCM 58–85, pp. 16–17; Pernal, interview, HCM 4–87, p. 4.

115. Personal communication, letter from Prof. Jacob Felberbaum, 14 October 1988, to C. G. Roland.

116. Happily, the lists of the martyred occasionally are erroneous. Dr. Henry Fenigstein is cited in *Martyrdom* as one who did not survive. He did, and meetings with him have been an important source for this study.

117. These specific figures all are taken from [Stanislaw Rozycki?], "The School System," in Kermish, *To Live with Honor*, pp. xliv + 790, illust., p. 514. According to Rudowski and Zablotniak, the students paid 200 zloty tuition and teachers earned up to 10 zloty for an hour's lecture, though these figures may refer to one of the Warsaw schools outside the ghetto, either the so-called Zaorski School (see Rudowski, "Clandestine Medical Studies," pp. 242–43) or the Paskiewicz School, which was functioning by 1940 (Janina Zaborowska, interview by Charles G. Roland, Oral History Archive, Hannah Chair for the History of Medicine McMaster University, Hamilton, Ontario, HCM 76–85, Oakville, Ontario, 12 September 1985, 34 pp., pp. 12–13).

118. These are the hours cited in what seems to be the sole extant document from the medical school.

119. [Rozycki?], "The School System," in Kermish, *To Live with Honor*, p. 514.

120. [Rozycki?], "The School System," in Kermish, *To Live with Honor*, p. 511.

121. [Rozycki?], "The School System," in Kermish, *To Live with Honor*, p. 514.

122. Borman, interview, HCM 23–82, Kingston, Ontario, 26 September 1982, 41 pp., p. 9.

123. Borman, interview, HCM 23–82, Kingston, Ontario, 26 September 1982, 41 pp., p. 21.

124. Tadeusz Stabholz, interview by Charles G. Roland, Oral History Archive, Hannah Chair for the History of Medicine McMaster University, Hamilton, Ontario, HCM 26–82, Cleveland, Ohio, 4 December 1982, 46 pp., p. 17.

125. Cited in Borman, interview, HCM 23–82, pp. 8–9.

126. Wygodzka, interview, HCM 1–88, p. 12.

127. Anonymous, "The School System," in Kermish, *To Live with Honor*, pp. 502-03.

128. L. Stabholz, interview, HCM 5–87, pp. 14, 31.

129. Balin, interview, HCM 7–83, p. 34.

130. Fenigstein, interview, HCM 17–82, pp. 3–6.

131. T. Stabholz, interview, HCM 26–82, pp. 21–22.

132. Borman, interview, HCM 23–82, p. 12.

133. Bakowska, interview, HCM 3–83, pp. 32–33.

134. Fenigstein, interview, HCM 17–82, Toronto, Ontario, 28 June 1982, 19 pp., p. 7.

135. Lewin, *A Cup of Tears*, p. 11.

136. Dawidowicz, *War Against the Jews*, p. 213.

137. Borman, interview, HCM 3–84, p. 19.

138. Fenigstein, interview, HCM 17–82, p. 15.

139. Apenszlak, *Black Book*, pp. 28–29.

140. Balin, interview, HCM 7–83, p. 28.

141. Bakowska, interview, HCM 3–83, p. 18.

142. Berg, interview, HCM 6–84, Milpitas, California, 14 September 1984, 49 pp., p. 7.

143. Borman, interview, HCM 23–82, Kingston, Ontario, 26 September 1982, 41 pp., pp. 1–2.

144. Gutman, *Jews of Warsaw*, p. 143.

145. They also disproved the gloomy predictions of Dr. Milejkowski, who claimed that due to the terrible conditions in the ghetto, "only incompetents will graduate these courses." Milejkowski, "Answers to a Questionnaire by Dr. Milejkowski," in Kermish, *To Live with Honor*, p. 744.

146. Horace, Book 3, Ode 30.

147. Wdowinski, *And We Are Not Saved*, p. 51.

148. Hirszfeldowna, *The Story of One Life*, p. 206.

149. Hilberg et al., *The Warsaw Diary of Adam Czerniakow*, p. 300, entry of 20 November 1941.

150. Anonymous, "B. Clandestine Schooling, Secondary Schools and Universities, Jewish youth," in Kermish, *To Live with Honor*, p. 460.

151. Anonymous, "The School System," in Kermish, *To Live with Honor*, p. 512.

152. Hilberg et al., *The Warsaw Diary of Adam Czerniakow*, p. 305-06, entry of 7 December 1941.

153. Wygodzka, interview, HCM 1–88, 8 January 1988, p. 25.

Chapter 11

1. Vladka Meed, *On Both Sides of the Wall: Memoirs from the Warsaw Ghetto*, trans. Steven Meed (New York: Holocaust Library, 1979), p. 276; p. 70.

2. Meed, *On Both Sides of the Wall*, p. 103.

3. Henry Shoskes, *No Traveler Returns* (Garden City, NY: Doubleday, Doran & Co., 1945), pp. xiii + 267; p. 136.

4. Abraham Lewin, *A Cup of Tears: A Diary of the Warsaw Ghetto* (London: Fontana/Collins, 1990), pp. xii + 308; p. 262, n. 95.

5. Jerusalem, YVA 03/398 0–3/2–2, testimony of Sabina Gurfinkiel-Glocerowa, "Szpital na Czystem," undated, ca. 1945, p. 54.

6. Karolina Borman, interview, HCM 23–82, 26 September 1982, pp. 27ff.

7. Abraham Shulman, *The Case of Hotel Polski: An Account of One of the Most Enigmatic Episodes of World War II* (New York: Holocaust Library, 1982), p. 240.

8. Halina Berg [pseudonym], interview, HCM 6–84, 14 September 1984, pp. 26–27.

9. Berg, interview, HCM 6–84, 14 September 1984, p. 32.

10. Marek Balin, interview, HCM 7–83, 16 May 1983, p. 26.

11. Meed, *On Both Sides of the Wall*, p. 82.

12. Meed, *On Both Sides of the Wall*, p. 194.

13. Nathan Gross, "'Aryan Papers' in Poland," in *Extermination and Resistance: Historical Records and Source Material* (Kibbutz Lohamei Haghettaot, Israel: Ghetto Fighters' House, 1958), pp. 79–85; pp. 79–80.

14. Balin, interview, HCM 7–83, 16 May 1983, pp. 26–27.

15. Zofia S. Kubar, *Double Identity: A Memoir* (New York: Hill and Wang, 1989), pp. 209; p. 18.

16. Hanna Krall, *Shielding the Flame: An Intimate Conversation with Dr. Marek Edelman, the Last Surviving Leader of the Warsaw Ghetto Uprising*, trans. Joanna Stasinska and Lawrence Weschler (New York: Henry Holt and Co., 1986), pp. xiii + 124; p. 15.

17. Dr. Bronislaw Wisniewski, personal communication, TLS 13 May 1898 to C. G. Roland.

18. Feliks Kanabus, "Address at the JNF, September 20, 1965" in Jacob Glatstein, Israel Knox, and Samuel Margoshes (eds.), *Anthology of Holocaust Literature* (Philadelphia: Jewish Publication Society of America, 1969), pp. 392–95.

19. Lewin, *A Cup of Tears*, p. 43.

20. Yisrael Gutman, *Jews of Warsaw, 1939–1943: Ghetto, Underground, Revolt*, trans. Ina Friedman (Bloomington and Indianapolis: Indiana University Press, 1989), pp. xxi + 487; p. 285.

21. Berg, interview, HCM 6–84, 14 September 1984, p. 33.

22. Berg, interview, HCM 6–84, 14 September 1984, pp. 35–37.

23. Janina Zaborowska, interview, HCM 76–85, 12 September 1985, pp. 7–8.

24. See, for example, Nechama Tec, *When Light Pierced the Darkness: Christian Rescue of Jews in Nazi-Occupied Poland* (New York and Oxford: Oxford University Press, 1986), pp. xv + 262, and Wladyslaw Bartoszewski, *The Blood Shed Unites Us (Pages from the History of Help to the Jews in Occupied Poland)* (Warsaw: Interpress Publishers, 1970), p. 244.

25. Gutman, *Jews of Warsaw*, p. 272.

26. Balin, interview, HCM 7–83, 16 May 1983, pp. 24–25.

27. Irena Bakowska, interview, HCM 3–83, 1 February 1983, pp. 40–42.

28. Eugenia Pernal, interview, HCM 4–87, 19 May 1987, p. 27.

29. Pernal, interview, HCM 4–87, 19 May 1987, p. 20.

30. Teresa Prekerowa, "The Relief Council for Jews in Poland, 1942–1945," in Chimen Abramsky, Maciej Jachimczyk, and Antony Polonsky (eds.), *The Jews in Poland* (Oxford: Basil Blackwell, 1986), pp. xi + 264; p. 167.

31. Jozef Garlinski, *Poland in the Second World War* (New York: The Macmillan Co., 1985), pp. xxi + 387; p. 166.

32. Gutman, *Jews of Warsaw*, pp. 355–56.

33. Meed, *On Both Sides of the Wall*, p. 89.

34. Jacob Sloan (ed.), *Notes from the Warsaw Ghetto: The Journal of Emmanuel Ringelblum* (New York: Schocken Books, 1974), pp. xxvii + 369; pp. 346–47.

35. AAJJDC AR3344, file 801, Report (Sept.) 1942–1943; from Report of the Jewish National Committee, Poland, to Dr. Schwarzbart, London, 15 November 1943.

36. Prekerowa, "The Relief Council for Jews," p. 162.

37. Władysław Bartoszewski, *The Warsaw Ghetto: A Christian's Testimony* (Boston: Beacon Press, 1987), p. 57.

38. Prekerowa, "The Relief Council for Jews," p. 171.

39. Meed, *On Both Sides of the Wall*, p. 204.

40. Chaim Lazar, *Muranowska 7: The Warsaw Ghetto Uprising*, trans. Yosef Shachter (Tel Aviv: Massada-P.E.C. Press Ltd., 1966), p. 341; p. 23.

41. Shoskes, *No Traveler Returns*, p. 95.

42. Lazar, *Muranowska 7*, pp. 136–37.

43. Raul Hilberg, Stanislaw Staron, and Josef Kermisz (eds.), *The Warsaw Diary of Adam Czerniakow: Prelude to Doom*, trans. S. Staron and the staff of Yad Vashem (New York, Stein & Day, 1982), pp. viii + 420; p. 382, entry of 19 July 1942.

44. Shoskes, *No Traveler Returns*, p. 107.

45. Gutman, *Jews of Warsaw*, p. 206.

46. Simon Wiesenthal, *Justice, Not Vengeance* (London: Weidenfeld and Nicolson, 1989), pp. xi + 372; p. 278.

47. Lewin, *A Cup of Tears*, p. 276, n. 209.

48. Gutman, *Jews of Warsaw*, pp. 209–13.

49. Gutman, *Jews of Warsaw*, p. 211.

50. Meed, *On Both Sides of the Wall*, p. 61.

51. Tadeusz Stabholz, interview, HCM 26–82, 4 December 1982, p. 34.

52. Stabholz, interview, HCM 26–82, 4 December 1982, p. 32.

53. Stabholz, interview, HCM 26–82, 4 December 1982, p. 33.

54. Anonymous, in Joseph Kermish (ed.), *To Live with Honor and Die with Honor!* . . . *Selected Documents from the Warsaw Ghetto Underground Archives "O.S." ["Oneg Shabbath"]* (Jerusalem: Yad Vashem, 1986), pp. xliv + 790; p. 691.

55. Gutman, *Jews of Warsaw*, p. 214.

56. Lewin, *A Cup of Tears*, p. 136, entry of 22 July 1942.

57. Lewin, *A Cup of Tears*, p. 139, entry of 26 July 1942.

58. Tuvia Borzykowski, *Between Tumbling Walls*, trans. Mendel Kohansky (Beit Lohamei Hagettaot, Israel: Hakibbutz Hameuchad Publishing House, 1972), p. 229; p. 86.

59. Noemi Makowerowa (ed.), *Henryk Makower: Pamietnik z getta warszawskiego, pazdziernik 1940-styczen 1943* (Wrocław, Warszawa, Kraków, Gdansk, and Lodż: Zakład Narodowy im. Ossolinskich Wydawnictwo, 1987), p. 213; p. 98–9.

60. David Wdowinski, *And We Are Not Saved* (New York: Philosophical Library, 1985), pp. xxi + 222; pp. 65–66.

61. Janina David, *A Square of Sky: Recollections of My Childhood* (New York: W. W. Norton & Co., 1964), p. 222; p. 193.

62. Frank Stiffel, *The Tale of the Ring: A Kaddish* (Toronto, New York, London, Sydney, and Auckland: Bantam Books, 1985), p. 348; p. 67.

63. Gurfinkiel-Glocerowa, "Szpital na Czystem," p. 31.

64. Pernal, interview, HCM 4–87, 19 May 1987, p. 19.

65. Pernal, interview, HCM 4–87, 19 May 1987, p. 18.

66. Sloan (ed.), *Notes from the Warsaw Ghetto*, pp. xxvii + 369; p. 311.

67. Gurfinkiel-Glocerowa, "Szpital na Czystem," p. 23.

68. Wdowinski, *And We Are Not Saved*, p. 66.

69. Lucy S. Dawidowicz, *The War Against the Jews, 1933–1945* (Toronto and New York: Bantam Books, 1986), pp. xxxx+466; p. 307.

70. Philip Friedman (ed.), *Martyrs and Fighters: The Epic of the Warsaw Ghetto* (New York: Frederick A. Praeger, 1954), p. 324; p. 160.

71. Krall, *Shielding the Flame*, p. 43.

72. Friedman, *Martyrs and Fighters*, p. 160.

73. Krall, *Shielding the Flame*, p. 7.

74. Krall, *Shielding the Flame*, pp. 35–36.

75. Gurfinkiel-Glocerowa, "Szpital na Czystem," pp. 27–29.

76. Gurfinkiel-Glocerowa, "Szpital na Czystem," p. 31.

77. Gurfinkiel-Glocerowa, "Szpital na Czystem," p. 32.

78. Gurfinkiel-Glocerowa, "Szpital na Czystem," p. 33.

79. Sloan, *The Journal of Emmanuel Ringelblum*, p. 311.

80. Ludwig Stabholz, interview by Charles G. Roland, Oral History Archive, Hannah Chair for the History of Medicine McMaster University, Hamilton, Ontario, HCM 5–87, Tel Aviv, Israel, 11 June 1987, 33 pp., pp. 27–28.

81. Balin, interview, HCM 7–83, 16 May 1983, p. 13.

82. Balin, interview, HCM 7–83, 16 May 1983, pp. 14–15.

83. Jerusalem, YVA 03/441, Marek Balin, "Selekcja w szpitalu," 1945, pp. 1–2.

84. YVA 03/441, Balin, "Selekcja w szpitalu," p. 2.

85. YVA 03/441, Balin, "Selekcja w szpitalu," pp. 3–4.

86. YVA 03/441, Balin, "Selekcja w szpitalu," p. 4.

87. YVA 03/441, Balin, "Selekcja w szpitalu," pp. 2–3.

88. Berg, interview, HCM 6–84, 14 September 1984, pp. 21–22.

89. Borman, interview, HCM 23–82, 26 September 1982, pp. 23–26.

90. Lewin, *A Cup of Tears*, p. 165, entry for 24 August 1942.

91. Adina Blady Szwajger, *I Remember Nothing More: The Warsaw Children's Hospital and the Jewish Resistance*, trans. Tasja Darowska and Danusia Stok (New York: Pantheon Books, 1990), pp. xx+184, illust., maps, p. 56.

92. Lewin, *A Cup of Tears*, p. 230.

93. Wilhelm Hagen, "Krieg, Hunger und Pestilenz in Warschau, 1939–1943," *Gesundheitswesen und Desinfektion* 8: 115–28; 9: 129–43, 1973; p. 130.

94. Zentrale Stelle der Landesjustizverwaltungen, Ludwigsburg, Polen 365d, pp. 654–72, Monthly reports by Lichtenbaum, the new chairman of the *Judenrat*.

95. Makowerowa, *Henryk Makower*, pp. 110–12

96. Henry Fenigstein, as Told to Saundra Collis, *The Holocaust and I: Memoirs of a Survivor* (Toronto: Unpublished MS, 1990), pp. 521+xlii; p. 156.

97. Hanna Hirszfeldowna (ed.), *The Story of One Life, from "Historia Jednego Zycia" by Ludwig Hirszfeld* trans. F. R. Camp and F. R. Ellis (Fort Knox, KY: Blood Transfusion Division, United States Army Medical Research Laboratory, n.d.), p. 368; p. 279.

98. Wdowinski, *And We Are Not Saved*, pp. 70–71.

99. Marek Edelman, cited in Bartoszewski, *The Warsaw Ghetto*, p. 41.

100. Pernal, interview, HCM 4–87, 19 May 1987, pp. 6–7.

101. Berg, interview, HCM 6–84, 14 September 1984, p. 25.

102. Fenigstein, *The Holocaust and I*, p. 147.

103. Lewin, *A Cup of Tears*, p. 154, entry of 12 August 1942.

104. Stiffel, *The Tale of the Ring*, p. 73.

105. Bartoszewski, *The Warsaw Ghetto*, p. 35.

106. Lewin, *A Cup of Tears*, p. 153, entry of 11 August 1942.

107. Lewin, *A Cup of Tears*, p. 213, entry of 22 November 1942.

108. Gurfinkiel-Glocerowa, "Szpital na Czystem," p. 34.

109. Gutman, *Jews of Warsaw*, pp. 268–69.

110. Anonymous, "Social Data for November, 1942," in Kermish, *To Live with Honor*, p. 165.

111. Lewin, *A Cup of Tears*, p. 217, entry of 27 November 1942.

112. Helena Szereszewski, "In the Financial Department of the Judenrat (Memories of the Warsaw Ghetto)," in *Extermination and Resistance: Historical Records and Source Material* (Kibbutz Lohamei Haghettaot: Ghetto Fighter's House in Memory of Yitzhak Katznelson, 1958), pp. 65–78; p. 65.

113. Szereszewski, "Financial Department of the Judenrat," p. 66.

114. Gutman, *Jews of Warsaw*, p. 274.

115. Howard Roiter, *Voices from the Holocaust* (New York: William-Frederick Press, 1975), p. 221; p. 85.

116. Gutman, *Jews of Warsaw*, p. 178.

117. Gutman, *Jews of Warsaw*, p. 236.

118. Wdowinski, *And We Are Not Saved*, p. 79.

119. Raul Hilberg, *The Destruction of the European Jews* (New York and London: Holmes & Meier, 1985), pp. xii + 1274; p. 508.

120. Wdowinski, *And We Are Not Saved*, p. 82.

121. Fenigstein, *The Holocaust and I*, p. xxxiv.

122. Wdowinski, *And We Are Not Saved*, p. 86.

123. Gurfinkiel-Glocerowa, "Szpital na Czystem," p. 45.

124. Wdowinski, *And We Are Not Saved*, p. 86.

125. Wdowinski, *And We Are Not Saved*, p. 89.

126. Leon Uris, *Mila 18* (Toronto, New York, London, and Sydney: Bantam Books, 1962), p. 563.

127. Balin, interview, HCM 7–83, 16 May 1983, p. 22.

128. Gurfinkiel-Glocerowa, "Szpital na Czystem," p. 47.

129. Gurfinkiel-Glocerowa, "Szpital na Czystem," p. 50.

130. Gurfinkiel-Glocerowa, "Szpital na Czystem," pp. 62–63.

131. Gurfinkiel-Glocerowa, "Szpital na Czystem," p. 50.

132. Gurfinkiel-Glocerowa, "Szpital na Czystem," p. 53.

133. Gurfinkiel-Glocerowa, "Szpital na Czystem," p. 49.

134. Krall, *Shielding the Flame*, p. 37.

135. Gutman, *Jews of Warsaw*, pp. 364ff; Juergen Stroop, *The Stroop Report: The Jewish Quarter of Warsaw Is No More!*, trans. Sybil Milton (London: Secker & Warburg, 1980), p. [230], illust., maps.

136. *The Stroop Report*.

137. Gutman, *Jews of Warsaw*, p. 365.

138. Zivia Lubetkin, *In The Days of Destruction and Revolt*, trans. Ishai Tubbin (Beit Lohamei Haghettaot, Israel: Hakibbutz Hameuchad Publishing House and Am Ovod Publishing House, 1981), p. 338; pp. 184–85.

139. Millie Eisen, interview, HCM 58–85, 20 June 1985, pp. 12–13.

140. Henry Fenigstein, interview, HCM 3–82, 21 January 1982, p. 9.

141. Inside the ghetto, even more than elsewhere, many pursued hedonistic escapes from reality. For some this was alcohol, for others sex; Fenigstein collected stamps. He was sought out by *Hauptstürmführer* Franz Konrad through the intermediacy of a Jewish stamp dealer, formerly from Danzig but then in the Warsaw ghetto. Fenigstein, *The Holocaust and I*, p. 116.

142. Fenigstein, *The Holocaust and I*, pp. 169–70.

143. Fenigstein, *The Holocaust and I*, p. 191.

144. Fenigstein, *The Holocaust and I*, pp. 181–82.

145. Stabholz, interview, HCM 26–82, 4 December 1982, pp. 29–30.

146. Stabholz, interview, HCM 26–82, 4 December 1982, p. 30.

147. Stabholz, interview, HCM 26–82, 4 December 1982, p. 31.

148. Tadeusz Stabholz, *Siedem Piekieł,* (Stuttgart, 1947), p. 300.

149. Balin, interview, HCM 7–83, 16 May 1983, pp. 22–24.

150. Balin, interview, HCM 7–83, 16 May 1983, p. 24.

151. Borzykowski, *Between Tumbling Walls*, p. 57.

152. Garlinski, *Poland in the Second World War*, p. 172.

153. AAJJDC AR3344, file 801, Report (Sept.), 1942–1943; from Report of the Jewish National Committee, Poland, to Dr. Schwarzbart, London, 15 November 1943. The committee consisted of Dr. A. Berman, Icchal Cukerman, and "D. Kaftor," a pseudonym for David Guzik of the Joint.

154. Joanna K. M. Hanson, *The Civilian Population and the Warsaw Uprising of 1944* (Cambridge, London, New York, New Rochelle, Melbourne, and Sydney: Cambridge University Press, 1982), pp. xiii+345; p. 15.

Chapter 12

1. Raul Hilberg, Stanislaw Staron, and Josef Kermisz (eds.), *The Warsaw Diary of Adam Czerniakow: Prelude to Doom*, trans. S. Staron and the staff of Yad Vashem (New York: Stein & Day, 1982), pp. viii+420; p. 232.

2. Joseph Kermish (ed.), *To Live with Honor and Die with Honor! . . . Selected Documents from the Warsaw Ghetto Underground Archives "O.S."* [*"Oneg Shabbath"*] (Jerusalem: Yad Vashem, 1986), pp. xliv+790, illust.

3. Emil Apfelbaum, (ed.), *Maladie de Famine: Recherches Cliniques sur la Famine Exécutées dans la Ghetto de Varsovie en 1942* (Warsaw: American Joint Distribution Committee, 1946), p. 264; Emil Apfelbaum (ed.), *Choroba Glodowa: Badania Kliniczne Nad Glodem Wykonane w Getcie Warszawskim z Roku 1942* (Warsaw: American Joint Distribution Committee, 1946), p. 265; and Myron Winick (ed.), *Hunger Disease: Studies by the Jewish Physicians in the Warsaw Ghetto*, trans. Martha Osnos (New York, Chichester, Brisbane, and Toronto: John Wiley & Sons, 1979), pp. xiv+261, illust.

4. Rose Klepfisz and Emil Lang, *Annotated Catalogue of the Archives of the American Jewish Joint Distribution Committee, 1933–1944* (New York: AJJDC, undated).

5. Hilberg et al., *The Warsaw Diary of Adam Czerniakow*.

6. Jacob Sloan (ed.), *Notes from the Warsaw Ghetto: The Journal of Emmanuel Ringelblum* (New York: Schocken Books, 1974), pp. xxvii+369, maps.

7. Abraham Lewin, *A Cup of Tears: A Diary of the Warsaw Ghetto* (London: Fontana/Collins, 1990), pp. xii+308.

8. E. P. Kulawiec (ed. and trans.), *The Warsaw Ghetto Memoirs of Janusz Korczak* (Washington, DC: University Press of America, 1979), pp. xvii+127, illust.

9. Henryk Fenigstein, *Varshever Yidisher Shpitol beisn di Nazi-Rezhim* (Frankfurt-am-Main: Buchdruckerei Joh. Wagner & Sohne, 1948), p. 20, map.

10. Mordecai Lenski, "Problems of Disease in the Warsaw Ghetto," *Yad Vashem Studies* 3: 283–93, 1975.

11. Isaiah Trunk, "Epidemics and Mortality in the Warsaw Ghetto, 1939–1942," *YIVO Annual of Jewish Social Science* 8: 82–122, 1953.

12. Trunk, "Epidemics and Mortality," p. 84.

13. Wilhelm Hagen, "Krieg, Hunger und Pestilenz in Warschau, 1939–1943," *Gesundheitswesen und Desinfektion* 8: 115–28; 9: 129–43, 1973.

14. Lenski, "Problems of Disease," p. 290.

15. These figures are derived from Julian Fliederbaum, Ari Heller, Kazimierz Zwei-

baum, and Jeanne Zarchi, "Clinical Aspects of Hunger Disease in Adults," Table 1, in Myron Winick (ed.), *Hunger Disease: Studies by the Jewish Physicians in the Warsaw Ghetto*, trans. Martha Osnos (New York, Chichester, Brisbane, and Toronto, John Wiley & Sons, 1979), p. 34.

16. Wilhelm Hagen, *Auftrag und Wirklichkeit: Sozialarzt im 20.Jahrhundert* (Munich-Grafelfing: Werk-Verlag Dr. Edmund Banaschewski, 1978), p. 255; p. 179.

17. Hagen, *Auftrag und Wirklichkeit*, p. 178.

18. Hagen, *Auftrag und Wirklichkeit*, p. 181.

19. Table derived from data in Hilberg et al., *The Warsaw Diary of Adam Czerniakow*, p. 310, entry for 29 December 1941.

20. Table derived from data in Trunk, "Epidemics and Mortality," p. 98.

21. Table derived from data in Trunk, "Epidemics and Mortality," pp. 95–97. These figures should be compared with statistics indicating that there were 1640 cases of typhus reported for all of Poland in 1930, 4149 for 1935 (Trunk, p. 97).

22. Trunk, "Epidemics and Mortality," p. 97.

23. Lenski, "Problems of Disease," p. 290.

24. Hagen, *Auftrag und Wirklichkeit*, p. 176

25. Hagen, "Krieg, Hunger und Pestilenz," p. 134.

26. Lenski, "Problems of Disease," p. 288.

27. Lenski, "Problems of Disease," p. 289.

28. Lenski, "Problems of Disease," p. 290.

29. Yitzhak Arad, *Ghetto in Flames: The Struggle and Destruction of the Jews in Vilna in the Holocaust* (New York: Holocaust Library, 1982), p. 500; p. 318.

30. Sloan, *The Journal of Emmanuel Ringelblum*, pp. 7–8.

31. Sloan, *The Journal of Emmanuel Ringelblum*, p. 172.

32. Sloan, *The Journal of Emmanuel Ringelblum*, p. 194.

33. Sloan, *The Journal of Emmanuel Ringelblum*, p. 173.

34. Lewin, *A Cup of Tears*, p. 188.

35. Joanna K. M. Hanson, *The Civilian Population and the Warsaw Uprising of 1944* (Cambridge, London, New York, New Rochelle, Melbourne, and Sydney: Cambridge University Press, 1982), pp. xiii + 345; p. 9.

36. Trunk, "Epidemics and Mortality," p. 116.

37. Trunk, *Judenrat: The Jewish Councils in Eastern Europe Under Nazi Occupation* (New York: The Macmillan Co., 1972), pp. xxxv + 664; p. 151.

38. Henry Shoskes, *No Traveler Returns* (Garden City, NY: Doubleday, Doran & Co., 1945), pp. xiii + 267; p. 55.

39. Yisrael Gutman, *Jews of Warsaw, 1939–1943: Ghetto, Underground, Revolt*, trans. Ina Friedman (Bloomington and Indianapolis: Indiana University Press, 1989), pp. xxi + 487; p. 65.

40. Trunk, "Epidemics and Mortality," p. 122.

41. Trunk, *Judenrat*, p. 154.

42. Lenski, "Problems of Disease," p. 293.

43. Trunk, "Epidemics and Mortality," p. 118.

44. AAJJDC AR3344, file 811, Publicity: General, (May) 1937–1942, 1944; from *Unser Tsait*, May 1942.

45. Trunk, "Epidemics and Mortality," p. 114.

46. Trunk, "Epidemics and Mortality," p. 113.

47. Emil Apfelbaum (ed.), *Maladie de Famine: Recherches Cliniques sur la Famine Exécutées dans la Ghetto de Varsovie en 1942* (Warsaw: American Joint Distribution Committee, 1946), Table XXIII, pp. 112–13.

References

Primary Material: Unpublished

Many documents, cited individually where appropriate in the text, were found during research in the following archival repositories:

Jerusalem, Yad Vashem Archives

Koblenz, *Bundesarchiv*, German Federal Archives

Ludwigsburg, Zentrale Stelle der Landesjustizverwaltungen

New York, Archives of the American Jewish Joint Distribution Committee

Dr. Bronislaw Wisniewski, New York City, personal communication, letter, 13 May 1989, to C. G. Roland.

Dr. Jacob Felberbaum, New York City, personal communications, letters, 30 September and 14 October 1988, to C. G. Roland.

Dr. Henryk Fenigstein, Toronto, personal communication, ALS, 8 February 1991, to C. G. Roland.

Dr. Wladaslaw Lewin, New York City, personal communication, letter, 15 February 1991, to C. G. Roland.

Primary Material: Published

Anonymous, *The German New Order in Poland* (London, Hutchinson & Co. Publishers Ltd. [1942]).

Apenszlak, Jacob (ed.), *The Black Book of Polish Jewry: An Account of the Martyrdom of Polish Jewry Under the Nazi Occupation* (New York: Howard Fertig, 1982).

Apfelbaum, Emil (ed.), *Maladie de Famine: Recherches Cliniques sur la Famine Exécutées dans la Ghetto de Varsovie en 1942* (Warsaw: American Joint Distribution Committee, 1946), p. 264.

Apfelbaum, Emil (ed.), *Choroba Glodowa: Badania Kliniczne Nad Glodem Wykonane w Getcie Warszawskim z Roku 1942* (Warsaw: American Joint Distribution Committee, 1946), p. 265.

Arad, Yitzhak, Yisrael Gutman, and Abraham Margoliot (eds.), *Documents on the Holocaust: Selected Sources on the Destruction of the Jews of Germany and Austria, Poland, and the Soviet Union* (New York: Ktav Publishing House, 1981).

Browning, Christopher R., and Israel Gutman, "The Reports of a Jewish 'Informer' in the Warsaw Ghetto—Selected Documents," *Yad Vashem Studies* 17: 247–93, 1986.

Faschismus-Gett-Massenmord (Berlin: Rütten and Loening, 1961).

Fracastorii, Hieronymi, *De Contagione et Contagiosis Morbis et Eorum Curatione*, Libri III, trans. Wilmer Cave Wright (New York and London: G. P. Putnam's Sons, 1930).

Hilberg, Raul, Stanislaw Staron, and Josek Kermisz (eds.), *The Warsaw Diary of Adam Czerniakow: Prelude to Doom*, trans. S. Staron and the staff of Yad Vashem (New York: Stein & Day, 1982), pp. viii+420.

Katznelson, Yitzhak, *Vittel Diary*, trans. Myer Cohen (Israel: Beit Lohamei Hagettaot and Hakibbutz Hameuchad, 1972).

Kermish, Joseph (ed.), *To Live with Honor and Die with Honor! . . . Selected Documents from the Warsaw Ghetto Underground Archives, "O.S." ["Oneg Shabbath"]* (Jerusalem: Yad Vashem, 1986).

Kulawiec, E. P. (ed. and trans.), *The Warsaw Ghetto Memoirs of Janusz Korczak* (Washington, DC: University Press of America, 1979), pp. xvii + 127, illust.

Lind, James, *An Essay on the Most Effectual Means of Preserving the Health of Seamen in the Royal Navy, and a Dissertation on Fevers and Infection* (1779), in Christopher Lloyd (ed.), *The Health of Seamen: Selections from the Works of Dr. James Lind, Sir Gilbert Blane, and Dr. Thomas Trotter* (London: Navy Records Society, 1965).

Milton, Sybil (trans. and ed.), *The Stroop Report: The Jewish Quarter of Warsaw Is No More!* (London: Secker & Warburg, 1980).

Remak, Joachim (ed.), *The Nazi Years: A Documentary History* (New York: Simon & Schuster, 1986).

Rubinlicht, Henryk, in Howard Roiter (ed.), *Voices from the Holocaust* (New York: William-Frederick Press, 1975), p. 221; pp. 110–11.

Sloan, Jacob (ed.), *Notes from the Warsaw Ghetto: The Journal of Emmanuel Ringelblum* (New York: Schocken Books, 1974), pp. xxvii + 369, maps.

Winick, Myron (ed.), *Hunger Disease: Studies by the Jewish Physicians in the Warsaw Ghetto*, trans. Martha Osnos (New York, Chichester, Brisbane, and Toronto: John Wiley & Sons, 1979), pp. xiv + 261, illust.

Zylberberg, Michael, *A Warsaw Diary, 1939–1945* (London: Vallentine, Mitchell, 1969), p. 220, illust., map.

Interviews

All interviews with the file code HCM were conducted by the author and constitute part of the Oral History Archive, Hannah Chair for the History of Medicine, McMaster University, Hamilton, Ontario. This information will not be repeated here or in the footnotes.

Bakowska, Irena, interview, HCM 3–83, Kingston, Ontario, 1 February 1983, 55 pp.

Balin, Marek, interview, HCM 7–83, Timberlake, Ohio, 16 May 1983, 46 pp.

Berg, Halina [pseudonym], interview, HCM 6–84, Milpitas, California, 14 September 1984, 49 pp.

Borman, Karolina, interview, HCM 23–82, Kingston, Ontario, 26 September 1982, 41 pp.

Borman, Karolina, interview, HCM 3–84, South Orange, New Jersey, 28 March 1984, 46 pp.

Brysk, Miriam, interview, HCM 5–84, Galveston, Texas, 31 May 1984, 42 pp.

Dover," "Grace [pseudonym], interview, HCM 36–85, Port Dover, Ontario, 4 April 1985, 42 pp.

Eisen, Millie, interview, HCM 58–85, Greyslake, Illinois, 20 June 1985, 58 pp.

Fenigstein, Henryk, interview, HCM 3–82, Toronto Ontario, 21 January 1982, 29 pp.

Fenigstein, Henryk, interview, HCM 11–82, Toronto, Ontario, 31 March 1982, 16 pp.

Fenigstein, Henryk, interview, HCM 17–82, Toronto, Ontario, 28 June 1982, 19 pp.

Karolowicz, Karolina, interview, HCM 10–90, Warsaw, Poland, 3 November 1990, 25 pp.

Pernal, Eugenia, interview, HCM 4–87, Toronto, Ontario, 19 May 1987, 36 pp.

Piszczek, Irena, interview, HCM 2–88, Montreal, PQ, 23 June 1986, 18 pp.

Stabholz, Ludwig, interview, HCM 5–87, Tel Aviv, Israel, 11 June 1987, 33 pp.

Stabholz, Tadeusz, interview, HCM 26–82, Cleveland, Ohio, 4 December 1982, 46 pp.

Tramer, Egon, interview, HCM 24–85, Winnipeg, Manitoba, 9 March 1985, 18 pp.

Wygodzka, Bronislawa J., interview, HCM 1–88, New York City, 8 January 1988, 28 pp.

Zaborowska, Janina, interview, HCM 76–85, Oakville, Ontario, 12 September 1985, 34 pp.
Zakrzewski, Kazimierz, MD, interview, HCM 9–90, Warsaw, Poland, 2 November 1990, 25 pp.

Memoirs

Adler, Stanislaw, *In the Warsaw Ghetto, 1940–1943: An Account of a Witness* (Jerusalem: Yad Vashem, 1982), pp. xviii + 334.
Arbus, Izak, *The Number on My Forehead: A Survivor's Story* (MS, 1990), p. 224.
Balicka-Kozlowska, Helena, "Konspiracyjne Studia w Getcie Warszawskim," in Aleksandra Dawidowicza (ed.), *Tajne Nauczanie Medycyny i Farmacji w Latach, 1939–1945* (Warsaw: Panstwowy Zaklad Wydawnictwo Lekarskich, 1977), pp. 243–54.
Bartoszewski, Wladyslaw, *The Warsaw Ghetto: A Christian's Testimony*, trans. Stephen G. Cappellari (Boston: Beacon Press, 1987), pp. x + 117, illust.
Berman, Adolf, "The Fate of the Children in the Warsaw Ghetto," in Yisrael Gutman and Livia Rothkirchen (eds.), *The Catastrophe of European Jewry: Antecedents, History, Reflections* (Jerusalem: Yad Vashem, 1976), pp. 400–21.
Birenbaum, Halina, *Hope Is the Last to Die: A Personal Documentation of Nazi Terror*, trans. David Welsh (New York: Twayne Publishers, 1971), pp. iv + 246.
Bolton, J. H., "Personal Experiences as a Prisoner of War, with Special Reference to Dietetics," in H. L. Tidy, (ed.), *Inter-Allied Conferences on War Medicine, 1942–1945* (New York: Staples Press Ltd., 1947), pp. 370–72.
Borzykowski, Tuvia, *Between Tumbling Walls*, trans. Mendel Kohansky (Beit Lohamei Haghettaot, Israel: Hakibbutz Hameuchad Publishing House, 1972), p. 229, illust.
Clare, George, *Last Waltz in Vienna: The Destruction of a Family, 1842–1942* (London: Pan Books, 1990), p. 274.
David, Janina, *A Square of Sky: Recollections of My Childhood* (New York: W. W. Norton & Co., 1964), p. 222, illust.
Dawidowicz, Lucy S., *From That Place and Time: A Memoir, 1938–1947* (New York and London: W. W. Norton & Co., 1989), pp. xiv + 333, map.
Donat, Alexander, *The Holocaust Kingdom: A Memoir* (New York: Holocaust Library, 1978).
Eisner, Jack, *The Survivor*, ed. Irving A. Leitner (New York: Bantam Books, 1982), p. 263.
Eliach, Yaffa, *Hasidic Tales of the Holocaust* (New York: Avon Books, 1982), pp. xxxii + 312.
"Extracts from the Warsaw Ghetto Diary of Chaim A. Kaplan, 1940," in Yitzhak Arad, Yisrael Gutman, and A. Margaliot, (eds.) *Documents on the Holocaust* (New York, Ktav Publishing House, 1982).
Fenigstein, Henryk, *Warshewer Yidisher Shpitol beisn Nazi Rezhim* (Frankfurt-am-Main: Buchdruckerei Joh. Wagner & Sohne, 1948), pp. 20.
Fenigstein, Henryk, as Told to Saundra Collis, *The Holocaust and I: Memoirs of a Survivor* (Toronto: Unpublished MS, 1990), pp. 521 + xlii.
Fluek, Toby Knobel, *Memories of My Life in a Polish Village, 1930–1949* (New York: Alfred A. Knopf, 1990), pp. 110, illust.
Goldstein, Bernard, *The Stars Bear Witness*, trans. Leonard Shatzkin (New York: Viking Press, 1949), p. 295.
Gray, Martin, with Max Gallo, *For Those I Loved*, 2nd ed., trans. Anthony White (London: W. H. Allen, 1984), pp. xvi + 349.

Hagen, Wilhelm, "Krieg, Hunger und Pestilenz in Warschau, 1939–1943," *Gesundheitswesen und Desinfektion* 8: 115–28; 9: 129–43, 1973.

Hagen, Wilhelm, *Auftrag und Wirklichkeit: Sozialarzt im 20.Jahrhundert* (Munich-Grafelfing: Werk-Verlag Dr. Edmund Banaschewski, 1978), p. 255.

Hartglas, Apolinary, "How Did Cherniakow [*sic*] Become Head of the Warsaw Judenrat?" *Yad Vashem Bulletin* 15: 4–7, 1964.

Hyams, Joseph, *A Field of Buttercups* (Englewood Cliffs, NJ: Prentice-Hall, 1968), p. 273, map.

Hirszfeldowna, Hanna (ed.), *The Story of One Life, from "Historia Jednego Zycia" by Ludwig Hirszfeld*, trans. F. R. Camp and F. R. Ellis (Fort Knox, KY: Blood Transfusion Division, United States Army Medical Research Laboratory, n.d.), p. 368.

Kanabus, Felix, "Address to the JNF, September 20, 1964," in Jacob Goldstein et al. (eds.), *Anthology of Holocaust Literature* (Philadelphia: Jewish Publication Society of America, 1969), pp. 392–95.

Katsh, Abraham I. (ed. & trans.), *The Warsaw Diary of Chaim A. Kaplan* (New York: Collier Books, 1973).

Karski, Jan (Jan Kozielewski), *Story of a Secret State* (Boston: Houghton Mifflin Co., 1944), pp. vi + 391; p. 334.

Kubar, Zofia S., *Double Identity: A Memoir* (New York: Hill and Wang, 1989), p. 209.

Lazar, Chaim, *Muranowska 7: The Warsaw Ghetto Uprising*, trans. Yosef Shachter (Tel Aviv: Massada-P.E.C. Press Ltd., 1966), pp. 341, illust.

Lewin, Abraham, *A Cup of Tears: A Diary of the Warsaw Ghetto* (London: Fontana/Collins, 1990), pp. xii + 308.

Lubetkin, Zivia, *In the Days of Destruction and Revolt*, trans. Ishai Tubbin (Beit Lohamei Haghettaot, Israel: Hakibbutz Hameuchad Publishing House and Am Ovod Publishing House, 1981), pp. 338, illust.

Makowerowa, Noemi (ed.), *Henryk Makower: Pamietnik z getta warszawskiego, pazdziernik 1940–styczen 1943* (Wrocław, Warszawa, Kraków, Gdansk, and Lodż: Zakład Narodowy im. Ossolinskich Wydawnictwo, 1987), pp. 213.

Meed, Vladka, *On Both Sides of the Wall: Memoirs from the Warsaw Ghetto*, trans. Steven Meed (New York: Holocaust Library, 1979), pp. 276, illust.

Meroz, Anna, *W murach i poza murami getta: Zapiski lekarki warszawskiej z lat 1939–1945* (Warszawa: Czytelnik, 1988), p. 76.

Orenstein, Henry, *I Shall Live: Surviving Against All Odds, 1939–1945* (New York, London, Toronto, Sydney, and Tokyo: Touchstone Books, Simon & Schuster, 1989), pp. xiv + 272, illust., maps.

Orlowski, Witold, "Tajne nauczanie chorob wewnętrznych na wydziale lekarskim Uniwersytetu Warszawskiego, w szczególności w 2 Klinice chorob wewnętrznych, w latach 1939–1944," *Polski Tygodnik Lekarski* 1 (25): 804–05, 1946.

Pankiewicz, Tadeusz, *The Cracow Ghetto Pharmacy*, trans. Henry Tilles (New York: Holocaust Library, 1987), pp. xi + 155, illust.

Penson, Jakub, "Dur Plamisty," *Polskie Archiwum Medycyny Wewnętrznej* 27:445–509, 1967.

Szajn-Lewin, Eugenia, *W Getcie Warszawskim: Lipiec 1942—Kwiecien 1943* (Poznan: Wydawnictwo A5, 1989), p. 59.

Shoskes, Henry [Henryk Szoszkies], *No Traveler Returns* (Garden City, NY: Doubleday, Doran & Co., 1945), pp. xiii + 267.

Stabholz, Tadeusz, *Siedem Piekieł,* (Stuttgart: 1947), pp. 300.

Stabholz, Tadeusz, *Seven Hills*, trans. Jacques Grunblatt and Hilda R. Grunblatt (New York: Holocaust Publishers, 1991), pp. 228, illust.

Starkopf, Adam, *There Is Always Time to Die*, ed. Gertrude Hirschler (New York: Holocaust Library, 1981), pp. 242, illust.

Stiffel, Frank, *The Tale of the Ring: A Kaddish* (Toronto, New York, London, Sydney, and Auckland: Bantam Books, 1985), pp. 348, illust.

Stypulkowski, J., *Invitation to Moscow* (London: Thames and Hudson, 1951).

Szereszewski, Helena, "In the Financial Department of the Judenrat (Memories of the Warsaw Ghetto)," in *Extermination and Resistance: Historical Records and Source Material* (Kibbutz Lohamei Haghettaot, Israel: Ghetto Fighter's House in Memory of Yitzhak Katznelson, 1958), pp. 65–78.

Blady-Szwajger, Adina, "Spital w Getcie (1939–1943)," in *Zeszyty Historyczne* (Paris: Instytut Literacki, 1988), pp. 83–148.

Blady-Szwajger, Adina, *I Remember Nothing More: The Warsaw Children's Hospital and the Jewish Resistance*, trans. Tasja Darowska and Danusia Stok (New York: Pantheon Books, 1990), pp. xx + 184.

Temchin, Michael, *The Witch Doctor: Memoirs of a Partisan* (New York: Holocaust Library, 1983), pp. 185, illust.

Turkow, Jonas, *Azoy iz es Geven* (Buenos Aires: CFPJ, 1948).

Vassiltchikov, Marie "Missie," *The Berlin Diaries, 1940–1945* (London: Chatto & Windus, 1985), pp. xii + 320, illust., maps.

Wdowinski, David, *And We Are Not Saved* (New York: Philosophical Library, 1985), pp. xxi + 222.

Wulman, Leon, "Between Two Wars: A Review of Social Medical Work for Jews in Poland, 1919–1939," *Jewish Social Service Quarterly* 16: 267–73, 1940.

Zawadzka-Wetz, Alicja, *Refleksje Pewnego Zycia* (Paris: Instytut Literacki, 1967).

Ziemian, Joseph, *The Cigarette Sellers of Three Crosses Square*, trans. Janina David (Minneapolis: Lerner Publications Co., 1975), p. 247, illust.

Zweibaum, Juliusz, "Kurs przysposobienia sanitarnego do walki z epidemiami w getcie Warszawskim w latach, 1940–1942," *Archiwum Historji Medycyny* 21: 355–56, 1958.

Zylberberg, Michael, *A Warsaw Diary: 1939–1945* (London: Vallentine, Mitchell, 1969).

Photographic Collections

Anonymous, *Scenes of Martyrdom and Fighting of Jews on the Polish Land, 1939–1945* (Warsaw: Rada Ochrony Pomników Walki i Męczeństwa, 1978), pp. [60], text in English, Polish, Hebrew, French, Russian, and German.

Anonymous, *The Warsaw Ghetto: The 45th Anniversary of the Uprising* (Warsaw: Interpress Publishers, 1988), pp. 92 + unnumbered illustrations.

Keller, Ulrich (ed.), *The Warsaw Ghetto in Photographs: 206 Views Made in 1941* (New York: Dover Publications, 1984), pp. xxv + 131, illust.

Milton, Sybil (trans. and ed.), *The Stroop Report: The Jewish Quarter of Warsaw Is No More!* (London: Secker & Warburg, 1980).

Secondary Sources

Adelson, Alan, and Robert Lapides (eds.), *Lodz Ghetto: Inside a Community Under Siege* (New York: Viking, 1989), pp. xxi + 526, illust., maps.

Almog, Shmuel, "What's in a Hyphen?" *SICSA Report* [Newsletter of the Vidal Sassoon International Center for the Study of Antisemitism, Hebrew University of Jerusalem], No. 2, Summer 1989, pp. 1–2.

Amery, Jean, "In the Waiting Room of Death: Reflections on the Warsaw Ghetto," in Sidney Rosenfeld and Stella P. Rosenfeld (ed. and trans.), *Radical Humanism: Selected Essays* (Bloomington: Indiana University Press, 1984), pp. 21–36.

Apfelbaum, Emil (ed.) *Choroba Glodowa: Badania Kliniczne Nad Glodem Wykonane w Getcie Warszawskim z Roku 1942* (Warsaw: American Joint Distribution Committee, 1946), p. 265.

Arad, Yitzhak, *Ghetto in Flames: The Struggle and Destruction of the Jews in Vilna in the Holocaust* (New York: Holocaust Library, 1982), p. 500.

Aziz, Philippe, *Doctors of Death*, Vol. 3: *When Man Became a Guinea Pig for Death*, trans. E. Bizub and P. Haentzler (Geneva: Ferni Publishers, 1976).

Bartoszewski, Wladyslaw, *The Blood Shed Unites Us (Pages from the History of Help to the Jews in Occupied Poland)* (Warsaw: Interpress Publishers, 1970), pp. 244, illust.

Bennett, John D. C., and Lydia Tyszczuk, "Deception by Immunisation, Revisited," *British Medical Journal* 2: 1471–72, 1990.

Bernheim, Mark, *Father of the Orphans: The Story of Janusz Korczak* (New York: Lodestar Books, E. P. Dutton, 1989), pp. xv + 160, illust.

Brill, Norman Q., "Neuropsychiatric Examination of Military Personnel Recovered from Japanese Prison Camps," *Bulletin U.S. Army Medical Department* 5: 429–38, 1946.

Browning, Christopher R., "Nazi Resettlement Policy and the Search for a Solution to the Jewish Question, 1939–1941," *German Studies Review* 9: 497–519, 1986.

Browning, Christopher R., "Genocide and Public Health: German Doctors and Polish Jews, 1939–41," *Holocaust and Genocide Studies* 3: 21–36, 1988.

Bruce-Chwatt, Leonard J., & Zbigniew Bankowski, "An Unknown Page in the History of Medicine," *Journal of the American Medical Association,* 201: 946–48, 1967.

Buffton, Deborah Darlene, "The Ritual of Surrender: Northern France Under Two Occupations, 1914–1918/1940–1944" (Ph.D. thesis, University of Wisconsin at Madison, 1987).

Celma-Panek, Jerzy, (ed.), *Warszawska Akademia Medyczna: History, the Present Day*, trans. Joanna Ciecierska (Warsaw: Akademia Medyczna, 1983), p. 120.

Cholavsky, Shalom, "The German Jews in the Minsk Ghetto," *Yad Vashem Studies* 17: 219–45, 1986.

Crosby, A. W., "Virgin Soil Epidemics as a Factor in the Aboriginal Depopulation in America," *William and Mary Quarterly* 33: 289–99, 1976.

Dawidowicz, Lucy S., *The War Against the Jews, 1933–1945* (Toronto and New York: Bantam Books, 1986), pp. xxx + 466.

Ding, Erwin, "Über die Schutzwirkung verschiedener Fleckfieberimpfstoffe beim Menschen und den Fleckfieberverlauf nach Schutzimpfung," *Zeitschrift für Hygiene und Infektionskrankheiten* 124: 670–82, 1943.

Donat, Alexander (ed.), *The Death Camp Treblinka: A Documentary* (New York: Holocaust Library, 1979), p. 320.

Donat, Alexander (ed.), *The Death Camp Treblinka: A Documentary* (New York: Holocaust Library, 1979), p. 320.

Dworjetski, M., "Jewish Medical Resistance during the Catastrophe," in *Extermination and Resistance: Historical Records and Source Materials*, Vol. 1 (Kibbutz Lohamei Hagettaot, Israel: Ghetto Fighters' House, 1958).

Favel, A., *Faithful Unto Death: The Story of Arthur Zygielbaum* (Montreal: Zygielbaum Branch Workmen's Circle, 1980).

Fein, Helen, *Accounting for Genocide: National Responses and Jewish Victimization during the Holocaust* (Chicago and London: University of Chicago Press, 1984).

Friedman, Philip (ed.), *Martyrs and Fighters: The Epic of the Warsaw Ghetto* (New York: Frederick A. Praeger, 1954), p. 324.

Garlinski, Jozef, *Poland in the Second World War* (New York: The Macmillan Co., 1985), pp. xxi + 387.

Gilbert, Martin, *Aushwitz and the Allies* (London: Michael Joseph/Rainbird, 1981), pp. xii + 368, illust, maps.

Goldbloom, A. Allen, Abraham Lieberson, and Charles D. Rosen, "Malnutrition and Vitamin Deficiency in Recently Released Prisoners of War," *American Journal of Digestive Diseases* 15: 115–18, 1948.

Goldstein, Bernard, *Die Sterne sind Zeugen: Der Untergang der polnischen Juden* (Munich: Deutscher Taschenbuch Verlag GmbH & Co., 1965).

Gross, Nathan "'Aryan Papers' in Poland," in *Extermination and Resistance: Historical Records and Source Material* (Kibbutz Lohamei Haghettaot, Israel: Ghetto Fighters' House, 1958), pp. 79–85.

Gutman, Yisrael, *Jews of Warsaw, 1939–1943: Ghetto, Underground, Revolt*, trans. Ina Friedman (Bloomington: Indiana University Press, 1989), pp. xxi + 487.

Hanson, Joanna K. M., *The Civilian Population and the Warsaw Uprising of 1944* (Cambridge, London, New York, New Rochelle, Melbourne, and Sydney: Cambridge University Press, 1982), pp. xiii + 345.

Harrison, Kenneth, *The Brave Japanese* (Adelaide: Rigby Ltd., 1966), pp. 280, illust.

Henry, Clarissa, and Marc Hillel, *Of Pure Blood*, trans. Eric Mossbacher (New York, St. Louis, and San Fransisco: McGraw-Hill Book Co., 1976), pp. 256, illust.

Hilberg, Raul *The Destruction of the European Jews* (New York and London: Holmes & Meier, 1985), pp. xii + 1274.

Hirschfeld, Ludwik, [*sic*] and Hanna Hirschfeld, "Serological Differences Between the Blood of Different Races," *Lancet* 2: 675–79, 1919.

Hirschfeld, Ludwik, "A New Germ of Paratyphoid," *Lancet* 1: 296–97, 1919.

Horace, Book 3, Ode 30.

Jakobi, Helga, Peter Chroust, and Matthias Hamann, *Aeskulap und Hakenkreuz: Zur Geschichte der Medizinischen Fakultät in Gießen zwischen 1933 und 1945* (Frankfurt: Mabuse-Verlag, 1989), p. 202.

Kater, Michael, *Doctors Under Hitler* (Chapel Hill, NC, and London: University of North Carolina Press, 1989), pp. xii + 426.

Kennedy, Robert M., *The German Campaign in Poland (1939)* (Washington, DC: Department of the Army, 1956).

Keys, Ancel, Josef Brozek, Austin Henschel, Olaf Mickelsen, and Henry Longstreet Taylor, *The Biology of Human Starvation* (Minneapolis: University of Minnesota Press, 1950), Vol. 1, pp. 1–766, illust., Vol. 2, pp. 767–1385, illust.

Klatskin, Gerald, William T. Salter, and Frances D. Humm, "Gynecomastia due to Malnutrition: I. Clinical Studies," *American Journal of the Medical Sciences* 213: 19–30, 1947.

Krall, Hanna, *Shielding the Flame: An Intimate Conversation with Dr. Marek Edelman, the Last Surviving Leader of the Warsaw Ghetto Uprising*, trans. Joanna Stasinska and Lawrence Weschler (New York: Henry Holt and Co., 1986), pp. xiii + 124.

Lendle, Ludwig, *Grundlagen der allgemeinen und speziellen Arzneiverordnung* (Berlin: Springer-Verlag, 1945), pp. viii + 276.

Lenski, Mordecai, "Problems of Disease in the Warsaw Ghetto," *Yad Vashem Studies* 3: 283–93, 1975.

Leslie, R. F., Antony Polonsky, Jan M. Ciechanowski, and Z. A. Pelczynski, *The History of Poland Since 1863* (Cambridge: Cambridge University Press, 1983), pp. xii + 499, maps.

Lifton, Betty Jean, *The King of Children: A Biography of Janusz Korczak* (New York: Farrar, Straus and Giroux, 1988), pp. 404, illust.

Lifton, Robert Jay, *The Nazi Doctors: Medical Killing and the Psychology of Genocide* (New York: Basic Books, 1986).

Lipscomb, F. M., "Medical Aspects of Belsen Concentration Camp," *Lancet* 2: 313–15, 1945.

Long, Esmond R., "Tuberculosis in German Prison Camps," *Military Surgeon* 97: 449–50, 1945

Maclean, Pam, "Control and Cleanliness: German–Jewish Relations in Occupied Eastern Europe during the First World War," *War and Society* 6: 47–69, 1988.

Major, Ralph H., *Classic Descriptions of Disease, With Biographical Sketches of the Authors* (Springfield, IL: Charles C Thomas, 1959), pp. xxxii + 679.

Marcus, Joseph, *Social and Political History of the Jews in Poland, 1919–1939* (Berlin, New York, and Amsterdam: Mouton Publishers, 1983), xviii + 569.

Mark, Edwarda, "Konspiracyjne wyzsze szkoly medyczne," *Sluzba Zdrowia*, 3, 1962.

Markowski, B., "Some Experiences of a Medical Prisoner of War," *British Medical Journal* 2: 361–63, 1945.

Marrus, Michael R., *The Holocaust in History* (Toronto: Lester & Orpen Dennys, 1987), pp. xv + 267.

Megaw, J. W. D., "Davis, W. A. [U.S.A. Typhus Commission]. *Typhus at Belsen*, 29 mimeographed pp., four tables and one map at Field Headquarters A.P.O. 887, U.S. Army, dated July 26, 1945," *Bulletin of War Medicine* 6: 398–99, 1946

McQuaid, Elwood, *Zvi* (West Collingswood, NJ: Friends of Israel Gospel Ministry, 1978), p. 202.

Mitscherlich, Alexander, and Fred Mielke, *Doctors of Infamy: The Story of the Nazi War Crimes*, trans. Heinz Norden (New York: Henry Schuman, 1949), pp. xxix + 172.

Nicolle, Charles, "Investigations on Typhus: Nobel Lecture," in *Nobel Lectures: Physiology or Medicine, 1922–1941* (Amsterdam: Elsevier Publishing Co., 1965).

Potter, Paul, (trans.), *Hippocrates*, Vol. VI (Cambridge, MA: Harvard University Press, and London: William Heinemann Ltd., 1988).

Prekerowa, Teresa, "The Relief Council for Jews in Poland, 1942–1945," in Chimen Abramsky, Maciej Jachimczyk, and Antony Polonsky (eds.), *The Jews in Poland* (Oxford: Basil Blackwell, 1986), pp. xi + 264, maps; pp. 161–76.

Proctor, Robert, *Racial Hygiene: Medicine Under the Nazis* (Cambridge, MA, and London: Harvard University Press, 1988).

Richet, Charles, "Notes medicales sur le camp de Buchenwald en 1944–1945," *Bulletin de l'Academie de Medecine* 129: 377–88, 1945.

Roland, Charles G., "An Underground Medical School in the Warsaw Ghetto," *Medical History* 33: 399–419, 1989.

Rosenthal, Harry Kenneth, *German and Pole* (Gainesville: University Presses of Florida, 1978).

Rostowski, J., *History of the Polish School of Medicine, University of Edinburgh* (Edinburgh: University of Edinburgh Press, 1955).

Rudowski, Witold, and Ryszard Zablotniak, "Clandestine Medical Studies in Poland, 1939–1945," *Journal of the Royal College of Surgeons of Edinburgh* 23: 239–52, 1978.

Schadewaldt, Hans, "Ludwik Hirszfeld," *Dictionary of Scientific Biography*, 1972, Vol. 6, pp. 432–34.

Schneider, William H., "Chance and Social Setting in the Application of the Discovery of the Blood Groups," *Bulletin of the History of Medicine* 57: 545–62, 1983.

Shulman, Abraham, *The Case of Hotel Polski: An Account of One of the Most Enigmatic Episodes of World War II* (New York: Holocaust Library, 1982), p. 240.

Spink, Wesley W., *Infectious Diseases: Prevention and Treatment in the Nineteenth and Twentieth Centuries* (Minneapolis: University of Minnesota Press, 1978).

Steiner, Jean-François, *Treblinka*, trans. Helen Weaver (New York: Simon and Schuster, 1967), p. 415.

Szlazakowa, Alicja, *Janusz Korczak* (Warsaw: Wydawnicto Szkolne i Pedagogiczne, 1978), pp. 146, illust.

Tannahill, Reay, *Flesh and Blood: A History of the Cannibal Complex* (London: Hamish Hamilton, 1975), pp. ix + 209.

Tec, Nechama, *When Light Pierced the Darkness: Christian Rescue of Jews in Nazi-Occupied Poland* (New York and Oxford: Oxford University Press, 1986), pp. xv + 262.

Trunk, Isaiah, "Epidemics and Mortality in the Warsaw Ghetto, 1939–1942," *YIVO Annual of Jewish Social Science* 8: 82–122, 1953.

Trunk, Isaiah, *Judenrat: The Jewish Councils in Eastern Europe Under Nazi Occupation* (New York: The Macmillan Co., 1972), pp. xxxv + 664, illust.

Tushnet, Leonard, *The Uses of Adversity* (New York: Thomas Yoseloff, 1966), p. 108.

Uris, Leon, *Mila 18* (Toronto, New York, London, and Sydney: Bantam Books, 1962), p. 563.

Watt, Richard M., *Bitter Glory: Poland and Its Fate, 1918–1939* (New York: Simon and Schuster, 1979).

Wheeler-Bennett, John W., *Brest-Litovsk: The Forgotten Peace, March 1918* (New York: W. W. Norton & Co., 1971), pp. xvi + 478, illust., maps.

Wiesenthal, Simon, *Justice, Not Vengeance* (London: Weidenfeld and Nicolson, 1989), pp. xi + 372, illust.

Winick, Myron (ed.), *Hunger Disease: Studies by the Jewish Physicians in the Warsaw Ghetto*, trans. Martha Osnos (New York, Chichester, Brisbane, and Toronto: John Wiley & Sons, 1979), pp. xiv + 261, illust.

Wulman, Leon, and Joseph Tenenbaum, *The Martyrdom of Jewish Physicians in Poland*, ed. Louis Falstein (New York: Exposition Press, 1963), pp. xii + 500, illust.

Yahil, Leni, "Madagascar: Phantom of a Solution for the Jewish Question," in Bela Vago and George L. Mosse (eds.), *Jews and Non-Jews in Eastern Europe, 1918–1945* (New York and Toronto: John Wiley & Sons; Jerusalem: Israel Universities Press, 1974), pp. 315–34.

Zablotniak, Ryszard, "Wydzial Lekarski w Getcie Warszawskim," *Biuletyn Zydowskiego Instytutu Historycznego* 74: 81–86, 1970.

Zablotniak, Ryszard, "Das geheime Medizin- und Pharmazie-studium in Polen in den Jahren 1939 bis 1945," *Zeitschrift für Arztliche Fortbildung* 83: 363–66, 1989.

Ziemian, Joseph, *Gevulot Geto Varsha Veshinuyehem* (Jerusalem: Yad Vashem, 1971), pp. 31 + [4], 7 maps.

Zinsser, Hans, *Rats, Lice and History: Being a Study in Biography, which, after Twelve Preliminary Chapters Indispensable for the Preparation of the Lay Reader, Deals with the Life History of Typhus Fever. . . .* (Boston: Little, Brown, and Co., 1935), pp. xii + 301.

Zweibaum, J., "Sur la survie de l'épithélium vibratile *in vitro*," *Comptes Rendus Hebdomadaires des Seances et Memoires de la Societe de Biologie et de ses Filiales* 93: 782–84, 1925.

Zweibaum, J., "Analyse histophysiologique de l'épithélium vibratile en état de survie *in vitro*," *Comptes Rendus Hebdomadaires des Seances et Memoires de la Societe de Biologie et de ses Filiales* 93: 785–87, 1925.

Zylberberg, Michael, "The Trial of Alfred Nossig," *Wiener Library Bulletin* 22: 41–45, 1969.

Tertiary Sources

Eitinger, Leo, and Robert Krell, *The Psychological and Medical Effects of Concentration Camps and Related Persecutions on Survivors of the Holocaust: A Research Bibliography* (Vancouver: University of British Columbia Press, 1985), pp. xii + 168.

Gilbert, Martin, *Jewish History Atlas*, 3rd ed., (London: Weidenfeld and Nicolson, 1985), pp. 128, maps.

Klepfisz, Rose, and Emil Lang, *Annotated Catalogue of the Archives of the American Jewish Joint Distribution Committee, 1933–1944* (New York: AJJDC, undated).

Sobotta, Joh., *Atlas der deskriptiven Anatomie des Menschen*, 3 Vols. (Munich and Berlin: J. F. Lehmanns Verlag, 1941).

Stanislawski, J., *McKay's English-Polish Polish-English Dictionary* (New York: Random House, 1988), pp. 463 + 416.

Index